The Daily T...

GW00374623

Meditations through the Year

Denis Duncan

367 Meditations for Daily Life

John Hunt
Publishing Limited

I dedicate this book of Meditations

- as I did the first (*Be Still and Know ...*),
the second (*Solitude, Stillness, Serenity*)
and the third (*Rainbows through the Rain*)
now combined in this volume - *with additional meditations*

to my wife Ettie, who died on 16 October 1993
and who was for 51 years my partner on the way.

As she served on the staff of the *Daily Telegraph*
for over twenty years, particularly as personal assistant
to Max Hastings, then Editor-in-Chief,
it is the more appropriate that these volumes of
Saturday Meditations from that paper
should be dedicated to her.

DENIS DUNCAN is a minister of the Church of Scotland, formerly editor of *British Weekly* and Director of the Churches' Council for Health and Healing. He was also Associate Director and Training Supervisor at Westminster Pastoral Foundation, Director of Highgate Counselling Centre and of Hampstead Counselling Service, all in London. Earlier he served in St Margaret's Parish in Juniper Green, Edinburgh, and in Trinity, Duke Street Parish, Glasgow.

The focus of his current ministry is "proclamation through preaching, writing and the ministry of healing".

Also by Denis Duncan:

Be Still and Know . . .
Solitude, Stillness, Serenity
A Day at a Time
Creative Silence
Health and Healing: A Ministry to Wholeness
Love, the Word that Heals
Here is my Hand
The Road Taken
Rainbows through the Rain

Books edited by Denis Duncan:

Through the Year with William Barclay

Every Day with William Barclay

Marching Orders

Marching On

Through the Year with J B Phillips

Through the Year with Cardinal Heenan

Copyright © 2002 John Hunt Publishing Ltd
46A West Street, Alresford, Hants SO24 9AU, U.K.
Tel: +44 (0) 1962 736880 Fax: +44 (0) 1962 736881
E-mail: office@johnhunt-publishing.com
www.johnhunt-publishing.com

Text: © 2002 Denis Duncan in conjunction with *The Daily Telegraph*

Typography: Nautilus Design, Basingstoke, UK

ISBN 1 84298 094 7

A CIP catalogue record for this book is available from the British Library.

Printed in the U.K. by Ashford Colour Press

Cover photographs courtesy of Powerstock

Contents

JANUARY

FEBRUARY

MARCH

Contents

Contents

Contents

Foreword

by Clifford Longley

We live in a culture which has reduced the spiritual to the psychological. That could even be the definition of the secular. At the same time, not many people would care to put their whole trust in psychology, as their ancestors placed their trust in God. As a result, we have become an orphan people, with nowhere to turn when we must turn somewhere.

Yet help is available under our very noses. It is not necessary to journey to the ashrams of India or delve into the exotic mysteries of Zen or Yoga, in order to discover our spiritual roots. The Christian tradition lays all its riches before us, if we could only recognise them for what they are. But often we need a guide; and those with the necessary skills are few.

One guide with these gifts in abundance is Denis Duncan. This book gathers together in one place his articles, which have been published in the *Daily Telegraph* under the heading "Meditations". For some of his readers this will be a reunion with old friends. Dr Duncan is a writer whose columns are cut out and kept, often to grow dog-eared within the folds of a wallet or purse. Such readers will find, to their pleasure, that in this case the total is even greater than the sum of its parts.

For other readers this will be a first introduction. It will be a rewarding encounter, not only for Christians, but for those of any religion or none. Good spiritual writing transcends denominations, and can readily cross the boundaries between faiths. The ability to speak to people of all sorts and conditions is a sure test of true spirituality. That mysterious thing we exchange when we love and are loved, here on earth, is not a different thing from the love of God, of which the spiritual writer writes. To better understand the one is to better understand the other. And they are the entrance to the understanding of suffering, when love turns to pain.

What denies us access to the ancient and modern wisdom of Christianity is our own ignorance or fear, or that over-familiarity which breeds contempt or indifference – or maybe, most of all, the hidden but pernicious influence of cultural fashion. Embarrassment at being thought "religious" may be a poor reason for turning away from the only thing that is likely to help us, but in the present age it is a common reason nevertheless.

In the sensitive hands of Denis Duncan, the Christian faith becomes much more than a collection of texts or doctrines, and the Christian life something much deeper than a habit of churchgoing. It becomes an exploration and spiritual journey. "Through prayer, meditation and contemplation our level of spiritual awareness can change too..." he writes at one point. And later he explains, "It is open to all who humbly seek and reverently ask, to be allowed . . . to touch and handle things unseen." There is a sense of beckoning on, a leading forth, in his writing which puts me in mind of some of the metaphysical poetry of George Herbert. Above all, neither of them makes religion "difficult" in a technical or intellectual way. Denis Duncan addresses people in their ordinary conditions and takes them as they are. I believe he also moves them on. It is a rare and extraordinary gift.

Introduction

BY DENIS DUNCAN

For the last twelve years I have had, and at the time of writing still have, the privilege of contributing 26 Meditations each year to the Saturday edition of The Daily Telegraph. To both Charles Moore, the Editor, and his predecessor Max Hastings, I express my appreciation for their making this ministry possible. Even if but a small percentage of the readership of the Telegraph turn to my contribution, it is still a very large congregation! The *Telegraph* has a circulation level of well over a million copies each day and that therefore becomes an estimated readership of more than three million. To have such a platform is a moving thought.

Two hundred and fifty of these Meditations have appeared in three volumes – *Be Still and Know ...*, *Solitude, Stillness, Serenity* and *Rainbows through the Rain*. All were published by Arthur James, now part of John Hunt Publishing, in association with the *Telegraph*. My publisher has now suggested that, with two of those titles already out of print, it would be useful to bring them all together in one volume. This book is the result of that proposal. John Hunt also suggested that the book be extended to a year of such meditations. This volume therefore includes all the Meditations that have been published in the *Telegraph* since *Rainbows through the Rain* plus an additional two months of further Meditations written for this book. Those months are August and September. I have based these Meditations on two of my earlier books, *Creative Silence* and *Love, the Word that heals*, both no longer on my publisher's list. In total there are 367 Meditations, that is 366 to allow for a leap year, and one extra one, which was written for the anniversary of the death of Diana, Princess of Wales; it comes between August 31 and September 1 as she died on August 31, 1997.

The Meditations, apart from August and September, are as they appeared in the newspaper. This means they were written not as a connected series, but simply as a reflection relevant to each week. I have tried to indicate in footnotes the context in which they were written where this is necessary. It also means, obviously, that over twelve years, repetition of phrases, references, favourite underlying themes, etc, must occur. Wherever I can, I have noted such associated references in the footnotes.

The late Bishop George Appleton, a previous contributor to this column, said that when he undertook the responsibility of writing Meditations, he was given only one guideline by the then editor, and that was that he must write about "the eternal verities". I have made that my guideline too. Bishop Appleton also gave twelve years to the writing of this column. It is again a privilege to be in such company.

I am grateful to Clifford Longley, a distinguished journalist indeed, for the Foreword which he so generously wrote for *Be Still and Know ...*, and which was reprinted in *Solitude, Stillness, Serenity*. I thank my publisher, John Hunt, for his encouragement and help in setting up and seeing through the project. I record my gratitude to Jillian Tallon (who turns up sometimes in the text!) for all she has done to make this book possible.

The sense of being "called to preach" is for me an over-riding one. As my ministry has evolved in so many varied ways, proclamation in print has taken its place beside proclamation in the pulpit. That I have had these two particular strings to my bow (though there are others) fills me with gratitude.

Denis Duncan
June 2002

The Bliss of Solitude

"I want to be alone," drawled the late Greta Garbo, the statement becoming a catchphrase for ever associated with that famous screen actress. It cannot have been a longing for loneliness. It must have been a plea for privacy.

To be alone means two different things. On one hand it describes a state which none can enjoy, some dread, and many experience. How awful is that utter loneliness which belongs, in John Betjeman's phrase, to "the poor, unbeloved ones" – their lot in this world. But the same phrase can refer to solitude, as positive a concept as loneliness is a negative one. The latter is enforced, the former chosen. One brings pain, the other peace.

The cry of the lonely for family, friends, fellowship is heart-rending. Bereft of living contact, they become resentful and bitter. Lost in an unloving world, they deserve our pity. Sadly it sometimes happens that, devoid of other relationships, they find the church too has let them down. Some survive, coping without complaint and accepting their aloneness with resignation. Others, inwardly angry over their experience of life, condemn themselves to isolation and project their problems on an uncaring world.

Solitude is totally different. It is something to be sought as creative and beneficial. The reasons for seeking it may not always be healthy. For some, increasing dependence on retreat becomes nothing more than a running away from the world and its problems. For others however, solitude is sought for profound religious reasons at the heart of which is the need to be alone with God and, in God's presence, with ourselves. "How sweet, how passing sweet is solitude," wrote William Cowper. It was something which he, with his inner turbulence, needed as much as any other. There is no experience more profound or valuable than being alone, in proper solitude.

The record of Jesus' life makes clear his need for withdrawal to the quiet place. He had to get away from the demanding crowds who waited for his teaching and yearned for his healing. He made solitude a habit. If it is a New Testament precept that "the disciple must be as his master", it is a precept all too difficult to fulfil. His thoughts and our thoughts, his ways and our ways, are far from each other. But the obligation remains. "Try to have the same attitude to life that Jesus had," Paul wrote to the Philippians. Like him, we need to practise as Wordsworth calls it "the bliss of solitude". It is only in the desert place and alone that we can discern the will of God. The saints know it. Those with a profoundly simple faith know it.

True religion begins with a confession of faith and develops in a commitment for life. Spiritual growth is of the essence of that commitment, which demands both devotion and discipline. A key factor in that process must surely be the practice of solitude.

A Time for Stillness

Jesus was a Jew, steeped in the wonder of his Bible, our Old Testament. His spirituality was shaped, humanly speaking, by the glory of the Law and the witness of the prophets. From such sources there came the bases of his thinking, the inspiration of his teaching, the depths of his ideas and the stimuli for his imagination. He was, naturally, very much aware of the deep longing of his people for the coming of the Messiah, the deliverer of his people. That hope lasted for a long period. Even at the time of his ascension, there were those among his disciples who were asking: "Will you now restore the kingdom to Israel?"

Following the divine affirmation given at his baptism by John in the Jordan, Jesus wrestled with the meaning of his calling. Through 40 days and 40 nights, he struggled with the temptations implicit in his call to be Messiah. There was much in the Old Testament that painted the accepted picture of the Messiah as a warrior king, a concept he ultimately had to reject. He found the image of the Messiah as a suffering servant in that same Old Testament, a concept that expressed what he felt about his calling. A moving, dramatic figure, the Suffering Servant would be despised and rejected by men and women, a figure of sorrow and acquainted with grief. When he entered Jerusalem in triumph, Jesus came not as the warrior king on a charger, but in humility, on an ass.

What a treasure-house of spirituality the Old Testament is! It provided for Jesus – as it did for Judaism, as it does for the Christian faith – a source-book of inspiration, a course-book on faith. And how important it was in relation to the Incarnation. It was the book that documented the on-going revelation of God to people. Jesus came "in the fullness of the time", a phrase which sums up that combination of history and geography which made Palestine the place in which he must be born. He came as a Jew because Judaism was spiritually so developed, so advanced in its understanding of the eternal dimension, so aware of its relationship to God that it had to be the cradle of the Incarnation.

The Old Testament is a book which has much war, violence and strife in it, but it is also the book that testifies to the value of stillness. Turn for example to Psalm 23 with its still waters, green pastures and the capacity to restore the soul; to Psalm 46 with its counsel to "Be still and know that I am God"; to the story of Elijah, under pressure from the prophets of Baal, being advised to heed not earthquake, wind and fire, but only "a still, small voice". It was surely from the Old Testament that Jesus learned the supreme importance of stillness in the devotional life.

If life today is to be tolerable and productive, it is essential to learn the meaning of stillness. We need a time not for talking but for listening; that time for total concentration on, and contemplation of, God.

SERENITY

If time is given to solitude, and attention is given in the stillness, then spiritual growth will reveal itself in greater inner peace and serenity. As a result, the ability to cope with the vicissitudes of life will be truly strengthened.

One of the occasions when Jesus deliberately sought solitude followed the feeding of the 5000 people. The disciples were sent on their way back across the Sea of Galilee. Jesus found stillness in his quiet place, but the disciples were experiencing turmoil on the water. As sometimes happened on that lake, a storm of considerable ferocity blew up, creating alarm for the followers of the Lord. It was in that crisis that Jesus appeared, walking on the water, strengthened by his time of solitude and stillness. With the authority he alone could command, he calmed the waves, stilled the storm and soothed the fearful disciples with his presence. "It is a spirit," they cried. "It is I," he said. "Be not afraid." The serenity of their Lord, and the authority he proclaimed, left them in wonder and admiration. As they said on another occasion, "Why, even the wind and waves obey him."

Jesus showed that same impressive serenity in his response to his accusers and to those who blasphemed against him. Tested, tried, taunted, he simply "answered them nothing". He managed to maintain serenity too under the harshest of provocation, when in Gethsemane he faced the ultimate test. It seemed, momentarily, that he wavered: "Father, let this cup pass from me," he cried – but immediately recovered that still, serene centre as, in trust, he prayed: "Nevertheless, not my will but thine be done."

The power of the church lies in the strength of its individuals. It needs for its corporate witness the spiritual power of its members. If the "spiritual blaze", of which Alexander Solzhenitsyn speaks as essential at the watershed of history marked by the millennium, is to be created it will come from the spiritual commitment and drive of individual people.*

When pupils reach the day of leaving at the Rudolf Steiner school in which they have learned the meaning and importance of the wholeness of life and the essential place of the spiritual in that wholeness, they are allowed to share in a traditional custom. Wisely, the school feels there is gain in keeping some experiences back in a world too much given to introducing young people to every experience too soon. Clothed in white gowns, and with burning torches in their hands, the departing pupils make their way in a line to a field beyond the school where a huge bonfire is standing, unlit. They form a circle round the pile and then, at a given moment, all plunge their flaming brands into the bonfire and a colossal blaze leaps up to illuminate the countryside for miles. And round that blaze, songs are sung.

Those who can best contribute to the spiritual blaze we need are those who, coming from the solitude and the stillness, reflect the serenity of Christ.

* See fuller reference in A Spiritual Blaze, May 28.

THE HOLY LIFE

The most effective contribution to the communication of the gospel is the genuinely holy life. If this principle was ever in doubt, it has been hugely re-affirmed through the ministry, in life and in death, of Cardinal Basil Hume. Across the denominations, from members of other faiths and those with none, from prominent people in high places to humble souls in every walk of life, has come the recognition of a spirituality that was indeed profound. Such goodness brings a response which has nothing to do with shared dogma or credal conformity. It is an instinctive reaction to demonstrated holiness.

Paul, writing to Timothy, was greatly concerned to ensure that, living in "crooked and depraved times", his commitment to the faith was essential. To hold on to sound teaching when false prophets seek to destroy the faith becomes a priority. "Guard the good deposit that was entrusted to you," he writes to Timothy, "guard it with the help of the Holy Spirit who lives in us." But it is not only a holding action that is needed. Spirituality must develop new depths. To ensure that growth a further step is involved: "Fan into flame the gift of God," he says.

To live what Paul calls "the holy life" within the security of the monastery is one thing, but to have to do it when walking the corridors of ecclesiastical power, surrounded by and subject to political pressures, is a wholly different matter. It was the capacity to hold to the life of devotion and retreat despite the conflicts of present day public life that Basil Hume demonstrated. His epitaph will proclaim his simplicity, his sincerity and his serenity in a world of confusion, intrigue and turmoil.

Of those gifts of simplicity, sincerity and serenity, it is the last that has so moved people everywhere. In a position of power in politics and public affairs, he was ever available to the man, woman or child in the street. That has touched the hearts of many. Insincerity in high places has in Ireland, in the Balkans, in the Middle East brought huge international problems and colossal human suffering. In a position where he had controversial issues to face, he could make mistakes yet never lose his sincerity. That was an enormous influence for good. But his final public testimony to his coming death evidenced a serenity that gave wings to his own words in his book, *The Mystery of the Cross.* * "Death is a formidable foe until we learn to make it a friend. Death is to be feared if we do not learn to welcome it. Death is the ultimate absurdity if we do not see it as fulfilment. Death haunts us when viewed as a journey into nothingness rather than a pilgrimage to a place where true happiness is found . . . Death is not the end of the road, but a gateway to a better place."

To attain to such authentic serenity is a triumph of grace indeed.

* Darton, Longman & Todd, 1998.
This Meditation was written in 1999. Cardinal Hume died on June 17 in that year.

Be Still and Know . . .

To be able to be still is to have found the secret of success in the struggle against the strains and stresses of this noisy, raucous and demanding world. It is a capacity made incarnate in the life of our Lord. When faced, as he often was, by criticism, hostility, opposition and, in the end, crucifixion, he never lost his serenity and tranquillity. Even in his darkest hours, he knew how to be still and *know* that God, his Father, was with him in that darkness.

There were times when Jesus' inner peace was severely challenged. In the Garden of Gethsemane, he sweated blood over the appalling events that faced him; on Calvary, where those events became reality he was strained to the limit to hold onto his faith and his peace. But he did. The disciple can never emulate the extraordinary spiritual strength of the Master, but the example remains to help us find our peace. We need, like Jesus, to be able under great pressure to be still and know that he is God.*

To develop his "still centre", Jesus went to quiet places . . . the Mount of Olives, the seashore, the desert place. Paul followed his example. In the desert of Arabia he wrestled with the consequences of the call that came to him on the Damascus road.

We too must repair to "the desert place" even if, literally, for us that is impossible. It matters not. "The desert place" is the sanctuary we create wherever we are, the place where we can meet God. It may be in the quietness of a church. It may be somewhere in the garden. Perhaps we cannot go anywhere at all through physical limitation so a corner of a room can be our sanctuary. There, selected symbols will speak to us of spiritual things. It may be simple or splendid, small or large. It is of no importance. "The desert place" is where we meet God in the stillness and know that he is there.

The desert place is also the place where we meet ourselves, where we face the pain of our weakness and our sin. It is here however, that a miracle takes place. It is at the very time when we face ourselves that we know that God is already there, forgiving, redeeming, assuring, renewing. It is in this experience of a loving God that we find the stillness we so eagerly seek.

True serenity comes from knowing God as a living, loving presence. Equipped with such peace, we can face life, a day at a time, with calmness and confidence. Aware of our weakness, physically, emotionally, spiritually, we become the more sure that the divine strength is flowing through our whole being.

Such stillness is not of our making. It is God's gift and it is on offer to all his people.

* Psalm 46, verse 10 (Psalm numbering throughout the book follows that of the Authorised Version of the Bible).

WAITING FOR GOD

For those who are emotionally and nervously exhausted, the first needs may well be rest and food. It is not sensible to make demanding decisions when we are physically worn out.

This certainly seems to be the message coming from the story (in 1 Kings, chapter 19) of the prophet Elijah's deep depression. Hounded by the prophets of Baal, facing the faithlessness and consequent hostility of the children of Israel, and having to fight for God totally alone, Elijah felt compelled to cry out: "I've had enough, Lord. Please take away my life." Wearied to death, he was asleep under a juniper tree when a ministering angel brought him food and drink. "Arise and eat," the angel said. Only then was Elijah ready to face the deep spiritual issues before him.

It was, however, precisely as he waited on God that he "got it all wrong". It was in the dramatic and the extraordinary that Elijah expected that God would presumably make himself known. God was not however, in the rushing wind, the cataclysmic earthquake or the scorching fire. What Elijah must do was simple: just listen to "the still, small voice".

There is a reminder of this same spiritual law in the story of the walk to Emmaus. It was in the commonplace process of "breaking bread" at an *ordinary* meal in an *ordinary* home that the risen Jesus made himself known.

God does, of course, sometimes reveal himself in dramatic events. Did not the Holy Spirit come, at the first Pentecost, with a "rushing, mighty wind" and "tongues of fire"? There was, too, an earthquake at the precise moment that Jesus died on Calvary. But more often the divine presence is made known in the everyday events of life – family, fellowship, loving relationship, quiet reflection, silent contemplation, the care of the carers, the courage of the strugglers.

He is there in forgiveness and encouragement when people fail. Was it not to Peter, who denied him, that Jesus wanted news of his resurrection sent? Was it not to Thomas who doubted him that he showed his pierced hands? It was to those same disciples who had "forsaken him and fled" that the Holy Spirit was given.

Seeking for God in the unusual can be a temptation – Jesus himself had to reject that very subtle pressure when he was "tempted of the devil". Finding Jesus in the commonplace was the blessing that came to the two who walked to Emmaus. So can it be for us all.

For further comments on the walk to Emmaus, see Emmaus Encounter, January 8; Preparing the Way, January 9; Transforming Vision, January 25.

CREATIVE SILENCE

"Silence is as deep as Eternity, speech is as shallow as Time." How apposite to any reflection on communication is Thomas Carlyle's comment! He is pointing to a paradox which illuminates the truth, aptly expressed by Christina Rossetti, that silence is "more musical than any song".

"The ministry of silence" has four aspects (at least): the silence we ought to maintain about other people; the silence which is an integral part of prayer . . . when we need not to speak, but to listen; the silence of dignity* when the only appropriate answer to abuse is no answer (remembering that Jesus, when faced by his accusers' blasphemies "answered them nothing"); the silence of awe, compelled upon us by the sheer mystery of the divine holiness. How important indeed then is silence to the religious life.

Communication involves the practice of preaching and the ministry of print; caring relationship expressed in a "being with"; the creative arts as instruments of communication to the imagination; the healing ministry, conveying strength and peace to body, soul, mind and spirit. Through each, God makes known his love. There remains however one other way in which truth is learned and grace is given. It is through the power of creative silence.

"That man's silence is wonderful to listen to," said Thomas Hardy. Consider then just how much can be said by silence . . . the sympathy that silence can convey when, in situations of tragedy and loss, words fail completely; the inner wonder experienced in the contemplation of the divine splendour, which "shallow speech" just cannot express; the feeling of being (in the words of the Psalmist) "dumb with silence", faced as we are by the daily horrors of violence, war, destruction, devastation, starvation, wounds and death. Sometimes only silence can adequately convey our inner feelings.

In this noisy, tumultuous world, it is right to remember the prayer expressed by Edmund Hamilton Sears

> O hush the noise, ye men of strife
> And hear the angels sing.

God is in the silence of "the desert place". It is there that we come to know ourselves. It is there that he meets with us. The revelation of the forgiving, renewing love of God in "the silence of eternity" makes it indeed a truly creative silence.

* This theme is developed in The Silence of Dignity, May 8.

EMMAUS ENCOUNTER

In Luke's Gospel there is the dramatic resurrection story which we know as "The Walk to Emmaus". It is profoundly moving in its demonstration of the reality and validity of spiritual experience but, because it is concerned with contemporary concepts such as changes to consciousness and levels of awareness, it is also very relevant today. The changes to which it bears witness are not, however, artificially created or drug induced. They are wholly the product of an encounter with the risen Christ.

Two followers, as they walked, had "reasoned together" about events that had taken place in Jerusalem relating to Jesus of Nazareth. As they told the stranger who joined them on their journey, they had been discussing his crucifixion and reports of his resurrection, yet even when he expounded their scriptures with authority they were completely unaware of his identity.

A little later on, as they shared their evening meal with the stranger, something happened that transformed their spiritual awareness. "Their eyes were opened," we read, "and they knew him." Returning to Jerusalem, they reported to the assembled disciples that the stranger, the risen Jesus, had been made known to them "in breaking of bread".

Symbols and rituals play an important part in every day life. To the development of the spiritual life of the individual and of the church, they are even more important. They are, however, means, not ends in themselves. When they become ends, they lose their purpose. Rightly used, they are aids to the growth of the spiritual life, for they become the point around which images and beliefs cluster.

The symbol has a special power. It is the ability to bring into consciousness the great themes gathered around it. To contemplate the symbol of the cross is immediately to be reminded of God's saving acts through the crucifixion and resurrection of Jesus.

Breaking of bread was a normal, natural action within that meal, but it was profoundly symbolic too. It brought flooding into the consciousness of the two followers that other meal in an upper room where Jesus shared with his friends not only his coming death and resurrection, but himself. So meaningful was the action that "their eyes were opened" and their level of awareness dramatically raised. They recognised their Lord.

The Emmaus experience lies beyond our reach, but through prayer, meditation and contemplation, our level of spiritual awareness can change too, and enable us to "touch and handle things unseen".

PREPARING THE WAY

Worship involves every aspect of our being, physical, mental, emotional and spiritual. It dare not be treated as if it were simply an intellectual exercise nor should it be turned into merely an emotional indulgence. Both intellect and emotions are, nevertheless, involved.

It is sad when deep emotional needs, such as grieving, are not met in worship. Equally, of course, the body should have an opportunity in worship for the expression of celebration and joy. "Dancing in the aisles", an ancient as well as a modern religious activity, will appeal to some but not to all.* It does, however, allow physical expression in worship. The fundamental point is the need for body, soul, mind and emotions all to be embraced in worship together.

I return to the story of the walk to Emmaus** for it contains "a cautionary tale" of some importance. The two followers of Jesus were "reasoning together" about religious matters. They were, in fact, discussing the crucifixion and reported resurrection of Jesus when "the stranger" joined them and expounded the scriptures to them. Amazingly, though they were engaged in theological discussion about Jesus, they were totally blind to his presence as "the stranger". That was indeed strange.

This is not a condemnation of theological debate. There is a need for more theology in the churches today, not less. It is simply a warning that we can discuss the great saving acts of Jesus intellectually but have no sense of the reality of his risen presence.

In worship, similarly, we can do all the technically right things, minds concentrated, emotions stimulated, but however correct our religious behaviour, if we are not aware of the Christ "in the midst", the basic purpose of worship has been missed, to our spiritual loss. Worship is the experience of a loving and "grace-full" relationship with Christ. It is his promise that where two or three – or more – gather together "in his name", he is there to meet with, and minister to them.

Those who lead worship have a great responsibility,*** for they are asked to create the ambience in which the Lord may meet with, and minister to people. Every item in an act of worship – praise, prayers, readings, sermon – must contribute to the transforming encounter with the risen Christ.

To lead worship is to have the privilege of "preparing the way of the Lord".

* See also Lord of the Dance, May 5.
** See also Emmaus Encounter, January 8.
*** See also January 10; February 25, 28 and 29; November 21, 24 and 26.

SERENE STABILITY

To know *about* God is one thing. To know God is another. Theology, once described as "the queen of the sciences", is an intellectual necessity and an invaluable discipline. May there always be those qualified and equipped to pursue it. It is not, however, the most important element in healthy religion. Religion is focused on and embedded in relationship and, primarily, on the relationship between God and humankind. It is in relationship that God reveals the essence of the divine love.

The wonder of worship is not confined to the intellectual element essential in its celebration, though that element is always present (we are to love God with our *minds* as well as our other faculties). It is rather a positive response to the One who, we are told by St John, "first loved us". It is a consequence of the divine initiative in that primary relationship that all other relationships are mandatory – love towards others, towards the earth from which we come, and to ourselves. From these relationships come the disciplines of pastoral care, ecological concern and that most important of pastoral attitudes, the need to accept ourselves "as we are". It is on that basis that God accepts us. What is equally important is that loving our neighbour "as ourselves" depends on a humble but loving self-acceptance.

Worship encapsulates that complex of relationships and roots it in *coming* to praise and *going* to serve. Jesus' invitation to the "weary and heavy-laden" to *come* and find rest and refreshment relates paradoxically to his command to *"go* into all the world" in mission and service. Liturgy is that relationship and its derivatives expressed in prayers of adoration, thanksgiving, confession and absolution, and of intercession. Mysticism is a being in touch with God in non-verbal but profound experiences of the divine presence. Indeed "true mysticism," writes Wyons Mauleverer, "is most intimately concerned with loving contact with him in whom we believe ... we find our rest in him."

Finding such rest in relationship takes us back to that great statement in the *Confessions* of St Augustine: "Thou hast made us for Thyself and our hearts are restless till they rest in Thee." Restlessness is essentially a negative spiritual condition, whether it be in Augustine's north Africa in the fourth century or here and now in the uneasy dis-ease of the late twentieth century. It is the church's function in an uncertain world to encourage men and women to "find God" and experience the relationship of love through which there is the possibility of stability today and serenity tomorrow.

"Oh that I knew where I might find him" is the heartfelt cry from Job. The mystic who wrote *The Cloud of Unknowing* points to the answer. It is related to the opening sentences of this Meditation: "By love may he be gotten and holden, but by thought never."

God is infinitely far away yet, paradoxically, very near: "Closer is He than breathing and nearer than hands or feet." Worship is the acting out of that sense of relationship with God and with each other, with ourselves and with the earth.

THE PURSUIT OF SIMPLICITY

One of the less attractive features of modern life is its liking for jargon words that do not enhance the beauty of our language. The word *downshifting* is certainly not an appealing one. The concept for which it stands should however engage our attention and fire our enthusiasm. It is that of *voluntary simplicity*.

I read with interest, surprise and pleasure that "downshifting had become Britain's fastest growing lifestyle trend".* There is no doubt that such a development will benefit the health of the nation entangled as most of its citizens are in a very complicated world. Add the menace of materialism and the gargantuan problem of suffering in the world today when, as the hymn says, "human hearts are breaking under sorrow's iron rod," and it is no wonder stress and strain, anxiety and breakdown are hallmarks of our contemporary society. What a valuable concept is that of *voluntary simplicity*!

Religious folk generally should welcome the trend to simplicity. Christians will feel it strikes a chord, for did not Jesus live the simple life? "Foxes have holes and the birds their nests, but the Son of Man has nowhere to lay his head." He had no property, no bank accounts, no mortgages, no hire purchase agreements, no credit cards. His was (in material terms) a simple life, but it was a simplicity that was entirely voluntary. Should not the disciple seek to reflect the Master?

The simple life, is of course, still lived in religious communities where poverty, chastity and obedience are life-long vows. Voluntary simplicity goes even further in the case of a nun I know who lives the life of a hermit. She tells me that the main features of the eremitical life are "frugality, silence, solitude and simplicity". The life of prayer to which the hermit is called, she says, "requires a quiet regular pace of life, conducive to recollection, guarding the imagination, avoiding the kind of external activity that could interfere with devotion." Few can pursue the hermit's life, but what she says about it can surely be translated into a voluntary simplicity which to embrace would in itself be an act of dedication or re-dedication.

Voluntary simplicity involves, as some see it, a retreat to rural places and natural conditions, but it does not have to take that shape. Many will have to work out the meaning of voluntary simplicity in suburbia, industrial town or city. Voluntary simplicity is not seeking an escape or dropping out. It is an act of obedience. "Simplicity of living means meeting life face to face ... without unnecessary distractions, without trying to soften the awesomeness of our existence or mask the deeper significance of life with pretentious, distracting and unnecessary accumulations ... It results in a more fulfilled and richer life that is not dictated by debt, junk and that never-ending quest for status and position."**

To change our way of life drastically demands a major effort of will – and faith. But it could be profoundly worthwhile, diligently to seek such voluntary simplicity. Or, less attractively, downshifting.

* Quoted in *Ethos, The Ethics in Business Magazine,* August-September 1997, from *Back to Basics* by Michael Green.
** Duane Elgin, *The Voluntary Society*, 1981.
See also January 12 and 13, and October 31.

HOLY SIMPLICITY

"We may be giants scientifically," said a contributor to a recent BBC Moral Maze programme, "but morally we are pygmies." That statement points to the discrepancy between the sophistication of scientific, technological and (thankfully) medical progress and our ability to cope with the moral and spiritual questions posited by such developments. Its basic validity should not however lead us, as it does some religious people, to dismiss contemporary life as wholly amoral or immoral, and modern people as increasingly corrupt. That is the injustice of over-generalisation. Despite the terrible crimes committed, especially against children; despite the rampant materialism in so much thinking and the unhealthy sensuality that provides so much news; despite the awfulness of persistent wars, the violence, rape and murders, the drug traffic, and the madness of irresponsible people with guns, what is wonderful about God's world is the amount of goodness shown by so many people, the high degree of moral awareness reflected at many levels and in the glorious spirituality of humble, anonymous folk. It is right to recognise the deficiencies in moral and spiritual life today. It is not right to see the world and its people as beyond redemption.

That said, it is necessary to recognise how easily we can be corrupted. Greed, for example, is highly infectious. We can all become "locked in" to contemporary materialism and the economic struggle to survive. The problem for all religious people is how to remain "untarnished by the world"; how to fulfil the injunction "not to be conformed to this world" but to be "transformed". Just here is a crucial point of witness for disciples.

In creating a "manual for Christians" today, four areas of current failure need attention. *Rule 1* concerns *the simple life*: the reference is the reminder that "the Son of Man had nowhere to lay his head". *Rule 2* deals with *priorities*: the reference here is to Jesus' instruction to "seek first the Kingdom and his righteousness and all these (other) things will be added to you". *Rule 3* lays down the importance of *perspective*: the reference is to the stance laid down by St Paul, "the things which are seen are temporal but the things which are not seen are eternal". *Rule 4* deals with the importance of *direction*: the reference is to the biblical exhortation to run the race of life, "looking unto Jesus".

However impossible is the achievement of it, it is important to hold on to the ideal of the simple life, to retain what Ben Jonson calls "the grace of simplicity". "Teach us delight in simple things," we sing in Rudyard Kipling's hymn. It is not wrong to be modern, to have and to enjoy the things that are part of life today, but it is good for the soul to keep alive the sense of simplicity. "Cultivate simplicity," wrote Charles Lamb to Samuel Taylor Coleridge. But perhaps simplicity alone is not enough. "I have always revered *holy* simplicity" said St Jerome. Those who have tried to get back to the way of the Lord have usually done so by seeking to reflect Jesus' simple life and practising holy simplicity. "*O sancta simplicitas!*" cried John Huss, as he died, "O holy simplicity!"

SILENCE AND SIMPLICITY

The more real the underlying unity of the church, the more it can tolerate variety – and even afford to encourage it. Genuine movement towards unity should not be felt as threatening to distinctive witness but rather as an opportunity to integrate into the evolving corpus of belief and practice valuable historic insights into the faith.

It has been a privilege and benefit to me that two-thirds of my ministry has been in ecumenical undertakings. The blessings of such wider sharing do not change my primary calling which is to be committed to the ministry of Word and Sacraments, a task I see to be of primary importance today, but my ministry has been enhanced indeed through my interdenominational experience.

To take something from another tradition and add it to one's own, if it is valid both biblically and theologically, does not deny or abnegate one's faith, just as making an effort to *understand* other faiths does not conflict with one's own "Christ-centredness".

There may however remain areas of spirituality that still lie largely outside our experience. One of these may be disciplined and, particularly, contemplative prayer. Contemplative prayer and its related lifestyle have four elements. These are, as Thomas Keating (Cistercian priest, monk, abbot) records: "Solitude, Silence, Simplicity, and a Discipline for Prayer and Action." That four-fold definition is in itself ancient.

It is manifestly easier to carry out these practices in the controlled (organisationally) ambience of the convent, the monastery or the religious community, but working out these elements of spirituality in our personal daily life still remains a highly desirable aim.

The cultivation of the benefits of solitude is a strength in the struggle against unconscious motivation, that process (all too familiar to St Paul) whereby negative inner pressures, coming from depths outside the reach of our memories, overrule our conscious desires for good. Father Keating, while holding that "the language of psychology is an essential vehicle in our time to explain the healing of the unconscious",* goes so far as to say that "only the passive purifications of contemplative prayer can effect this profound healing. Only then will the reservoir of interior silence, built up in periods of contemplative prayer, never run dry." That statement will not necessarily be accepted in all psychotherapeutic circles but it deserves deep reflection.

Simplicity of faith can be a strength, too. It is not an attitude of simplistic naïveté that skates superficially over the great problems of life. It is a clear-sighted vision, a spiritual understanding, not necessarily able to be put into theological terms or philosophical argument, that has been vouchsafed to the earnest seeker, educated or less educated, articulate or inarticulate.

A young woman I have known for many years wrote to me to say that so hectic was her life – work, family etc – that, in her spiritual life, "God is getting the short straws." A dedicated woman, committed to service of great value, she reminds us, as she reminds herself, that to keep the spiritual balance right, we do need that fourth element, a discipline for prayer and action.

* The psychoanalytic concept of the unconscious is referred to in a number of Meditations but more fully on May 2 and 22. The "collective unconscious" is mentioned in those for June 17 and August 31.

FINDING PEACE

Those who follow Jesus want to take him at his word. After all, it was said of him that, unlike others, he spoke with authority. But trying to be obedient to his words can bring severe problems to some people. He said, for example, "If you ask any thing in my name, I will do it." There are sincere people who have become bitter when the "any thing" for which they pleaded "in his name" was not given.

What then did Jesus mean when he said: "Take no anxious thought for tomorrow"?* Given the realities of life today, how do you do that? When cuts in jobs are predicted and family responsibilities are great, can you be other than anxious about the future? When paedophile rings threaten the safety of the children, is it not a worry? Insurance companies prosper just because of anxiety about the future: is it not prudent to prepare for risks over property and life? The loss of a partner will bring not only loneliness, but worry about tomorrow. When temptation persists and inner pressures compel the repetition of abhorred sins, guilt can bring overwhelming anxiety. An anxious world teems with anxious people. Advice that seems over-simplistic cannot meet such deep needs.

"How blessed is he who leads a country life, unvex'd with anxious cares," wrote the poet John Dryden. Perhaps in the simpler world of Palestine, in Jesus' time, it was easier to "consider the lilies of the field, how they grow," and contemplate "the fowls of the air" fed by "your heavenly Father". It is less easy to take no anxious thought for tomorrow in the relentlessly demanding, often depressing, actively threatening world that is ours today.

The importance of Jesus' exhortation surely lies not in a literal interpretation of his words but rather in a recognition of the principle which he expounds. Anxiety is unprofitable and unhealthily negative. Just as fear casts out love, so worry destroys inner peace. Concentrating on illnesses only encourages ill-health. Even in prayer it is not good to focus on problems rather than God. It is love which casts out fear. Giving out does us much more good than giving in. We cannot, by an act of will, banish anxiety. We can reduce its pressure by reflecting deeply on "the things which we most surely believe".

There is so much to encourage us in the doctrine of Providence, its wonders seen through the eye of faith. The glory of the doctrine of forgiveness is its capacity to demolish persistent anxiety over guilt. Salvation is not a merit to be earned. It is a gift of grace, and anxiety is eased thereby. To believe in the healing Christ is to know God's will for us is wholeness. And if there is anxiety as to where energy can come from, remember that first Pentecost when promised power filled the disciples.

* See also Coping with Anxiety, April 14 and Prescription for Anxiety, April 15.

TWO ARE BETTER

"Well! My poor heart, here we are, fallen into the ditch which we had made so firm a resolution to avoid; let us implore the mercy of God, and that he will help us to be more steadfast in future ..."

These words from the great mystic, Francis de Sales, will touch a nerve in us if we are honest people. It is the story of the spiritual life as it has been experienced by seekers throughout the ages. Julian of Norwich expounds the same theme. In the parable of the servant who "hurried off so hopefully to do his Lord's will" she writes: "And anon he falleth into a slade and taketh full hurt."

The vocabulary of religion describes this experience as "temptation". The language of psychotherapy will think of it as negative pressures coming from the "shadow" side of the unconscious. The effect is the same. There is nothing more discouraging in the development of the spiritual life than the persistent sense of failure in thought and, even worse, behaviour when self-discipline falters, and faults believed to have been overcome are repeated. For the alcoholic dedicated to overcome his or her "problem", but who falls again, the sense of despair can be devastating. Someone struggling against sexual temptation experienced as intense inner pressures not always understood, can be made nearly suicidal by another "failure". What is even worse is the fact that such moments of weakness may follow times of heightened spiritual activity when the sense of grace is strong. How vulnerable we can be at such times!

Such falling into the ditch or slade must not however lead to a persistent dwelling on, and analysis of, failure. Brother Lawrence, in *The Practice of the Presence of God*, offers spiritual common-sense for our comfort and encouragement. He was much "aware of his sins but was not discouraged by them; he confessed them to God and did not ask him to excuse them. When he had done so he returned in peace to his ordinary business of love and worship." Add 'she' to 'he' each time, and we have practical spiritual direction of great value for us all.

It is in the same spirit that Francis de Sales offers his prescription for temptation in the quotation with which I began:

> "Here we are, fallen into a ditch": admit it
> "Let us implore the mercy of God": confess it
> "Trust that He will help us": have faith
> "God shall help us": leave it, forgiven.

"Two are better than one," said the Preacher (Ecclesiastes), "for if they fall then one will lift up his fellow." The battle for spiritual progress can be carried on privately with the help of God, but it is also the very purpose of spiritual direction and/or pastoral counselling to provide support on the spiritual journey. Sharing and caring is a God-given way to forward spiritual growth. Use it!

THE JOY OF GROWTH

When I had the responsibility for selecting potential trainees for training [course] in counselling on an analytic model, I was always impressed by the fact that a very high percentage of these 'mature' applicants were people who had themselves experienced counselling or psychotherapy as 'clients'. In other words, having themselves gone through problems and experienced the pain of growth in doing so, they wanted now to help others find the joy of growth too.

Whatever our undertakings in life, it is almost always necessary to endure pain to achieve success. Behind the musician, gloriously interpreting music in song or with an instrument, there lie hours of practice, scales, arpeggios, exercises, discipline. The ecstasy in performance is worth the agony of preparation. For athletes who are to perform at the Olympic Games there are the long routines essential to build up muscles, sinews, stamina. For footballers seriously injured, there may be years of painful recovery programmes before the joy of public performance is possible again. The Formula One driver faces discomfort, danger and death to have the joy of knocking part of a second off his lap-time. Across the whole field of human endeavour – what pain there is in preparation! What joy in achievement!

Growth into maturity psychologically and/or spiritually, reflects the same process. Blocks have to be cleared. Knots have to be unravelled. Defences have to come down, perhaps a little, probably a lot. Creative growth depends on the pain of self-awareness and self-discovery and, in this process, the first steps may be the most demanding ones.

St Paul speaks of present suffering and future glory when he exclaims: "I reckon that the sufferings of this present time are not worthy to be compared with the glory that shall be revealed in us!" As with a woman in childbirth, the pain is now, the joy is to come. When the Psalmist proclaims that "God has put a new song in my mouth," he is testifying to the joy of growth. Zacchaeus, an unhappy man, ostracised by the people because he was a tax-gatherer, shows the inner pain that made him climb up a sycamore tree to see Jesus, who might help him.* To read his story is to feel his pain. To hear his declaration of recompense and reconciliation is to sense his incipient joy. The process is a glorious one.

"All through my life I have been aware of the power of God, guiding me," writes Lin Berwick,** cerebral palsied, blind and in a wheelchair, in her book *Inner Vision*, *** "displaying all too clearly how He wants me to use the dark, as well as the joyful, periods. Adversity can be changed to joy so long as we accept the will of God."

"Weeping may endure for a night, but joy cometh in the morning."

Worship should reflect the joy of growth. Rightly and properly worship includes the essential element of confession, but the ultimate purpose of all worship is uplift and encouragement. For at the heart of it is praise and thanksgiving for his promise of the miracle which can bring newness of life and the joy of growth.

* References to the story of Zacchaeus occur in Meditations for February 21, April 5, June 2 and 4, July 15, October 6 and 23, and December 12.
** See Rejoice and Sign! for more about Lin, July 21.
*** Available only from The Lin Berwick Trust, 4 Chaucer Road, Sudbury, Suffolk CO10 1LN.

THE PAIN OF GROWTH

It was Sunday morning. The hymn, enthusiastically sung, was *The Church's one foundation*. A line in a verse not printed in all hymnaries had a searing impact. "The cry goes up 'How long?' " Saturated as we are by images of suffering, it seemed to express the anguish so prevalent today. The context – the line relates to disunity in the church – was temporarily overlaid by mental pictures of the hurt, harried, homeless people in, for example, Bosnia, leaving loved ones behind to their fate. The cry does indeed go up: "How long, Lord? How long?" Will the suffering of the world and such people never end? Can it at least be diminished?

To offer, unasked, religious platitudes to those overwhelmed by human tragedy is spiritual insensitivity of an indefensible kind. How can the simplistic text be relevant to, or "heard" by, the husband who has just lost his young wife to cancer? To the survivor whose loved ones have been killed in the accident? To the parents of the child who has died through illness, cot death, murder, suicide? It will therefore probably be with anger that the following words are read:

> The person who truly wishes to be healed is the one who does not refuse
> treatment. This treatment consists of the pain and distress brought on by
> various misfortunes. He who refuses it does not realise what they accomplish
> for him in this world or what he will gain when he departs this life.

The language is dated – this statement was in fact made a very long time ago by St Maximus the Confessor. It was made the focal point in a talk given by a friend, an Anglican priest, when addressing colleagues on "Healing through Dying". His purpose was to bring some hope in relation to the problem of suffering, and to do it not in terms of doctrinaire, academic theology, but through the theology of experience.

Saxon Walker's wife, Sheila, knew for a year that she was dying of cancer but, as Saxon tells us in his book, *Sheila – a Healing through Dying*,* that year was to be for them both the most spiritually creative year of their lives. They deliberately and consciously lived out the Christian Year, with its painful parts and its glorious parts, discovering as they did so such growth, healing and wholeness that Sheila's last year became not a failure but a victory, not a death but a new life.

The same principle, the creative power of pain, was something that had to be firmly put to the many applicants I had to interview over their desire to be trained in a psychotherapeutic model of counselling. The pain of growth had to be faced. My German colleague in Frankfurt, Dr Werner Becher, a psychotherapist, told me: "If you ever want to experience hell, undertake analysis." The statement may be exaggerated but it makes its point. The road to (in Jung's word) "individuation" or wholeness runs through the vale of tears.

In the spiritual life, the way to sanctification also involves the pain of spiritual growth. If, in St Maximus's word, the "treatment" is resisted, maturity is postponed. It can never lightly be claimed that suffering has an inherently creative component, but it is always true that the journey from the despair of the Garden of Eden to the wonder of the Garden of the Resurrection passes through the Garden of Gethsemane.

* Published by Arthur James, 1985.

THROUGH PAIN TO PEACE

There is something very dramatic about a statement in the story of doubting Thomas, the disciple whose belief in the resurrection of Jesus had to be "evidence-based". "*And Jesus came, the doors being shut.*" In literal terms, it is simply the record of a fact. The risen Lord did appear in their midst although the doors were closed. What is moving about the phrase is the symbolic truth encapsulated in it. It is another way of saying that "*Man's extremity is God's opportunity.*" It is in the depths of our despair, when we do not know where to go or what to do, when all the doors to progress seem shut, that Jesus comes in grace to be "*God with us.*"

It is that very point which is expressed with great power by St Paul in his second letter to the Corinthians, a letter which keeps in close relationship, hopelessness and hope. "*We are under pressure on every side,*" he writes (in William Barclay's translation), "*but never without a way out. We are at our wit's end, but never at our hope's end. We are pursued by men but never abandoned by God. We are knocked down but never knocked out.*" It is, Paul tells the Corinthian Christians, when they are at the lowest ebb that they will find that "*the supreme power belongs to God and does not have its source in us*".

It would be easy to dismiss such language as pious talk or religious sentimentality were it not the case that so many would willingly testify to such an experience. People who, because of their physical disabilities, emotional agony or even spiritual torment, have found that meeting the pressures and the knockout blows with faith, somehow discover precisely there at the point of crisis, are the seeds of victory. A seriously disabled woman, incapacitated from birth and later totally blind, is somehow able to say that "*the best things I have done for God have been done since – and because – I became blind.*" A victim of acute suffering and appalling pain can manage a radiant smile as she talks of the privilege of "*sharing in the sufferings of my Lord*". It is so often in the depths that the journey of discipleship has its source, the experience of (in the words of the Psalmist) emerging from "*the miry clay*" to find one's feet "*on the rock*". It is the Psalmist again who declares that it is when people are "*at their wits' end that they cry unto the Lord*".

The journey to inner peace may well be through the experience of pain. It does not however need to be so. If we return to the story of Thomas, we will remember the encouragement conveyed by Jesus' words to Thomas. The disciple was blessed in that he could base his faith on experience, but greatly blessed too, said Jesus, are those who believe without such evidence. It is possible to learn the glorious truth about the "supreme power of God" without having to journey through despair and pain. Fortunate are those who have come to such a faith.

DARKNESS, MY FRIEND

No matter how often you read the Bible, a verse, a text, a passage will strike you as completely new. It may be its relevance at that particular time and in that particular place. Some psalm of praise reflects your joy. Some word of encouragement meets a need. Some anguished cry touches your own pain. It happened like that yesterday.

It is part of the pastor's life to encounter the pain and anguish of his or her people. It may be, as last weekend, a plea to "please pray for my parish priest for his father has an inoperable cancer." The condition is, sadly, not unusual but the particular circumstances made it poignant. It may be the letter that came a few days ago from "friends of a friend". Their 11-year-old daughter died in an horrific home accident four years ago, and now their 20-year-old son has died from Sudden Death Syndrome.

But back to the passage which I happened to read yesterday. It was Psalm 88, a psalm of anguish that ended (in the New International Version) with the compelling cry: "The darkness is my closest friend." How descriptive this is of the anguish experienced by priest and parents. "Psalm 88 is the utterance of one who, in unrelieved anguish, 'cleaves to God most passionately when God seems to have withdrawn himself most completely'," writes one commentator on this psalm of loss and bereavement, the loss of friends and the absence of God: "You have taken my companions and my loved ones from me: the darkness is my closest friend." Such anguish!

Anguish involves the feeling that "whatever you thought was the beneficent power of creation is a childish error ... so that, finally, you give up hope and say there is nothing positive in life whatever." Dr Martin Israel, pathologist and priest and a long-time friend, wrote these words from his own experience of deep depression (described in his book *Dark Victory**) and more recently, of the sheer physical weakness that led him towards near-death. In his later book (*Doubt, the Way of Growth,***) he writes of the necessity of suffering anguish. "Until you have experienced anguish, you have not lived a full, proper life." That is something that can only be said by one who has suffered greatly and come to see that somewhere within the suffering there can be a hint of light.

A theatre visit this same week movingly underlined the anguish of suffering. My long-time friends, Sylvia Read and William Fry *** present *Shadowlands* in which C S Lewis's faith struggles with the fact of his wife's terminal cancer. It is not wrong to rail against the injustice of such suffering, but thanks be to those who, like John Milton in his blindness, see in the darkness a glimpse of light. "So by this infirmity," he wrote, "may I be perfected, by this completed. So by this darkness, may I be enclosed in light." Darkness, my friend!

* Mowbray, 1995.
** Mowbray, 1997.
*** Theatre Roundabout, 859 Finchley Road, London NW11 8LX.

THE ROAD TO GROWTH

The statement in the letter to the Hebrews in the New Testament which says: "Jesus, the Son of God . . . was tempted like as we are," is very important. Theologically, it underlines the truth that he is truly and fully human. Psychologically and spiritually, it brings great comfort. The Master, like the disciples, experiences severe temptation. We can then be assured of the divine understanding of our human failures.

While the experience of temptation is common to us all, the focus of it will vary from person to person. Human susceptibility in matters of "the flesh" is, for example, a common failing, but for Jesus it was something different. His three temptations, as recorded by both Matthew and Luke, all relate to that which was unique to him, his awareness of his divine power and gifts. Was he willing to forward his purpose by winning followers through turning stones to bread; creating publicity for himself by leaping from the temple only to land, miraculously, unharmed; engaging in worldly empire-building?

Those subtle inner pressures, tempting him to abuse his power, were firmly resisted and finally rejected. Of the reality of his experience of temptation there is no doubt. That enables him the more to be "God-with-us".

There are two insights in the story of Jesus' temptations that can help us with the pain of spiritual growth. First, it is important to be aware that severe temptation may follow times of spiritual elation. Matthew seems to be suggesting this by his placing the story of Jesus' temptation so close to his greatest spiritual experience, namely the affirmation at his baptism in Jordan: "This is my beloved Son in whom I am well pleased." It is immediately after the recording of this high point, spiritually, that the retailing of the temptation story comes. The closer people get to God the more urgent is it (to personalise the matter) for Satan to step up the attack.

Second, Luke makes a note not recorded in Matthew, but it is a significant one. "When the devil had ended all the temptation, he departed from (Jesus) *for a season*." To this the spiritual struggle in Gethsemane and on the cross surely testifies. It is realistic to recognise as a fact of spiritual life that future failure is always potentially present in us. The graph of the painful journey to spiritual growth is not symbolised by a simple straight line, going onward, rising upward. It is a jagged picture of heights and depths, hills and valleys, peaks and pits, spiritual elation and abject failure. But there is no need to be discouraged. Jesus is "God-with-us"; forgiveness is assured and new life promised.

DEVOTIONAL DISCIPLINE

James S Stewart was a prince among preachers. Whenever it was made known – in the forties, fifties and sixties – that he would be in a particular pulpit, the crowds would gather, not in the sermon-tasting context of other years, but simply to hear his profound biblical exposition and its penetrating application to life. Although he spent the later part of his ministry as an academic – he taught New Testament language and literature in the Faculty of Divinity in Edinburgh University – he always remained the quintessential pastor and preacher. An exceptionally shy man (as some of the best pastors are), his genuine saintliness showed itself in the quality of his personal ministry and the manifest strength of his disciplined devotional life.*

In discussing that necessary element of discipline in the spiritual life, I take very seriously Augustine's cautionary word: "He is a vain preacher of the word of God without, who is not a hearer within." To that I say "Amen". None of us finds it easy to be devotionally disciplined.

When writing (in 1980) a devotional book of prayers and thoughts for each day called *A Day at a Time*, I asked James S Stewart, whom I had known for many years, about his devotional discipline. With typical graciousness, he shared his practice with me.

Before prayers in the morning, he read (1) a lectionary passage from the Bible; (2) an excerpt from *Pray Today*, published by his church and mine, The Church of Scotland; (3) the appropriate reading from "my father's well-thumbed copy" of *Daily Light*; and (4) a section from the late John Baillie's *A Diary of Private Prayer*. After evening prayers, he used three aids – first something from *The Upper Room*; secondly, one of the Psalms; and finally a chapter from a specifically devotional writer (he gave Evelyn Underhill as an example). This may feel to be a rather demanding devotional programme – and a little dated – but it indicates the sort of spiritual exercise to which we could usefully aspire. In the end, of course, *our* programme must be matched to *our* needs.

Religious , that is monks and nuns, live "in community" and therefore have the benefit of a devotional structure to help them maintain their spiritual priorities. One of the pleasures of being at Taizé was the sound of the bells regularly summoning all, community members and visitors alike, to prayer. In the ordinary world, it is less easy to give a proper priority to devotional obligations. Time, duties, business pressures, responsibilities, anxieties, lack of energy, can combine to prevent consistency in the spiritual life; yet deep down we know that there cannot be a living faith if the needs of the inner being are ignored and the means of grace neglected.

"Time set aside for the inner life is an essential part of our spiritual development," says my friend and colleague, Dr Martin Israel, pathologist and now priest. The late Christopher Bryant writes encouragingly: "It is of great importance to persevere with set times of prayer and not give up." The form, length and content of our spiritual exercises must be our own. There is certainly, Jesus tells us, no need for "much speaking". Long or short, articulate or inarticulate, what really matters is that our worship is from the heart. But that devotion will always be enhanced by the exercise of discipline.

* There is a similar reference to James S Stewart in April 24, and another on October 31.

THE JOURNEY OF LIFE

When David Livingstone volunteered for missionary service, he was asked where he was willing to go. "I will go anywhere," he replied, "so long as it is forward."

One of the glories of the Christian faith is its offer to all of the possibility of a new beginning. Deep in the heart of most human beings is the desire to "wipe the slate clean", to be forgiven, to be "made new". The doctrine of forgiveness presents that opportunity to all who sincerely seek it.

Jesus made it clear that, where there is genuine penitence, God's forgiveness is total and unconditional. Whatever we have said or done or thought or felt that is unacceptable to him, to the church, to society or to ourselves is embraced in the miracle of grace, and we can go forward with confidence. To engage, then, in continuing self-condemnation, and endless recrimination is to deny the forgiveness given and the freedom of spirit received. To know, when we are in deep despair over both our personal failures and the corporate darkness in the world around us, that everything can be made new is the greatest possible encouragement on the spiritual way.

On the journey of life, it is not achievement that matters most; it is sensing that you are travelling in the right direction. Paul had, as he himself claimed, a life that was full of achievements, moral, ethical and religious, but he came to realise – particularly through his experience on the road to Damascus – that he was going in the wrong direction. Conversion was the process by which the whole direction of his life was changed. From then on, he had to "run the race . . . looking unto Jesus". The secret of success in the spiritual life lies in our ability (as the old chorus says) to "turn your eyes upon Jesus", for he is, in the words of the letter to the Hebrews, "the author and finisher of our faith". He gives direction.

"Do you see yonder wicket gate?" asked Evangelist of Christian in John Bunyan's *Pilgrim's Progress*. The answer was "No." Then said Evangelist: "Do you see yonder shining light?" "I think I do," was the reply. Evangelist said: "Keep that light in your eye and go up directly thereto, so shalt thou see the gate; at which when thou knockest, it will be told thee what thou shalt do."

With that light in your eye, in faith, go forward.

THE RIGHT DIRECTION

All that I knew about the hotel in Budapest, to which I was driving from Prague, was its name. It could be anywhere in the city. I spotted a man, standing at a busy junction, studying a map. Extracting myself carefully from the seemingly unending traffic flow, I parked (as others did) on the pavement. Communication, I assumed, would be a problem. In fact, it wasn't. The gentleman was from Croydon. There on his map was the hotel, duly marked, across the river in Pest. I now had my marker and concentrated solely on visualizing the most direct route to it; straight to the river, along the bank until you reach a particular bridge, cross the bridge and that road should lead to the hotel. I kept my eye resolutely on the goal, looking at nothing on the way, however potentially interesting. So long as I held to the right direction I would arrive. I did.

The spiritual life is not a state but a journey. To reach the goal it is essential, as we saw in yesterday's Meditation, to ensure that you are travelling in the right direction. The New Testament makes clear the secret of a successful pilgrimage. You must keep "looking unto Jesus, the author and finisher of our faith".

From the beginning of the Bible to its end, the recurring themes are change and growth. Genesis begins with the image of the spirit of God moving on the face of the waters, bringing order out of chaos. Revelation declares the God who "makes all things new".

It does not ultimately matter whether the great themes of redemption and renewal are expounded in profound theological language or as the simple faith of the one who "takes Jesus at his word". Real living (which the New Testament calls "life abundant") begins with change and issues in growth. The process is dramatically portrayed in the Damascus road experience of Paul which pointed the former persecutor of Christians, Saul of Tarsus, in an entirely new direction. From then on, his aim was spiritual maturity.

In the kind of world we face today, where materialism and secularism abound, we need to keep to the way of life, focus on the great landmarks of the faith, build a sound theological structure and evolve a philosophy of life that will replace alienation with relationship, meaninglessness with purpose, lostness with rediscovery, fear with love, death with life.

The Garden of the Resurrection demonstrates how death becomes life when you look in a different direction.* Mary Magdalene, loving her Lord, stood there gazing disconsolately at the place of death. A voice behind her made her turn round. It was the risen Christ. She was no longer looking at death but at life, for she was now looking in the right direction.

* Referred to also in The Power of Prayer, February 13.

INNER VISION

That politicians, like policemen, seem to be getting younger may be a sign of advancing years! The fact that there are young men and women in high office is, nevertheless, a trend not to be discouraged. The President of the United States, the last Prime Minister, the present Prime Minister and the Chancellor of the Exchequer* are all men of youthful vigour. When that is combined with vision, it should be a healthy combination. This year's General Election** produced a plethora of youthful parliamentarians. If the element they lack is experience, what they bring must be awareness of the attitudes and ideals of younger generations. If they can learn quickly (and there is nothing like heavy public responsibility to encourage that process), they can bring into politics not only the traditional "breath of fresh air", but a vibrancy and verve relevant to contemporary needs. It was a man who was put to death at 33 who transformed religion for all time.

A proper appreciation of youthful endeavour should not however decry the value of experience, especially in spiritual things. Those who most clearly sensed the significance and wonder of the birth of Jesus included the venerable Simeon and a 90 year-old prophet, Anna.

Pastoral responsibility has many rewards and one of them is the privilege of spending time with the aged saints whose bodies are failing greatly but whose spirituality is deep and keen. That depth comes from long and intimate acquaintance with their Lord, usually arising from the time for reflection that immobility brings. I have experienced often the depth of their inner vision. The most accurate comments I ever heard on the spiritual life of the congregation to which she was attached, came from a 90 year-old woman, confined to a wheelchair, living alone and for years unable to attend church. The "closer walk with God" that the life of virtual solitude brings seems to strengthen the spiritual instinct and intuition of some people to a point where it can result in true prophecy.

Age, not always crabbit, and youth, given the gift of grace, can surely "live together". Each has something to offer the other. There is a tendency, at least in western society, for age to be discounted, even disparaged, but it is a mistake not to be willing to listen to the wisdom of the years. Quantity in years alone does not, however, necessarily bring about the evolution of spiritual quality. A very young man had to tell a senior citizen, the Pharisee Nicodemus, that "you must be born again". It was for that same young man to tell a much older fisherman: "Get thee behind me, Satan, for thou savourest not the things that be of God but those that be of men."

For young people to see visions and for older people to dream dreams, said Peter at Pentecost (quoting the prophet Joel), can be evidence of the outpouring of the Spirit. In the economy of the kingdom, inner vision in older and younger people together could be a powerful instrument for good.

* Mr Bill Clinton, Mr John Major, Mr Tony Blair, Mr Gordon Brown respectively.
** 1997.

TRANSFORMING VISION

"Why do you stand there, gazing up to heaven?" There is an implied rebuke in the question put to the disciples on the first Ascension Day by "two men in white apparel". Surely they know that, as he promised, he will "in like manner", come again. It is time to stop gazing heavenwards, come down to earth and go back to work for his kingdom.

There is a place in religious life for both contemplation and activity. If, however, involvement in the world "in his name" is to be effective, it must be founded on vision. Faith without works easily becomes false piety. Activity without faith is no more than useful service.

The two followers on their journey to Emmaus, experienced a heightened level of spiritual awareness. As we have noted earlier,* through the symbol of "breaking of bread" they became conscious of the presence of the risen Lord. He had joined them on their walk, an unrecognised stranger who had expounded the scriptures to them. In a moment of evening wonder, they recognised the risen Christ.

It was a combination of circumstances that created the context in which the miracle was possible. As the three men approached Emmaus, night began to fall. With traditional hospitality the two followers invited "the stranger" to stay the night. He, however, "made as if he would go further", but they "constrained" him, insisting that he would tarry with them. It was that insistence that led to the situation in which the miracle could occur. So overwhelmed were the two men by what had happened to them that they immediately returned to Jerusalem to share the news of Jesus' resurrection with the apostles.

Mystic experience cannot be achieved, only received. It is, nevertheless, open to all who humbly seek and reverently ask, to be allowed as I said before to "touch and handle things unseen". Circumstances can then combine, in spiritual synchronicity, to open the way for a transforming vision.

It may come in an act of worship; in the solitude of the mountain top; in the serenity of green pastures and by still waters; in the awesome holiness of some silent sanctuary; in an intimate relationship with a loved one; in "the desert place" where we meet with God and with ourselves. However momentary the experience, the result is grace and renewal . . . as the transforming vision surely was for the two who walked to Emmaus.

* See Meditations for January 8 and 9.

GOD'S GENEROSITY

"It is in the silence of the desert that the battle for the life or death of the soul will be decided, for there the false, the trivial, the decorative is stripped away and human beings come face to face with themselves and with God." I wrote these words in 1980,* and they remain true in terms of subsequent experience. It is indeed in the silence that we come to terms with ourselves and with God. I had not then, however, come across a statement seeming to confirm this analysis of the spiritual life in the writings of the great reformer, John Calvin. He wrote "Nearly all the wisdom we possess, that is to say true and sound wisdom, consists of two parts. These are 'knowledge of God and of ourselves'." He continues: "Although they are closely connected, it is difficult to say which comes first. Knowledge of ourselves not only stimulates us to seek God but, as it were, also leads us by the hand to find him . . . We never achieve a clear knowledge of ourselves unless we have first looked upon God's face and then descended from contemplating him to examining ourselves."

The desert place experience** (and "desert" means wherever that personal, private sanctuary is), ought to be profound. It may well create a sense of apprehension because the process is a threatening one and should be healing. No process of self-examination in the light of God's presence can be other than painful. Laid out behind us is the seemingly endless sequence of personal failures, innocent errors, wilful disobediences, the repetition of surrendered sins, the sense of incomprehension at the depths to which publicly personable people can sink. But it is precisely here that the time – or rather timeless – factor is crucial. The self-analysis takes place in the presence of the utterly forgiving God. The divine presence – which, like Moses, Isaiah and so many of the Old Testament prophets, we approach with a sense of awe – is, in fact, on the authority of Jesus, the forgiving Father. In the very moment of acknowledgement and repentance, the generosity and graciousness of God is active. So every aspect and consequence of our honest self-knowledge is embraced and encompassed in the knowledge we have of God as Jesus Christ revealed it. To those who say, with John Donne, "But I have more", there comes simultaneously: "My grace is sufficient for you."

The search for other metaphors to describe the indescribable God must go on; metaphors relevant to our language, experience and culture. God is always contemporary, but whatever concepts are found, whatever images prove useful, they must never set aside that factor of personal relationship, marked by honesty on the human side and forgiving grace on the divine side. This is of the essence of the divine-human encounter.

True religion, in the light of God's revelation in Jesus, must always be comforting, always encouraging, endlessly invigorating. That "other Comforter", the living and abiding presence of Jesus, always brings power and creates strength. That message is, by derivation, within that word, Comforter, itself.

* Creative Silence, 1980 (Ecclesia Services, 80a Woodland Rise, London N10 3UJ).
** See also Meditation for January 5, Be Still and Know . . .

THE DIVINE PATIENCE

How privileged were Peter, James and John to share in two great moments – one glorious, one dark – in Jesus' life! One was his Transfiguration, the other his agony in the Garden of Gethsemane. Peter's excitement at the mountain top vision of Moses and Elijah, as well as the sight of Jesus embraced in radiant light, was manifest and understandable. Less easy to comprehend was the inability of the three disciples to remain awake while Jesus agonised in Gethsemane over his coming suffering and death. How sad his words sound: "Could you not watch with me one hour?" They could not, and so did not see the sweat "like drops of blood" that indicated the tension he was experiencing in that strife of prayer.

That searching phrase, "the strife of prayer", comes from Jacques Loew, the Dominican monk who pioneered the worker-priest movement in France. In his book *Face to Face with God** he pinpoints the prime "characteristics of all prayer and all struggle: patience, perseverance and constancy". The element of patience is a crucial one.

"Though God take the sun out of heaven," wrote George Herbert, "we must have patience." Paul certainly counselled Timothy to "follow after patience" and in the second letter of Peter it is strongly emphasised as a virtue.

It is, however, its association with suffering (both words come from the same Latin root) which is significant. Patience is, in fact, writes Robert Llewellyn, "that quality of life which makes suffering creative". How appropriate it is then to reflect on patience, for the sacrifice of Jesus, and his understanding of it in terms of the great Old Testament concept of "the suffering Servant", incarnate the compassion of a God of love "who suffers long and is kind".

The divine patience is a prominent biblical theme. Of many references to it, the most glorious description comes surely from the Psalmist: "Thou, Lord, art a God, full of compassion and gracious, long-suffering and plenteous in mercy ..." (Psalm 86) The Greek work for "long-suffering" is *makrothumia*. It is the word used by Paul to tell the Romans of the goodness, forbearance and long-suffering of God. It is the attitude personified by the waiting father, ready to receive his prodigal son, not with anger or judgement, but with heart-felt love. That picture encapsulates Jesus' portrayal of the patient God.

The church, in its proclamation of the gospel, must surely present not the God of wrath but the God of compassion, whose love, in the words of the benediction, "passeth understanding". Redemptive love unites patience and passion.

If the religious life is an attempt to reflect divine qualities and attributes, George Herbert is right: "We must have patience." In so doing, we mirror in some small way the divine patience, our example and our joy.

* Darton, Longman & Todd (1977).
For a further Meditation on this theme, see August 3, The Love that is Patient.

IN THE MOOD

What to say and do to bring about changes of mood is the challenge that faces preachers, pastors, spiritual directors, psychotherapists, counsellors and politicians. "Mood," in dictionary terms, is a "contemporary state of the emotions". Additionally, it means "a prevailing spirit, disposition or set of attitudes". The first definition takes mood out of the realm of rational control. The second points to the problems that arise for politicians.

Much evidence is offered by politicians to show that the recession is over and economic growth is at hand. There is, however, a major difference between that public presentation and the actual mood of ordinary people. Daily experience in small businesses involves worry about survival, jobs, homes and families. Confidence in the future is unsteady and statistics, on their own, just do not take away the mood of despondency.

The Irish situation illustrates the same dilemma. Assurances about the cessation of violence are just not strong enough to meet the deeply ingrained lack of trust in some people – as the debate about the word "permanent" in relation to a cease-fire has shown. It will need more reassurance than has so far been given to remove doubt from the collective unconscious of some groups. Indeed, something of a conversion experience may be necessary to close the gap between public pronouncement and private misgiving.

In the religious field, conversion needs to be as thorough as anywhere else or moods may well hold us back. Jesus pointed to the dangers of superficial religious experience in the parable of the sower. Seed that cannot root properly because there is no depth will endure for some time but ultimately fade away. Pastors and preachers need to be aware that, unless conversion reaches the unconscious level, it will not hold. Indeed the transformation required is effectively re-birth, Jesus said to Nicodemus. Bringing about the "new creation" of which Paul speaks involves radical and total change. Only then will attitudes, relationships and behaviour be affected.

Moods are a problem in our personal lives too. We can suddenly find ourselves "spiralling downwards" into gloom and depression, and not understand why it is happening. Perhaps some event has acted as a trigger and activated feelings of rejection, lack of worth or bereavement. Other causes may be unconscious and beyond our reach. We cannot simply will ourselves out of that dark mood but, hopefully, we can find help in two directions. If some new factor enters the situation (the dreaded interview was in fact highly successful, for example), a dramatic change in mood is possible. Our other lifeline may be the love of a friend or the expertise of a counsellor. Most people need company to be strong enough to look at and then face the factors that pull us down.

We also need to draw on the resources of our faith. There is, or ought to be, in our religion access to the spiritual energy that can lead us away from decline into depression and disease, and take us towards health and wholeness. Historic Christianity calls that energy the Holy Spirit who at Pentecost, so dramatically changed the mood of the disciples.

The background references in this Meditation refer to 1997.

HOLY DETACHMENT

It is not money itself but the love of it that is said to be the root of all evil. But there is much evil caused too by the extreme lack of money that genuine poverty represents. There are obvious links between unemployment and social misbehaviour, desperation and delinquency, homelessness and hopelessness. Poverty as a vow, voluntarily made as an act of Christian obedience, is a noble virtue. But the poverty that is forced on people by social policy or political circumstance is another matter. Whether it is seen in the poverty present in our own society through vast differences in the distribution of wealth or at its horrific worst in underdeveloped parts of the world, concern for the needs of the poor represents a fundamental response inseparable from the demands of the gospel.

The Christian faith can never be other than a radical faith, rooting out whatever creates unacceptable inequality. The infinite value of every created being is built into the fabric of the Christian message. Equality may be an impossible aim, but equality of opportunity is not. Everyone must be given the chance to make the most of their creative potential, and any system which defeats that purpose deserves prophetic denunciation. Offending one little one merits both divine displeasure and human condemnation.

To come to feel that money is of less and less importance is a sign of maturing spirituality. That is, of course, more easily said in comfortable financial circumstances than in dire straits . "The best thing about getting old," writes L S McCandless however, "is that all those things you couldn't have when you were young, you no longer want."

That practical thought can be taken to a deeper level. "Be not conformed to this world," Paul wrote to the Ephesians. "Be ye transformed." Growth in spirituality is demonstrated by the attitude we have to "the world". It is not that we grow away from involvement in this world, for no proper understanding of the doctrine of the Incarnation would allow that to happen. You are "in the world," Jesus told his disciples. But he went on: "You must not be *of* it." Jesus shared the pain, the pressures, the suffering, the cruelty, the admiration, the criticism of the world as one who was "truly human", but he demonstrates for all the world to see and from it to learn, the vibrant concept of holy detachment. It does not mean leaving the world and its needs behind. Indeed, the greater the depth of true spirituality, the more will compassion for the world flow out. But it does involve finding the right relation between the "temporal" and the "eternal", between the kingdom and the "other things".

Holy detachment may be for most of us a later experience of life, but it needs to be a real and a growing area for all.

THE HERMIT'S WAY

"I rise at 3am for the office of Vigil at 3.30am, returning to my hermitage thereafter for further devotions alone. Mass is at 6.30am followed immediately by a further hour of solitary prayer." And so a normal day in the life of a hermitess unfolds. To read this programme of the holy life of a long-standing friend, formerly a specialist in her own professional field, compels respect and admiration. Hidden away in a holy island, inner happiness reigns. Is it escape from reality or a pilgrimage towards it?

Reading her letter, takes me back to a visit last autumn to the village of Sachselm, near Lucerne in Switzerland. In the mountainous region east of the Lake of Sarnen, I visited the village of Flüeli. Nicklaus of Flüeli, peasant farmer, politician, magistrate, statesman, founder of Swiss unity and a creative originator of Swiss neutrality, lived in the fifteenth century and was married to Dorothea, with whom he had ten children. He served on the town and cantonal councils and became a judge, yet, at the age of 50, and with the agreement of his wife, he took Jesus' words literally: "No man is worthy of me who cares more for father or mother, son or daughter, than for me." From that day he became Brother Klaus the hermit, living the disciplined life, sleeping on a bench or the bare floor, wearing a simple woollen cloak, using on cold nights an old patched blanket, until his death in 1487. The long path down to the hermitage in which those twenty years were spent is a journey through nature's splendour, a road now enjoyed by the streams of pilgrims who come to visit Brother Klaus's home. Not everyone will feel comfortable with a father leaving a family of ten children (however well provided for materially), but the call to leave all and follow the hermit's life was crystal clear to Brother Klaus.

The kind of choice made by hermitess and hermit does not realistically face many church members today. But it does remind us that the primary purpose of the church, is to provide the "stabilising power of the enduring spiritual realities". The church does not exist to fulfil social functions that are "of less and less relevance to, or indistinguishable from, those carried out by secular institutions" says the spiritual writer, John Main. What a tragedy it is if the church is so preoccupied with its problems, its image, its personnel, its structures, its committees that it is not available to "fan into flame the gift of God". It is, or should be, a lively organism, firing up the holy life.

It is not a past experience that the church exists to proclaim, but a present and powerful one. The risen Christ in its midst creates its stabilising power today. The presently active Holy Spirit is dynamic power, the divine energy at work in the world. It is to that great reality the hermits witness by trying to practise what they preach.

RAINBOWS THROUGH THE RAIN

A memorable image, one that is worthy of being carried over into a new century, is that of the rainbow over the Rheinfall in Switzerland. It was on an October day that Jillian and I sailed across the Rhine in a small boat to take a closer look at, and pictures of, the turbulent waterfall at Schaffhausen. For thousands of years the cascade has thundered down to create stormy waters and swirling torrents, but when the sun shines brightly - as it did that day - it projects through the vast spray thrown up by the waterfall, a striking rainbow. It seems so close, possibly 100 feet above the water, colourful and complete. That rainbow, shining through the turbulence, is not only a wonderful sight, but a dramatic symbol.

The rainbow above the churning waters is an appropriate image for a new year, a new century, a new millennium, for just such a symbol was offered for the new world, in the Old Testament story, after the flood. "I will set my rainbow in the clouds," God said to Noah, "and it will be the sign of the covenant between me and the earth. Whenever the rainbow appears in the clouds, I will see it and remember the everlasting covenant ..." The rainbow proclaimed God's continuing presence despite the clouds and storms.

The Incarnation was no mere form of words. It was pulsating action, expressing love and compassion. These qualities, divine in their nature, became incarnate in living encounters with people. That Jesus suffered as human beings do, was tempted like as we are, shared our lot, is made known in his miracles of healing, his empathy in bereavement, his understanding and forgiveness of human failure. Caring was fundamental to his mission, whether he talked tenderly but firmly to a woman caught in an act of adultery, immortalised the tears of the woman who then dried his feet with her hair, loved a reluctant rich young ruler, conversed patiently but authoritatively with a respected senior citizen like Nicodemus or ministered to a woman from Samaria. In every human situation where there is panic, pain or peril we are not alone; "God with us" indeed.

The new century will increase efforts to find the contemporary language and the meaningful metaphors needed to make the credal truths on which faith is based, relevant to the people of the new millennium. It is however the language and the images that need to change, not the faith, "the things which we must surely believe". They, like the One to whom they relate, are "the same – yesterday, today and for ever".

At the heart of belief is the divine-human relationship, proclaimed in the Old Testament and confirmed by Jesus, a relationship expressed in the eternal triangle of love between God, ourselves and our neighbour. It exists because "He first loved us." The rainbow in the rain is the symbol of the promised presence of God whatever our situation. Look carefully and you will be able to trace rainbows through the rain.

SET OBJECTIVES

It can be disconcerting to lose touch with your roots, dangerous to remove your landmarks, disastrous not to determine your objectives. This somewhat alliterative sentence evolved out of reflection on two Old Testament passages. The first and third phrases come from the prophet Jeremiah, the middle statement from the book of Proverbs. Roots, landmarks and goals are important.

The experience of losing your roots is emphasised by an image in Jeremiah 50, verse 6. It is a pastoral one common in the prophetic books: "My people have been lost sheep ... They wandered over mountain and hill, and *forgot their own resting-place.*" That is lostness indeed. It is important for nations that they do not lose touch with their foundations; this makes the way that history is taught crucial. It is important that the church thinks and acts "in remembrance of Jesus"; that emphasises the need for the traditional as well as the novel in worship and theology. It is important that as individuals we are aware of the people who have shaped us.

The loss of landmarks endangers the fabric of life. The words in Proverbs (chapter 23, verse 10) no doubt refer to literal landmarks, but the metaphor is relevant to contemporary life. It is not the intention of the proposed change to the Armed Services rule relating to the affairs members have with non-Service people (distinct from affairs between Service people, which will remain an offence) to lower standards and diminish values, but the current trends in relationship ethics cumulatively create a feeling of erosion that threatens the health of society. When traditional landmarks disappear, contemporary approaches to social and ethical problems (including the fields of both medical and Christian ethics) tend not to set up the markers which society needs and individuals miss. It is not universal immorality that is the danger for today, but a widespread a-morality.

The ability to "determine set objectives" is the mark of great statesmen – as R A Butler once pointed out in a reference to Ernest Bevin and Winston Churchill. It is a concept that meant much to a Church of Scotland minister for whom I have always had the greatest admiration and respect, the Rev John Brown, who died recently. He once preached a sermon on the Jeremiah passage to which I have referred. The exact text (chapter 50, verse 5) was: "They shall ask the way to Zion and turn their faces towards it." Should not all of us determine set objectives, he asked?* (One of Mr Brown's sons is, significantly, the Chancellor, Gordon Brown.)

It was said of Jesus that he "set his face steadfastly towards Jerusalem". He had determined his objectives. The result is Christian history. His roots were in the Old Testament and the Jewish law. His landmarks were the commandments, both old and new. His purpose was the well-being, salvation, wholeness of people. It is no wonder that his followers are asked to keep "looking unto Jesus" for their roots, landmarks and objectives are in him.

* *Gordon Brown, The Biography* by Paul Routledge, Simon and Shuster, 1998.
This Meditation was written in 1999.

SENSE OF IDENTITY

The late and great George MacLeod, when illustrating a theme or point, had a flair for apt story-telling. One such anecdote concerned a soldier in the First World War (in which MacLeod himself – later known for his pacifist stance – won the Military Cross for his bravery). As a result of a bomb exploding nearby, the soldier suffered severe injuries and a total loss of memory. MacLeod, concerned about the man, took him to a Services boxing match which would be, he thought, attended by many of his friends and acquaintances. Between two of the rounds, MacLeod led the soldier into the ring and asked the audience if any one recognised him. There was no response of any kind. Desperate, the soldier in his acute distress, cried out "Will nobody tell me who I am?"

There is nothing more important than a sense of identity. With it self-confidence is created; without it, a sense of worth is usually missing, as is a lack of self-respect and sense of value. The latter can lead to psychological and personality problems.

To come to know one's identity will involve a determined exercise in self-awareness. Some may achieve this through self-analysis though the difficulties in this process are real. We all have the ability to block out anything that seems to be threatening or uncomfortable so that we will not reach such material. For many, then, the process of self-knowledge is better effected through a relationship of a professional kind. It may be through counselling or possibly spiritual direction. Because of the pain of self-knowledge, the process is a demanding one but a worthwhile one. To know who you are is, at best, a very affirming process.

Making it possible for people to discover themselves and their value was something Jesus did particularly well. The statement in St John's Gospel that Jesus "knew what was in man" was a tribute to the sensitivity and insight he showed in his personal dealings with people of so many different backgrounds. To each and all he gave a sense of dignity and worth. He acknowledged their identity.

It was, interestingly, about his own identity that Jesus asked his disciples: "Who do you say that I am?" Receiving the answer that he did from Peter with his heart-warming spontaneous response: "You are the Son of God!" he was moved to exclaim (I paraphrase) "Peter, you have spoken, not in terms of human knowledge on the level available to flesh and blood. You have done it by spiritual intuition, by divine revelation!" It is a magic moment in the Gospel story and one that identified him in such a way that Jesus could now let it be known that he would suffer and die. Identified as the Messiah, he could now show that Messiah to be the Suffering Servant.

The search for identity is a psychological one, but it is also a spiritual one. For a sure faith we need to know who we are as well as whom we serve.

DAYS OF DOUBT

"I'm struggling," said the voice on the phone, 400 miles away. It was Mary.* I had known her since she was fourteen years old, watched her through her formative years and conducted her wedding to John* 39 years ago. Two months ago, when Mary rang me early in the morning, I had to assume it was bad news. It was. John had died from a heart attack during the night. Mary had faced the bereavement and funeral with courage, faith and dignity, but two months on, the depth of her loss was being felt. She was indeed "struggling".

When death comes suddenly, preventing long suffering, it must be a blessing to the one who has died, but it brings wounding hurt to those left behind. But how much worse is "dying by inches".

A devout Christian, for whom I have unreserved respect, used that phrase recently. She was referring not to the slow deterioration which is a normal part of ageing, but to her own experience of terrible suffering. Crippling deafness had brought her specialised ministry to young people to an end – and her to personal isolation. Surgical mismanagement had led to severe restrictions on mobility and appalling pain. Her ability to serve had been continually reduced. Dying by inches, with its combination of physical and spiritual agony, must test the faith of even the most committed saint. What can the will of God be in such a situation?

"Days of darkness still may meet me, sorrow's path I oft may tread," says F H Rowley's hymn. He goes on: "But his presence still is with me, by his guiding hand I'm led." But in days of doubt, can this feel real?

When sweat "like drops of blood" fell from Jesus in Gethsemane, it was his day of doubt. He prayed that he might be spared the agony, but was able to add: "Thy will, not mine, be done." But the doubt seems to have remained: "My God, my God, why hast thou forsaken me?" he cried from the cross.

It would be insensitive and arrogant for one unacquainted with such suffering to tell others to make the ultimate commitment and "surrender all to Jesus". How can one theorise on the spiritual benefits of "detachment" or advocate in such circumstances "catharsis", the spiritual process whereby an individual is "cleansed or freed from such impediments – sensible, intellectual or spiritual – which block the quest for authentic existence and union with God" (Professor J D Jones)? How can one tell people to accept positively the darkness which is both the condition and the quality of the true knowledge of God (Denys the Areopagite)? Much more likely than "surrender" is our taking to ourselves King Agrippa's words, "Almost thou persuadest me ..." Yet the weight of the counsel from the saints is that light comes out of darkness.

The darkest part of the night is the "night of spirit". St John of the Cross declares that that is "the dark night of the soul" in which the self is stripped of any remaining spiritual gratification and of every consoling image of itself. Only beyond this, he says, does the dawn of illumination break into the final union.

It is a daunting, demanding journey, but the end of it is consolation, not desolation. It is, perhaps, "growing by inches".

* For privacy reasons, the names have been changed.

HALF AND HALF

What a glorious book is that of the Old Testament prophet, Ezekiel. No wonder my old Principal in New College, Edinburgh – the late Professor W A Curtis – advised us all to give it very special attention. It is the book which gives the most accurate definition possible of a healing, pastoral or counselling relationship. "I sat where they sat." It is the book which offers that dramatic death and resurrection story, the utter desolation of the valley of dry bones transformed into new life by the inspiration of God's spirit. It is the book which, particularly in the *New English Bible* translation, presents the most remarkably tender picture of the infinitely caring love of God: "I myself will tend my flock, I myself pen them in their fold, says the Lord God. I will search for the lost, recover the straggler, bandage the hurt. . ." It is the book in which this same God "sought for a man among them that should . . . stand in the gap" for him, only for the sad, bathetic "punchline" to follow: "But I found none."

The God of Ezekiel is a God of huge tenderness and infinite loving-kindness, but he is also the God who makes that "absolute demand"* to which I have referred elsewhere. The demand is for nothing less than complete commitment. The demand is echoed in the New Testament in the words of Jesus to actual and potential disciples: "Whosoever will come after me, let him deny himself, take up his cross and follow me."

There is a fascinating translation of Psalm 119, verse 113, in one of the early "new translations", that greatly respected one by James Moffatt. It runs: "I hate men who are *half and half*." That is a clear statement about failure in individual commitment. Corporate failure is equally condemned in one of the letters to the seven churches at the beginning of the Book of Revelation. The language is strong and the condemnation devastating, leaving the church of the Laodiceans in no doubt of the divine view of failure in commitment: "I know thy works, that thou art neither cold not hot. So then because thou art lukewarm, and neither cold nor hot, I will spit you out of my mouth."

Commitment, if willingly and voluntarily given to a proper cause or a leader of integrity, is a great gift. But the choice of the subject or object of commitment is crucial. Directed to a wrong cause or a flawed leader, such blind commitment turns into fanaticism. The results of that are all too visible in the world today . . . terrorism, persistence in violence and war whatever suffering they bring to the innocent. The world has suffered too much from uncritical adherence to destructive activity for false motives.

There is no doubt, however, of the value of commitment for religious faith so long as it is freely and responsibly made, objectively understood and enthusiastically offered. Alas, it was just this which the admirably honest, rich young ruler could not give, departing sorrowfully as a result. This, too, made King Agrippa's comment to Paul interesting in its context but ultimately irrelevant. "Almost," he said, "thou persuadest me to be a Christian." But "almost" and "commitment" bear no relation to each other. Half-and-half people will never make disciples.

* See Meditation for February 12.

BUT . . .

What a difference the conjunction "but" can make! It has the capacity to convert a flat statement of fact or opinion into a dramatic declaration of great significance.

Let me illustrate this by quoting one of five "but" statements by Jesus in the Sermon on the Mount. "Ye have heard that it hath been said 'Thou shalt love thy neighbour and hate thine enemy', *but* I say unto you 'Love your enemies, bless them that curse you, do good to them that hate you and pray for them that despitefully use you, and persecute you' ..."

What a powerful point that "but" makes, one that is important as we now reflect on the need for a sense of perspective. There are human perspectives, *but* there is a divine perspective. And they are very different. "My thoughts are not your thoughts," God declares through Isaiah, "neither are your ways my ways."

Paul makes the same kind of point when he stands the human perspective about what is real on its head and emphasises that "the things that are seen" are only ephemeral and "temporal". It is that which is "not seen" which is "eternal". In other words, material things, however important, are nevertheless transitory. It is the invisible spiritual dimension that constitutes ultimate reality. Jesus' point about the priority of "seeking the Kingdom and his righteousness" is another statement of the divine perspective. We human beings invariably demonstrate that it is the "other things" which come first. However important those other things are, it is a false perspective that gives them primary significance.

Spirituality, like holiness, is not expressed in sameness, but in difference; not in closeness to human standards, attitudes and ways but in radically different attitudes. Believers are told by Paul: "Be not conformed to this world, *but* be ye transformed." The doctrine of the Incarnation is a fundamental statement about the total involvement of God in human life and in the life of the world, with all its passion and pain, its trials and temptations, but Jesus still emphasised the stance that disciples must take. Certainly they are *in* the world, but they must not be *of* it.

"There is nothing ugly," said the artist, John Constable, "for let the form of an object be what it may, light, shade and perspective will always make it beautiful."

There is something here that feels akin to the gospel in that, in the divine perspective, every human being, made in the image of God is of infinite value in his eyes. Humanity may be damaged, *but* there is always on offer the grace that transforms the ugliness of sin into the beauty of holiness. The divine perspective, as a model, may be very demanding, *but* it is never discouraging. Reach for it!

CHARGED WITH GRANDEUR

"A wider universe demands deeper awareness of the dimension of the spirit and of spiritual resources available for man, of the infinity of God, and of the divine knowledge and understanding still to be claimed." This statement (quoted in Templeton Trust literature) is particularly relevant when set against the materialism that characterises contemporary living. Breadth, depth, development, growth . . . these are liberating words and concepts. They contrast starkly with so much that is negative in the world today – declining standards in relationships and behaviour, the constant glorification of the trivial, tunnel vision expressed in narrow views and intolerant attitudes, the selfish individualism that works against real community and social health.

Current political, ethical and even theological confusion is contributing to much of the prevalent "doom and gloom". The gradual removal of what the Old Testament calls "the ancient landmarks" is, metaphorically, affecting public values, personal morality and social standards. Religious people are additionally threatened by the statements of theologians which seem to them to run counter to "all that they must surely believe". And it is all taking place in a world that seems topsy-turvy. Footballers are sold for millions, while starvation reduces its victims to skeletons; the phrase "love child" seems to be reserved for babies born in relationships other than marriage; entertainers and "stars" are celebrated (especially at their deaths) as cult heroes or heroines despite their having lived lives far removed from either the norms of society or from those of the church in particular. No wonder so many feel disillusioned with such a world.

It is imperative, however, that those who strive for better things should lose neither their sense of objectivity nor proportion. The world is, as Gerard Manley Hopkins, proclaims it to be, "charged with the grandeur of God!". The amazing beauty, mystery and wonder of creation is revealed to us in ever more dazzling ways by modern technological equipment. In reality, the world is not populated by monsters, murderers, rapists and criminals. It is mostly made up of honest, hard-working and law-abiding people who seek – often against great odds – to create and maintain healthy family life, observe civilised attitudes and value personal loyalty. There is, moreover, a large number of socially responsible human beings, many of them young men and women, whose conscious purpose is to feed the hungry, minister to the sick, look after the old, the frail and those who are disabled, serve the afflicted; who strive, in sum, to create a better world. So the great unfinished conflict between good and evil goes on. While, in our more depressed moments, it may feel as if evil is triumphant, there is an enormous amount of goodness being fed into the world.

It is essential that people of faith and purpose should not be overwhelmed by (as Paul calls them) "the powers of darkness", the negative forces so present in the atmosphere. That atmosphere needs to be healed by prayer and practical loving. Those who are aware of those "spiritual resources available for human beings", dare not withdraw in disillusionment, from the battle for goodness, beauty and love in this world which in creation was good and which, through grace, can be better.

WINE INTO WATER

It was unusual for water to be turned into wine as happened in Jesus' miracle at the wedding in Cana of Galilee. It is all too commonplace in our world today for wine to be turned into water. Trivialisation too often typifies our contemporary culture.

Awe and wonder in the presence of holiness lie at the heart of true religion as great Old Testament characters such as Moses and Isaiah understood so clearly. Moses's face "shone" when he descended from Mount Sinai where he had "talked with God". Isaiah was moved to profound confession for himself and his people when his "eyes had seen the King, the Lord of hosts". The New Testament reflects the same sense of mystery and wonder. Peter, asked who Jesus was, is moved to cry: "Thou art the Christ." Thomas, his doubt defeated, declares: "My Lord and my God." Paul, "caught up to the third heaven . . . heard unspeakable words". Mary Magdalene's response to the risen Christ was a devout "Master." No wonder adoration undergirds all Christian worship.

It is the church's responsibility to stimulate the sense of the spiritual and nourish our awareness of the grandeur of God. Paradoxically, the greater the sense of divine love, the deeper the involvement of God's servants in the problems of people.

Wonder, love and praise are not escapist emotions. They are the grounds from which love in action comes. The glorification of the trivial endangers the centrality of that which is inherently important. "Behold, they have taken away my Lord, and I know not where they have laid him," says a broken-hearted Mary Magdalene, seeking the crucified Jesus. What she says literally has profound symbolic importance. We can "lose" the Lord in ecclesiastical organisation, institutional minutiae or a super-abundance of activities.* The letter of dogmatic theology can obscure the spirit of love and compassion. Yet the priorities of the Christian community do not change. They are proclamation, fellowship and service. The prime task of the church is to be a healing community. Where pride of place is given to activities not closely related to mission and evangelism, the church's work is in danger of trivialisation.

If the grandeur of God is diminished; if limits are set to his all-embracing love; if the sense of the numinous ceases to enliven the human heart; if the Lordship of Christ is taken to the circumference of faith, we are in danger of that trivialisation so typical of sport, entertainment, the media and politics in the ill-balanced life of the world today, often represented by a sensationalism that destroys people and is contrary to love. For, says Paul, "love finds nothing to be glad about when someone goes wrong, but is glad when truth is glad."**

* This point is also made in Meditations for January 23 and February 14.
** William Barclay's translation of 1 Corinthians, chapter 13, verse 6. This theme is developed in the Meditation August 13.

Amazing Grace

St Paul's Grotto and the catacombs of Rabat, close by the walled city of Mdina in Malta, are present-day reminders of the apostle's unscheduled visit to the island. He and his companions were on their way to Rome when they were shipwrecked. The disaster, in providential hands, brought blessings. The winter sojourn of three months affected Malta profoundly. It also provided a specific healing miracle for Publius, the chief magistrate. The curing of his father's dysentery made such an impression that others, too, came for the laying on of hands and – the doctor-reporter Luke records – were healed. When the party could at last leave, he also comments that "they heaped honours upon us". Had the shipwreck not happened, Malta would have missed an experience.

When I visited the grotto, I wondered how he and his friends had coped with the claustrophobic conditions in that confined area. But Paul's belief in a Providence that brings the best out of the worst enabled him to effect a miracle of transformation. He made that prison-like abode (there is evidence on its ceiling that it had been used for that purpose) into a place of prayer. A bleak cave was now a chapel. What felt like a cell had become a sanctuary.

When the risen Jesus promised his disciples that they "would receive power after that the Holy Spirit is come upon you", he was pointing to the divine energy that can change both people and situations. It is the "gracious" gift of which John Newton spoke when he wrote of "amazing grace". The divine-human encounter is a healing relationship in which God, in love, takes the initiative. We, graciously receiving, "love him because he first loved us". It is grace that is at the heart of that divine initiative. The aim is our wholeness. Salvation is therefore a gift to be received, not a merit to be earned.

A theology of grace is needed today to prevent our falling victim to the facile optimism that considers human progress inevitable if only we can create the right environment, provide universal education, apply sound psychology, explore new technology. It is a dangerous delusion. These disciplines, each valuable in itself, just cannot reach that deep, dark side of our inner being, corrupted by what both Testaments describe as sin. It is only grace that can deal with our spiritual dilemma, our inability to find God on our own.

"You have made of my life not a tavern, but a temple" wrote the poet* in gratitude for human love. How much greater must be the transformation effected by "the grace that is sufficient". Prisons become sanctuaries. Darkness turns to light. Death becomes resurrection.

* *I Love You*, attributed to Roy Croft

THE GARMENT OF HUMILITY

The moment I entered the room at Quarrier's Homes, I realized that I was in the presence of true greatness. There stood a little man who had a reputation worldwide for his witness and his work. His ministry was to proclaim the Christian message in the slums of Kobe in Japan, but it was for more than that that his name was held in honour. Toyohiko Kagawa had always incarnated his message in his offering of loving care to the poor, the sick, the destitute and the dying. Despite his own serious illnesses and frequent weakness, he had never ceased to give himself totally to the people whom, in Christ's name, he loved. In our brief conversation, I was so aware that the greatness of his man lay not in his fame but in his humility.*

"There's nothing so becomes a man as modest stillness and humility" – at least in times of peace, said Shakespeare (in *Henry V*). There is certainly no quality so deeply rooted in the New Testament as true humility. Paul writing to the Philippians, explains why this is so. "It would have been no robbery" for Jesus to have "claimed equality with God", but what in fact did he do? "He made himself of no reputation and took upon himself the form of a servant, and was made in the likeness of men." But there is more. "Being found in fashion as a man, he humbled himself and became obedient unto death, even the death of the cross." There is no doubt as to the implications of this for his followers. Paul puts it clearly: "Let this mind be in you which was also in Christ Jesus." Christians are called to don "the garment of humility".

There is no place for arrogance* in either individual or corporate religion but, for individuals and groups alike, this is a hard undertaking. Was not arrogance the primal sin in the Garden of Eden? Adam and Eve, our representatives, wanted to be "like God".

It is humility, not arrogance, that will win not only the attention of the world, but also its heart. The harvest of the Spirit was evidenced in the life Kagawa by the power of his humility. So must it be with us all.

* See also Meditation for March 1.

OF LITTLE FAITH

Many find it hard these days to adhere to Jesus' exhortation "to take no anxious thought for tomorrow". Our world, obsessed by the need for security at one level, is at other levels incredibly insecure. "Few people in the work place, from the most senior to the most junior, now have security of employment" claims the Industrial Committee of The Church of Scotland in its report to the General Assembly. It goes on: "Security of work has become a casualty in the last ten years or so." That insecurity leads to financial insecurity, which in turn creates mental and emotional insecurity. The result is widespread stress. It needs a strong faith to cope with life's pressures today. But even those with a real sense of inner security must find it hard not to be anxious about the future.*

There are religious people who feel guilty because they will particularly worry about the dilemma because of the import of the gospel message about faith and faithlessness. Those "of little faith" are sternly rebuked by Jesus. When Peter, walking on the water towards Jesus, began to sink he found the low level of his faith to be blamed. The disciples, petrified by the storm, are asked: "How is it that you have not faith?" When the disciples cannot cure a boy with epilepsy it is associated with the failures of a "faithless and perverse generation". Highly commended by Jesus, on the other hand, are people of admirable faith – those who brought the man who was "sick of the palsy", the Canaanite woman who pleaded for her daughter's healing; the one Samaritan leper who returned to give thanks; the woman with the haemorrhage. Is it then just a matter of simple faith and all will be truly well? A priest I knew, a saintly man, died broken and bitter because he had all the faith possible for one human being, but he was not healed. There are many like that.

Our uncertainty increases when we read in the letter of James that "faith without works is dead". He writes pragmatically: "Suppose a fellowman or woman has not clothes to wear and no food for a daily meal, and suppose one of you says in such a situation: 'Go, and God bless you! May you have a fire to warm yourself and a meal to eat.' And suppose you do not give that person enough to keep body and soul together, what use is that? If faith does not issue in action, if it is all alone by itself, it is dead."** The exhortation to "have faith in God" can, alas, seem no more than empty religious words to the starving, the unemployed, the poor, the bruised and battered of society.

But still that sense of unease about being of little faith remains. Indeed it will be increased when we look at homes of loving like William Quarrier's Homes in Bridge of Weir (to name but one). Founded on faith, operated in faith, Quarrier's makes its needs known and leaves the rest in God's hands. God has marvellously honoured its faith. Are we too often of too little faith?

* This theme is also explored in Meditations for April 14 and April 15.
** *William Barclay's Translation of the New Testament* (Arthur James).

LITTLE MIRACLES

It was from a hill above Tiberias that I first had sight of the Sea of Galilee. There, in reality, was the stretch of water of which I had heard and read since Sunday School days. It was deeply moving, for was it not round these shores that Jesus had walked and talked, preached and healed? And, of course, it was the water on which, on a stormy night, he had so dramatically walked.

It is not really necessary to try to explain rationally this or any other miracle. The story is a record of the disciples' *experience*. Significantly it is present in all four Gospels. And as one of them notes, so traumatic was the effect of Jesus' presence and actions, that it reinforced their awareness of his divinity.

Miracles are, as the Latin derivation of the word indicates, "wonder-full" happenings. If, however, it feels difficult to accept the miraculous element, look on the story as a teaching parable and you will find it points to familiar but important aspects of Jesus' ministry and teaching. It follows that his approaches to ministry must be made incarnate in his church, the healing community too.

First, Jesus comes to frightened men with a *calming word*. "It is I! Be not afraid!" 3am is – especially for the sleepless, the anxious, the fearful, the doubting and those distressed by guilt – the darkest hour. It was, in fact, in "the fourth watch" that Jesus came to still the storms, internal as well as external. That, the distinguished New Testament scholar and my student colleague of long ago, Dr Robin Wilson, tells us "would be about 3am".* The calming word comes in the darkest hour. May the healing community continue to convey that blessing to anxious people.

Second, Jesus stretched out to frightened Peter, faithless and sinking, a *helping hand*. Those who choose to follow the one who stilled the storm must constitute themselves not only the *worshipping* community, but also the *serving* community. This, theologically, the doctrine of the Incarnation compels. That service includes, of course, the personal helping hand, but must be expressed in a total involvement in the life of the world, its pain, its poverty, its problems and its politics. For what is politics but the discipline that deals with human concerns, the people's health and homes, education, social welfare, personal needs?

Third, it was the *lack of faith* on the part of the disciples that most concerned Jesus. He spoke in terms of the need to have faith that would "move mountains"; but the level of his expectation was too high for his disciples. Not surprisingly, it is for most of us. Bitter experience, unanswered (as we feel it) prayer, overwhelming suffering, bereavement and/or perhaps rejection may have created the crisis of faith and doubt which leaves us with the "little faith" which Jesus so often found around him. In the sophisticated, materialistic world of today, simple faith feels facile and the so-called power of prayer irrelevant. And yet there are those like the little crippled lady who spoke to me after the service on Sunday about each day's "little miracles" to which she testified so movingly.

"Be not faithless, but believing," said Jesus to his disciples then, and he says it still. It is a tough demand. But taken seriously, as the Lord's commands must be, little miracles may well come.

* Commentary on the Gospel of St Mark in *Peake's Commentary on the Bible* (Thomas Nelson).

ABSOLUTE DEMAND

Those who claim that the church should be more "in tune with the times" seem to imply that, by accommodating the gospel to today's needs, the faith becomes more "attractive". There is however little evidence that, by making entry to the Christian life easier, the number of those who come into the church is likely to increase. The reverse is, in fact, closer to the truth. It is in the churches that emphasise the *demand* of the gospel that growth shows most clearly.

Jesus, in his attitude to life and to people, made clear the "absolute demand" (to use a phrase from the late Professor H H Farmer) of the gospel. Those who love father, mother, son or daughter "more than me" said Jesus are "not worthy of me". Discipleship means "leaving all", taking up the Cross and following him.

Jesus asked much of his disciples, but he founded the "absolute demand" which he made of them on his own acceptance of that demand by himself. This commitment he expressed in his attitude to his coming death. Luke tells us that he "steadfastly set his face to go to Jerusalem", knowing the consequences. He had, he said, to do the will of the Father who sent him. While in the Garden of Gethsemane, the human part of him rebelled at the suffering he had to face ("if it be possible, let this cup pass from me"), the "absolute demand" that was involved in fulfilling "the will of my Father" compelled him to add: "Nevertheless, not my will but thine be done."

The language of faith has many words in its vocabulary that remind us of the *corporate* nature of Christianity . . . community, congregation, fellowship, kingdom, body, etc. Remembering that basic aspect of the church will help to prevent any over-emphasis on individualism in religion. That said, however, personal obedience remains an absolute demand from which no follower can claim exception.

Jesus, in declaring his own attitude to life, asks his disciples to reflect his lifestyle. It is one in which there is an absolute demand to "seek first the Kingdom" and let all other things fall into their proper place. It was to Peter, concerning himself with what would happen to another disciple in the future, that Jesus' demand was made crystal clear. "Peter," he said in effect, "don't worry about what is to happen to others. *You follow me!*"

THE POWER OF PRAYER

"To travel hopefully is a better thing than to arrive," wrote Robert Louis Stevenson. The religious journey has something of this "feel" about it. It is not that spiritual goals are unimportant, of course, but the great blessing is really to know that you are travelling in the right direction.

If this is true for individual pilgrimages, it applies to corporate situations too. "Where there is no vision, the people perish," it says in the book of Proverbs. Where there is no sense of direction in events, the same is true. How desperately we all try to see the right direction for the greater peace of what used to be Yugoslavia, but confusion and contumacy reign. In Ireland over the years of "the Troubles", direction has been lost in sectarian feuds and traditional but unquestioned religious hostility. There was a sense of puzzlement throughout the nation on a certain Wednesday when interest rates went up and down in rapid but perplexing succession. Had we lost our economic direction? When we lose our way in both personal and corporate situations, we can experience a lostness and a meaninglessness that is devastating.

There was a time when Mary Magdalene found herself looking in the wrong direction. Her weeping eyes were focused on the tomb and her missing Lord. Then she turned round and, looking in the other direction, she found herself face to face with the living Lord. This was a turning-point indeed for Mary.*

One of the fundamentals of faith is the belief that God's grace and power can completely change the direction of lives. "I met a man," said the late and great Dr John White, referring to his encounter with Jesus. That was the secret of his robust conviction. The vocabulary of faith includes, as I have said before, words such as renewal, regeneration, redemption and reconciliation. They testify to the fact that, through grace, everything can change – aims, attitudes, reactions, relationships, even indeed our whole philosophy of life.

Change is the action of God, but Jesus encouraged and indeed commanded his followers to contribute to the possibility of change in people and in situations by importunate prayer. "The prayer of a good man is powerfully effective," said James, as is equally the prayer of a good woman. Intercessory prayer is the process through which we co-operate with God in bringing about change, in providing direction.

No wonder Paul says to the Thessalonians: "Pray without ceasing", or Tennyson to us all, "More things are wrought by prayer than this world dreams of."

* This change in direction by Mary is referred to elsewhere, e.g. in Meditations for January 23, and March 28.

CLOSED MIND, HARD HEART

There are two negative, destructive factors, as evident to Jesus in his time as they are towards the end of this millennium. One is the closed mind, the other the hardening heart. The first is a denial of the on-going creative activity of God. The second represents a declining spiritual sensitivity which reduces our capacity to "touch and handle things unseen".

The closed mind restricts the possibility of growth intellectually, emotionally and spiritually. Openness to new aspects of understanding is not a threat to faith, nor a denial that we have been given, through revelation and "the Word of God", "all that we need for our salvation". Nor is it an invitation to re-write the basic doctrines of the faith. It is an invitation to those who, secure in their religious convictions, want to learn more of the infinite wonder of a world created by a God whom we often tend to make (in J B Phillips' words) "too small".

The more sinister process is the hardening heart. The classic Old Testament example of this destructive development is the continual refusal of Pharaoh to let the children of Israel go, despite the sequence of plagues sent on him and his people. The repeated rendering of the phrase "Pharaoh hardened his heart" underlines the subtle process of spiritual deterioration.

The ultimate result of the heart-hardening process is dramatically described by Jesus when he spoke of those who called his demonstrations of divine power in healing miracles the work of Beelzebub, that is the devil. When the heart is so hardened and the spirit is so sterile that the ability to distinguish between evil and good has been lost, spiritual sensitivity has become so low that the capacity for repentance must be nearly dead. And where there is no penitence, how can forgiveness be given? It is in the context of the hardening heart that Jesus speaks of the possibility of the unforgivable sin.*

If there is spiritual sterility in our times, let this not be seen as a criticism applicable only to others. It is a confession of feelings we all share. The materialism expressed in the ruthlessness of market forces, the dominance of money in the problems of international relationship, the revolution in information technology and its influence on hidden persuasion, the dominant themes of everyday living – health, cosmetic improvement, invitation to greed – all this and more stifles the spirit, if we allow it to do so, and spiritual sensitivity declines.

The church has many responsibilities – religious ordinances, social witness, prophetic proclamation, a concern for justice and reconciliation – but it must not forget that its primary task is the nurture of the spirit. Spiritual sensitivity and ruthless materialism cannot live together. It is imperative that the church works to secure the triumph of the former over the latter and, as Paul wrote to Timothy, to "fan into flame the gift of God".

* Also referred to in the Meditations for March 15 and August 13.

IF ONLY . . .

"If only . . ." What feeling is contained in this simple phrase! Regret, remorse, sadness, self-criticism, guilt; so much lies behind the almost involuntary expression of these words. The feeling is always uncomfortable, always pain-full.

The actress, Sylvia Read, uses the phrase "if only" a dozen times in rapid succession as she wrestles with the horror of her son, Jonathan's, suicide at the age of 33. "Those near to a dead friend or relative," she writes in *Sharing a Grief** "are beset by 'if only'. In the days following Jonathan's suicide, I began unpicking days, weeks, years." There were so many things that perhaps could have been done differently, things that perhaps contributed to his death. "The threads of the past got unpicked till they lay scattered all around me. The past was broken up in little pieces, and the pieces seemed to be pointing tiny hands at me and whispering '*Guilty!'* "

I was recently involved in a workshop at the residential weekend of The Compassionate Friends,** an organisation of which people become members only for the saddest of reasons, namely that they have lost a child (at any age, and in whatever circumstances) through death. The purpose of the workshop was to help each other with the problems of anger and guilt. The commonest theme was the *if only* one. Whatever the cause of death in each situation – road crash, illness, suicide – the pain was the guilt over believed failure to take some action that might have prevented that fatal situation arising. Many people have their own *if only*s.

I cannot find an example in scripture of the literal use of these words in the sense which I am describing, but there is one situation in which they are, effectively, used. It occurs in St John's Gospel (chapter 11, verse 21). Lazarus had died three days earlier, and although Jesus knew of his death, he had decided not to come to Bethany where Lazarus and his sisters lived. It was Martha who made the plaintive plea: "If only you had come, my brother would not have died." Jesus wept.

There are many reasons why that sense of remorse over things we believe we have failed to do in relation to someone who has died, will linger, perhaps for ever. In most cases, however, the reality is that we did what we could at the time; that we are not omnipotent and may not have been able to act in a different way in the circumstances in which we feel we failed. It is so often only with hindsight that possible alternatives, if any, can be seen.. Yes, we did what we could. To persist in "unpicking the pieces" gives no benefit to those who have died and, in emphasising guilty feelings to the point when they become inappropriate, we alone will be hurt.

It is particularly important for those with a religious faith to believe in the forgiveness of sins, for it is a primary doctrine of the Christian faith. It is in the infinite divine forgiveness that the failures of the past lose their power to hurt and to destroy. Then we can move forward.

* ISBN 0 9529160 0 2.
** Also referred to in Meditations for March 19, July 9 and December 10.

PATCHES OF GODLIGHT

"One moment of ecstasy can transform your life." The psychologist Margo Anand wrote this in relation to particular human experiences, but because the word *ecstasy* relates to religious experiences too, the statement becomes important for spiritual development. In the university of life there is a profound need for the transforming moment.

Ecstasy is (according to Professor E J Tinsley*) "an overwhelming experience wherein the sense of individual selfhood is transcended, the primary tense dimensions of time, past, present and future, are blended in an overwhelming sense of the eternal now and there is an unforgettable experience of serenity, well-being and joy". Theoretical as that may sound, it nevertheless describes the experience of the saints and mystics, those who, as the spiritual writer Baron von Hügel testified, "are never so fully active, so truly and intensely themselves, as when they are most truly possessed by God".

Such ecstasy, and the mysticism with which it is closely associated, lie outside the experience of most of us. Nor are they experiences that we can choose to achieve for they are gifts to be received gratefully and graciously. There is, however, at the heart of them what everyone on the spiritual journey needs, an experience which is life-changing.

The biblical record contains many transforming experiences. When Moses came down from Mount Sinai with the tables of stone, his face was "radiant," as Aaron and all who were with him testified. Forty days and forty nights "with the Lord" had clearly changed his life. The prophet Isaiah was moved to commitment because "his eyes had seen the King". St Paul was "caught up in Paradise" in a mystical experience, "heard inexpressible things" and received "surpassingly great revelations". It was an experience that enabled him to learn of "the grace that is sufficient". The Transfiguration was for Jesus himself such an experience, his face "shining like the sun". The experience of the two who walked towards Emmaus and met the risen Lord must surely have found their lives transformed for ever.

The level of our spiritual life will be much less than the peak experiences of those of biblical times. But, then or now, the world is essentially the same. "A garrulous and facile generation needs the mystic quiet" claims a writer of the thirties. It could be a statement for today. In a world where charities ask for £2 a month to save a child while footballers are paid £40,000 a week; where a garrulous generation gossips over titillation and trivia; where a facile world fails to root out injustice, discrimination and abuse, the value of transforming personal experiences remains. It brings what C S Lewis describes as "patches of Godlight in a sad, dark world".

Transformation comes in many ways - through loving relationships, lively people, lasting memories, "patches of Godlight". "I have toward heaven breathed a secret vow to live in prayer and contemplation."** To fulfil such a vow can only bring a blessing to this superficial world.

* Article 'Ecstasy' in *A Dictionary of Christian Theology*, edited by Alan Richardson, SCM 1969.

** *The Merchant of Venice*, Portia, Act III, scene iv.

DISTRACTIONS FROM DISCIPLESHIP

There is a danger that very public introspection in church circles over personal relationships, combined with confusing ecclesiastical messages in relation to sexual morality, could blunt the authority of the church in matters spiritual. The media prominence given to both processes may well divert the church from concentrating on its primary tasks of mission, evangelism and the nurturing of personal and corporate commitment to its head, Jesus Christ. In other words, we are in danger of fostering distractions from discipleship.

Jesus found it necessary to emphasise to disciples the need for unqualified commitment to him. He asked people to "take up the cross" and follow him in total obedience. To the man who asked for time to bury his father, Jesus responded sharply: "Let the dead bury their dead: follow me." To the disciple who wanted first to say goodbye to his family, Jesus pointed out that "no man, having put his hand to the plough and looking back, is fit for the kingdom of God." These were hard sayings, but the message is clear. Distractions from discipleship cannot be tolerated.

Peter was another who found himself on the receiving end of a similar rebuke. Having betrayed jealousy towards "the disciple whom Jesus loved" and been irritated by Jesus' persistence in questioning his commitment ("Simon Peter, lovest thou me?" he had asked three times), Peter asked, "And what shall this man do?" In effect, Jesus said bluntly, "Mind your own business and don't be distracted by what affects others. *You follow me!*" (John chapter 21, verse 22).*

As with the danger of distraction in relation to personal obedience, so the church must ensure that it too is not distracted from its primary aims. "No sound ought to be heard in the churches, but the healing voice of charity," wrote Edmund Burke. The church's stated duty is to preach and heal. Its pastoral responsibility is to "search for the lost, recover the straggler and bandage the hurt" (Ezekiel chapter 34, verse 16, *New English Bible*). The church is built on the rock-like confession of Peter at Caesarea Philippi that "Jesus is Lord" and so the first duty of the church is to proclaim that message. Of course the church must be concerned about political matters – health, education, justice, poverty, homelessness, war, the proper stewardship of power, the things which affect "citizens". If, however, it so concentrates on political involvement that it loses touch with its primary purpose, it has been distracted from its corporate discipleship. The church must use every insight it can gain from psychology and related disciplines, but if that leads to its being no more than a psychotherapeutic clinic, it has been diverted from its fundamental spiritual purpose. The church must engage in social welfare (and there are branches of the church which do it magnificently), but if it ends up being simply a social service it is less than the church ought to be.

Religion, Jesus made clear, is essentially a matter of getting priorities right. If what he calls, in the Sermon on the Mount, the "other things" (often good things) are promoted to first place and "seeking the kingdom" is relegated to second place, there have been distractions, whether in personal or corporate discipleship, that disturb proportion. Our inner security and peace depend on getting our spiritual priorities right. That achieved, the "other things" will fall comfortably into their proper place.

* Words also quoted in Meditation for February 12.

STRENGTHEN THE STAKES!

What a wonderful resolution is to be found in the Old Testament prophet, Isaiah! If your vision is narrow; if your sense of adventure is diminishing; if your circle of interests is decreasing; if (as J B Phillips puts it) "your God is too small", then listen to this:

> Enlarge the place of your tent, stretch your curtains wide.
> Do not hold back; lengthen your cords, strengthen your stakes.
> Do not be afraid . . . (Isaiah chapter 54, verse 2)

What could be a more stimulating and encouraging resolution than that?

The context relates to Israel's history but here let us simply reflect on the words themselves. If it is true that "there's a wideness in God's mercy like the wideness of the sea"; if the characteristic of God's love is its "length, breadth, depth and height", then our focus must be not on diminishment but on expansion; not on exclusiveness but on inclusiveness; not on negativism but on that which is positive. The characteristic of the divine love is not its restrictive boundaries, but its all-embracing essence. Enlarge, stretch, lengthen and strengthen. And have the faith to match!

Asked to deal with one of those currently popular forms of magazine article, the personal portrait type of feature, one of the questions put to me was "What causes you the most difficulty when it comes to believing in God?" I found myself spontaneously saying that it was encountering those who publicly and professionally claim to be God's servants and are totally lacking in humility, sensitivity and compassion. It is not so much the human failures or personal peccadilloes of which we all are or have been guilty that are the real worry within the church, but much more those unpleasant trends too frequently found there – small-mindedness, intolerance, petty jealousy, unwillingness to listen and consider, envy of position, dogmatism, impatience of weakness, blindness to goodness (the most serious sin of all, according to Jesus). If the church is to proclaim with conviction the gospel of love in a too-often unloving world, it must demonstrate its own ability to be a living, loving fellowship.

Those who saw the disciples fulfilling their ministry were impressed by the "boldness" of their preaching, and the success of the healing miracle, but even more it seems by the radiance of spirit they expressed. The people "took knowledge that the disciples had been with Jesus". Was there ever more telling testimony to the effect, albeit unconscious, on the life of the disciple?*

Some may feel anxious that emphasising expansion and enlargement may lead to a weakening of the faith; that inclusiveness implies the acceptance of fringe features; that there is danger in an over-liberal attitude; that the enlarged circle may not be as Christ-centred as it should be. But the theme contains the answer. If you enlarge and stretch and, in particular, lengthen the cords, *you must strengthen the stakes*. To be expanding and inclusive demands not less emphasis on basic beliefs, but more.

The firmer the foundations, the greater the expansion can be. The deeper the roots too, the taller is the tree.

* This point is dealt with further in the Meditation for October 21.

THE SILENCE OF THE EARS

"Love finds nothing to be glad about when someone goes wrong," St Paul tells the Corinthians, "but is glad when truth is glad."* It is a text that needs to be writ large in every editorial and production office in the world of the media for it condemns outright the exploitation of human failure for the sake of commercial gain as well as sensationalism, scandal-mongering and the intimate gossip that is founded on rumour rather than fact. It would be naïve to expect the world of commercial communication to be governed by the principles of love, for circulation and viewing figures depend on much more worldly motives in a cut-throat competition. Bad news provides most of the news of the world. There is a difference however between the recognition of that human fact and the deliberate and persistent pursuit of unhappy people, victims of their own folly or others' failure and being "glad when someone goes wrong". "There but for the grace of God go I" is a necessary reminder of the universality of human weakness. We should be careful what we say about other people.

Mother Teresa, in her long life, often emphasised the importance of silence. "We cannot put ourselves directly in the presence of God," she once said, "if we do not practice internal and external silence."** On the significance of silence in personal life she comments: "Souls of prayer are souls of great silence." Commending the silence "which gives a new outlook on everything" she encourages the development of inner silence by practising the silence of the eyes, the silence of the ears, the silence of the tongue, the silence of the mind and the silence of the heart.

Consider Mother Teresa's concept of the silence of the ears.

James, practical disciple that he was, made the necessary point that we cannot do two contrary things together. He points to obvious examples. A fountain cannot gush with fresh and salt water at the same time. A fig-tree cannot yield olives, nor a vine figs. It is a principle which holds good in the silence of the ears. Concentration on rumour, gossip and uncharitable words and other elements that (Mother Teresa again) "come from fallen human nature", blots out the possibility of doing what those who serve God must do – that is, listen. The prophet Elijah learned this lesson. The drama of earthquake, wind and fire deafened him to the still, small voice within. It was the necessary silence of the ears which enabled him to set aside despair and go back to the work he was called to do.

It is the silence of the ears which will make those in search of their salvation listen to the voice of God within and the cry of the poor without. Only in the silence can we learn the priorities of discipleship. Without such listening, discipleship will lose its purpose, and love to God and neighbour will be denied its full expression.

* This text is discussed in greater depth in the Meditation for August 14.
** *In the heart of the World*, Mother Teresa, New World Library, 1997.

TOO HARD FOR GOD?

Jesus not infrequently accused his disciples of having "little faith" and criticised their failure to believe that "the things which are impossible with men are possible with God", that "with God all things are possible". But are they? The human dilemma is the conflict between an obedient desire to believe in divine omnipotence and the harsh realities of life experienced in natural disaster, murder, accident or any other of the forms of human suffering that tie faith in knots.

For a very specific declaration of the omnipotence of God, turn to Genesis and Sarah, Abraham's wife.* The promise of a child in her old age by a centenarian husband was too much for her mind or even her imagination. Her response was laughter.* It was through Abraham that God conveyed a rebuke for such a lack of faith with the clearly rhetorical question: "Is anything too hard for the Lord?"

Is it? Those bereaved in Turkey's earthquake, the broken-hearted parents who have lost a child, the cancer victims facing terminal illness may find it hard to give the expected answer. Despite faith, prayer, perhaps life-long commitment and obedience, the sought-for deliverance has not come – because God did not so will it? because there are some things God cannot do?

Those who ridicule religious faith by pointing to massive human suffering, corporate or personal, always ask how a loving God can permit such suffering. That accusation will continue. What is more trying is the profound crisis of faith and doubt that suffering can (though it does not always) bring to the genuine believer, brought up to accept words of authority which claim that nothing is too hard for the Lord (as God told Abraham), that with God all things are possible (as Jesus told the world).

Having given the gift of free will and freedom to human beings, God is bound by the gift and cannot necessarily prevent the results of that freedom. If human freedom is a reality, human suffering is an inevitable consequence.

Those with faith will however see the providential presence of God in the way human situations develop. There is no doubt that, in the deliverance of the Israelites at the Red Sea, it was in that way that the event was interpreted for the eternal importance of Israel's history. Divine synchronicity can say something very important through suffering and many will bear personal testimony to such experience.

When Jesus wept over Jerusalem, it was the irony of what he could have done but they would not allow him to do that caused his tears. There are some things that are "too hard", even for God. Disaster, be it naturally caused or through human failing – or a combination of both – leaves us with the mystery of suffering unsolved. It was not however frustration alone that made Jesus cry. He also felt profound compassion. Here is a glorious paradox! It is from the deep wells of human suffering that compassion freely flows.

* See also the Meditations for July 7, October 30 and December 1.

REAL CHANGE

Changed people change situations. They do. Things begin to happen when change takes place not only in the minds of people but in their hearts; when it affects their inner being, when it reaches "the unconscious". Why do so many people then believe that, in some people and some situations, change is impossible? The arrogance with which so many commentators and critics who had no personal contact with the recently executed American murderess but dismissed the reality of her conversion is disturbing. Guards who were in continuous contact with her, who acknowledged that Death Row conversions are often (perhaps usually) insincere, opportunist or manipulative, testified that in this case the change was real and total; yet distant observers dismiss the possibility of change! Of course it does not alter her guilt or the need for some punishment, but the change was manifestly real.*

The evidence of change is in the difference it makes to attitudes, temperament, actions, relationships, life. Such change was there for opponents and critics to see when the despised tax-gatherer, Zacchaeus,** emerged from his private encounter with Jesus and issued a public apology (which must have been desperately hard to make), backing it up by changing wrong situations which were the result of his past actions. There were those who were "baffled" by the preacher Paul in Damascus (Acts chapter 9, verse 21): "Isn't this the one who carried on a merciless campaign against those who call on the name of Jesus?" It seems to be difficult for so many to believe in the possibility of genuine change. But the positive proof is in the changed situations that follow. How glorious is the witness of those who, because their lives have been transformed, set out to change the world and its ways.

Jesus spoke about the nature of change – or conversion – in the parable of the sower. The seed that falls on the rock finds no depth and so the plant withers. So is it when change is superficial and does not reach the deep places. New life simply dies. The seed that lands among thorns is choked and destroyed. So is it with the superficial conversion that is undermined by the pleasures and material attractions of the world. It is only the seed that falls on good ground that flourishes for it is deep-rooted. So is conversion complete when it moves on to total commitment, when change brings fruit of some kind, whether it be 30, 60 or 100 per cent. Conversion is real when it embraces the unconscious as well as the conscious, when it touches the heart as well as the mind.

To be able to judge when change is real is not easy. To be glad when it is demonstrated is to reflect the joy felt over the prodigal son: he "was dead and is alive again". To deny it is to join with the thoroughly virtuous but stubborn elder brother who could not believe that his brother had changed. He had! His father certainly knew it. The right response to profound change for the better is not half-hearted hesitancy or cynical condemnation. It must be "Hallelujah!".

* This reference is to an incident in 1999.
** There are other references to Zacchaeus in Meditations for January 16, April 5, June 2 and 4, July 15, October 6 and 23, and December 12.

TRUE GREATNESS

It is not often that you feel that you are in the presence of true greatness; greatness, that is, in the New Testament sense of the word. I experienced that feeling acutely when, many years ago, I was introduced to a physically insignificant but spiritually colossal man, famous for his work for the poor and deprived in the slums of Kobe in Japan. He was, of course, Toyohiko Kagawa. Himself racked by ill-health, he had fired the spirit in so many of us in our younger days. "Lives of great men all remind us," wrote Longfellow, "that we can make our lives sublime, and, departing, leave behind us footprints on the sands of time." How powerful is the influence of the truly great!

There was an occasion when Jesus' disciples disputed among themselves as to who should be the greatest. Jesus answered by placing a child amongst them. "It is the one who thinks as little of his importance as this little child," he said, "who is the greatest in the kingdom of heaven." The greatest are those who, like Kagawa, are least conscious of being great.

In Paul's letter to the Philippians there is a profound theological statement about the Incarnation. It encapsulates the wonder of the humility of God. Paul writes: "Christ Jesus … did not regard his equality with God as a thing to be clutched to himself but … took upon himself the form of a servant. He humbled himself and became obedient unto death, even death on a cross." Here is a statement about the true greatness of Jesus framed in glorious terms! The corollary is specific: "Let this mind be in you which was also in Christ Jesus," he says. True greatness involves true humility in us all.

Reflecting on the theme of greatness, I cannot but refer to the lamented death of Rabbi Hugo Gryn.* I was in his presence only once, but the sense of his greatness was borne in upon me. Others have now made it clear how great he was. "Men like him happen only once in a lifetime," wrote two of his friends. "We are fortunate it happened in ours."

The breadth and depth of Hugo Gryn's outlook was so much part of his stature. "He was a born ecumenist," said the writer of his obituary in this newspaper,* "a man who spent his professional career searching for common ground between all faiths." To do that was not a denial of his Jewish faith, just as it is not a denial of Christ-centred Christianity to sense glimpses of the truth in many places. Indeed, the firmer the convictions of the Christian, the more there is confidence in genuine exploration. J B Phillips was so right. We must not make our God too small.

Encounter with true greatness is always life-enhancing – as I felt after my meeting with Kagawa.** Be moved deeply then by what others wrote of Huge Gryn: "We are a group of Asians, Blacks and Jews who were inspired by Hugo Gryn to laugh together, grow fond of each other and air our harmonizing views as he did, forcibly and regularly."

It is only the truly great who enable others to leave such footprints.

* The *Daily Telegraph*, 1997.
** This incident has already been referred to in the Meditation for February 9.

TREASURE-STORE

The Bible is, by any standards, an extraordinary book. It is of immense literary value, abounding in both memorable poetry and abiding prose. It is a documentary concerned with human relationships and divine encounters. It recounts profound prophetic activity, solid social history and marvellous mythology (in the technical sense of that word). It is a book respected and admired by many, irrespective of religious adherence. It contains the wonder of the Old Testament scriptures and the glory of the New Testament Gospels. It provides, in the form of letters to Christian communities, incisive theology and deep pastoral concern and care. It enshrines, for the perpetual record, the history of the life and teaching of Jesus Christ. For many, it is "the supreme rule of faith and life, the inspired authority, the Word of God". What a wonderful book the Bible is!

All who love the Bible in its entirety will, nevertheless, have favourite parts. Those who value the Psalms and mark in red memorable phrases or verses will draw comfort, inspiration and devotional power from a true manual of the spiritual life. Who is not moved by the twenty-third psalm with its green pastures, still waters and restoration of soul? A favourite prophet – and it might well be Ezekiel – will provide passages pulsating with spiritual stimulation and profound pastoral care. Those who appreciate St Paul (and there are those who don't!) will differ over his greatest contribution, but is it not remarkable that one and the same man can write a manual of theology such as his letter to the Romans is and at the same time produce the glorious analysis of love in his first letter to the Corinthians, or his striking spiritual insight into the humility of Jesus in Philippians? And at the heart of the New Testament lie the three Synoptic Gospels which provide the essence of the record of Jesus – his teaching, preaching and healing, his encounters and relations, the flesh and blood Christ, the man of Nazareth, the prophet from Galilee, the Messiah as he saw himself, who came to his own who "received him not" – and St John proclaiming the cosmic Christ, the incarnate Christ, the crucified Christ, the risen Christ, the Christ who makes his continuing and abiding presence felt through "another Comforter", the Holy Spirit.

"If I could have the privilege," writes E V Rieu (in *The Four Gospels*) "of a few moments talk with the four evangelists, I must confess that it would be St Luke whom I would confront with the longest set of questions." Many would perhaps share that view, and for several reasons. For me there would be one area above all others on which I would want to hear St Luke, and that is on Jesus' healing ministry. For it is a doctor who records and reports on the healing miracles. That gives an authenticity and an authority to those "signs of the Kingdom" of a very special kind. How glorious it is to hear from a doctor's lips informed testimony to the reality and validity of those miracles in a way that only a physician could do it.

THE GLORY OF LIFE

"Do you know Bosshardt?" It is the question I always want to ask anyone from Holland – as I did when a guest of friends in Vienna. The young man's answer was typical. "Everybody knows Bosshardt," he said.

In other Meditations I have referred, in passing, to Major Alida Bosshardt.* Referred to publicly simply by her surname, she is officially retired, having given her life's ministry to serving those caught up in the sordid environment of Amsterdam's Red Light district.

She knew by name virtually every prostitute in the area. She was known to, and respected by, the owners of every pub and club, however unpleasant. She was loved by "the girls". She was never refused entry to *any* establishment to sell *War Cry*. A Salvation Army officer and evangelist, she was also a social worker. She believed a Salvationist should be professional in both disciplines. Profound and articulate when lecturing on theology, she saw it expressed best in the simpler form of the poster on her living-room-cum-office-cum-study-cum-chapel. It reads:

> The Glory of Life is to give, not get:
> to serve, not be served;
> to be a strong hand in the dark
> to another in time of need;
> to be a strength in a crisis of weakness.
> This is to know the glory of life.

When I reflect on the word "enthusiasm", it is Bosshardt who comes leaping into my mind. Although that word is sometimes used in the secondary sense of emotional over-exuberance, it means (by derivation) "possessed of God". Bosshardt is, indeed, the enthusiast!

"Quench not the Spirit!" Paul wrote to the Thessalonians. To "restrain" (*Good News Bible*) or "suppress" (*Jerusalem Bible*) the Holy Spirit, the source of true enthusiasm is, in William Barclay's rendering, "to try to stop the activity of God", whether in oneself or in others. To be sure that we do not stifle the Spirit in ourselves demands self-examination and self-discipline. To destroy genuine spiritual enthusiasm in others – whether by discouraging their vision, denigrating the style of their ministries, or opposing every proposed change – is a sin not always absent from religious circles.

As we walked back to the Goodwill Centre in OZ Voorburgwal in Amsterdam, I heard Bosshardt say to two of "the girls" we met: "This is the Scottish preacher who is writing a book about me."** They approached me, hands outstretched. "You won't do the Major any harm, will you?" one of them said. "We love her." That I could not do, for in Bosshardt I have found true spiritual enthusiasm, the Spirit unquenched.

"Sometimes I can point to success," writes Bosshardt, "for people have changed; men and women and children to whom you mean something. You do what you must do. You try hard. You care for all your co-workers. The result? It is God who does the book-keeping."

Such ministry is indeed the glory of life.

* I refer to Major Bosshardt in the Meditation for November 18.
** Published in 1977 as *Here is my hand!* (Hodder & Stoughton, now long out of print).

ENJOYING GOD

One of the most memorable phrases from the largely forgotten Shorter Catechism comes at the very beginning of that seminal work. "Man's chief end is to glorify God" it says, "and to enjoy him for ever." It is the use of that word "enjoy" that attracts attention. God is to be "enjoyed". That word means to receive pleasure from something or someone. Its synonyms are "like", "love", "relish". This is indeed a very positive statement about the attitude to God we are allowed to have and the way in which we are free to express it. It is also, in effect, a description of the way people should approach worship. If worship is essentially enjoying God, it cannot be other than characterised by enthusiastic love and an exuberant faith.

Worship is for many simply church attendance, a somewhat passive experience of listening rather than active involvement in an enjoyable experience. Certainly many of the Old Testament psalms convey a real sense of celebration. The whole book vibrates with songs of praise and shouts of joy. At the same time the psalms, like the Bible itself, represent every aspect of human experience. As well as exaltation, dereliction, despair, doubt, deprivation are but some of the living themes relating to real people. But this surely is the wonder of the Word of God as a whole as well as of the Psalms in particular. The Bible speaks with many voices, ministering to many needs. It can rejoice with those who rejoice but weep with those who weep. It can offer the authoritative word, but contains a preacher who feels "all is vanity", that there is no purpose or meaning to life. It is this very comprehensiveness that makes the Bible a living book, able to meet the needs of all who worship.

To enjoy God fully means loving him with our whole being. Worship is not confined to any one aspect of our personality. It involves physical, mental, emotional and spiritual pleasure. This means that worship must offer the opportunity to every part of us to enjoy relationship with God. Intellectual effort will be involved in true worship as the mind wrestles with the deep things of faith. The emotions will, as one of the seats of enjoyment, seek ways of expressing feelings – the joy of celebration, the catharsis of confession, the glory of forgiveness, the sense of relaxation and peace. The needs of the soul with its "sincere desire" must be touched through the imagination, through intuition and through inner nourishment. And, not least, the body must share in "relishing" God which makes song, dance and movement part of the offering of worship.

The task is great, the approach to it of necessity humble. But if the purpose of leading worship is to be fulfilled, it will need to enable all who come to enjoy God. The added blessing in the process for all who conduct worship is that of enjoying oneself in God.

THE PILOT LIGHT

"And God said, Let there be light, and there was light." The beautifully told story of the Creation in Genesis records a striking fact. Light was created on the *first* day. Not until the *fourth* day were the two "great lights" created; "the greater light (the sun) to rule the day and the lesser light (the moon) to rule the night". The stars were created then too. Light is therefore the primary element in creation, existing in its own right. No wonder the divine presence is so often described in terms of light! "God *is* light" John writes and "in him is no darkness at all."

When he wrote the theological introduction to his Gospel, and sought to describe the eternal Word which was "in the beginning with God", John turned again to the concept of light. John the Baptist insisted that he "was not that Light" but was sent to bear witness to that Light. "That was the true Light which lighteth every one that cometh into the world." It is no surprise then to hear Jesus describing himself as "the light of the world".

If light is a form of energy, having in certain circumstances "as if it were a single continuous wave of energy" (my scientific text-book tells me); if all created things are made up of energy, we have a model or image which can perhaps help modern people to conceptualise the notion of spiritual power. *Energeia* is one of the Greek words used to translate the Hebrew word *ruach* (spirit, wind, breath) and is in William Barclay's view more appropriate than *dynamis* (power). Have we not then a highly positive image of the coming of the Holy Spirit, those first disciples filled with the divine "energy" and transformed into men of conviction, courage and action? With light and energy so related, certain New Testament precepts take on great importance: "Walk in the light as he [Jesus] is in the light," said John; "because Christ shall give you light," says Paul. Inner light is offered to all as a gift by "the Light of the world".

The necessity of the continuing presence of that light within is stressed in Jesus' graphic statement: "If the light that is in you be darkness, how great is that darkness!" That would mean that our inner light level – our pilot light – had dropped too low for our inner health's sake. The causes may be stress, strain, anxiety, doubt, lack of faith, emotional exhaustion or spiritual dryness. What has happened, writes Agnes Sanford (from whose book *Healing Gifts of the Spirit** I have drawn this image) is that we need, through prayer and waiting on the Holy Spirit, to ensure that our pilot light is re-lit. "It is from the pilot light all the burners of creativity can be lit, from which our latent abilities and powers are so swiftly brought into new life that we can, indeed, be called a new creation."

What a blessing is the Old Testament benediction! "The Lord lift up the light of his countenance upon you." "Walk in the light!" for it is the healing light indeed.

* Published by Arthur James Limited (as is her book, *The Healing Light*).

INNER RESOURCES

It would not be surprising if counselling agencies, psychotherapeutic clinics, psychiatric departments in hospitals and not least doctors' surgeries find themselves under pressure at this time. If this is so, it will not only be because it is the season for winter ills and "blues". It has to do with the possibility of post-millennial deflation and depression. And this is related to very basic psychological and spiritual realities.

The millennial experience was, individually and corporately, a memorable one. The splendour of the televised displays on London's Thames, Paris's Eiffel Tower, Edinburgh's Princes Street, Belfast City's Square and countless other places around the world brought elation and excitement to millions. The services in cathedrals in London, Edinburgh and Belfast, and the outstanding *Songs of Praise* from the Millennium Stadium at Cardiff (where 66,000 people were present) paid a triumphant tribute to the religious significance of the event. Words of hope and encouragement; messages about love and service; exhortations commending new beginnings and new opportunities – altogether a high level of excitement was created, making a unique occasion (in an individual life) an unforgettable one.

Then life has to return to "normal". The human spirit cannot remain at a perpetual psychological or spiritual peak; reality, with its stress and struggle, grief and sadness, fear and frustration, pain and suffering is there as it always is. The post-millennial experience may portray, in an acute form, the alternation so often present between elation and depression, ecstasy and desperation.

There is no need to use the term "manic depressive" to describe the mood swings which are part of being human. That concept is confined to extreme cases of personality disorder where elation and depression are acted out in extreme and unhealthy behaviour. It is simply part of our common experience that we can, on occasion, reach the heights of spiritual experience and for various reasons (traumatic events, combinations of negative circumstances, relationship crises, etc) touch rock bottom too.

The variation in moods and the alternating of elation and despair in the flow of life need not lead us to despair. The important part is to recognise the reality of our temperamental and spiritual frailty. If caught up in such negative feelings, there are three directions in which help lies. The first is the importance of the will to change attitude. Depression is by definition not something which can be cured by act of will, but the attitude we take to the situation in which we find ourselves is important. The second is to seek help from pastoral adviser, spiritual director, therapist or counsellor, creating a context in which fears and feelings can be looked at in safety. The third is to realise anew "the grace that is sufficient for all our needs". "I have learned to find resources in myself whatever the circumstances" wrote St Paul.* Within religious faith, the means of grace are always there, and the reality of the power of the Holy Spirit to change and renew can be acknowledged.

* Philippians chapter 4, verse 11 (*New English Bible*).

TRUE WORSHIP

"Let us worship God," I said on Sunday morning as I called the congregation to praise and prayer. I must have used these words around 3000 times in my years of ministry. But therein lies a danger. The sheer familiarity of the words may make us unaware of the problems people feel over religious terms taken for granted. "Worship" is a difficult word for some people.

The point was brought home to me by a business executive who read a Meditation in which I described worship as an acting-out of the relationship of love which is at the heart of faith. In a gracious and thoughtful letter (he is by profession "an ideas and implementation planner"), he writes: "I find it impossible to build such a word (worship) into any meaningful relationship between man and God if that relationship is built on a relationship of love. Even if one accepts the (in my view) wholly misleading metaphor of Father in place of God, I still find worship an impossible ingredient in that relationship. Did you worship your father, or encourage your children to worship you?"

The word "worship" creates different images. I am sure it is our interpretation of the word itself that causes difficulty. "O come, let us worship and bow down" cried the Psalmist. "Let us kneel before the Lord our maker, for he is our God ..." As with so many Old Testament images and metaphors drawn from contemporary ideas and institutions, worship appears to involve two levels: monarch and subjects, "almighty" God and his servants, omnipotence and powerlessness. This encounter between divine authority and human weakness certainly feels inappropriate to a relationship of love. But such a form of relationship on two levels is, in fact, encouraged by the Hebrew word used 86 times in the Old Testament to translate "worship". It means "to prostrate oneself". Perhaps the difficulty over the word "worship" relates to the associations it has with an emphasis on the divine sovereignty. Are such attitudes what we expect people to feel in response to the call "Let us worship God"?

It is better to look in another direction and that is to the Anglo-Saxon root of the word; worship is derived from *weorthscipe* which means "honour". Recognition of worth prompts respect, reverence, admiration, even love, and it is those words which point to the essence of worship. To worship God is to honour God and that leads us happily to Alan Richardson's definition of the purpose of worship: "to offer praise to God for his grace and glory." How appropriate this is to the relationship of love and familial bond.

How we honour God "for his grace and glory" is a matter of tradition, temperament, choice and style. What is all-important is that worship reflects the best that we can offer – liturgically, musically, intellectually and spiritually.

"God is a Spirit," said Jesus to the Samaritan woman. "They that worship him must worship him in spirit and in truth." Whatever we offer in worship must represent our utmost for the highest.

BEAUTY AND HOLINESS

Every act of worship should magnify beauty and holiness. Whether two or three gather together or a multitude assembles for praise and prayer, the Psalmist's exhortation is "Worship the Lord in the beauty of holiness." He would surely accept too, the holiness of beauty. No one should leave an act of worship without experiencing the wonder that leads to awe, reverence and re-dedication, a new realisation of the presence of the risen Christ, and gratitude for the comfort that comes from the God who is with us. The privilege of worship is, for those who come to it, the opportunity to touch and handle things unseen, but it is also a mighty responsibility for those who are asked to lead it, those who, with true humility, extend the great invitation: "Let us worship God."

The created world is a very beautiful place. To watch the extraordinary sunrises and sunsets seen this winter in Scotland can only result in a grand "Amen". The flowers that bloom so brilliantly in the spring, birds on the wing, animals running wild . . . we all have our own evidence of the wonder of creation. And in the world of the arts, magnificent writing, striking sculpture, "poet's pen and painter's hand" lift the human spirit above the mundane and the ordinary. The genius of Mozart, a Beethoven symphony, a Bach motet, a Schubert sonata can provide inspiration that touches the deep places of the soul. Why is it then that the world has to be cursed by the tawdriness and triviality of so much modern activity? that the lives and loves of so-called celebrities are made more important than the suffering of Afghanistan? that the sacred intimacies of relationships and the grief of bereavement become the butt of comedians' humour? that a conscious desire to push the boundaries back as far as possible typifies many approaches to entertainment? There is an ominous phrase in the book of Judges – "every man did that which was right in his own eyes." In a society where religion and politics were intertwined, such crass individualism could only lead to anarchy. There are many today who claim that we too have the right to do whatever we like. But that will bring moral and spiritual anarchy.

Unless there is some objective standard against which to test our intentions, motives, behaviour and policies, the danger of moral, ethical and spiritual anarchy is real. It is through religion that for most that standard is provided. For Christians the very core of Jesus' teaching demands that because human beings are made in the image of God, they must never be used as a means to an end. Any behaviour or policy that demeans or damages someone else must always be questioned. It is responsible community, not rampant individualism, that is at the heart of the gospel.

Keep ugliness at bay or beauty and holiness will be its victims.

A Meditation for Lent

THE DIVINE HUMILITY

It is hard to believe what we read in the twenty-sixth chapter of Matthew's Gospel! He has just described the poignant Passover meal of which Jesus partook with his disciples before his approaching suffering. It is a time remembered down the ages in millions of celebrations of the sacrament there instituted when Jesus broke the bread and shared the cup. It was a profoundly moving occasion. But how extraordinary! The incident Matthew next records after the Last Supper is the disciples' discussion about which of them should be the greatest. The response to the divine humility was human arrogance.

Arrogance, whether encountered in politician, preacher or crusading group, is simply unacceptable. If, in an individual, it is unattractive and indeed offensive, how much more damaging it is when corporately present, for example, in racial or religious prejudice. It reeks of assumed superiority. It is an unpleasant characteristic of people who seek to control, limit or even ban those with whom, or with whose views, they disagree. It is a fundamental aspect of intolerant fundamentalism, of whatever kind. None of these destructive aspects of arrogance should however surprise us, for it is, as the Genesis story makes clear, the primal sin in the Garden of Eden. The tempting serpent appeals directly to human arrogance. "You shall be as gods" he urges. It is that factor that brings about "the fall" and the consequent damage to relationships as it is detailed in Genesis, relationships with God, with others, with the earth, and within ourselves.

"God so loved the world that he gave his only begotten Son" in order to restore a right relationship with him and consequently with others. The answer to human arrogance is the divine humility, expressed in the wonder of the Incarnation. Jesus (says Paul) "made himself of no reputation and took upon him the form of a servant. (He was) found in fashion as a man. He humbled himself ... " If mere human words can describe divine mystery, this surely proclaims the humility of God.

In washing the disciples' feet, Jesus deliberately demonstrated humility to be the mark of both the individual follower and the church corporate. "The churches must learn humility as well as teach it," said George Bernard Shaw (in his Preface to *St Joan*). It is a quality that still needs to be proclaimed and practised in high places, ecclesiastical and secular. Certainly there can be no ministry of reconciliation where arrogance is displayed, nor is a ministry of healing possible if those seeking to be channels of God's power lack humility. Those who claim they follow Jesus must, in their self-presentation, relationships and evangelism, be "clothed in the garment of humility".

Lenten reflection will include thanksgiving for him who "really and truly became a servant". How strange it is that those who actually sat with him in that upper room should so soon turn to a selfish and arrogant concern with personal greatness! But, alas, how human!

A Meditation for Lent

THE SPIRIT'S SHRINE

That smoking is a danger to health is common – if often unheeded – knowledge in an age when legislation compels health warnings to be associated with the advertising of tobacco. But strong criticism of smoking was published 400 years ago! The collected works of James VI of Scotland and I of England contains *A Counterblast to Tobacco*, a book that, like many others of historic interest, is to be seen at the first free lending library in Scotland, Innerpeffray Library, opened in 1682 near Crieff in Perthshire. No longer exercising its original function, the collection of 3,000 books published before 1801, and a further 1,000 thereafter, can be seen at the library, beautifully situated beside the ruins of Innerpeffray Castle on the banks of the Earn.

Smoking is, we read, "a custom loathsome to the eye, hatefull to the nose, harmefull to the braine, dangerous to the lungs ..." The works of Joshua Sylvester, published in 1621, offered a similar view in a contribution entitled: "Tobacco battered, and the pipes shattered about their ears that idly idolizes so base and barbarous a weed." Smokers may be somewhat mollified to know that a much more common "addiction", tea-drinking, is strongly condemned in *The Farmer's Letters to the People of England,* while *A Journal of Eight Days Journey ... to the Thames* by "A Gentleman of the Partie" describes tea drinking as "pernicious to health, obstructing industry, and impoverishing the nation".

As a preparation for the approaching season of Lent, with its emphasis on discipline in the spiritual life, reflection on the need to discipline the body – in the light of these solemn warnings – is not un-useful. St Paul's attitude to the body is deeply rooted in the divine purpose and it is to the Corinthians that he spells it out: "Are you not aware that your body is the temple of the Holy Spirit?" or, as the *New English Bible* renders it, "a shrine of the indwelling Spirit". We cannot do what we like with our bodies because they belong to God. "You are not your own; you are bought with a price." The case for physical self-discipline in the service of God is built into faith.

Ultimately, however, spiritual and physical discipline belong together. Growing in grace is the spiritual process that refers not to our spirit only or to the body only, but to our whole being. "I pray that you may be kept sound in spirit, soul and body" is Paul's blessing on the Thessalonians.

What we do with our bodies is our responsibility, but the ultimate criterion lies in our awareness of the One to whom we owe our stewardship, and of the body as the shrine of the indwelling Spirit. "No athlete ever relaxes his self discipline. They discipline themselves to win a crown that must fade" Paul tells the Corinthians (in William Barclay's translation). "We do so to win a crown that cannot fade."

A Meditation for Lent

PRAYER WALK

"Enoch walked with God." Twice this simple statement is made. That, added to the fact that these words are not used about any others mentioned in that Genesis chapter, suggests that Enoch had evident spiritual quality. Later in the Old Testament it would be said of Noah and of David that they too walked with God. Pilgrimage, the journey to wholeness, two disciples walking together to Emmaus in religious discussion – the image of the spiritual journey is an important feature in devotional experience.

Something of this is expressed in the fascinating "Prayer Walk" through the beautiful grounds of All Saints Pastoral Centre at London Colney in Hertfordshire. It provides 40 minutes of reflection on nature and has "stops" at particular points where the pilgrim is encouraged to meditate on the unchanging love of God by reflecting on trees, sculpted or real, some of the latter gnarled with age, some lush and leafy, some newly-planted saplings. There are deep roots to some trees, while the branches reach heavenwards. And, as in the book of Revelation, trees and river are found side by side.

There is history too, again emphasising the span of time. At Stop 3, the invitation is to look across the meadow to a woodland where Alban, the first Christian martyr in Britain, is reputed to have been arrested by the Romans in AD 209. He was taken in place of his friend, Amphibilus, and died rather than deny his Lord. In the quiet and peace of the gardens, and while those on the walk are wholly engaged in contemplation and prayer, you become aware that you do not hear the sounds of the nearby M25, but its presence reminds each pilgrim that spiritual devotion and the real world are intertwined.

Lent is again approaching to remind us of the journey we take with Jesus on the way to Calvary and the Garden of the Resurrection. The 40 days of Lent are indeed a prayer walk, an opportunity for re-dedication by sharing Jesus' journey.

There are those whose pain, the result of traumatic tragedies or repeated sorrows, is so great that they can, in some way, compare their suffering to crucifixion, but for most of us that connection feels wholly inappropriate. The journey with Jesus through all he endured is nevertheless a spiritually maturing experience as the truth, however we explain it or interpret it, makes a fresh impact upon us. "We may not know, we cannot tell what pain he had to bear, but we believe it was for us he hung and suffered there." Our understanding of the atonement is a personal matter. Background, tradition, temperament and experience all play their part in the way we interpret Jesus' death, but that a divine gift of grace of enormous importance lies at the heart of the Easter story cannot be in doubt. The Lenten prayer walk provides the opportunity to realise again the wonder of the life, death and resurrection of Jesus.

A Meditation for Lent

CRUCIFIED GOD

There is always a sense of drama as the world rings out an old year and rings in the new. It is the opportunity given to regret, reform and resolve. That process touches the inner being, if it is allowed or encouraged to do so. A painful but cathartic end result of it is renewed determination, re-kindled vision and the energy, emotional, mental and spiritual, to "go forward".

2002 has been made into something even more traumatic by events since last September. An all-pervading anxiety exists. The festive lights may have been bright but the darkness around them is intense and still is as we journey through Lent towards Easter.

The words on the sticker in the car parked in front of me seemed to bring a calming new year message to just such a world. "Don't worry," it said, "God is in control." It needs a parenthesis of silence to ponder the implications of that statement. If it is true, it can only be in an eschatological sense, that is a long-term sense related to the coming of God's kingdom. "God is working his purpose out as year succeeds to year" we sing in Arthur Campbell Ainger's hymn. "He holds the whole world in his hands," expresses the same profound sense of providence as do the words that reporter Naomi Wolf herself heard from carol-singing children in New York, the sirens blaring outside the church: "He rules the world with truth and grace." The grand picture of the Christ whose kingdom replaces "the kingdoms of this world" is deeply embedded in faith and those intimations of providence that are part of our personal experience reflect that Christian hope. But what do those words on the sticker say to the relatives of those in hi-jacked crashing planes, to those crushed in the dust of collapsing towers, to those who became the victims of the fires they fought? What do they say to destitute families in war-stricken Afghanistan? What do they say to the parents of their just murdered child, the senior citizen mugged for a pittance, the relatives of a family killed by a drunken driver?

It is because of situations like these that the existence of a God of love is vociferously questioned and the irrelevance of the Christian faith proclaimed. But precisely here the great paradox lies! The faith is not irrelevant; <u>suffering is at its heart</u>. The One who felt the full weight of human pain, who was despised and rejected, a man of sorrows, acquainted with grief, reviled and abused, condemned to death though totally innocent, physically nailed to two pieces of wood, he is the lynch-pin of that faith. If ever there was a demonstration of the divine understanding of human suffering, it is in Jesus.

The answer to the problem of suffering lies beyond our human grasp, but in this season of Lent a shaft of light illumines our darkness. It is the profound awareness that in Jesus we see, in Jürgen Moltmann's dramatic phrase, "the crucified God". That is the God who is with us.

A Meditation for Lent

TOWARDS MATURITY

On Jesus' journey towards Jerusalem, and during the events which happened there, characters of whom little is known played their minor but positive parts on his behalf. There was, for example, Simon of Cyrene.

Cyrene in Libya was the home of numerous Jews. They shared with others a synagogue in Jerusalem (the book of Acts tells us) so Simon, not unnaturally was there to celebrate the Passover. All we know about him however is in the one verse which each of the Synoptic Gospels allocates to him. Mark, whose Gospel was based on memories of the dictated words of Peter, does mention that Simon had two sons, Alexander and Rufus, giving the impression he was known to the disciples. But that is about all. Each simply records that Simon of Cyrene was enlisted by the Roman soldiers (as they had the 'legal right' to do) to carry Jesus' cross when he stumbled, exhausted, under its weight.

Interesting too is the otherwise unmentioned wife of Pilate who, with a woman's intuition and following unpleasant day-dreams, "begged" her husband to "have nothing to do with that just man". History has recorded her personal plea on Jesus' behalf when all around seemed hell-bent on destroying him.

This is the sinister element in the journey towards Calvary and one which no individual intervention could contain. Corporate pressure and institutional prejudice on the part of the authorities (and not least the religious authorities) had taken over. The strength of the forces of hostility is expressed in the pathetic ritual of Pilate washing his hands of responsibility. There was by now a tidal wave of uninformed, uncritical, unjust corporate antipathy, determined on the destruction of Jesus. This is indeed a frightening example of the corporate "shadow", that interplay of negative irrational feelings which no rational argument can contain. It leads towards the public choice of the release of the murderer Barabbas rather than that of the innocent Christ. What greater sin could there be than this!

Corporate hostility in the form of institutional prejudice still afflicts society. We would all, if asked, make clear our dislike of racism as we would of violence, but deep, hidden, unrecognised – because unconscious – feelings can, under pressure of circumstances, be ignited by believed threats to territory and possessions.

Lent is a time for confession, repentance, reconciliation and spiritual regeneration, the acknowledgement of our need to face the negative forces that spoil our lives and, too often, the lives of others. Lent is the time for re-creation.

The Lenten "spring-clean", in which all that is negative is thus changed into that which is positive and beautiful for God, will advance our spiritual maturity, deepen our faith and make us more of a blessing to others.

A Meditation for Mothering Sunday

A MOTHER'S HEART

My mother went to school with D H Lawrence. She said later: "He was a very strange young man." She was a disciplined Victorian lady, so her reaction to him was not really surprising. She was trained by a strict father, whose stern personality was evidenced by the way he treated my mother's brother, his only son. For some misdemeanour, he was expelled from the family home for ever. He went abroad and was never seen again (though my mother did maintain correspondence contact with him). My mother, an artist and a musician, accepted the discipline in which she had been schooled. Lawrence, keen to extend the boundaries of current thought and behaviour, was not a natural soul-mate for her.

Mothering Sunday has stimulated these reflections on the questions my mother's passing reference to Lawrence raised. They focus on the concepts of discipline and freedom. Not mutually hostile, they can be so when each is taken to an extreme. Discipline (not in my mother's case, but possibly in her father's) can descend into judgementalism and dogmatism. Freedom, if it is abused, becomes not liberty but licence. Because we live in the "anything goes" society, entertainment constantly reflects the desire to push the boundaries of acceptance further and further. Is not the greater need at the beginning of the twenty-first century for personal and public self-discipline, less irresponsibility and more responsibility, less violence, cruelty and brutality and more of the gentle graces of women?

Jesus' mother, Mary, was human. When Jesus went missing in the temple in Jerusalem, her annoyance at his giving his parents anxiety was clear. She was distressed but dignified as her son was crucified and she was loyal to his cause by being involved in the disciples' post-ascension meetings. But there was in her too a profound humility and spiritual sensitivity. What she said on realising her calling as the mother of one who would "redeem Israel" cannot help but move: "I am the Lord's servant. Be it unto me according to your will."

Mary journeyed with Jesus through tragedy to triumph. The former was not unexpected for had not Simeon told her when he gave thanks for Jesus that "a sword would pierce through her own heart too"? From then on she was involved in events she could not understand. What she had was the capacity to "keep all these things – the puzzling words, the surprising actions (as at the marriage in Cana of Galilee) – and "ponder them in her heart". It was an act of faith and of commitment beyond the bounds of maternal responsibility.

"The loveliest masterpiece in the heart of God," said the nineteenth-century Carmelite nun, Thérèse of Lisieux, "is the heart of a mother." Mary is surely the Incarnation of that truth. In an all too heartless and cruel world, let us give thanks for the dignity, self-discipline and sensitivity of Mary, and for the gentle graces of women. The world greatly needs them.

A Meditation for Lent

THE REAL LENT

Without the falling rain, rivers diminish, mountain streams dry up, reservoirs become empty. Without the gentle breeze or mighty wind, the windmills remain motionless. Without appropriate food and drink, bodily strength falters. Without sleep, energy ebbs away. It is the same in the spiritual life. It can be healthy only if properly nourished. In order to *give out* we must *take in*. Without replenishment in the deep places, our spirituality will be arid and lifeless.

This is a spiritual law which not only prophets and preachers but also every individual will ignore at their peril. If all the emphasis in life is on activity, be it in the personal, corporate or even church spheres, and prayer and stillness are squeezed out, there will be much busy-ness, but little effectiveness. Feverish activity may impress some people, but over-concentration on *doing* seriously damages *being*.

If Jesus himself felt the need for isolation as a preparation for involvement, how much more do ordinary human beings need physical, mental, emotional and spiritual relaxation as a precursor to further endeavour. It is just here that that necessary sanctuary, the "desert place", comes in. The wilderness is the place of preparation, confession and self-awareness of divine grace. Luke therefore records that Jesus returned from the wilderness "in the power of the Spirit".

Lent, says Harry Williams,* "has nothing to do with giving up sugar in your tea or trying to feel it's wicked to be you ... Our Lent is going with Jesus into the wilderness." It is the place of trial and testing but it is also the place of ultimate victory. In that desert place, we encounter ourselves, "warts and all", but in the same moment become aware of the forgiving, renewing, grace-full love of God. It is indeed the place where we *take in*.

Surprisingly, perhaps, it is the Spirit who created Jesus' wilderness ordeal. Matthew records it thus: "Then was Jesus led up *of the Spirit* into the wilderness." Luke goes further; Jesus was *driven* there by the Spirit. The one who was to give out supremely to the world in words, love and blood, found in the ordeal in the wilderness, the grace and power he needed to fulfil his mission.

The church exists to forward that mission. It must never then allow itself to be drawn away from its primary task. That responsibility is to offer the bread and water of life to the spiritually hungry and thirsty. If it fails to offer the gifts of grace "in Jesus' name" it will become a sterile, irrelevant and insignificant organisation.

"Accept your wilderness," says Harry Williams. "From the story of the Son of Man, realise what your Lent really means. Then the angels will minister to you as they did to him." Indeed, they will.

* *The True Wilderness* (Constable, 1965).

A Meditation for Lent

EXPECTANCY

When Jesus was driven by the Spirit into the wilderness immediately after his baptismal experience, he encountered his first spiritual crisis. In Chinese, as I have noted elsewhere, the word "crisis" is made up of two ideograms. One means *danger* and the other *opportunity*. The wilderness crisis brought these themes together. There were, Mark reports, the wild beasts, but the ministering angels were there too, present with Christ as he defied the dangers, both physical and spiritual. That he grasped the opportunity to grow in grace through his encounter with temptation is evidenced by his returning into Galilee "in the power of the Spirit". The wilderness was a positive experience through which he clarified the nature of his mission.

If our Lent means going with Jesus into the wilderness, we can expect both testing and triumph. Deep within our inner being, powerful negative pressures, called in religious terms temptations, threaten to break through our defences, seeking to be "acted out" in our behaviour. It is a time of trial and spiritual danger. But because the wilderness is the place where we encounter God and his redeeming love, it is also the place of opportunity. It is in that encounter with ourselves and simultaneously with God that we discover – or rediscover – "life abundant".

Critic and journalist Michael Ignatieff tells us that Winston Churchill called melancholy "black dog" (it is not far from wild beast!). Ignatieff goes on: "These days we all seem to be in black dog's grip. Nations, like individuals, can get it too. The sound I hear around me is a low sigh of despair." Ignatieff is speaking of the prevalent depression that seems presently to be paralysing people and stifling corporate endeavour.

Such depression is very dangerous. It represents a constantly downward spiral. We need, urgently, an upward spiral, and this we will get when we recover that sense of *expectancy* that seems to have so deserted us. Our Lent has within it the opportunity to recover just such expectancy and faith. As Jesus returned "in the power of the Spirit" from the wilderness, so may we through our Lent with him, recover vision and hope.

There is much in the Bible about the spiritual law of expectancy . . . in its emphasis on "waiting on God"; in Jesus' instruction to us to ask, seek and knock; in his commendation of the faith of the woman from Canaan who sought her daughter's healing. Jesus created expectancy wherever he went. It is in such situations that miracles happen.

Going with Jesus into the wilderness to share his presence, purpose, power and peace, will lead to our positive return to the world, regenerated, renewed, expectant, grace-full. Lent is not a time for doom and gloom. It is an opportunity to learn – or re-learn – the disciplines of faith and hope.

THE GENTLE GRACES

It must be a privilege to be called "Mary". To share that name with the mother of Jesus surely brings the kind of blessing that comes from contact with real holiness. But there is so much more to be said. Not only was Mary the most important person in relation to Jesus' birth but, at his crucifixion (John tells us) there were *three* Marys (including his mother) present. Then, when his time for resurrection came, whom did he encounter in the garden but Mary of Magdala. In other words, *at each of the great saving acts of redemption for the world, there was a Mary present. His mother Mary was at the Incarnation, the Marys were at the crucifixion and Mary Magdalene was at the resurrection.*

Not surprisingly, yet another Mary to whom he was close (for "Jesus loved Martha and her sister") demonstrated the spiritual concern that led him to say in commendation: "Mary has chosen that good part which shall not be taken away from her."

"You are blessed among women," the angel told the Mary who was to bear the Son of God. Surely blessed by association are those who bear the name "Mary" today, for it is a name that mattered greatly to our Lord.

The fourth Sunday in Lent, Mothering Sunday, is a thanksgiving for motherhood. And rightly so. But perhaps, as we reflect, we can see it as more than that. It is a time of gratitude not only for "the handmaid of the Lord" but also for the ministries offered by women to Jesus in his suffering. It is a time too, to recognise the gentle graces of femininity.

In this "macho" world, we sorely need these graces … sensitivity, gentleness and compassion. The glorification of violence, the worship of the trivial and the ruthless materialism that so subtly infects us all, stimulating greed and the desire for gain, are making our world a darker, more threatening place, a vale not only of tears, but of fears. It is a time to re-establish the strength of gentleness.

The sensitivity and intuitiveness of Mary, the mother of Jesus, the compassion of the Marys who waited by the cross and the tenderness of Mary Magdalene in the Garden of the Resurrection, demonstrate anew the gentle graces of femininity so needed today.

In every human being there are both masculine and feminine components. Although the exact nature of their relationship is unique to each individual soul, there must be a creative balance between them for it is essential to our wholeness. Let us then be glad that the celebration of motherhood has its place in our real Lent, for it does something to emphasise, to our sad and needy world, the gentle graces of womanhood.

A Meditation for Lent

THE WILL OF GOD

It can be so difficult to discern the will of God. All kinds of pressures, external and internal – self-interest, rationalisation, wishful thinking – impinge on our understanding of God's will and our ability to hold to our conviction. It may, then, be helpful to reflect, in a moment, on an Old Testament cautionary tale.

Mr Bumble clearly did not rate highly the intelligence of an ass! In a withering comment on an expressed legal opinion (in Dickens's *Oliver Twist*), he said (somewhat ungrammatically): "If the law supposes *that,* it is a ass, a idiot." Palm Sunday puts a different value on this (at least in Bible times) invaluable beast. Jesus, consciously and deliberately, chose it to bear him into Jerusalem. The presence of that ass could not fail to make an impact on many, amid the loud hosannas and waving palms. This was exactly what the Old Testament prophet, Zechariah, had foretold: "Behold, thy King cometh unto thee – lowly, and riding upon an ass."

Recall, now, an Old Testament passage, that cautionary tale which brings credit to an ass, this time the one used by Balaam, the prophet. Balak, King of Moab, sent ambassadors to enlist the support of Balaam (*per pro* God) in overcoming his enemy. Balaam, in his second response to the request (we shall return to this) seriously displeased God by his ambivalence over the divine will. He set off with Balak's messengers only to be halted by his beast's refusal to go further. For its assumed stubbornness, it suffered from Balaam's violent temper (his cruel actions suggest an inner turmoil). But what dramatic irony! The prophet of God is blind to "the angel of the Lord" barring his way, while the much-maligned ass is sensitive to and wholly aware of the divine presence!

But back to the story recorded in Numbers, chapter 22. It focuses on the need accurately to discern God's will and be obedient to it. Balak's representatives had asked Balaam to "curse this people" for "they are too mighty for me". God told Balaam to send them away, saying: "The Lord refuses to give me leave to go with you." In Balak's eyes, however, even a prophet has his price so "more honourable" ambassadors carrying "the rewards of divination" are to be dispatched to Balaam. It was no use. "If Balak would give me his house, full of silver and gold, I cannot go beyond the word of the Lord." Well said, indeed! Then comes the fatal *but.* Let me think about it overnight, Balaam says in effect, and I will give you my decision tomorrow. The damage was done. The first judgement had been God's will, the second Balaam's wish. Balaam went with the messengers only to find the angel of the Lord barring his way.

"Jesus set his face to go to Jerusalem." He knew God's will for him. Neither the pain of Gethsemane nor the agony of Calvary would divert him from obedience to his calling. Would that we all had something of that strength when instinctively we know God's will for us.

A Meditation for Lent

ROAD TO HOLINESS

Lent is not a time for dreariness. It is a time for the development of the spiritual life; a time for journeying with Jesus and therefore making proper preparation for Easter; a time for reflection on what it means to be in but not of the world; a time for meditating on the need, paradoxical though it sounds, both to separate (for separateness is an essential element in holiness) and to be involved (which the doctrine of the Incarnation demands); a time for sharing in Jesus' suffering and preparing to rejoice in his resurrection. Lent is a time when the hope of an enhanced spirituality is high. This makes it an opportunity.

High hopes and hard spiritual realities come into conflict when we try to be in but not of the world. Spirituality must always be earthed in reality lest it becomes false piety or sheer escapism. There is a connection between faith and works for feelings of faith must be expressed in acts of love. Those spiritual eyes that "gaze up into heaven" can be allowed only to those whose feet are firmly on the ground. The necessity of a lively spiritual life is stressed by Michael Ramsey when he comments: "A church which starves itself and its members in the contemplative life deserves whatever spiritual leanness it experiences." The "longest journey in the world," writes Dag Hammarskjold, "is the journey inwards." But he goes on: "The road to holiness inevitably goes through the world of action." It is imperative that we touch and handle things unseen. It is equally imperative that we serve the widow and the orphan in their affliction. That, says James, in his New Testament letter, is genuine religion.

There is, as says Ezra Pound of his times, a "tawdry cheapness" about the world today. Opportunism, not opportunity, characterises its life. The world of publishing has been shown to be like so much else, driven by the money market. So increasingly is the world of sport. Mega-mergers dominate the financial news, ever bigger units are deemed to be essential to economic survival. The lottery brings hope to the people – or, more likely for most, despair. How hard it is to attend to the spiritual life when we are so focused on mammon. It may be part of the responsibility of our personal and corporate Lenten reflection to take notice of the reminder from Jesus at the time of his temptation: "Man does not live by bread alone." Life must be built on the solid rock of a living faith, not the shifting sands of shares and dividends.

"Wherein lies happiness?" asks John Keats in 'Endymion'. His answer? "In that which becks our ready minds to fellowship divine." "Happiness," said the blind and deaf Helen Keller "is not obtained through self-gratification but through fidelity to a worthy purpose." If Lent can bring us benefit, it may well be through the grasping of the opportunity to realise anew the validity of the claim of virtually every faith that it is the things which are not seen that are lasting yet ultimately immensely practical.

A Meditation for Lent

THE LENTEN PRIVILEGE

Lent is a time of opportunity. Observing it in the appropriate devotional spirit enables us to focus on the great events of Jesus' life and their relevance for our lives. The Lenten pilgrimage provides the stimulus for a determined and disciplined effort to concentrate on spiritual growth. We should grasp that opportunity and see it as a privilege.

Progress in the spiritual life is a gift of grace, but the grace comes only if we create the prepared context in which to receive it. To hear what God will say means deliberately being in a position to listen. To do what God requires us to do is dependent on our expectant attention. Jesus discouraged "much speaking" in prayer. He encouraged the simplicity of genuine faith. The quality of the devotional life is not determined by the number of hours or minutes we spend in prayer and meditation, but by the capacity to receive and obey, to watch and wait, to assimilate and act. The child Samuel articulates the proper response for all of us: "Speak, Lord, for thy servant heareth."

Waiting on God demands dedication, discipline and concentration. But, as Hamlet would say in another context: "Ay, there's the rub." How hard it is to concentrate in the stillness, for any length of time, on spiritual things! There are always those dreaded distractions – tomorrow's problems, family demands, mounting bills, undefined anxieties – the fears and worries that are different in degree and detail but are common to us all. It is inevitable that the pressures which dominate life in a stressful world and which occupy much of our waking attention, should break through into that time reserved for deeper contemplation. It is a human problem, not a sin.

Those who practise meditation find that there are helpful ways of trying to defeat distraction. Some, for example, take an object – a flower, a candle, a familiar symbol, an appropriate picture – so that whenever the mind begins to wander it can be quickly brought back to the focus of spiritual attention. Some take a passage from the Bible and are ready to return to it if external thoughts intrude. Some hold a verse or a text in mind – "Be still, and know that I am God", or "Jesus is Lord", for example – repeating it in mantra form to aid concentration.

It was of Principal D S Cairns' spirituality that his son, Professor David Cairns, wrote movingly and inspirationally: "My father has left the outsides and circumferences of those who write about the meaning of things, and he is bent at the centre, to see with his own eyes and touch with his own hand the pearl of great price." He was indeed focused fully on the kingdom and unlikely to be distracted by unimportant things.

We travel far behind the saintly Cairns on the spiritual journey, but at least we can sense the aim of it. Whatever distracts us in our quiet times needs setting aside, and that not with over-earnestness but with good humour.

A Meditation for Lent

A NEW BEGINNING

Lent originally meant spring. The festival that runs from Ash Wednesday to Easter really, then, relates to new life and spiritual growth. The popular association of Lent with "giving up" something, while rightly pointing to the need for Lenten discipline, becomes too narrow a concept, for the real Lent is a time of sanctification and inner growth through self-examination, contrition, forgiveness, renewal, commitment and the restoration of "the soul's sincere desire". Journeying with Christ towards his death and resurrection and feeling the purpose and pain of that journey ministers to the spirit and nourishes wholeness. It is a time to take seriously Paul's exhortation to the Philippians to "fill your minds with ... the things that are good and lovely and of good report." It is a time for a new beginning.

Striving for personal holiness in the world of today is an enormous task. Evil seems to be so prevalent and pervasive – and so infectious. "Sleaze" in politics and "bungs" in sport are part of a new and unpleasant vocabulary. The level of what is acceptable in entertainment slips ever downwards and, recently, dramatically so. There are series which trawl the gutters of human behaviour in the name of novelty and comedians whose only stock-in-trade seems to be dirt. This is not a call for censorship. It is a plea for self-discipline, for licence is liberty without discipline. It is the licence that says "anything goes" which is sought today. We are allowing a downward spiral to evolve and take us to levels from which it will be difficult ever to return. The cultivation of the beauty of holiness is a genuine Lenten task, both individually and corporately. There is a responsibility laid on all, whatever their religious stance, to proclaim in their words and to present in their lifestyle the beauty of holiness, a holiness not prudish and restrictive but healthy and wholesome, a holiness which values the good and the lovely, the things worthy of praise.

It must be a matter for concern that so much that is trivial, trashy and tawdry is shaping the ambience in which young lives evolve today. Only in contact with the truly holy – that is the good and the lovely – can spiritual growth develop into maturity.

Nowhere is the value of influence more demonstrated than in the doctrine and practice of infant baptism. To take vows, consciously and deliberately to ensure that a child is brought – through membership of Christ's body, the church – within the sphere of holy happenings and holy things is to bless that child's future. However unaware consciously of the grace that is mediated through the sacrament, that child is in contact, if vows are fulfilled, with the wonder of goodness and people of faith. There surely must follow in that developing life a sensitivity to the beauty of holiness and a desire to express it.

To have been put in touch, at an early age, with the means of grace is to have received a splendid benediction.

A Meditation for Lent

THE SOUL RESTORED

Jesus gave a very serious warning to those who sought to "gain the whole world" at the cost of their souls. Erasmus, the Dutch scholar, certainly saw the danger: "The supreme disaster," he wrote, "is the death of the soul." We would be wise to heed these warnings because we are living in soul-destroying times. Terrorist bombs do not only bring bereavement, injuries, damage to property and public chaos. They strike at the heart of crucial peace processes. They are, therefore, soul-destroying.

It is not easy today to cultivate the grace of "whole-souled loveliness".* So many factors are working against it – the pressures from materialism and secularism, the cult of possessions, the competitive ruthlessness of the acquisitive society, the outrageous financial values put on so-called celebrities in sport and entertainment, sleaze in public life, inequality of opportunity, unemployment and the threat of redundancy. How difficult it is to maintain and develop the spiritual life in face of such soul-destroying forces!

The darkness, the Bible tells us, cannot extinguish the light. For that we thank God. There is, after all, so much that is glorious in his creation, so much in the arts that is inspiring, so much to be admired in truly loving relationships. Add then the conviction that divine grace can make all things new, and hope really does "spring eternal". The cultivation of the spiritual dimension is a primary obligation in the religious life. "As to the spiritual direction of my soul," writes Simone Weil, "I think that God himself has taken it in hand from the start and still looks after it." God gives us the means of grace to help us restore our souls.

The Lenten pilgrimage provides an opportunity to do just that. The "interior disturbance" which, according to Jean-Pierre de Caussade, "renders the soul incapable of applying itself to devotional exercises," will be alleviated in the company of Jesus whose peace the world cannot give – or take away. The "guilt of dust and sin," which George Herbert confesses "draws back the soul", will be forgiven in the company of him whose grace is sufficient for us. The fear that is soul-destroying will be cast out in the company of him who is perfect love.

Enfolded in love, we journey through Lent, ready surely to say with the Psalmist: "Unto thee, O Lord, do I lift my soul."

* This phrase comes from a Celtic blessing.

A Meditation for Holy Week

FROM DEATH TO LIFE

The divine humility, so movingly demonstrated when Jesus washed the disciples' feet, is further proclaimed in the event remembered each Palm Sunday, the triumphal entry into Jerusalem. Jesus planned it deliberately to declare publicly his understanding of his Messianic role. Zechariah, the Old Testament prophet, had proclaimed: "Behold, thy King comest unto thee . . . lowly, and riding upon an ass . . ." Jesus was entering the city not as a warrior but as a servant.

The spontaneous acclaim given to him by what Matthew called "a very great multitude" simply underlined to the authorities, ecclesiastical and temporal, the threat which Jesus presented, especially if he had the support of "people power". The comment of his preaching and the integrity of his practice threatened the spiritual vested interests of the religious leaders. His destruction was essential. As the hosannas of his welcome were replaced by the unfolding events of Holy Week, people power was harnessed to the demand for his death. The shout "Crucify him, crucify him!" rang through the streets.

Jesus, however, had long been aware of the dark face of reality, expressed in conscious hostility to him by his opponents and, more seriously, of the subtle unconscious factors coming from the negative shadow side of his enemies. He accepted the dark face of reality and therefore saw his coming death as within God's will. From the time "he set his face to go to Jerusalem", he knew he must be "obedient unto death".

Each year as we travel through Holy Week, we see anew, with all its frightening intensity, the shadow side of fallen human nature at work. That same negative side of the unconscious – sometimes individual, now collective – has been horrendously demonstrated in events like the bomb in Warrington, despite the severe biblical warning about "offending these little ones". That same shadow is present in power when the people deliberately chose the robber Barabbas and rejected the innocent Jesus.

It is just such an action that sheds light on the sin which is described in the New Testament as "unforgivable". That sin,* as the context makes clear, is essentially a state of mind so depraved that it can no longer distinguish between good and evil. The description of Jesus as Beelzebub (a demonic power) is so contrary to the truth that those who made the accusation had reached a condition which is effectively spiritual death. In such a condition repentance is impossible, and without repentance how can there be forgiveness?

The glory of Holy Week is its demonstration of the divine omnipotence. That power is not an ability "to do anything". It is the capacity to take the evil that human beings do and make it praise God. In Holy Week that happens. Out of death comes life. It is there we see the divine humility and the divine omnipotence in concert. Let, then, the people say: "To God be the glory, great things He has done!"

---

* Also referred to in the Meditations for February 14 and August 13.

A Meditation for Lent

THE ABSENCE OF GOD

It is not recorded in the Gospels that Jesus laughed, only that he wept. When he learned of the death of his friend, Lazarus, and felt deeply the sorrow of Lazarus' sisters, Martha and Mary, the tears flowed. That emotional reaction to his bereavement proclaimed his true humanity. Described variously as "God incarnate", "the Word made flesh" even "God with us", here was a true human being who knew the meaning of grief, could feel others' pain and was able to weep over his and their loss. What a momentous declaration of the divine empathy with every distraught soul!

St John, at the end of his Gospel, underlines how little we know of what Jesus said and did. "Jesus did many other things as well," he writes, adding enthusiastically: "If every one of them were written down, I suppose that even the whole world would not have room for the books that would be written." Perhaps amusing events are among those that went unrecorded.

The Lenten journey is not primarily a time for laughter. It is a time of pain. The road towards Jerusalem will end with the agony of crucifixion. It will become the way of suffering to which Jesus always knew his obedience would lead. Even as a 12-year-old boy he had bemused his parents by declaring, in seeming rebuke, that he "must be about his father's business". Following Peter's confession: "You are the Christ, the Son of the living God," he deliberately began to explain to his disciples "that he must go to Jerusalem – and be killed". Moved by the picture of the suffering servant so dramatically portrayed by the prophet, Isaiah, he recognised that he would be despised and rejected, a man of sorrows and acquainted with grief. But it was not only physical suffering he anticipated. He would become too the victim of institutional prejudice on the part of "elders, priests and teachers of the law". He would face the conflict between self-interest and obedience in the garden of Gethsemane. He would even cry from the cross in utter dereliction: "My God, my God, why have you forsaken me?"

It is precisely Jesus' experience of suffering that is his greatest gift to troubled people. His tears for Lazarus speak with love to the bereaved partner or parent. His agony as he faced the conflict between a longing for life and the need to give it up will touch the heart of those who want to live but contemplate their self-destruction. His own distress over the seeming absence of God in his darkest hour will strike a chord with those who, at their wits' end, cannot feel the divine presence at all.

Those who travel the Lenten way in his company can only be grateful that, sharing human pain, he suffered as he did. To all who weep, agonise, mourn, the tears of Jesus make real the sympathy of God.

LIFE'S MUSIC

Whether it be the conducting of an orchestra, the managing of a football team or the leading of a congregation, it is the skill and ability of the leader in bringing the best out of each individual involved that leads to success. Those who carry such roles have a great responsibility but they also enjoy a sense of satisfaction and fulfilment. In dealing with individuals, the teaching profession particularly remains a vocation in that it offers the opportunity to "educate" young people, that is (by derivation) to "bring out" the potential gifts and talents of each girl or boy, stimulating a developing human being, mentally, physically, emotionally and indeed spiritually. Whatever socially, politically or economically impedes that process must be a matter of concern.

Such an ability characterised the way in which Jesus dealt with individual people. Whether choosing disciples or encountering people in need, his capacity for hearing a cry for help, ministering to a need, touching a nerve led the apostle, John, to comment that "Jesus knew what was in man." People grew taller in his presence, be it an extrovert outspoken fisherman or his introvert brother; an anxious Pharisee seeking spiritual help by night or a Samaritan woman at a well by day; a ruler of the synagogue pleading for his dying daughter, or a Syro-Phoenician woman expressing a level of faith beyond his expectation. Jesus sensed, drew out and developed the strength and potential of those he encountered in his ministry. Indeed nothing is more dramatic than the extraordinary change that compelled his scattered followers to seek to "conquer the world" in his name. The transformation was brought about by that "other Comforter", Pentecost's proof of Jesus' continuing presence and power.

There is in Christianity a proper emphasis on sin as a negative factor, conditioning all we are and do. Consciousness of sin properly forms part of each act of worship in prayers of confession. But respect for, and belief in, the corrupting effect of (as Genesis presents it) "disobedience to the divine will", should never blind us to the wonder of creation and the reality of human potential. A dramatic reminder of that comes in the words of Jolan Chang, words which compel us to ask questions about our achievements, especially when seen within the context of a faith which makes weakness strong, turns darkness into light, speaks of death and resurrection: "Most of us are like owners of a precious Stradivarius violin that we have never learned to play." What a gift of creation is human "be-ing"! What potential the Creator has implanted in stamping us with the divine image! What grounds for hope and encouragement lie there! Life is more than "being". It is "becoming".

Those outside a religious faith may hear this challenge to "learn to play" as a call to positive thinking, renewed endeavour, recovery of energy and purpose. For those who acknowledge a divine power, it is a reminder that it is never too late to take further lessons in how to create life's lovelier music.

A Meditation for Lent

"DEARE LENT"

"Welcome, deare Feast of Lent!" wrote George Herbert. It is a cry so vigorous and enthusiastic that it compels reflection on the meaning of the Lenten season. There are those who associate Lent with doom and gloom, denial and self-negation, unwelcome and restrictive discipline, yet for others, like that poet priest in the seventeenth century, Lent is a celebration. Perhaps no season in the Christian year so attracts both negative attention and positive proclamation. Lent is fasting and feasting, discipline and delight, pancakes and pilgrimage, burden and blessing. Lent is, like love, a many-splendoured thing. It is rightly welcome.

Associated with the Lenten season are many facets of the faith and the spiritual life. Its primary link is with spring, so it positively points to new beginnings. Early church links are with training for discipleship. It was associated with forgiveness and reconciliation, consciously expressed in the receiving back into communion of true penitents. The journey from Ash Wednesday to Easter is a pilgrimage profoundly touched by the sufferings of the Lord. It is the search for "whole-souled loveliness" (as a Celtic blessing describes it) in journeying with Jesus through the pain of Calvary, the gross darkness of the descent into hell and the glory of the Garden of the Resurrection.

"Deare Lent" is then welcome not as a time of giving something up (though that is not an un-useful discipline) but of grasping something new and life-giving. Its prime purpose is the pursuit of holiness. "There is nothing negative or killjoy about holiness," the late David Watson assures us. Mother Teresa puts it in a marvellously positive and exciting way: "Holiness consists in doing the will of God ... with a smile."

But there are times when it is hard to smile, and such times are now. Horrific pictures of human tragedy, in war and earthquake, push our ability to watch and absorb it to the limit as the sights of suffering are brought into our safe and comfortable homes. There is suffering on a scale so vast and unbelievable – as was the Holocaust 60 years ago. We cannot travel the Lenten way without facing, yet again, the sheer mystery of suffering. Yet at the same time we are in the company of him who turned death into life, defeat into victory, hopelessness into hope. Welcome, deare Lent, for your coming takes us to the deep places where the worst has to be encountered while we are assured that the best is yet to be.

"Practical holiness and entire self-consecration to God are not sufficiently attended to by modern Christians in this country." That was said even before the twentieth century began, by the famous Anglican, Bishop Ryle. If it is equally true today, then let the world – but not least the church – welcome deare Lent and its invitation to travel on the Lenten road to holiness. And to do it, if it is possible, with a smile.

SHARING THE PAIN

Those who seek to care for others pastorally must have the ability not only to sympathise with them but also to empathise with them, that is to understand their situation and to share their pain. This is especially so in times of loss and bereavement. To go on to identify with them may, however, be going a step too far. Every grief is unique, and no one else can fully enter into that suffering.

The danger of over-identification or being, as it were, taken over by others' problems, is a matter for constant attention in the supervision of counsellors and care professionals. That danger acknowledged, there is however the need to do everything possible to (as the Old Testament prophet Ezekiel put it) "sit where they sit". To identify as closely as possible with others' pain is to demonstrate a true empathy.

I found it necessary to recognise the important distinctions made above in talking recently to just under 200 bereaved parents. Every one had lost a child (or children) of whatever age, and in whatever circumstances, and many of them had been recently bereaved. I spoke on 'Healing relationship: growth through friendship', a concept at the heart of the national and international organisation of which very sadly (for membership means your child has died) they are members, The Compassionate Friends. Being the only person there who was not a bereaved parent laid a heavy responsibility on me over every word I used. In particular, it would have been very insensitive to say *I know how you feel*. I can't, for I have not been in their position.

That I was very nearly a bereaved parent is not relevant. Our son, when a few days old, contracted cellulitis and was saved by an experimental use (so far as very young babies were concerned) of the then new discovery of penicillin. But he was brought back from near death. That he is still alive constitutes the crucial distinction. Nor does my lifelong vocational involvement, or my personal experience of bereavements, allow me to say to those who have suffered the greatest loss of all, the death of their son or daughter, "I know how you feel." What it does allow me to say, in empathy, is "I feel for you."

If sensitivity is ever needed, it surely is in times of bereavement. You cannot tell bereaved parents that "time is a great healer, and you will get back to normal." Whatever that normality was, it is gone for ever. You cannot assure people that they will "get over it". They never will. You cannot even assume that parents will "come to terms with it"; most never do. You can only speak and act in such a way that, in that darkest hour and the long, dark days that follow it, you feel for them and with sensitive empathy try to say or do something that will comfort, encourage, sustain them; in other words, to offer a healing relationship.

CREATIVE COMPASSION

I cannot walk along Edinburgh's Princes Street, past the tall monument to Sir Walter Scott without remembering – and yet it is so very long ago – a good man, a devoted pastor of many years in a parish just outside the city, who threw himself to his death from the top of that monument. Ruddy and cheerful of countenance, gracious in manners, gifted in the pulpit – and yet for some reason it happened. The anguish behind that decision is painful to imagine.

I passed that monument only a few days ago. The sight of it, with its memories, took me back to a sermon preached in St Paul's Cathedral some time ago. The occasion was the Festival of the Sons of the Clergy, a situation that moved the preacher, the Very Rev Michael Mayne, to tell of his own father's death. "On a Saturday afternoon in May, my father wrote a note to my mother who was out, climbed the tower of the church beside the rectory, removed the boarding from the belfry and threw himself down. He died almost immediately."

It is never right to say to anyone who has gone through torment or suffered tragedy "I know how you feel." All experience is unique. If you have never lost a child, it is impossible to know what such an experience is truly like. For the same reason, only those who have taken their own lives can have known the anguish that leads to such a drastic decision. It is a time when nothing you have ever believed in seems to have any relevance to you and the situation in which you find yourself.

In the days of Michael Mayne's father's death – some 60 years ago – he tells us that a suicide was allowed no proper burial, no marked grave or memorial. The coroner at that inquest commented: "I cannot conceive of a clergyman desecrating holy ground as Mr Mayne has done." And, adds Michael Mayne, "no one ever spoke of my father again." From the parish in which Mr Mayne had served, almost a life-time later, has come a statement by the Rector that "few people in your father's village remember him, and the traumatic event" and "we would like to see a simple memorial to him erected". It was. It is a kind of healing of which Michael Mayne said in his sermon: "We and the local body of Christ which are my father's parish are saying to him: 'We shall never know why you did what you did, for that is known only to you and to God; but your desperate cry for help came out of so much anguish of spirit that it demands not our judgement but our compassion'."

It is in line with the spirit of the Master that his followers, when faced by events they cannot accept or understand, should choose not the rigours of judgements, but the creative power of compassion. If such an attitude is considered a risk to standards and values, it is nevertheless the risk we need to take.

A Meditation for Lent

INNER SPRINGTIME

"It is not only the will to win that is necessary," said the athlete, who had just broken a long-distance world record, "it is the will to prepare." It is a thought relevant in the season of Lent. The spiritual journey involves the discipline of preparation.

Lent in the early church had strong connections with preparation. It was the time set aside for the teaching and training of baptismal candidates. But the Lenten discipline was not confined to them. Church members too were exhorted to engage in spiritual practices, especially praying, fasting and studying, and to do so with humility. A sense of the importance of a period of focused spiritual discipline as a preparation for the remembrance of the sufferings of Jesus and the wonders of the resurrection rightly continues today. Journeying with Jesus through his wilderness and along the Lenten way, in sincerity and with humility, is found by most pilgrims to enrich the spiritual life. "Travelling together" (the theme of one Lenten address in the current* series in York Minster, led by Sisters of the Holy Paraclete) aptly describes the significance of the Lenten journey.

Lent is a time of positive spiritual endeavour involving the discipline of preparation and leading to the discovery of new life. It is here that its association with spring becomes excitingly relevant. Even now, as that season approaches, shoots and buds proclaim new life, renewal, creation and re-creation. Lent is our inner springtime. It is not a time to dwell gloomily on our failures, our darkness, our spiritual inadequacy (though a healthy recognition of our weakness is appropriate). It is a time to point to the potential for our growth towards spiritual maturity if we travel with the Lord on his journey towards Jerusalem and all that lay at the end of it.

"This day may I re-connect with the springtime within me," prays the author of the section "Inner Springtime" in *Catching the Dream*.* The writer goes on: "In our inner preparation for the great festival of Easter, we need to balance the focus in our shortcomings with a focus on the springtime within us. Whatever our chronological age, we each have an inner child within that longs to be invited out to play, to skip like the lambs, to express the creativity that the child finds so natural and the adult so often finds blocked by inhibitions." So the true Lent speaks of hope, of spiritual progress, of the new creation for ever possible through grace.

"For heaven's sake – keep on" is the final title in the York series referred to above. Lent involves the discipline of preparation and the determination to keep going, to "run the race that is before us". Jesus is our inspiration on the Lenten journey and our companion on a pilgrimage through suffering to victory.

* 1999.
** *Catching the Dream*, New Start for the Millennium, a Lenten study published by ACTS, Scottish Churches House, Dunblane, FK15 OAJ, 1999.

TRAVELLING ON

I was moved by the frail, elderly lady who spoke to me after the service on Sunday. "I could not hear you," she said, "because I am deaf. Nor could I see you because I am nearly blind. But how I sensed the Spirit in the atmosphere!"

My dictionary defines religion as "belief in, recognition of, or an awakened sense of a higher, unseen controlling power or powers ..." It was to this sense of the numinous, the inner consciousness of another dimension, that this lady surely testified. It is something experienced through what Paul describes as the "knowledge which is beyond knowledge". It relates to the reality of "the things which are eternal". This world is, alas, deeply affected by materialism, conditioned by public relations, market forces, political, economic and social pressures. All canvass the value of wealth and possessions. Sadly, such pressures relentlessly force those who cannot cope with such demands towards poverty and repossessions. How essential it is then to proclaim to such a world – and this is a primary task of the churches – the need for the recognition of the dimension within which Jesus lived and on which the early church was founded, the dimension of the Spirit.

When John Baillie entitled one of his books *Invitation to Pilgrimage*, he pointed to the nature of the journey of faith. We are, says William Wordsworth, "travellers between life and death", travelling on to our spiritual destiny. It means taking risks even to the extent of being thought "fools for Christ's sake". But it is an exhilarating process involving purpose, direction and movement. The pilgrimage is never easy. There will be peaks of spiritual experience and deep troughs of despondency and despair. "My marks and sores I carry with me," said Mr Valiant-for-Truth in John Bunyan's *The Pilgrim's Progress*, "to be a witness for me that I have fought his battles." Whether our pilgrimage be seen as a race (as Paul saw it) or a struggling plod, it is a journey of destiny and excitement so long as we "keep looking unto Jesus".

The pilgrim goes where the Spirit leads. It is a journey made in freedom, with spiritual growth and increased inner awareness the symptoms of forward movement. How beautifully the dove, the image of the Holy Spirit, symbolises both movement and freedom! The Genesis picture, too, is of the Spirit *moving* upon the face of the waters, while both Testaments speak of the Spirit in terms of wind and breath, elements invisible and unable to be grasped, but energising and free-flowing. That Spirit must not be quenched or contained by hidebound dogma, ecclesiastical regulations, spiritual censorship or the privatisation of belief. Like the wind, the Spirit "blows where it wills". And if freedom has its risks, the word of God is always that against which we test our experience.

Perhaps, in the end, Wordsworth's claim that we are all "travellers between life and death" needs emendation. We are, in fact, travellers from death to Life.

A Meditation for Holy Week

LIFTED UP

Robert C Roberts tells of a lady who was deeply disappointed with most of the literature on spirituality that she found in Christian bookshops. "It is a little like a down pillow," she said. "If you are sleepy, it may be just what you need, but if you want something to stand on, to enable a higher reach, it 'squooshes' down too easily. You need something firmer ..." She then tried academic theology, and took an adult education course in religion. "There is intellectual firmness often," she said, but added, again with disappointment, "but what can be reached by standing here is not food for the spirit. The stool is strong enough – but I opened a cupboard looking for food and found only various tools and games."*

It is a sad story for, after all, it is the main purpose of religion to minister to the spirit; that is, in George Steiner's striking phrase, "to nudge (people) into the neighbourhood of the transcendent".** There is a gap that needs to be filled and a deep need that must be met, and one of the ways to spiritual sustenance is surely through the Lenten pilgrimage when we journey with Jesus, in reflection, towards Calvary and on to the Garden of the Resurrection. As we take that journey in imagination and memory, we grow into a greater awareness of the divine presence.

If the study of the Master and his ways is the training course for the pupil, let the disciple watch Jesus as he responds to people in need with words and compassionate actions; as he explains and interprets "the signs of the times"; as he meets hostility with the silence of dignity. After all, is it not recorded that, faced by his accusers, "Jesus answered them nothing"?

When Jesus entered Jerusalem, a king riding on an ass, "all the city was moved". What a complex of emotions he stirred up! There were the happy hosannas and waving palms that we recall each Palm Sunday. There were the Pharisees, sullenly complaining about the disciples' exuberance. There would be, soon, the crowd calling for Barabbas' freedom and Jesus' crucifixion. And still to be faced was the spiritual agony of Gethsemane, the betrayal and denial by two of his disciples, and the physical agony of the cross. And yet he forgave his murderers who "know not what they do", promised paradise to a penitent thief and committed his mother, Mary, into the safe keeping of the disciple he loved. All this was done though he was despised and rejected, a man of sorrows who "hung and suffered there". What manner of man, indeed is this?

To be, in imagination and awareness, in the company of Jesus as Holy Week unfolds is surely indeed to be nudged into the neighbourhood of the transcendent, to be sanctified by such a demonstration of the divine love.

Let Holy Week bring benediction through feeling the blessing of such amazing grace. How rightly he said that if he were to be "lifted up from the earth", he would draw everyone to him.

* From *Spirituality and Human Emotion* by Robert C Roberts (Eerdmans/Paternoster Press, 1982).
** Quoted by Stewart Todd in *Theology in Scotland*, Spring 1996.

A Meditation for Passion Week

LET THERE BE LIGHT!

Seldom can the threat of impending darkness have been proclaimed as clearly as in the words of Lord Grey of Falloden with the First World War approaching. "The lamps are going out all over Europe," he said. "We shall not see them lit again in our lifetime." He died in 1933, the year Adolf Hitler became Chancellor of the Third Reich. Darkness was coming. There are times when darkness feels very dense.

Such a time is recalled when Passion Week, the week from Passion Sunday to Palm Sunday, is followed by Holy Week as part of the journey with Jesus towards Calvary and crucifixion. Matthew, Mark and Luke unite to record the fact that as Jesus' life moved to its close "there was darkness over all the land from the sixth until the ninth hour". It was "gross darkness", significantly symbolic, silently overwhelming. Such darkness descended on the people of Dunblane in a few moments of madness.

The Bible associates darkness with wickedness, sin and suffering. The crucifixion was all of these – the murder of the innocent one who "hung and suffered there". Yet the cross is the focus of the glorious paradox that throbs at the heart of faith. Its "genesis" reaches back to the creation story: "Darkness was on the face of the deep," it says, but goes on "Then the Spirit of God moved on the face of the waters. And God said 'Let there be light.' And there was light." Perhaps the paradox is presented most pointedly when we read in Exodus that Moses "drew near to the darkness *where God was*". God did not will the murder of the children of Dunblane and their teacher, said the minister of Dunblane Cathedral, Colin McIntosh, to the parents and people of Dunblane; it is rather that, in those awful moments of darkness, "God's heart was the first to break." God is in the darkness. God shares our pain. Somehow in the heart of the darkness of Dunblane, a light began to show. "The darkness and the light are both alike to thee," cries the Psalmist exuberantly.

> Aye on the shores of darkness, there is light,
> And precipices show untrodden green,
> There is a budding morrow in midnight ...
>
> (John Keats, *To Homer*)

Jesus presented himself as the light of the world, a light which, St John tells us, "shines in the darkness and the darkness has never extinguished it" (William Barclay's translation). The corollary is unavoidable. Disciples, then and now, must "let their light so shine ..." that God is glorified thereby.

Let the words of a child sum up the call of Jesus to his followers. They come from the young Robert Louis Stevenson who, waiting for his supper and looking out on the Edinburgh street in which he lived, was watching the old-fashioned lamplighter on his rounds, lighting each city light. His nurse called him to his meal, but the young Robert refused to take his gaze away from the lamplighter. "Look, look," he cried, his face pressed against the window pane, "there's a man out there punching holes in the darkness."

So must we all.

VOCABULARY OF LOVE

There is a curious comment in W H Auden's poem on the death of W B Yeats. "*Poetry makes nothing happen,*" he writes. Can this be so? Just because poetry is the literary form that uses so much of the imagination allied to the harmony of words, it surely is capable of "moving" someone and indeed of moving them on. From the huge range of poets from every age and place, we choose our favourites, a choice almost certainly based on the poets' capacity to encourage, challenge, inspire or change us.

That capacity to develop us in profound ways is shared with other literary forms. The play, the novel, the film, has as its primary purpose our entertainment, but the playwright, the film-maker, the novelist, can also bring a crusading element to their work. That is likely to be implicit rather than explicit, subtle rather than patent, but it is the factor which may make things happen by presenting new perspectives on old problems and critical analyses of public attitudes and mores.

It is the purpose of religion to bring about change in the human condition, both at a personal and a social level. The Old Testament and the New Testament both encourage repentance and the renunciation of past weakness and exhort men and women to renew their commitment to obedience to God, that is to raise the level of their spiritual awareness. But the means to achieve this aim is almost always a book. The Christian faith, like the Jewish faith, has its Word of God and the function of that literary work which includes history, poetry, parable and drama, is to make things happen in the lives of people. "*The sword of the Spirit which is the Word of God*" is, in St Paul's view, an essential element in any campaign to bring about change.

Change, conversion, renewal if they are to take place must touch the "inward parts" of our being. In more contemporary language, that means that to be effective, change must happen at the unconscious level of our personality. Unless "*deep speaks to deep*", unless grace touches the parts beyond the reach of human systems of education or philosophy, the miracle of interior change will not take place. The turning-point in spiritual renewal comes when both conscious and unconscious levels are touched by grace. Then things happen.

Mother Teresa talked of "*a vocabulary of love*". She was not thinking only of the power of words – in poetry or any other literary form – though she used them to great effect in changing attitudes. The vocabulary of love is words in action. However much her words struck home at all levels of society, it was the vocabulary of love incarnate in action which so influenced the world – the multitude of hospitals, clinics, orphanages, hospices that she created. The greatest effect of all in "making things happen" remains the life of the servant of God who is a vocabulary of love incarnate.

A Meditation for Lent

"Behold the Man"

"Lord, is it I?" What drama is encapsulated in that cry uttered, virtually in unison, by the disciples! It happened at the Passover meal, the meal which was to become the Last Supper. There he made the statement that bewildered and saddened the disciples: "One of you shall betray me." It was then that "every one of them" asked that uncomfortable question, anxiously questioning their behaviour and attitudes without understanding why they felt guilty. Each in his heart wondered if he had failed in his discipleship.

The journey of Jesus towards Jerusalem, Calvary and the Garden of the Resurrection has always aroused emotion and passion, and has led to so much great music which, this and every Easter, will draw crowds not only to cathedrals and churches, but to concert halls of many kinds. The events of Holy Week touch the minds, hearts and souls of millions. The sheer greatness of a good man (whether or not he can be called Saviour and Lord), the unfairness and injustice of his appalling suffering, the sense of his involvement with people in their pain (because he understood it through sharing it), touch a human nerve and create a spontaneous response. There is a sense in which Jesus belongs to the whole world and the world acknowledges it. If it cannot bring itself to say "my Lord and my God" as Thomas did, it may well say "*Ecce homo*", "Behold the man."

There is an irony in the nature of the responses to Jesus' suffering. Often his followers failed him. Yet strangers supported him. Judas's betrayal, foreseen and prophesied by Jesus, led to his self-inflicted death, an act of remorse and profound guilt. Peter's denial was also foretold by Jesus. The tears Peter shed reflected his sense of failure. There was corporate failure too at the time of Jesus' arrest. "*All the disciples forsook him and fled.*"

But there were positive responses to Jesus from people outside the category of formal discipleship. There was Joseph of Arimathea, a secret disciple, and a member of the Sanhedrin, the court of Justice which tried Jesus. Did Joseph protest? Was he present when Jesus was condemned? Was he another failure? But he did redeem himself and pay his own tribute by receiving Jesus' body from Pilate and giving it a seemly burial. There was the centurion on guard by the Cross who felt moved to cry in tribute: "Surely this man was a son of God." There was the penitent thief, ready to acknowledge the innocence of Jesus and seek his blessing. There was Pilate's wife, imploring her husband not to be involved in the death of "that innocent man". All in some way came from the world outside his circle to acknowledge and honour a good man.

And so the man from Nazareth belongs both to the church and to the world. If not everyone feels able to "crown him Lord of all", each can offer thanks, praise and admiration in their own way for the man for others.

A Meditation for Lent

PARDON, POWER AND PEACE

The question is not whether the church is relevant today but whether most people feel it to be relevant to them. My instinctive reaction to that latter question is a "No", a reaction somewhat confirmed by the presence of but six of us at the early morning Eucharist in a parish church on Christmas Day. But other factors bring that judgement into question.

For example, a pre-Christmas survey found that 41 per cent of those interviewed said that they might well go to church during the Christmas period. Carol services obviously inflate this figure but, compared with accepted average levels of church attendance in this country, that is a remarkable percentage. It surely says something about the felt need for contact with the Christian faith today. An earlier survey, moreover, showed that in 1994 the percentage of those who were more concerned with the spiritual aspects of Christmas than with the commercial and social aspects had increased significantly since 1993.

These insights suggest that, although the institution "church" – with its own language, thought-forms, traditions, "eccelesiasticism", concern with theological minutiae, etc – may not seem relevant to many people (though many Christians, clergy and lay, work hard, sincerely and with imagination to make it so), the desire for faith and grace draws people towards that for which the church stands, the gospel of Jesus Christ. There is a sense that, within religion, personal needs can still be met, and perhaps increasingly so. There is a relevant faith for today available to all and, deep down, many people know it. The word "relevant" comes from a Latin verb meaning "to raise up", "to relieve". It is (the dictionary says) "associated with the notion of helping". To be relevant, then, means having the capacity to bring relief to people, to raise spirits, to encourage. The Christian faith is relevant today because it can respond to real human needs ... the longing for a new beginning, that second chance, perhaps even Jesus' "seventy times seven" level of forgiveness. The experience of that forgiveness and the new opportunity it brings is the most healing aspect of a faith founded on the belief that God is Love.

Inner peace will not solve the problems of the world or even our personal problems but, with the gift of that peace which, Jesus said, "the world cannot give or take away", it is more possible to cope with them. And for those who need resources, the promised, transforming spiritual power experienced by the disciples at that first Pentecost remains on offer to all who ask for it.

There is a faith for today that offers pardon, peace and power to all who seek it. The church must do all it can to ensure access to it for all who want such blessings.

NOT FEAR, LOVE

To say, as John does in the first of his three New Testament letters, that "perfect love casts out fear" is to describe ideal achievement rather than real possibility. To fear is human. To have perfect love is, even with the help of grace, beyond human reach in this life. But within the statement there is an important element of truth that is both practical and relevant. It is that the more we are concerned for others, the less will we be anxious about ourselves. One attitude is inward-looking and threatening, the other outward-looking and positive. There is between fear and love an attainable balance. The greater our sense of committed love, the less will be our self-centred fear. "When our hearts are filled with love," says Ann Morrow Lindbergh, "there is no room for fear."

Given this relationship between fear and love, blessing will follow if we consciously seek that attainable balance. We must take steps to ensure that we are facing in the right direction. In Christian terms that means "looking unto Jesus" and in other forms of religion giving attention to the spiritual dimension in life, however it is understood within that faith. Once direction is established, faith focused and an attitude of dedication and commitment to achieving that proper balance confirmed, mentally, emotionally and spiritually we shall be in good health. Physical health may well benefit too as we increase love and decrease fear.

Mary Magdalene, struggling to find Jesus in the Garden of the Resurrection, realised that she was in fact looking in the wrong direction. Her eyes and her attention were focused on the tomb and death. Only when she "turned round", changed direction and looked the other way did she encounter the risen Lord. That physical gesture made all the difference. It is symbolically true too. To be looking in the right direction is imperative for those who seek to develop their spirituality. When direction has been determined, focus maintained and dedication applied, the journey to real life has begun. In that combination of words – direction, focus and dedication – lies the clue to growth in grace and maturity.

Strength of will supported by the gift of grace is needed to maintain that spiritual journey as the pressures of life and the negative feelings from within us strain our commitment. But the purpose is, like recovering the lost coin and finding the treasure hidden in the field in Jesus' parables, worth the utmost effort. As happened over the finding of both coin and treasure, satisfaction and joy will follow. We shall be fulfilling anew the great command to love God and our neighbour. We will serve, give, fight and labour no longer counting the cost, heeding the wounds, seeking reward. Loving more, we shall be less afraid. It is in such circumstances that religion becomes real for it is not fear that should dominate our lives, but love.

The Gift of Wonder

"The world will never starve for want of wonders," said G K Chesterton, "but only for want of wonder." How right he is! "Nothing is more needed by humanity today ... than the recovery of a sense of 'beyondness' in the whole of life to revive the springs of wonder and adoration," says John Taylor. These words underline the dilemma of our times. We are surrounded by wonders but in danger of losing our sense of wonder.

Part of the reason may be the negative effect of the wonders of today for they can be used not only to bless society, but to curse it. The internet has opened doors even wider to pornography. The conquest of space brings not only the fascination of knowledge of the universe but the frightening possibilities of star wars. The "wonder-full" world in which we live reflects perennial paradoxes – the tyranny of traffic, the tawdry nature of so much contemporary entertainment, the obsession with sex, the greed that pays homage to dividends rather than the needs of ordinary people. "New wonders each returning day" will continue in our world, and for many of them properly used, we give thanks, but dare we lose our capacity for wonder?

Bishop John Taylor's words, quoted above, are incomplete. His concern over the loss of awe and "beyondness" relates not only to society at large. That loss must be rectified, he says, *particularly by the church*. If secular society should suffer a loss of the sense of wonder, it can, in terms of human failing, be understood, but that the body which sets out to be the guardian of the spiritual dimension should fall prey to that same deficiency must sound warning bells for an institution which exists to enhance the sense of "wonder, love and praise". That is the very heart of the purpose of the church. It can only fail miserably if it has lost the capacity for "beyondness" itself.

"Whoever is devoid of the capacity for wonder," wrote Albert Einstein, "whoever remains unmoved, whoever cannot contemplate or know the deep shudder of the soul in enchantment, might just as well be dead, for he has clearly closed his eyes upon life." It is a solemn warning to the church too, for wonder is after all the basis of worship. To nourish the sense of the numinous, to open minds and hearts to what Rudolph Otto called "the idea of the holy", to underline the reality of, as Paul described them, "the things not seen, the things that are eternal", is the aim of every act of worship.

Wonder is a gift the church must nourish, by its music and its meditation, its proclamation of the gospel of unconditional love, its compassion for the world, its miracles of grace, its pursuit of healing and reconciliation and its practice of the presence of Jesus. The church is failing the world if it has itself lost the capacity for holy wonder.

TOWARDS TRANSFORMATION

"The church which is married to the spirit of its age," wrote the famous Dean of St Paul's Cathedral, Dean Inge, "will be a widow in the next." It is a comment that relates deeply to the current debate on the much publicised terminal illness of the church. Nor is it only the institutional church which appears to be "nearly vanquished". It is, Cardinal Cormac Murphy-O'Connor pointed out last year,* Christianity itself that is in defeat in that it no longer has any impact on the majority of British lives and their moral decisions and no influence on modern culture and intellectual life.

It is obvious that a large number of old-fashioned and unattractive buildings have become a burden on the church. Much of the language, liturgies and music are meaningful only to older generations. "I have no objection to churches," wrote Brooks Anderson, "so long as they do not interfere in God's work." It may be that now many have become, unintentionally, obstacles to living religion. But the constant sniping by media writers and presenters does not give proper credit to the faithful and effective service across the land of parish priests and ministers, of devoted lay people, of lively congregations well aware of the need for change and active in bringing it about. Reports of the death of the church are, as was that of Mark Twain, "greatly exaggerated".

It is not a new experience for the church to be attacked, criticised, written off. Centuries of history have demonstrated its capacity for revival, renewal, reformation, resurrection. Taking seriously informed criticism of its weaknesses, its best response will be a return to its basic beliefs. Too much of the church's contribution today is social commentary on current problems. It sometimes seems unwilling to do what the first Christians took for granted, "preach Jesus Christ and him crucified". Those words must of course be translated into the language and concepts of today, but they remain the heart of the gospel and that which the church must proclaim.

Lent, a time for personal self-examination, is also a time for corporate assessment; and especially the need to sense when conforming to the ways of the world – be it in relation to power, the attraction of force, love of money, or indefensible moral licence – blocks the transformation that faith demands.

There is a time for out-of-date structures, irrelevant language and attachment to buildings to die, a time to set aside all that interferes with the work of God. If the church believes, as it should, that the Holy Spirit is the agent of reform, then change and renewal are always possible. It is the evidence of history that miracles happen, that the faith which has been lost can be found, that religion which was dead can come alive again. But it all depends on the church making central the reasons for which it was created, the proclamation of the gospel and the care of people.

* 2001.

A Meditation for Lent

BEWARE CONFORMITY

Lent is a time to reflect on the meaning of holiness. The experience may, however, be an uncomfortable one for honest self-appraisal could well disclose our failure in demonstrating the difference in standards, values, attitudes and fundamental perspective expected of those who are called to serve God. "Election" to such service, whether individually as a disciple or corporately as "the chosen people", involves separation from the world and demands evidence of holy difference.

The necessity for engagement with the world but disentanglement from it is spelt out forcibly in Jesus' valedictory prayer for his disciples. They are *in* the world, but not *of* it. They are bound by their calling to engage with the life of the world, sharing its pain and suffering. It is however, part of the mandate on holiness not to become entangled with the world. Beware conformity.

The distinction between an improper worldliness and a proper holiness is a prominent biblical theme. It is an important part of the covenant relationship between Israel and its God. St Peter, too, is reminded of the difference between Jesus' and the world's ways after he has spontaneously drawn his sword in his Lord's defence. "Those who take the sword shall perish by the sword," he is told. The Old Testament prophet, Zechariah, underscores the same theme in his words to community leader, Zerubbabel: "Not by might nor by power but by my Spirit" says the Lord.

Jesus' Incarnation was the expression in time of God's engagement with the world. The ministry he offered as "God with us" was his total commitment to people. The church as the body of Christ is bound by that same commitment. The problem today is that, under severe economic, political, social and cultural pressures, the church can become so entangled with the ways of the world that disentanglement is more and more difficult. Corporately we are being sucked into policies of "power and might" as the "war on terrorism" develops. Individually we find ourselves enmeshed in money-market competitiveness, overwhelmed by the hidden persuaders of advertising and commercial promotion, open to compromise on issues of moral and ethical importance. It is presumptuous to generalize in terms of individual spiritual success or failure, but reflection on the level of our holiness may well reveal the degree of our entanglement with the world.

"Do not be conformed any longer to the pattern of this world" Paul wrote to the Romans. Contemporary pressure to do exactly that makes for internal conflict for us all today. The dilemma of moral man in immoral society (to use Rheinhold Niebuhr's phrase) may make the literal application of the gospel ethic seem naïve and irrelevant, but dare the church set aside its distinctive beliefs in the power of the Spirit, the healing ways of God and the call to holy obedience? The temptation to conform is present and powerful but reflection on the meaning of holiness compels our resistance to it.

FOOLS – FOR CHRIST'S SAKE

"Start a huge foolish project like Noah," wrote the Persian poet of the thirteenth century, Rumi, "it makes absolutely no difference what the world thinks of you." Delighted I was indeed to come across these words for they expound a theme dear to my heart, that of *creative irresponsibility*.

Long-standing readers of these Meditations will recognise the phrase. "Creative irresponsibility," I wrote in 1994, "springs from the sense of adventure which lies between prosaic responsibility and indefensible irresponsibility." I pointed to an example of it in Abraham who, in obedience to his God, "went out not knowing whither he went", taking risks with his family in the interests of a great cause. I recalled Paul's demand that we must be "fools for Christ's sake" willing to be a public spectacle, insulted, persecuted, starving, for the sake of our convictions. "Giving without counting the cost" can be creative indeed even if it is, in worldly terms, irresponsible. To be a fool for Christ is an appropriate thought on April 1.

Two examples of such risk-taking compel further reflection on this great concept and the need to re-emphasise it.

The first refers to a project called *The Icebreaker Mission* and was recalled last year* when its leading adventurer, Professor Jack Perry, died. That mission was undertaken by a group of businessmen – sixteen of them – who in 1953 travelled to Peking to establish trade agreements with China, shortly after the People's Republic of China had been proclaimed. The "cold war" made contact with China near impossible. It was widely believed that the People's Republic would collapse, but Perry, a profound political thinker and prophet, took the opposite view. The stance made him unpopular in high places, unacceptable in official quarters, the subject of criticism and opposition that endangered his business and his career. What can be achieved in and with China today remains unclear, but that which many saw as irresponsibility on Perry's part has done much to create opportunities for Sino-British relations in many spheres today.

The other example – and it was in this context that I quoted Rumi above – was the sheer irresponsibility of reconstructing Shakespeare's Globe Theatre on the banks of the Thames. The late Sam Wanamaker, the American actor who dreamed dreams and saw visions, started what many saw as "a huge foolish project" and, though he was not to see its completion, inspired many others to press forward that endeavour. It is a moving example of creative irresponsibility.

Age dims the radicalism of youth, just as it can discourage risk and adventure, spiritually and mentally. But a living faith involves risk; theological risk in the endeavour to find relevant images and meaningful metaphors for contemporary seekers; ecumenical risk in the pursuit of not uniformity but unity; pastoral risk in seeking to minister to the relationships of the modern world. Launching out into the deep may sometimes be considered to be irresponsible. If it is a risk taken in obedience to the will of God, it will almost certainly have profoundly creative consequences for active religion involves risk.

* 1996.

A Meditation for Mothering Sunday

THE QUIET PRESENCE

"There was standing the sorrowing Mother, beside the cross, weeping while her Son hung on it." The thirteenth century hymn, *Stabat Mater dolorosa*, attributed to Jacopone de Todi, plaintively conveys the pain of history's most revered mother as she shares the suffering of her son. It is the pain that every mother – and father – knows who loses a child through death, however it comes. It is heart-breaking. Somewhere, today, someone is going through that pain – waiting, watching, worrying, weeping. Yet, so often, as supremely in Mary, it is borne with dignity.

It is natural to think of Mary on Mothering Sunday. However varied may be the ways in which she is acknowledged in different branches of the church, Mary was, in Jesus' life and death, the quiet presence. She was always there, saying little, giving much.

Mary proclaims her relationship with God through the *Magnificat*. Faced with an unbelievable proposition by the angelic messenger, her humble, glorious response was "Yes." Her words: "Be it unto me according to thy word" constitute an act of obedience and faith. She gives the "Yes" that is essential – as it is in prayer, the sacraments and healing – for God to effect a miracle. This is surely the most crucial "Yes" the world has heard. It makes the Incarnation possible. Elizabeth, her cousin, exclaimed in admiration: "Blessed are you among women!" How right she was!

The obviously profound relationship between Jesus and Mary was one that she had to learn. So much about her son was unusual – the things he said and did, the way people spoke of him, the expectations he created. As experience succeeded experience, Mary showed her profound sensitivity as (according to St Luke) she "kept all these things and pondered them in her heart". She was puzzled but open, instinctively aware if unable to comprehend. The "devout and just" Simeon, waiting for "the consolation of Israel", knew that with her child, that "consolation" had come. Anna, the prophetess, confirmed it. Confused parents, understandably concerned that their boy was missing in Jerusalem, were (as it must have felt) rebuked by the 12-year-old Jesus: "Do you not know that I must be about my Father's business?" Puzzled servants are told by Mary to "do as he says", and water is turned into wine. At Calvary, Mary was there, the quiet presence, weeping as any other mother would in such awful circumstances, but believing. Jesus' words from the cross show the nature of his relationship with his mother as he commits her to the care, in a mother and son relationship, of "the disciple whom Jesus loved".

Beyond the cross, the quiet presence continued. As the disciples gathered in an upper from for prayer, women were present too, and among them specifically mentioned, is "Mary, the mother of Jesus".

"Mary, at the foot of the Cross," writes Tina Beattie,* "represents the hope of those who continue to believe, even when there is nothing left in heaven and on earth to make sense of their faith … In her heart she keeps God alive although He is absent from all awareness and reason."

Let Mary's quiet presence be with you on Mothering Sunday.

* *Rediscovering Mary* (Burns and Oates/Dove, 1995).

A Meditation for Passion Sunday

DIGNITY IN SUFFERING

"Mary, you are specially dear to God!" So William Barclay translates the salutation of the angel who came to announce to the mother of our Lord that she would bear the child Jesus. Her cousin, Elizabeth, was the first to underline how special Mary was, and down the ages that sense of respect and admiration for Mary has continued. Ecclesiastical traditions may vary in the nature of the place given to Mary, but what all can share is admiration for the quality of her womanhood and motherhood. "I am the Lord's servant. Whatever you say, I accept," said Mary to the angel. It is her profound humility and vibrant obedience that makes her special.

On Passion Sunday, we reach the point in Lent when the suffering that Jesus had to face begins to impinge heavily on us. But it is Mary's torment too. Her dignity in facing the suffering of her son and the pain it brought to her own heart is moving beyond belief. Could there be anything more awful for a mother than having to watch her son being nailed to a cross, totally innocent of any crime, yet crucified with criminals? How could any woman bear such acquaintance with grief? Yet the record if brief, is touching indeed. "Jesus' mother … standing beside the cross." In the hour of his extremity, she was there.

The Norwegian sculptor, Gustav Vigeland, has among his hundreds of sculptures a remarkable commentary on responses to suffering. The snow was deep in Oslo as Jillian and I stood in Vigeland's Sculpture Park, the very bleakness of winter seeming to underline the burden of life depicted in his sculpture – six life-size male figures, supporting a large saucer-shaped basin. It holds "the water of life". The figures express, by their attitudes and postures, the sheer effort involved in bearing life's suffering. Some seem to be near to coping. Others, weighed down and crushed, are finding life and its pain a burden "grievous and heavy to be borne". It is life as we all know it. Some cope better than others. Some struggle not to go under. Some cannot manage at all. There are those who are ground down by the mystery of suffering, puzzled over "the bad things that happen to good people". There are those who are the victims of the seemingly irrational and unfair distribution of suffering, and feel resentment and bitterness at the endlessness of their pain. But there are those too who are able to sense the creative possibilities of their suffering, and are able to grow in grace and maturity through their experience of life. How blessed they are!

Mary, with the dignity of her suffering, is an inspiration to us all as we struggle to cope with life. If Mary with her gentle graces was remembered on Mothering Sunday, it is worth recalling that that Sunday is also known as Refreshment Sunday. It is refreshment indeed to be encouraged by one who, dignified in suffering, was "specially dear to God".

A Meditation for Mothering Sunday

A Good Mother

"God could not be everywhere and therefore he made mothers." So runs a Jewish proverb, happily to be recalled on Mothering Sunday. Motherhood at its best reflects the divine goodness.

The significance of Mary, the mother of Jesus, varies in different branches of the church but, whatever attributes are accorded to her across the Christian family, all would surely agree that she is, in the language of today, a superb role model. The hymn of praise known as the *Magnificat*, which she uttered on learning of her unique place in God's purpose, testifies to her innate humility while her spiritual sensitivity is beautifully summed up in her reaction to the events surrounding the Nativity, noted two days ago: "Mary kept all these things and pondered them in her heart." "Highly favoured" she was, "blessed among women," she was told. She is honoured today for her purity and spirituality by so many. To give thanks for the goodness of Mary is indeed an appropriate way of marking Mothering Sunday.

As is the case with so much in the spiritual life, the more we try to achieve goodness, the less attainable it becomes. It is, in fact, not an achievement at all. It is a product of the active presence of the Holy Spirit, a fruit in the harvest of the Spirit. If it manifests itself in an individual life, that is evidence of, in New Testament terminology, life "in Christ". Goodness flows from the "Christ within". It was said by those who heard the disciples preaching and saw their miracle of healing that "they took knowledge of them that they had been with Jesus". In other words, their goodness showed. Such goodness is more visible to others than it is to ourselves. We influence the world most when we are unaware of the goodness we have been given.

This truth lies at the heart of our belief in "justification by faith alone". Goodness is not the merit we create in order to claim the divine approval. It is that which develops within us, in the process of sanctification, through "amazing grace". If goodness is seen by others to be part of our contribution to the world, the credit for it is not ours. It is due to, as Thomas Binney's hymn says, "the Holy Spirit's energies". That makes the possession of goodness, as Mary made clear, a matter for profound humility.

Among the many blessings Jesus brought when "the Word was made flesh and dwelt among us", was his shining goodness. The rich young ruler recognised this and was moved to address Jesus as "Good Master". Jesus felt it right to divert such sincere admiration away from himself, saying: "Why do you call *me* good? There is only one that is good, and that is God." The point is understood, but the young man whom Jesus so admired for his honesty was only putting into words the impact of Jesus on those who met him.*

As Mothering Sunday comes again, it is right to suggest that some of the Lord's goodness was, surely, the result of his having a good and wonderful mother.

* This important story of the rich young ruler is referred to in several Meditations, for example May 24, June 8 and 25.

HOLY PASSION

It was after Jesus' triumphal entry into Jerusalem that there came some Greeks to the disciple Philip with the plea: "Sir, we would like to see Jesus." The action somehow expresses the need for some kind of a saviour. So often people sought him out; Nicodemus, the Pharisee, by night secretly; Zacchaeus, the despised tax-gatherer, up a tree, openly; the crowds, pursuing him when he needed a quiet place with his disciples. And so it has been down the ages. Those who "hunger and thirst after righteousness" have sought him out to learn from him as teacher, to be made whole by him as healer, to be inspired by him as preacher, to be drawn to him as the supreme example for living.

"He came unto his and his own received him not" yet, nearly two millennia later, his name is universally spoken, his words revered and his teaching treasured by millions. He was "despised and rejected", and yet his name is honoured not only within the religion he founded, but in others as well. For some he will simply be the carpenter of Nazareth to be honoured as a human being unique in goodness, proclaiming a profound but simple message about a way of life. To others he will be God incarnate in human life who "by his holy passion and his endless love" offers the salvation so needed by a corrupt world. Some will see him as the cosmic Christ who "in the beginning was the Word and the Word was with God and the Word was God." Here surely is the magnetism that draws seekers, searchers and sinners to him. In whatever way, at whatever level, he "being lifted up" draws people to him. In whatever language each finds it appropriate, and relevant, traditional, contemporary, academic, simple, every one can say "May Jesus Christ be praised!". The church may be deemed irrelevant by those outside it and many within it, but the "king and head of the church" never will be. In every time and every age there are those who will say with longing, hope and expectation "We would like to see Jesus."

When Mary Magdalene went to the Garden of the Resurrection, she cried broken-heartedly: "They have taken away my Lord and I don't know where they have laid him."* Is this, metaphorically, the theme at the heart of recent accusations made from within the church about the irrelevance of the church that the essential Jesus to whom so many have been, are and will be drawn, has been taken and hidden in unnecessary ritual, theological confusion, ecclesiastical minutiae, tedious assemblies, synods and conferences, the pursuit of personal power, the trivia of personal failings, disunity round altar and table?

We are not told if the Greeks did meet Jesus, but his answer to the disciples through whom the request was conveyed was to say that his hour had come, and to point to his passion, for him the core of his mission. As Passion Sunday comes round again, it is for us all to keep "looking unto Jesus", his holy passion and his endless love.

* This point is also referred to in the Meditation for February 7.

A Meditation for Holy Week

PASSION'S PRIORITIES

The word "passion" has several meanings. One of them relates to Jesus' suffering. As Holy Week approaches, his *Passion* is, properly, a focus for reflection. But *passion* also means "an abandoned display of emotion, especially of anger", while a third meaning is "strong sexual desire".

Was Jesus a passionate man? So far as the last dictionary definition is concerned, Jesus does not seem to have been passionate, certainly from the records that we have. This does not mean that the affection he felt for close friends – Lazarus, Mary of Bethany, Mary Magdalene – was not profound. It is simply noting that passion in the sexual sense of that word was not a demonstrated part of his life. Taking passionate in the sense of "emotional reaction", however, the story is quite different. Told of the death of Lazarus, and the sorrow of his friend's sisters, Mary and Martha, the tears flowed as Jesus wept. There were other events that made him very angry and led him to act with passion. They involved insincere religion and disrespect for God.

The disciples, like the experts in the Law and some Pharisees mentioned in the story of "the woman taken in adultery", had difficulty in knowing how Jesus would respond to situations. The latter group of people demonstrated that uncertainty in their seeking his reaction to adultery. Producing the woman "caught in the very act", they expected a passionate defence of the law of Moses on a matter which demanded stoning as the appropriate punishment. No such display came, and the silently retreating line of accusers, led by the eldest, indicated their failed expectations.

A similarly strong response seemed to be expected from Jesus over another "woman that was a sinner".* As she washed Jesus' feet with her tears and dried them with her hair in a genuine act of love, the host, Simon the Pharisee, railed at the one who claimed to be a prophet but apparently did not know the woman's unacceptable background. The disciples too grumbled "with indignation" at the waste of expensive ointment. Would Jesus share in such criticisms of either the woman or the waste? Certainly not. Simon was rebuked, and the woman commended.

It is clear then that it was not the personal peccadilloes, the "sins of the flesh" that aroused Jesus' passion. But there is no doubt what did – the sins of spiritual intolerance, of self-righteousness and of hypocrisy, especially shown by the official representatives of religion. The disrespect shown to God by temple consumerism and individual greed also moved him to passion. Money-changers and traders were driven out of the temple, their tables overturned. He used strong language too to condemn the "play-actors" on the religious stage. "Woe to you hypocrites," he said. It was this kind of sin that aroused Jesus' passion.

"Passion, I see, is catching", says Mark Antony in Shakespeare's *Julius Caesar*. The response to Jesus' Passion can only be the passionate pursuit of the things that were important to him. These surely include human rights for all, the expression of the value of every soul in their having the right to fulfil their potential, and the effort to replace corporate and financial greed with the simpler values of the One who had no place to lay his head.

---

* This incident is also mentioned in the Meditation for July 12.

HOLY SATURDAY

Jesus, according to the Apostles' Creed, was "crucified, dead and *buried*". It was on Holy Saturday, in fact, that he lay buried. The day between the crucifixion and the resurrection is a day of darkness and despair.

Despite the repeated emphasis on *three* days in the Gospel story, virtually nothing is said about the day between Good Friday and Easter Sunday. The concept of the descent into hell with its positive note about the ministry of Jesus to "the spirits in prison" is of much later origin. The late Alan Lewis underlines "the brief, inert void" in his book *Between Cross and Resurrection** which that day represents; it is a "non-event surely ... only a time of waiting in which nothing of significance occurs and of which there is little to be said. The day that follows Calvary is not an in-between day which simply waits for the morrow; it is an empty void, a nothing, shapeless, meaningless and anticlimactic, simply the day after the end."

It is difficult for us, with our knowledge of the glorious, triumphant ending to the Easter story, rightly re-told each Holy Week, to sense the apparent finality of that day when Jesus lay "buried". Try therefore to follow the story as it unfolds without turning to the last page ... the entry into Jerusalem, the agony in Gethsemane's garden, utter humiliation and rejection before those who held the right to judge, the dreadful journey to Golgotha, the sheer physical pain of the crucifixion, the anguished cry "My God, my God, why have you forsaken me?" No wonder darkness covered the land as the One who came to preach the good news, heal the sick and offer a new way of life to all, died an ignominious death between two thieves. As the disciples forsook him and fled, as weeping women stood near the cross, as the heavens were rent and thunder rolled, there could, from the stance of Holy Saturday in the unfolding story, be no other than Alan Lewis's conclusion: "If at this moment, a person who lived so close to God is lying in a criminal's grave, rejected, relationless and God-betrayed, what reason is there to believe that, even on the best of days, God is with us?"

It is therefore valuable, spiritually, to re-live the story *as it happened* in order to feel the weight of the darkness and despair of the second day because it throws into greater relief, the surprise, puzzlement and, ultimately, exceeding joy of the resurrection in all its glorious splendour. Prophecies are fulfilled. Promises are redeemed. The good news is given to the world. Jesus is risen! Jesus lives!

Varied are the views of believers on the nature of Jesus' rising from the dead but all can unite in the true resurrection and the power it had to change the world.

To feel the despair of Holy Saturday is to magnify the wonder of Easter Sunday. "The strife is o'er, the battle won." Hallelujah!

* Published by William B Eerdmans, 2001.

A Meditation for Easter

RESURRECTION JOY

"The Lord is risen, is risen indeed." So the cry of "Alleluia!" rings out in exultation and joy wherever Christians come together on Easter Day. And rightly so. The sad and sombre feelings aroused by the repetition of the journey through Holy Week have given way to a sense of triumph. "Thanks be to God who giveth us the victory through our Lord Jesus Christ!" There may be disagreements among believers on literal aspects of the resurrection story, but of the reality of his continuing presence as risen Lord, there is no doubt. The resurrection is a corner-stone of the faith.

Those who today have difficulties in believing that, as the Apostles' and Nicene Creeds assert, "on the third day, he rose again" will feel their doubts were shared even within the circle of the disciples. Perhaps Thomas speaks for many when he records his inability to believe that such an event could happen. I need proof, he cries. And, of course, he is given it. It will not perhaps convince contemporary doubters but it did Thomas. Those who, as Jesus commented, have believed without seeing such proof are blessed, have made an act of faith. This is what believing in the resurrection is.

Although Jesus had shown himself as risen to various individuals and groups in apostolic circles, there is a sense of uncertainty in the days between Easter and Pentecost. The wrong questions – for example about the restoration of the kingdom to Israel – were still being asked (Acts chapter 1, verse 6). Nevertheless efforts to stay together and to stabilise the groups were made. They maintained their group strength by shared "prayer and supplication". They were "of one accord". "The women, and Mary, the mother of Jesus", were involved in such devotions. The group did necessary practical things like appointing, by lot, a successor to Judas Iscariot in the apostolic band. That mutual support continued until "the day of Pentecost was fully come".

The coming of the Holy Spirit is an event similar in kind to the resurrection. Belief in that presence is an act of faith. The proof of its reality is the extraordinary effect of the coming of the Spirit on the disciples. A perplexed and puzzled group, holding together – but it feels only just – are transformed into an evangelisitic team, ready to take on the world "in Jesus' name". So amazing was the effect that we who claim the name Christians today are such as a direct result of that Pentecost of long ago. To the gathered throng, Peter's proclamation is crystal clear. "God has made that same Jesus, whom you have crucified, both Lord and Christ."

The transformation of the disciples from weak uncertainty to strong conviction and infinite courage is an event that needs an explanation. It cannot lie anywhere other than in the mysterious (in the biblical sense) events of the first Pentecost, the birthday of the church.

It is the resurrection joy that moves onto the power of Pentecost that is the life-blood of the faith.

"HE IS RISEN!"

"Death is going back-stage to meet the Author." Only someone from the world of entertainment could have said that – and did. The words are Donald Swann's. He died last week.*

I knew Donald as a friend of many years and respected him enormously. When, in the sixties, I wanted to explore the possibility of "communication through the arts", it was to Donald, his great friend Sydney Carter, Nadia Cattouse, Sylvia Read and William Fry (Theatre Roundabout) and others that I turned. Donald's contribution was particularly important because he was an explorer of "the things that are eternal", and did just that in his own presentation for us, *Soundings by Swann*. He is remembered, however, mainly as the (Sydney Carter's affectionate word) "hobbit-like" half of that famous partnership, Flanders and Swann. How extraordinarily successful were their shows, *At the Drop of a Hat* and *At the Drop of Another Hat*, with those familiar songs and gently satirical lyrics! I last heard Donald play and sing *Mud, Mud, Glorious Mud* publicly less than a year ago. He was "backed" by a distinguished chorus – Ian Wallace, John Amis, Frank Topping, Sydney Carter and others. How marvellous it was, for he was then very ill! But Donald needs to be remembered for his own serious work in composition, his passion for peace, his sense of the spiritual.

In the Coda which he added to his autobiography *Swann's Way: A Life in Song* (the paperback edition*), Donald writes of the cancer against which he battled so courageously for so long. "Thou famished grave" he quoted defiantly (from Edna St Vincent Millay), "I will not fill thee yet." And there is triumph too in his closing paragraph: "There is continuity at every point ... Nothing is finished ... The stream flows ever on ..."

How fitting it felt to quote these words at Eastertide (he died in March).* The disciples too were pointed *forward* by the message from the Garden of the Resurrection: "He is risen: he is not here ... he goeth before you into Galilee." It brings a ring of truth to the assurances from Jesus: "Lo, I am with you always"; "I will not leave you comfortless: I will come to you." And from Paul: "O death, where is thy sting? O grave, where is thy victory? Thanks be to God who giveth us the victory through our Lord Jesus Christ." Nothing, truly, is finished.

The theme of salvation focuses on three gardens. The first is the Garden of Eden, the garden of human failure where, as that profound Genesis story demonstrates, God's gift of freedom was abused in deliberate disobedience to his will. The second is the Garden of Gethsemane where Jesus feared, faced and accepted that he is "the Lamb of God who takes away the sin of the world". It is in the wonder of the third, the Garden of the Resurrection, that the seal is set on his victory over sin and death. The empty tomb proclaims his resurrection. The stream flows on.

Nothing is finished. The Garden of the Resurrection is not the place of ending, but of beginning.

"He is risen!" Alleluia!

* Published by Arthur James, 1994; Donald died in March 1994.

A Meditation for Easter Day

RESURRECTION

Jesus instructed his disciples to preach the gospel, heal the sick *and* "raise the dead". The first two exhortations are taken seriously, but boundaries of credulity and of faith are indeed reached when the resurrection of the dead is contemplated. Though some evangelists, particularly of an African background, claim such extraordinary miracles, the possibility of raising the dead goes beyond even the most fervent expectations of faith-full people. While Jesus did carry out such a miracle in the case of Lazarus, we are in a realm in which the disciple just cannot be "as the Master". Raising the dead just does not happen today. There was however an occasion some months ago when the word "resurrection" came into the context of healing ministry.

We were offering thanksgiving for the success of an operation to a lady to relieve excruciating long-term pain and to improve her walking. She is someone of great faith and lifelong dedication. One respected surgeon had felt it essential to decline to operate as the risk to life was much too great. Then came into the situation a year or two further on another surgeon of reputation and calibre who reconsidered the whole problem. To avoid surgery would leave this lady with perpetual pain and deteriorating movement. He put the crucial question to the patient: "Are you ready to have this life-or-death operation?" It was no rhetorical question. The possibility of death was very real. "I shall have to go and pray about it," she said. "Yes," said the surgeon, "and when you do, pray for the two guys who have got to carry it out!" The long, complicated and extremely tricky operation took place. The patient very nearly died. Giving thanks in our service and in her presence, I found myself talking about a rising from the dead, a resurrection. She truly had new life.

New life is the theme of Easter Day. There are many who believe implicitly in the resurrection of Jesus as scripture records it. There are those who, although they can only interpret the events of the first Easter metaphorically or mythologically, believe in a "true resurrection". All share the wonder of the story about new life in Jesus. At the heart of the Christian faith there is the promise of life instead of death, strength in place of weakness, hope in place of despair, victory in place of defeat.

Easter Day is a day held in honour of the gift of new life. Mary Magdalene knew it in the Garden of the Resurrection when she turned to meet the risen Lord. The disciples knew it when, having contemplated an empty tomb, they received the power of the risen Lord at the first Pentecost. The church knows it as it reflects on the miracles of grace that have brought new life to myriads of people down the years. Each one of us knows it when, in Easter adoration, we say with Thomas: "My Lord and my God."

> The powers of death have done their worst.
> But Christ their legions hath dispersed;
> Let shouts of joy outburst –
> Alleluia!

A Meditation for Easter

A TIME TO DANCE

Easter Day is a day not for argument but for affirmation, not for discussion but for dance. It is the triumphant end of the Lenten pilgrimage with Jesus. It is the beginning of his resurrection life.

Recording the fact that Jesus was "crucified under Pontius Pilate", the Nicene Creed bears witness to the reality of thorns, wood, nails and pain. It is a fact of history that Jesus was "crucified, dead and buried". Then, however, comes the leap from historic fact to personal conviction. The evidence for the resurrection of Jesus is persuasive in its intensity, but it is the evidence of faith, not logic. As such, it does indeed bear the ring of truth. We have, however, moved into what St Paul calls "the knowledge which is beyond knowledge" (Ephesians chapter 3, verse 19, *New English Bible*); to a level which goes beyond rational understanding. It is a level of spiritual awareness in which miracles, that is wonder-full things, become possible.

Pilgrims on the Lenten way will have drawn spiritual strength from their journey with Jesus to Calvary's hill, but some will find the next step, where the Creeds say that "he rose again", difficult for it involves not intellect but intuition, not reason but revelation. Peter's confession of his Lord, Jesus points out, is of that latter nature. For Peter to affirm "Thou art the Son of the living God" could not be a response "flesh and blood", but could only come as a revelation "from my Father which is in heaven". The disciple, Thomas, could not believe in Jesus' resurrection without proof. Given the evidence, he could exclaim: "My Lord and my God!" Significantly, Jesus told him, it involved an act of faith: "Blessed are they who have not seen, yet have believed." It is not the logic of events but inner conviction which compels belief in the resurrection.

Many today have to wrestle hard with the paradox which the Creeds present, namely that Jesus was, as the Nicene Creed puts it, "truly human" but at the same time "true God of true God". The search for new language, new concepts, new metaphors that will help them to hold these two truths together, will go on, for they are fundamental to Christian faith. "The Word became flesh and dwelt among us," so eucharistic devotion will gratefully acknowledge "the Lamb of God who takes away the sin of the world". To them Jesus says: "I am the resurrection and the life." This is the victory.

"Jesus' resurrection makes it impossible for man's story to end in chaos," writes Carlo Carretto (in *The Desert in the City*). "It has to move inexorably towards the light, towards life, towards love." Or, as my friend Sydney Carter puts it enthusiastically in his famous *Lord of the Dance*, "They buried my body and they thought I'd gone, but I am the dance and the dance goes on."

Easter Day is, indeed, not a time for discussion. It is a time to dance.

A Meditation for Easter

ASCENT FROM HELL

"I now know what hell is like." It was a Serbian mother speaking after a night of bombing in Belgrade. The same cry of despair could equally come from the innocents who suffer in the killings of Kosovo where civilians have been used as human shields in front of Serbian tanks: where "killing is a stark reality" in Albania. The language of the conflict in the Balkans seems to reflect a descent into hell – "unstoppable killings", "reported executions", "refugees in their thousands", "the biggest human disaster in Europe since World War II". It is the burden of human suffering that brings the stark realities of war and of the cross together. The suffering servant was a man of sorrows, acquainted with grief. In being "God with us" he will surely weep over the pain of the world until the ascent from hell can come.

The descent into hell, remembered between Good Friday and Easter Day, is very important. The two specific references to it in the New Testament give no clear guidance to its meaning, but intuition recognises its glorious significance. It points to the completeness of Christ's saving act. There is no depth beyond the reach of the divine love. No one can, in the words of John Greenleaf Whittier, "drift beyond God's love and care". Whether we feel, like St Paul, "chief of sinners"; or we shed inner tears over the failure of our life and service, the knowledge that Christ in his love has penetrated the very depths of human misery and pain is somehow made clear in that descent. From the very gates of hell, there is a road through him that leads towards heaven.

George MacLeod, in typically powerful words, makes clear the context in which the good news should be proclaimed. "The cross should be raised at the centre of the market-place," he said, "Jesus was not crucified in a cathedral between two candles, but on a cross between two thieves, on the town's garbage heap; at a crossroad so cosmopolitan they had to write his title in Hebrew, Latin and Greek at the kind of place where the cynics talk smut and thieves curse and soldiers gamble … That is where he dies. That is what he died for."

The gospel will be proclaimed in peaceful pulpits and comfortable churches this holy season. And rightly so. But the message of Holy Week cannot be confined to officially spiritual places. It belongs to the market place, the high street, the workshop, the battlefield. For it is at the point where the stark realities of the world meet with the awful reality of Calvary's tree, that the gospel of grace, love and reconciliation is most present.

Jesus' descent into hell is followed by resurrection day. Death is swallowed up in victory. The Easter prayer must be that the Balkan darkness will somehow be followed by an ascent from hell to lasting peace.

OUT OF THE ASHES

The moving and exciting final item in Walt Disney's Fantasia 2000 is Stravinsky's ballet music, *The Firebird*. Presented as it was on "the largest screen in Europe"* (some 60' high), the impact of the images accompanying the music is dramatic indeed. In this myth, the theme is "life, death and renewal". That is a sequence familiar in other areas of life. We see it annually in nature's seasons. We have it specifically in the great Christian themes of life, crucifixion and resurrection. It is a stimulating, encouraging theme because the end of it in each instance is triumph.

The symbol of fire is hugely present in the Bible. Fire can, as it did in *The Firebird*, bring devastating destruction, but it is also a symbol of God's presence in the story of Moses and the burning bush, a symbol of God's providential companionship on the journey through the desert when the children of Israel were guided by a "pillar of fire" and a symbol of the cleansing, renewing Spirit of God at the first Pentecost. Charles Wesley sings out the place of fire in the renewal of life when he writes: "O thou who camest from above, the pure celestial fire to impart, kindle a flame of sacred love on the mean altar of my heart. There let it for thy glory burn with inextinguishable blaze …"

If renewing fire is seen to have a part in reviving and re-directing the mission of the church, its destructive aspect should be recognised and respected. Radical renewal and reformation demand the letting go and leaving behind of cherished but irrelevant attitudes, familiar but faulty ways, and established but out of date habits. But that process must never be allowed to go too far, and all the glorious benefits of the past be lost for ever. The Benedictine nun, Joan Chittester, while pleading for disciples to "turn into fire" also helpfully defines the role of the fire in the ashes in her illuminating book.** She does this with the help of the term *grieshog*. Gaelic speakers tell us *grieshog* is "the process of burying warm coals in ashes at night in order to preserve the fire for the cold morning to come. Instead of cleaning out the cold hearth, people preserved yesterday's glowing coals under beds of ash in order to have a fast starting fire the next day … The old fire did not die; it kept its heat in order to be prepared to light the new one."

It is the great combination of a proper assessment of past values, and an adventurous risk-taking in the future, that brings fire from under the ashes. Language, concepts, images tied to the past may have to be consumed, but the fundamental convictions founded on the One who is the same yesterday and forever, buried in the ashes will, when fanned into flame by the Spirit, bring the "celestial fire" so essential for a needy world.

* IMAX Cinema, Waterloo.
** *The Fire in These Ashes*, published by Gracewing, 1997.

COPING WITH ANXIETY

One of the privileges of pastoral ministry is close contact with the "aged saints", those who, far advanced in years, are physically so weak, yet spiritually so strong. In their "closer walk with God", they have gained deep insights into human need and divine grace. But one thing concerns many of them. Their helplessness means they can *do* nothing to ease the world's pain. But they can and do pray fervently. I always suggest that they should bless the world by praying for "the healing of the atmosphere".

"Doom and gloom" is a phrase constantly used today as economic, social and international problems escalate; as the financial constraints bring worry to individuals and businesses; as many struggle to keep homes and families together. An infectious despair pervades large areas of society. With so much that is negative seeping into the atmosphere, we are becoming an increasingly unhealthy people, with widespread stress, nervous illnesses, debilitating depression, individual and corporate anxiety abounding.

The great Methodist preacher, Leslie Weatherhead, coined a phrase for his time and many years ago made it the title of one of his numerous books. What he offered, through uniting the insights of psychology with the truths of religion, was a "prescription for anxiety".* That it was a relevant prescription for many human needs was demonstrated by the numbers who came to hear him preach; at the same time he offered them a psychotherapeutic, analytic approach to healing. It is even more relevant today.

The pain of facing the inner, unconscious world from which so many of our "problems" come is, although invaluable for some, difficult for many. It is, however, possible to offer, even if it is in a much simpler, more limited way, a charter of encouragement to creative attitudes. It comes from Paul's first letter to the Thessalonian community, and offers five positive principles:

> Rejoice evermore: the Christian theme is resurrection and therefore victory. A theology of joy is an antidote to doom and gloom.
> Pray without ceasing: this is not an instruction to pray without stopping. It is a reminder that prayer is a way of life, that which maintains and develops relationship with Christ. The fruits of such a relationship can only be creative.
> In everything, give thanks: a grateful heart is life-enhancing.
> See that none renders evil for evil: revenge is negative and destructive. Reconciliation is positive and creative.
> Quench not the Spirit: how sad it is that so often, even within the religious community, spontaneity is discouraged, enthusiasm dampened, initiative discounted, change consistently opposed. How much more is enthusiasm a mark of the Spirit's presence, for "enthusiasm" is a word with God (theos) at its heart.

Joy, prayer, gratitude, reconciliation and enthusiasm – these attitudes by themselves cannot deal with severe anxiety, but they may offer some kind of simple prescription for a more creative life.

* *Prescription for Anxiety* (Arthur James). A Meditation on that theme follows tomorrow.

PRESCRIPTION FOR ANXIETY

Levels of anxiety, both personal and public, have reached new heights in our currently uncertain world. For those with a personal faith, the natural place to which to turn for a prescription for anxiety is the Bible. Those who do, may well find three important elements there that would provide support.

Take first the practical advice given by Jesus in the Sermon on the Mount, counsel reflected in the words of Thomas Carlyle who wisely said: "Our main business is not to see what dimly lies ahead, but what lies at hand." This seems exactly what Jesus had in mind. "Tomorrow will worry about itself. Each day has enough trouble of its own," he said. If we begin to look far ahead, it is all too easy for the imagination to create a sense of apprehension and foreboding, as pressures and problems, ill-defined and unidentified, come together to create inner turmoil. The advice is simple but valuable. Live a day at a time.

The second element in the biblical prescription for anxiety comes from Jesus' instruction to disbelieving disciples to "launch out into the deep". They were professional fishermen who had already "toiled all night and taken nothing", so the advice seemed futile; but they were, so far as Jesus was concerned, men of obedience. They launched out and made an enormous catch. Action can be an antidote to anxiety. Deep involvement in a project can greatly help to take attention from persistent personal anxiety and bring relief from pent-up tension and concentration on symptoms that is of real benefit.

Behind this piece of advice lurks an important equation expressed by the apostle John. "Perfect love casts out fear," he wrote. Fear is centred on self while love is expended on others. The more outgoing love dominates us, the less room there is for fear. While anxiety cannot of course be dealt with by an act of will or simply engaging in physical action – the source of the condition lies much deeper than that – this practical element of losing oneself in serving others or initiating an adventurous project can help to allay that personal concern with self that so easily develops into real anxiety.

The third element in this prescription comes from St Paul's response to adverse circumstances: "I have learned," he wrote, "in whatever state I am therewith to be content." This, the *Authorised Version* rendering, seems however to suggest resigned acceptance and we need more than that. Turn therefore to the *New English Bible*'s translation and feel the positive effect of what Paul says there: "I have learned to find resources in myself whatever my circumstances." The inner resources we have in ourselves are often more than we realise and, when they are supported by the resources which come from outside ourselves through our faith, we have indeed something that can profoundly allay our anxiety.

These three elements together provide a powerful prescription for anxiety in times of stress.

OUT OF THE DUMP

It is not surprising that the Jesus who came "down to earth" (this is what the Creeds call the Incarnation) was strikingly practical in spiritual matters. That was certainly true of his dealings with his disciples in his life, but the same "down to earthness" is shown in what he said to them after his resurrection. To bemused followers, asking if the time was at hand "to restore the kingdom to Israel", he dismissed the disciples' irrelevant question with a reminder that it was not for them "to know the times and dates" which are God's business, but rather to point them to immediate, practical priorities, to get on with the work of the Kingdom through preaching the gospel bequeathed to them.

Still bemused by Jesus' ascension, the disciples stood, "gazing up into heaven". The theme of practicality was then taken up by "two men in white" suddenly standing by them. Their rebuke is peremptory as they make it clear that this is no time for impractical puzzlement and wonder. "Why do you stand gazing up into heaven?" they ask. Jesus will return, in due time. But meantime action is needed. As Margaret Silf has put it: "If we look for signs in the heavens, we may easily overlook God's footprints in the High Street."* It is time for the disciples to be down to earth and get on with the Lord's business.

The practice of the presence of God, the development of the devotional life and the creation of true spirituality depend on such means of inner growth as meditation, contemplation and, for those so favoured with the gift, mystic exhilaration. We must touch and handle things unseen. But spirituality is not mere evanescent spiritual excitement. It is the down to earth love that will not let people go, that lifts human beings "out of the dump".

That last phrase is the title of a book of remarkable photographs taken in Guatemala City. Its cover picture is of three lovely, lively little girls, smiling and serene. They have been rescued out of the dump in that city where some 1,500 people 'live', most of them children who struggle to collect cardboard, plastic, glass – indeed anything that can be recycled. They scavenge for bits of food to eat and items to re-sell.

A professional American photographer, Nancy McGirr, photographing the dump and its inhabitants, became aware of the children's interest in cameras and decided to create a project whereby she takes small groups of children and teaches them a marketable skill that will help lift the next generation "out of the dump". The book and the cheerful cover children are the result.

There is a part of our spirituality which relates to heavenly things, but it only becomes mature when it is expressed in the high street, the dumps, the places where human need is greatest. It is part of true spirituality to be able to descend into hell, in Jesus' name.

* *Taste and See: adventuring into prayer* (Darton, Longman & Todd).

HEART OF HEALING

The Bible is an astonishing book. It throws up glorious statements the full impact of which has previously passed us by. This is, surely, testimony to its abiding inspiration.

Here is an example, possibly long familiar to some, but never so far noticed (that is, taken note of as distinct from physically seen) by others, including me. It is a wonderful verse in the fiftieth Psalm, and it shouts aloud God's love for creation. *"For every creature of the field is mine and the cattle on the hills. I know every bird on the mountains and the creatures of the field are mine."* God so loved the world!

Relationship is at the heart of religion – in four directions. There is relationship "upward" with God. There is relationship "outward" with our neighbour, with the world. There is relationship "inwards" with ourselves, and all of these three are part of that eternal triangle of love encapsulated in the great commandments above love to God, to neighbour and to ourselves. But the fourth direction in relationship is "downwards" to the earth.

It was that fourth direction which became the focus of my attention when I was asked to speak on "healing and farming". It compelled thought on the part of one, 99 per cent of whose ministry has been in the city, about this vital part of our relationships, that with the created world.

When Genesis tells us in that wonderfully profound story of the creation that at each step "God saw that it was good", you feel, humanly speaking, a divine sense of pride in each stage of the process. The Psalms exult in the joys of creation, in the heavens which declare the divine glory, in the firmament which is God's "handiwork". The prophets reflect this exhilaration too; Isaiah, talking about the greatness of God whose thoughts and ways are so different from ours, speaks in lyrical terms of singing mountains and trees which clap their hands in joy in the great restoration of relationship with God that follows repentance. And nature will reflect that happy state. "Instead of the thorn shall come up the fir-tree and instead of the briar shall come up the myrtle tree." In Genesis the results of Adam and Eve's sin of arrogance are "thorns and thistles" that symbolise the corruption of the earth, but it is of the redemption of that same earth that Isaiah speaks. There in the natural world of creation is the presence of the healing work of God.

The essence of the faith is restoration to a right relationship with God, whatever we within our own backgrounds call it – salvation, redemption, eternal life, entering the kingdom, finding meaning. This is the heart of healing. How right it is then to think of the healing of the earth and our relationship to it as rounding off that complex of relationships which are expressed in words like health, shalom, integration, wholeness. The earth is indeed the Lord's and everything in it.

DOGMATISM AND DRIFT

There are two approaches to religion that are not only unhelpful but positively unhealthy. One is that of dogmatism, the other that of drift. Both are represented by characters in David Hare's play, *Racing Demon*. Tony is the dogmatic, judgemental curate who undermines his vicar's standing. Lionel, the vicar, is very conscious of pastoral needs, but seems – at least to his curate – to present a laid-back attitude to ministry that suggests a drift away from the true faith. What he offers is a too liberal gospel that lacks both evangelical content and theological conviction. His favourite phrase is "as it were". Neither of these attitudes helps to make religion real (to use a phrase much loved by that gracious theologian, Nels Ferré).

Dogmatism differs from conviction and faith in its belief that the only right view on any matter is one's own view. There is therefore within such an attitude a self-righteousness in conflict with "walking humbly with God". In corporate terms, it is represented in society today by an unacceptable exclusive militant fundamentalism inconsistent with "real religion".

The drifter, on the other hand, has no clear goal. He or she responds to every new fashion in thinking, to every wind of intellectual change. The result is a lack of direction and focus. Lionel as I have already noted, was accused by his curate of adding the words "as it were" to every doctrine he discussed.

The unhealthy aspect in these polarised positions is the inflexibility of the dogmatic believer and the susceptibility to changing fashions of the drifter. Indeed both are susceptible to breakdown because of their attitudes. Under pressure, over-dogmatic people have been known to break down (one distinguished academic completely disintegrated when his theological mentor wholly revised his view on a particular aspect of doctrine). The drifter, confronted by life's turbulence, can become uncertain, unanchored and afraid.

Real life needs a combination of conviction with appropriate flexibility. That is not a new position, for it is firmly incorporated into the standards of the reformed faith with reference to the Westminster Confession of Faith. The firm basis is the Word of God which is the "supreme standard of faith and life" while the appropriate flexibility is the permission to have "freedom of opinion on such points of doctrine as do not enter into the substance of the faith". That is a valuable combination of strong conviction and necessary flexibility.

Being open to the Holy Spirit implies a readiness to receive new insights, learn from experience, benefit from contemporary insights, sift and weigh fresh aspects of truth. A mature and enthusiastic faith, one that is needed to cope with the pressures of twenty-first century living, requires a mind constantly enlightened by the Holy Spirit within a committed discipleship. Healthy, that is real, religion is founded on conviction supported by a Spirit-led ability to learn and to grow.

SEEDS OF GROWTH

The journey to the far country was undertaken by the free if wilful choice of the so-called prodigal son. The parable about him is a huge encouragement to all who, like him, take their lives into their own hands but end in disaster. If, as Jesus intended, the father in the parable is giving us a picture of God, we are being told of unconditional forgiveness, always available to those who "come to their senses" and return seeking a relationship restored. So overwhelming is the father's welcoming embrace and so enthusiastic his call for celebration, that the young man's prepared speech of sorrow and repentance is smothered by loving words and actions. Such an experience of unconditional, forgiving love is one of religion's greatest gifts. It compels acceptance of the credal statement in all its intensity and fullness: "I believe in the forgiveness of sins."

Unconditional love must be unconditionally received. To feel any continuing sense of guilt in the inner depths of our being is a denial of the forgiveness that has been received. If such inappropriate guilt* festers at the unconscious level of our personality it will perpetuate personal misery. In doing so we actively deny the reality of the unconditional pardon we have received. The grace we have received should rather be so integrated into our future outlook that the redemptive aspect of the divine forgiveness can begin to work. "Your failure," wrote Harry Williams, "will bring you raw material capable of being woven into a richer, more rewarding life."** How profoundly he knew that from his own experience. How strongly we should recognise it too. There lie the seeds of growth.

Experience of failure, despair, even desperation, if frankly faced, honestly assessed and recognised as wholly forgiven, can be profoundly creative. This is the wonder of the "personal redemption" expressed in unconditional love. It does not mean that evil, or any acts of unholiness in our past cease to exist. They are part of our history. It does mean that their power to hurt and harm us has gone away; they can now contribute to our growth. We may even find that we want to give thanks for our experience, for through it so much has been learned. Our failure has become a victory.

The mature Christian is a wounded Christian, but it is through wounds healed that faith comes. Saul of Tarsus went to a far country indeed and reached unholy depths in his murderous intentions towards the disciples. He too, by grace, "came to his senses" and found the relationship which made him St Paul, "a man in Christ".

Spiritual growth is a journey that weaves its way through darkness, pain and even despair, but all of these, embraced by the love of God, can be transformed into means of grace, wounds that heal. What a glorious experience it is to be led through the darkness into God's marvellous light. That surely is the Spirit at work.

* Guilt, appropriate and inappropriate, is referred to in several Meditations; see especially May 7.
** In a sermon published in *Sermons from Great St Mary's, Cambridge*, selected by Hugh Montefiore; Fontana 1968.

A Time to Weep

There is a time to weep. That time is now. Seldom in our lifetimes can there have been, within two weeks, events that have invaded the human heart with such intensity that tears cannot but flow . . . tears of sorrow, sympathy, concern, compassion, but tears of anger too.

St Matthew, recording King Herod's act of inhumanity in the slaughter of the innocents quotes from the prophet Jeremiah: "A voice was heard in Ramah, weeping and great lamentation, Rachel weeping for her children, and refusing to be comforted, for they were no more." How plaintively the grief of one mother is conveyed in these words. How representative it is of anyone who has lost a child, in whatever way. There is nothing so awful as the suffering of a child.

It is a time to weep for the children of Belfast, the frightened, tearful face of one particular little girl imprinted on our memories for ever from so many pictures of her. Those children will never forget their first days at school, as abused, spat on, they are introduced in their earliest years to violence and hatred, having become (as Ron Ferguson of Kirkwall Cathedral has described it) "suffering pawns in adult games". That any community could inflict such damage on children must bring tears not only of sorrow, but of anger too, to any normal human being. Moreover, when individuals, groups or nations, whoever they are, hurt, in war or terrorism, any country's children; when children in any land are taught to hate and gloat in suffering, tears cannot but flow.

Jesus wept over Jerusalem and will weep again for that war-torn city, but it is, at this moment, time to weep over New York and Washington and every city attacked by terrorists, fanatical in their misguided beliefs, without any feeling for perhaps thousands, killed, injured, bereaved; innocents in jet planes flown unwillingly and in terror to their doom; innocents in offices and on the ground; members of emergency services doing their dangerous work. History is littered with acts of appalling evil, but the enormity of this week's events seems to stand out in an all too violent world. It is a crying shame.

For politicians and governments huge problems lie ahead. In the church this is not a time to offer bland theological theories explaining the nature of suffering. One of the believed weaknesses of the church is its perceived inability to offer explanations of why such awful things happen to human beings. But people of every faith must pool their tears and bring the impact of the faith they hold to bear on removing evil from the world. Perhaps the Christian faith has made its contribution by pointing to the fallen nature of man and the need for the transforming power which it finds in Jesus Christ. It must continue to offer that insight to a world that, this week, sorely weeps.

This Meditation was written in the wake of "September 11" 2001.

CLEAR VISION

When Jesus found, in the words of the prophet Isaiah, a statement that summed up the purpose of his ministry, he read them publicly to the synagogue congregation in Nazareth with profound conviction. In that statement he committed himself not only to the proclamation of the Good News and the pastoral care of people, but to the healing ministry, pledging himself to give the blind their sight. It was no empty promise as both Bartimaeus and "a man born blind" could gladly testify.

Physical blindness touched the heart of Jesus, but spiritual blindness upset him even more. "You are blind guides," he told the Pharisees in a blistering denunciation of their hypocrisy. "You roam sea and land to make one convert," he raged, "and when he has become a convert, you make him as hell-begotten as yourselves. Tragic will be the fate of you experts in the Law and you Pharisees with your façade of ostentatious piety."*

The American philosopher, George Santanya, said that "a fanatic is one who redoubles his efforts when he has forgotten his aim." Fanaticism is a form of blindness and, because it is often related to religion, can be spiritual blindness. The irrational element in fanaticism destroys clear vision. Santanya's definition does not accurately describe those who perpetrated destruction and death in the horrific events in America; the suicide pilots were all too clear about what they were doing. But it does strike a chord in the Irish situation where so-called adherents of religion, Protestant and Catholic, continue to bring pain and death to human beings and damage, perhaps irretrievably, the physical and emotional health of children.

If ever there was a time for clear vision on the part of leaders, politicians and indeed all of us, it is now. The inevitable (in human terms) response to the suffering which fanatics have brought on so many people is a demand for vengeance and retribution. When a "red mist" takes over, however, clarity of vision departs, perspective is disturbed, rationality endangered. Leadership in a world so battered as this, needs clear vision, profound wisdom, disciplined determination and strength of will.

It is of the essence of the faith to believe that in every human situation God is present. George Fox, the Quaker, spoke of seeing "an ocean of darkness and death but (at the same time) an infinite ocean of light and love that flowed over the ocean of darkness." "And in that also I saw the infinite love of God," he says. In a time in which one American commentator speaks of a sense of divine abandonment, light and love combined with clarity of vision and profound wisdom are needed to take us forward.

* William Barclay's Translation of the New Testament
This Meditation was written in September 2001.

In Weakness, Strength

Re-reading a familiar story sometimes points up a detail that has not been noticed previously. Nowhere indeed is this more true than when we are going through the Bible. A quite new insight leaps up from the familiar text, often with creative results. It may be that something stands out for the first time and the question arises whether the writer has made just a passing comment or was drawing attention to something very significant. It is more than likely that a reference has been included because it is important.

Just that applies to a re-reading of two verses. One is from St Mark and the other St Luke. They relate to two quite different events. They deserve reflection:

> As they approached Jerusalem, Mark reports, Jesus sent two of his disciples, saying to them: "Go to the village ahead of you, and just as you enter it, you will find a colt tied there, one which no one has ever ridden."

> Luke writes: (Joseph of Arimathea) going to Pilate, asked for Jesus' body. Then he took it down, wrapped it in linen cloth and placed it in a tomb cut in the rock, one in which no one had yet been laid.

Just what had the Gospel writers in mind when each felt it necessary to make the point that the colt and the tomb were used *for the first time*? Is it that whatever is required for a holy purpose must be, as it were, unblemished?

The need for unblemished offerings was certainly stressed in the sacrificial rituals in the Old Testament. In Exodus, Leviticus and Numbers there are many instructions about the offering of lambs, goats and bullocks *without blemish*. There is in both Numbers and Deuteronomy a reference to sacrificing a heifer that has "never been worked and has never worn a yoke". It is a valuable theme: only the best is good enough for God.

That, by itself, could however cause concern to many people. If the qualification for ministry, discipleship or ordination is to be unblemished, how can human beings be called to service? If the prophet has to be someone who practises totally what he or she preaches, from whence can come the preachers? It must therefore be with gratitude and relief that a second principle, much emphasised in the New Testament, comes into play. It is one summed up in the wonderful concept of the wounded healer who has known what it is to be broken and beaten. Those who carry wounds make understanding healers. It is not a bar to discipleship, service or ministry to have descended into hell. It is grace received in the ascent from hell that becomes the very energy of ministry and discipleship.

It is those who have travelled through the awfulness of life who best can testify to amazing grace. Paul said, thankfully, that it was when he was weak that he was really strong.

UNCOMFORTABLE WORDS

Every sermon should end with words of comfort to ensure that the gospel is presented as it should be, positive, encouraging and reassuring. "Speak comfortably to Jerusalem" proclaimed the prophet Isaiah or, as several translators render it, "Speak tenderly". Every preacher should remember the need for "comfortable words".

While a proper emphasis on the tenderness of God is to be greatly valued, it is also the prophet's role to be, as Elijah was described by King Ahab, a "troubler". That function is indeed to bring discomfort by representing God's demand both in terms of personal obedience and corporate responsibility. It was therefore necessary that a prophet like Isaiah should condemn devotional superficiality ("to what purpose is the multitude of your sacrifices?"), bribery ("everyone loves gifts and follows after rewards"), rachmanism ("woe to them that join house to house and field to field until there is no place"), alcoholism ("woe to those who follow strong drink and that continue until night till wine inflame them") and the spiritual blindness that "calls evil good and good evil". These are uncomfortable words, intended to confront and challenge. They deliberately disturb the peace.

In the New Testament, the coming of Jesus is stated to be an uncomfortable fact. What is presented as his purpose is, in effect, a consequence of his coming. He will divide households and strain family loyalties. "He that loves father or mother more than me is not worthy of me. He that loves son or daughter more than me is not worthy of me. I am come to turn a man against his father, a daughter against her mother ... a man's enemies shall be the members of his own household." Uncomfortable words indeed.

"Preaching should break a hard heart and heal a broken heart." In that sentence, John Newton, prolific hymn-writer at the turn of the nineteenth century, encapsulates the responsibilities of the preacher. They are to challenge and to comfort. The latter may be the ultimate priority as the great Scottish preacher of yesteryear, George Johnstone Jeffrey, made clear in the words with which this meditation begins. The more onerous task is, however, that of confronting individuals and society with their neglect or rejection of the will of God. The counsel given is not a personal judgement for prophets and preachers must be aware of Jesus' stricture: "Do not judge or you too will be judged." In the prophet's role and under the direction of the Holy Spirit alone is it legitimate to bring uncomfortable words.

It is in the pursuit of proper change that the preacher becomes the troubler, the disturber. Often sung at ordination services, James Montgomery's hymn states the task:

> To warn the sinner, cheer the saint,
> Nourish thy lambs and feed thy sheep.

But he rightly puts the preacher's responsibility within the power of the Spirit, "poured out from on high" to provide graces and gifts, wisdom, zeal, faith and firmness. The prophet, then or now, has no easy task.

LISTEN TO THE WIND

Conversations with Jesus could be confusing as the woman from Samaria found when she met him at the well at Sychar. Offered "living water", she completely missed the point. All she could think of was the practical problem of drawing water without a bucket.

Nicodemus, the Pharisee who came secretly to Jesus by night, had the same problem. Though a "master of Israel", a theologian and teacher, he was a man who needed a rational explanation. To the challenge that "you must be born again" all he could think of was how you "entered a second time into your mother's womb". Jesus did not argue the point but simply looked for an illustration that might help Nicodemus to "connect". The evening breeze was rustling through the trees. "Listen to the wind, Nicodemus," said Jesus, "listen to the wind."

Jesus made it easier for one steeped in Jewish tradition by pointing to the Hebrew word, *ruach*. It meant, as Nicodemus knew, both wind and spirit. It was a word full of significance – the breath of life, the elemental wind that sweeps the earth, and the Spirit of God. The Spirit, Jesus told Nicodemus, was like the wind, invisible yet unmistakable, imperceptible yet powerful, untouchable but real. It was an exciting image.

Though unseen, the Spirit is always at work in the world. The Bible begins with the image of the Spirit "hovering over the waters", bringing order out of chaos. It ends as "the Spirit and the bride say 'Come!' " Everything in between is the record of the Spirit of God, active in the world. The Spirit may come like a gentle breeze in comfort and encouragement; come to confront and to challenge; come with extraordinary power as happened at the first Pentecost, to hesitant, perplexed disciples. "Listen to the wind, Nicodemus."

The source of that Spirit? It is in a true sense a mystery. We do not know where the Spirit comes from, Jesus tells Nicodemus, and what is more we do not know where the Spirit, like the wind, is going. But we know its reality. We can hear the wind, feel it, be blown over by it. The evidence of the Spirit is in changed lives, miracles of grace, situations revitalised. Flattened trees testify to the power of the wind. Transformed people testify to the power of the Spirit.

"Quench not the Spirit!" Paul said to the Thessalonians, or as William Barclay translates it, "You must not try to put a stop to the activity of the Spirit." "The Spirit blows where it pleases," Jesus told Nicodemus. There is here a solemn warning to us all. "No act of Convocation or Assembly can circumscribe the Spirit," declared the great Scottish preacher, James S Stewart. "No rooted personal prejudice (dare) patronise it." It is in this invisible, untouchable, unclassifiable divine energy that the possibility of change in the world and its people lies. No wonder the fervent cry of the ages is "Come, Holy Spirit, come!"

SPIRITUAL SUPERFICIALITY

What a welcome Jesus had when he rode into Jerusalem on a borrowed ass! Palm branches waving, garments laid in his path along the way, it was indeed a triumphal journey for the One who "came in the name of the Lord". And yet so soon in that same city he would be despised and rejected. Beads of sweat like drops of blood would moisten Gethsemane's garden. The struggle along the *Via Dolorosa* under a heavy cross would drain his strength. The crown of thorns would pierce his brow. The cruel nails of Calvary would be driven through his hands and feet. The acclamation he received was superficial and ultimately empty. The awful reality was, rather, summed up in the words of the Creed: "He was crucified, dead and buried." No wonder darkness, both real and symbolic, enfolded the land.

Spiritual superficiality is referred to in both the Old and New Testaments. The prophet Isaiah spoke of those who were "ever hearing but never understanding, ever seeing but never perceiving". Jesus himself recalled these very words because "though he had done so many miracles in their presence, they still would not believe." It was a phenomenon of which the prophet Ezekiel took notice in his devastating comment:* "My people come to you as they usually do and sit before you to listen to your words, but they do not put them into practice. With their lips they express devotion, but their hearts are greedy for unjust gain. Indeed to them you are nothing more than one who sings love songs with a beautiful voice and plays an instrument well. For they hear your words and do not put them into practice." How perverse people are! How shallow we can be! How poor the perception of the people of Jerusalem. There was no depth, no real understanding, no insight, no spiritual sensitivity in that city in what has come to be called Holy Week. "Which of the two, Barabbas or Jesus, do you want me to release to you?" Pilate asks. "Barabbas," they answer. "What shall I then do with Jesus who is called Christ?" In unison they cry: "Crucify him! Crucify him!" It is a shameful story, but it is our shame too. So often we crucify the Son of God afresh and put him to an open shame.

Spiritual superficiality is a failure in the process of growing into Christ, that sanctification of the whole being which constitutes true discipleship. Grace has not touched the deeper levels of inner being. Put in psychological terms, it means allegiance is only at the conscious level but has not reached and transformed the deeper unconscious level. It is however that inner conversion that conditions behaviour, shapes attitudes, determines the level of commitment.

Reflection will be worthwhile indeed if it lays bare the ease with which we fail to open our whole being to the renewing, regenerating power of the Spirit. As the Didache counsels, "Let grace come."**

* Also referred to in the Meditation for May 9.
** A second-century book of Christian teaching.

POWERFUL SYMBOLS

The impact of a symbol is wonderfully illustrated in a story told by Archbishop Desmond Tutu. He was walking with his mother down a street in the poverty and squalor of the black township in which he was brought up when a white man, dressed in a long white cassock and wearing a black hat, approached them. As he passed by, the stranger raised his hat to Tutu's mother. The fact that a white man in South Africa at that time should so acknowledge a black woman made a profound and indeed life-changing impression on young Desmond. It was a symbolic action which shaped his attitude to relationships between black and white people for ever. That man was the late Trevor Huddleston.* There is power in a symbol.

The unfolding story of Jesus' last journey to Jerusalem is a time to reflect on the symbols and symbolic actions forever associated with his self-offering for humanity. The bread and wine, the washing of the disciples' feet, the crucifix, the empty cross . . . to bring these dramatic symbols to mind is to open the door to reverent appreciation of "the mighty acts" of salvation. Passiontide is not a time for intellectual analysis of such acts of redemption nor for academic theories about the atonement. It is a time for worship, prayer and devotion. However we try to explain the atonement, the common factor, whatever our personal understanding of it, is a profound sense that, whatever happened in the death, burial and resurrection of Christ, it was an act of love bringing us back into a proper relationship with God that we could never do for ourselves. "We may not know, we cannot tell what pains he had to bear, but we believe it was for us He hung and suffered there." How wonderfully the symbols serve us by, in a flash, recalling the essence and extent of his sacrifice and so move us to greater faith, livelier hope and deeper love.

It was the late and great Dr Archie Craig, as Ron Ferguson reminds us in *Love your crooked neighbour*,** who, reflecting on the frailty of our spiritual condition, once said: "The paradox of the pulpit is that its occupant is a sinner whose chief right to be there is the perpetual sense that he/she has no right to be there." Every honest preacher, ordained or lay, will empathise with that confession. But it is not an awareness only applicable to those who are called to preach. It is the humble acknowledgement every sincere and sensitive soul will feel compelled to make before the cross.

"Too soon we rise: the symbols disappear" wrote Horatius Bonar. "The feast though not the love is past and gone." Symbols and symbolic actions serve a purpose, but it is the purpose, not the symbols which ultimately matter. If they have helped to bring us to the heart of Easter, they have served us well, by enabling us to touch and handle things unseen.

* Related by Professor Robert Davidson in *Go by the Book*, thoughts on biblical themes (Saint Andrew Press, 1996).
** Saint Andrew Press, Edinburgh, 1999.

Good Centurions

How fascinating it is to realise that so many of the Roman centurions mentioned in the New Testament are presented in such a favourable light! Although they were soldiers in the army of an occupying foreign power, they are referred to with respect; each one shows an unexpected measure of sympathy with Jesus, or with his servant, Paul. There was Cornelius, the centurion, who was used to help Peter to understand the inclusiveness of the gospel. There was the centurion who prevented soldiers taking Paul's life when he was shipwrecked on Malta. Another centurion cared for Paul when he was on trial before the Governor, Felix. Yet another, having learned of a Jewish plot to murder Paul, did what he could to foil the attempt. And there was the centurion who, suddenly discovering that Paul was a Roman citizen, saved him from the mob. Good centurions indeed!

A particular reference at the time of Jesus' crucifixion demonstrates a sympathy and sensitivity so lacking in those responsible for his death. "Surely," cried the centurion on guard-duty near the cross, "this was a righteous man." It was a tribute, not from the religious community, but from the world outside it.

That pattern was much repeated in the life of Jesus. The penitent thief sensed the innocence and goodness of his companion on Calvary. "This man has done nothing wrong," he declared boldly. It was a tribute the ecclesiastical establishment had refused to pay. "Do not have any thing to do with this innocent man," pleaded Pontius Pilate's wife as her husband sought to wash his hands of the Christ. It was a warning from the secular world to which the religious community was blind. Jesus was a good man, constantly harassed, consistently accused, and finally condemned to death by orthodox religion, yet seen as a friend by "publicans and sinners," as a prophet by a woman from Samaria, as a healer by a woman from Syrian Phoenicia. Those without formal training in spiritual disciplines somehow sensed the wonder of Jesus. Pharisees could descend as far as to accuse him of working miracles through the power of Beelzebub. What perversity is this!

This is for all involved in formal religion a cautionary tale. His rejection should not have happened then, but it did. It ought not to happen now, but it could. If Christ is to be proclaimed to the world, the body created to do that must engage, not least in Lent, in a searching examination of its own faith, priorities and purpose. Those concerned formally or professionally with religion can be diverted from the heart of the faith by obsession with theological niceties, liturgical details, over-concern with organisation and structure, maintenance rather than ministry, and in so doing hurt the world by taking away the Lord and forgetting where they have laid him. "If the light that is in you is darkness," Jesus said ominously, "how great is that darkness." It could after all "crucify the Son of God afresh and put him to public shame".

WHERE VIOLENCE BEGINS

Violence is not a new phenomenon. It is in fact endemic in the life of the world where human beings are free to choose evil, but the evolution of a so-called civilised society has failed to eliminate or even reduce the levels of violence. Indeed, stimulated by "entertainment", violence has become the most serious stain on our common life. The inevitable consequence of our current wallowing in the deep, dark recesses that condition human behaviour is a greater insensitivity to goodness and beauty and particularly to suffering and death. The loss of one life, especially that of a child, through violence is not just a headline, a statistic or an everyday event. It is an offence against God. The appalling abuse that children trying to get to school in Belfast suffered is certainly that too.

All responsible members of society would say they were against violence, but in our proper condemnation of violence, it is essential that we are aware how near the surface violent feelings can be in all of us. People of gentle and stable natures can, in certain traffic situations, demonstrate incipient or very active forms of road rage. There are those – are we among them? – who would be deeply offended if they were accused of racial prejudice or intolerance but whose reactions change perceptibly if those who are putting them – or us – under pressure, physical or otherwise, belong to another culture, nation or race. The confessional and the counselling room are places where domestic violence is revealed or acknowledged in the most unexpected of people. There are writers who would campaign strongly against all forms of violence, but do it in the most violent and aggressive language possible. While physical violence would be claimed to be totally abhorrent to them, verbal violence carries no such stigma.

There are examples of violence, from the crucifixion of Jesus to the death of Damilola Taylor, which seem to stem directly from sheer evil intention. Perhaps only through grace can transformation come. But there are large areas of violence and anger which we may recognise in ourselves, as well as see clearly in others, which demand determined self-awareness, a genuine desire to change unhealthy ways and a decisive act of will to alter patterns of behaviour detrimental to healthy relationships and the welfare of society.* We have a responsibility to make greater efforts to understand the sociological as well as the psychological causes of violence, to change a violent society into a non-violent one.

From where does violence come, asks that practical New Testament letter-writer, James. "From within," he replies. It may seem naïve to offer grace as a possible counter to excessive violence, but none should forget that one, Saul of Tarsus, who, according to the Acts of the Apostles, was "in a frenzy of murderous threats against the disciples of the Lord" and who "thoroughly approved of Stephen's murder" became St Paul, the least of all the apostles but, from then on, "a man in Christ".

* The Everyman Project, 40 Stockwell Road, London SW9 9ES exists for this purpose in relation to male violence.
This Meditation was written in September 2001.

TALES OF THE UNEXPECTED

If ever there was a time when light was needed, it is in the "gross darkness" of today. If only the divine light would illuminate brightly this dark, uncertain, anxious, confused world, a theophany or manifestation of God perhaps, dazzling in its penetration! In reality, all we can look for, seeing things as we do through a glass darkly, is to be blessed by shafts of light that give us glimpses of God at work in continuing creation and enfolding providence.

There is an unexpectedness that characterises much of the divine activity. Faith too is found in unexpected people. A fresh insight comes in wholly unexpected ways. God is "a God of surprises". There is the element also of unexpectedness over the *parousia*, Jesus' final coming ("you know neither the day nor the hour"), so that factor of surprise characterises both the life and teaching of Jesus.

It is present, for example, at the very heart of the mission of Jesus. That the Messiah should enter Jerusalem as its king riding on an ass is indeed a surprise. Classical expectations of the coming Messiah were, as some among the disciples continued to believe even after the resurrection, of the militant kind of Old Testament expectations. Instead the Messiah came in humility as the suffering servant, not a man of war but a prince of peace, not a monarch in splendour but a suffering servant. This is a tale of the unexpected indeed, but it points to the very heart of the gospel and calls disciples not to wealth and glory, but to suffering and self-sacrifice, not to possessions and property but to humility, poverty. What could have been more unexpected than that the "saviour" should be born in a stable, that the one described at his crucifixion as "King of the Jews" should be nailed to a cross and buried in a loaned grave?

The same element of surprise permeates the teaching of Jesus. The qualification "but I say" that characterises the Sermon on the Mount, hinted at the unexpected. The Jews had no dealings with the Samaritans, John records in his Gospel, but Jesus deliberately spoke with not only a Samaritan but a Samaritan woman. Surprisingly (to his listeners), it was a member of that same people that would for ever be known as "the good Samaritan". How taken aback Simon the Pharisee was to be told that he had shown no loving care ("you gave me no water for my feet") while a "notoriously bad woman" (William Barclay's translation) had demonstrated unconditional love by washing his feet with her tears and drying them with her hair. How confounded were those scribes and Pharisees who brought "the woman taken in adultery" for Jesus' judgement; to their surprise it was they who left condemned.

Quiet times are for both spiritual exploration and expectation. Increased spiritual awareness may well bring one of those shafts of light that bring surprise and encouragement.

THE POWER OF LOVE

The congregation was singing the traditional prayer, sometimes attributed to St Francis: *Make me a channel of your peace.* It contains the words: "Master, grant that I may never seek so much to be consoled as to console." To my later horror, I was heard by my neighbour to sing (though I knew it not) "... never seek so much to be controlled as to control." It was a Freudian slip, but a worrying one.

A desire for power lies deeply within the unconscious of many of those who are called to leadership, despite Lord Acton's well-known warning: "All power corrupts and absolute power corrupts absolutely."

The contemporary theologian, Sally McFague, writes in *Models of God:* * "At the heart of all the issues, the nuclear issue and issues of political and social oppression, is the question of power; who wields it? of what sort is it?" It is a personal issue too ... and always has been. The source of the cardinal sin which brought expulsion for our archetypal ancestors, Adam and Eve, from the Garden of Eden was the desire for power. They sought to be "as gods".

The question of power, and how it is incarnated in individuals and corporate groups, lies at the root of many problems; in politics, be it in a democracy or a dictatorship; in economics, especially in the abuse of wealth; in media control and ownership; in the church which has its own "corridors of power"; in professional relationships, therapeutic, psychiatric, medical, analytical; with the mass media-backed evangelist, exorcist or "healer". "The greater the power, the more dangerous the abuse," warns Edmund Burke.

Religion is not wholly helpful in guiding us on issues of power. In the biblical story of creation, man and woman are given "dominion" over birds, beasts, fish and "every creeping thing," but, as recent incidents have again shown, that power can be abused. A great deal of the language of the Old Testament is expressed in images of power and subservience, where concepts like kingship and lordship are used as models of the divine-human relationship. That is one of the reasons why contemporary theologians search for other models and metaphors more meaningful to modern believers. The liturgical language of public prayer employs a term like "almighty Father" which, on reflection, seems self-contradictory. Do "almighty power", and the "divine love" revealed in Jesus, sit comfortably together?

"The love of power," wrote William Hazlitt "is the love of ourselves." It is that which concerns me over that Freudian slip. If we possess, personally or in some corporate context, the privilege of power, it must be expressed in terms of outgoing love to God and neighbour. "All power is given to me in heaven and in earth," said Jesus after his resurrection. Power is only in safe hands when it belongs to "love incarnate, love divine". To have the privilege of power is therefore to need the gift of grace. Only then will it be expressed, not in domination, but in love.

* SCM Press, 1987.

Breaking News

A new phrase has entered our vocabulary. It is "breaking news". This appears across the television screen as some major event is unfolding. Until recently, "The News" has been a reporting of events that have happened. Now, such is the wonder of information technology, we are able to see things as they are happening or hear about things as they take place, events so far incomplete but believed to be of major news importance. Whether this facility is of human benefit or not, time will tell. What it does mean is that sitting in front of a screen makes it possible to travel with troops into battle, be present as tragedy strikes at a school or hospital on the other side of the world, witness the grief of the victims of accident or natural disaster, observe politics by being present at Question Time in the House of Commons.

The phrase "breaking news" itself carries with it a hint of apprehension because it has evolved in the most devastating of modern events, the terrorist attack on New York's World Trade Center and the Pentagon, and on a fourth aeroplane. "Breaking news" brought the unbelievable sight of a plane, passenger-laden, heading straight for the second of the Twin Towers. Such are the images of that day of breaking news that even now the sound of a low-flying plane or the unexpected noise of an explosion touches a nerve of anxiety.

The negative associations of breaking news in the twenty-first century need not however destroy the excitement of breaking news in the New Testament. It came in more natural, possibly even supernatural ways, but the effect in every case was electric. Reflect then, without fear, on the breaking news that marked the Incarnation. It was the angelic throng that broke the news of the birth of Jesus in Bethlehem. Wise men too had sensed there was breaking news in the stars and acted on that intuition. They succeeded in being in Bethlehem just after Jesus was born. Thus was the "Good News" brought to the world.

As it was in the coming of Jesus into the world, so was it when his life ended on Calvary. Soon there would be mysterious but glorious breaking news. Mary Magdalene was the bearer of it as, instructed by Jesus, she went "quickly to tell the disciples that he has risen from the dead". That breaking news sent Peter running, John (being younger) outrunning him, to the empty tomb. At the heart of faith is the good news of Jesus' resurrection.

The magic of the faith goes on. It was Pentecost when Peter, exhilarated by the coming of the Holy Spirit with symbols of wind and fire, publicly proclaimed the breaking news that would energise the church. The Spirit has come!

Breaking news in our time will continue to contain feelings of apprehension. The breaking news of the New Testament brings nothing but joy and praise.

THE SPIRIT COMES

I met Canon Andrew Glazewski just once, and that for only one hour, but I recall the occasion with pleasure. He showed me what it means to say: "The Spirit comes!" He died shortly after we met, so I had no opportunity to meet him again. In a snack bar, over a cup of coffee, Glazewski expounded the article in the church's creed which Pentecost Sunday celebrates: "I believe in the Holy Spirit!"

That doctrine was, for him, rooted in the Old Testament. To show me how, he took a spare sheet of paper from his briefcase, folded it corner to corner and then tore it in half, leaving him with two equal triangles. The first he placed, base at the top, pointing downwards; the other he put below it, pointing upwards. The two triangles met at the apexes, looking rather like an angular egg-timer.

Glazewski pointed to the upper, upside-down triangle. That, he said, symbolises the Holy Spirit (it was indeed "like the form of a dove"). Its ever-widening upward flow suggested the infinity of "grace abounding". The lower triangle, pointing upwards, Glazewski saw as the symbol of human "being". He drew two parallel lines across the triangle, creating three layers. The top area represented the conscious part of personality; the middle layer was that hidden, buried part of us known, in analytical terms, as the (individual) unconscious. We will come to the third layer in a moment.

The unconscious (seeking help from a modern analogy) is a recording of all our experiences since birth (and some would also say preceding birth). What is on that tape shapes our adult actions and reactions, determines our feelings and conditions the way we relate to others. Positively, the unconscious is the source of our creativity. Negatively, unhealed hidden feelings exert pressure on us from within and, breaking through, may be "acted out" to our discomfort, unhappiness and even tragedy. Paul knew what this "shadow" side of his nature meant: "The good that I would, I do not; and the evil that I would not, that I do," he confessed.

The third, deepest layer, wider still, is the collective unconscious, that reservoir of corporate conditioning which, for better or worse, contributes to what we are.

"The Spirit comes!" said Glazewski, as he pushed the top triangle slowly downwards to indicate the Spirit's penetration and permeation of our whole being, conscious and unconscious. That transforming, renewing process is salvation at work.

"Look now at the inter-twined triangles," said Glazewski. I did. There was the Star of David!

That is why Jesus came of the Jews. Only the spirituality and depth of their, and his, religion could at that time comprehend what happens when the Spirit comes.

A Meditation for Pentecost

A WORLD "SMUDGED"

Gerard Manley Hopkins, in his poem "God's Grandeur", speaks of a world that is "seared with trade; bleared, smeared with toil, a world which wears man's smudge and shares man's smell". Yet, for Hopkins, there is hope. "Nature is never spent: there lives the dearest freshness deep down things." And the ground of hope?

> Because the Holy Ghost over the bent
> world broods with warm breast and ah!
> bright wings

A recent survey among professional people demonstrated the unease so prevalent today. Fears, anxieties and stress were found to be widespread. Personal and family insecurity was rife because of the dread of unemployment. A large number of those questioned could not rule out the possibility of redundancy within a year. But there was a greater threat – inner insecurity. Was society itself "breaking up"? Did the future offer any hope of quality of life? The world was perceived as one which glamorises the trivial and minimises the spiritual; as one which abounds in goods but not in grace; a world where corruption is cutting confidence, where violence and perversion make their presence felt; a world "smudged" indeed. But people with faith cannot abandon hope, for it is over this "bent" world that the brooding Spirit moves, with warmth, to heal and to save.

There are many, too, who feel disconsolate over the institution "church". Insiders grieve that years of enthusiasm, commitment and prayer yield only discouraging results. Outsiders dismiss the church as irrelevant. Yet here there is a paradox that will stimulate and excite those able to see the presence of the brooding spirit in it. There are many signs that the desire for the spiritual dimension is alive and strong, especially among younger people. It is a quest which, sadly, so often by-passes the "official" church, but the indicators provide evidence of its reality – the immense interest in contemplation and especially meditation; the large number of people who fill retreat houses, healing homes and centres for prayer; the demand for spiritual direction. Many seek to make "the inner journey" through contact with eastern religion, the pursuit of esoteric philosophies and even curious cults. Not all these roads are safe (some forms of meditation, for example, carry risks), but these indicators point to the need for "deep calling to deep", the depth of human need crying out for a ministry to those deep down things.

The primary task of the church is to proclaim and demonstrate the wonder of life in the Spirit, to offer the resources of the faith to the needy and to present the opportunity of "new life". It is surely not an accident that the most obviously growing churches are those expressing Pentecostal fervour and offering charismatic renewal, churches which seem to meet the desire for a living, loving fellowship concerned with spiritual needs known and unknown.

In an age of overwhelming suffering, it is essential that the ministry of Jesus to the whole person – physical, mental, emotional and spiritual – be fully recovered. Jesus reaches deep down things. Is it not the "brooding, warm spirit" that is pressing on the churches the importance, as a normal part of its witness, of the healing ministry?

SPIRITUAL GIFTS

The coming of the Holy Spirit at the first Pentecost was a dramatic and exciting happening. The imagery described in that story – rushing wind and tongues of fire – enhances the sense of mystery. The behaviour of the apostles was wrongly interpreted as drunkenness by puzzled observers but there was no disorder among the disciples. Indeed Peter, as their accepted leader, delivered a clear and coherent description of the significance of what was happening, rooting it in the Old Testament scripture and offering an impromptu declaration of the meaning of the event in relation to Christ, crucified and risen.

These characteristics of order and coherence are important in assessing the validity and value of contemporary expressions of what are claimed to be movements of the Spirit. Many have found help in what has been described as "the Toronto Blessing", for example, but features of that experience are not justified by scripture. This is not to deny the element of renewal in "The Blessing", but to ensure that any movements of renewal must be tested against scripture and by their fruits.

The question of speaking in tongues, seen as a manifestation of the Spirit's activity, had created difficulties in the Corinthian church. Paul did not deny the validity of speaking in tongues as a spiritual gift, but he did minimise its importance among the range of gifts. He compares speaking in tongues unfavourably with prophecy. There seems too to have been some disorder created in that church by the abuse of speaking in tongues.

Paul is concerned to establish two principles. The first is that the Spirit creates not disorder but order, and the second is the importance of intelligibility. Neither disorder nor unintelligibility are for the edification of the church. He therefore recommends that when speaking in tongues takes place, there must be someone there who is able to interpret. If that condition is not met, what is being said brings no benefit to the community and really becomes a form of spiritual self-indulgence. Paul seeks to emphasise the communal nature of the faith. While the need for personal decision on central matters of belief must always be recognised, it is important that the corporate nature of the church is understood. Whatever gifts we have, for example the gift of healing, must be used *within* the body of Christ and for the benefit of the whole church. If a healing gift exists in someone, that gift should be tested and, once recognised by the church, should be used within it as a contribution to its total ministry.

It is no accident that it is in this context Paul proclaims (in 1 Corinthians 13) the centrality of love. Love is the guiding principle in every aspect of the church's life and work. If that principle abounds, no one in the church will use any aspect of its life for selfish purposes, even if genuine spiritual gifts are involved. Whatever is done must be done to the glory of God and be a blessing to people.

LORD OF THE DANCE

My abiding memory of Sydney Carter's poem "Lord of the Dance", set to an old Shaker tune, is of a magnificent rendering of it at the thanksgiving service for the life and work of my wife. Having often shared in the singing of this hymn at conferences, services, weddings and funerals, it came alive as I have never experienced it before, in London's Crown Court Church of Scotland on that occasion.* The poignancy was undoubtedly increased by Sydney's presence with us. Ettie had known him and worked with him over many years.

Sydney is a poet of distinction. His personal search for faith and belief, and the insights he has shared from that probing, have influenced many, not least younger people, and especially the folk-singers of the sixties in whose company he revelled. Who is not aware of his hymn of compassion: "When I needed a neighbour, were you there?", with its haunting refrain "and the creed and the colour and the name won't matter – were you there?"? His eightieth birthday was rightly celebrated by an event in Westminster Abbey in May, 1995. He deserves our thanks.

The New Testament has few references to dancing, although Jesus' mention, in the parable of the prodigal son, of the elder brother's anger when he heard music and dancing at the welcome-home party brings no disapproval of it. The Old Testament is much more specific on dancing and also very positive. There is a splendid picture of David dancing "before the Lord", and there are specific exhortations to dance in Psalms 149 and 150 – "Praise him in the dance!"

When "dancing in the aisles" entered (or re-entered) worship in recent decades, many Christians reacted with unease and discomfort. Tradition, temperament and reserve discouraged such phenomena. The charismatic renewal movement, however, with its more spontaneous and less inhibited ways, encouraged arm-raising, "happy clapping" and expressed affection. In many denominations, too, liturgical dance and movement have more recently been given a place.

It is part of discipleship to love God with "heart, soul, mind *and* strength", that is with our emotions, spirituality, minds and bodies. The involvement of the physical aspect of us in praise and worship should be seen as positive and creative. Christianity has often been confused and ambivalent over the human body (as problems over sexuality seem to suggest). Yet what more glorious affirmation of the body can there be than that "the Word was made flesh and dwelt among us." The Incarnation sets the seal on God's attitude to the body.

"Your body is the temple of the Holy Spirit." Paul's words determine our attitude to the body and demand that we treat it – ours and others' – with sensitivity. Just this points out the theological difficulty with boxing. If the body is the temple of the Spirit, can it be right, for sport or gain, deliberately to damage the body of another to the point of collapse and even virtual destruction?

"What greater calamity can fall upon a nation, than the loss of worship?" asked Ralph Waldo Emerson in an address to Harvard School of Divinity in 1838. Involving the whole person in worship may well make it a more attractive activity for many.

"Praise him with the dance" indeed!

* October 1993.
See also A Time to Dance, Meditation for April 11.

COPING WITH CHANGE

What incredible changes have taken place in my lifetime! As I look back to life in the Scottish village where I started school, I am amazed by its simplicity. We had no electric light or gas, only oil lamps. Ours was the first house in the village to have a wireless. The large draughty Overland car my parents owned required strenuous cranking to start it.

It was a way of life unbelievably far from the world we know today with its scientific and technological wonders, jet-age travel, space exploration, laser beams. The degree of change, development and so-called progress has been phenomenal.

There have been other revolutions too: the medical world is an example. The tuberculosis that sent a considerable number of people from my Glasgow church of the 1950s to sanatoria and Switzerland is, now, virtually a thing of the past (but cancer is now the unconquered scourge). For the benefits of that medical revolution we must be grateful.

The sexual revolution is as real but more controversial. Attitudes to marriage, divorce and personal relationships have changed dramatically. Some will welcome what they see as greater honesty and openness in relationships today. Others will feel ill at ease with these developments.

How have we coped with such a process of change? Can we cope with it unless there has been significant spiritual development too?

I cannot demonstrate it but feel instinctively that corporately, socially, nationally, even ecclesiastically, spiritual awareness, sensitivity and power have declined over recent years. That does not mean that all is negative. There are many people of grace and goodness among us today, the equal of those in any other generation. There is also a spiritual searching in many, a feature more marked in the later years of my ministry. Crowded retreat houses and busy spiritual directors testify to that welcome situation.

Nevertheless the overall impression remains. So steeped is our world in materialism and secularism that spiritual receptiveness has been dimmed and the real presence of the spiritual factor in decision-taking and policy-making has been diminished.

When, in the Old Testament, the sense of the numinous declined or disappeared, the prophetic call was to repentance. The New Testament effectively opens with the same demand: "Repent for the kingdom of heaven is at hand!" cried John the Baptist to the faithless. If ours is a world spiritually bereft and in need, then renewal is a priority for both world and church. But the church can lead the way in renewal only if it is itself willing to be renewed.

It is the prophet Ezekiel's vision of the miracle of resurrection in the valley of dry bones* that, though it comes from another age, perhaps best points to the basic elements required to bring about renewal. They are the sense of the presence and power of God, the need to found faith on the Word and the awareness of the power of the Spirit as the agent in revival. These eternal verities are relevant for renewal today.

* Ezekiel, Chapter 37.

INFINITE LOVE

Wilt thou forgive that sinne, where I begunne
Which is my sin, though it were done before?
Wilt thou forgive those sinnes through which I runne
And do run still, though still I do deplore?
When thou hast done, thou hast not done –
For I have more

The pain of confession and the plea for forgiveness in John Donne's *Hymne to God the Father* (also quoted in Meditations dated August 30 and 31) will find a response in those who similarly suffer an overwhelming sense of guilt and cry out for re-assurance. Others might feel that the presentation of the gospel by some preachers and evangelists puts too much emphasis on the creation of guilt feelings in leading people to "decision" and "surrender".

Confession, in that it is "good for the soul" is healthy, but concentration on guilt (for it is often complicated by "unconscious" factors) can create such a sense of personal unworthiness that anxiety, fear, "nervous breakdown", inability to cope and even suicidal feelings can result.

"The eternal verities" include, as I have said earlier, the doctrine of forgiveness. It is in the Apostles' Creed because it is of the essence of the faith. Practised as well as proclaimed by Jesus, it is the heart of the gospel.

Paul, in his dramatic confession of inner failure ("the good that I would, I do not, and the evil which I would not, that I do") certainly reflected the feelings of John Donne. His answer to his dilemma was a triumphant cry: "Who can deliver me from this body of death? I thank God through Jesus Christ our Lord." It is the reality of forgiveness, as part of God's infinite love, that makes people feel better and be better.

Guilt is a valid and necessary feeling. When we hurt someone by word or action, we ought to feel guilty and seek forgiveness. We are bound to share in corporate guilt over our part in the failures that produce war, racism, pollution and starvation, So long as guilt is "appropriate", it is proper and right. There is, however, "inappropriate guilt" which is a "neurotic sense of guilt over those experiences of feeling guilty which are not explicable in terms of the patient's conscious values" (Charles Rycroft).

It is simplistic to assume that declarations of forgiveness can dispose of complicated psychological problems. Nevertheless, the transforming power of grace and love can reach the inner hidden depths in ways difficult to define. It is, therefore, always relevant to bring the forgiving love of God into situations wracked by guilt.

To those who say with John Donne *"For I have more,"* the New Testament responds *"My grace is sufficient for you."*

THE SILENCE OF DIGNITY

The Christian emphasis on the value of silence is increasingly important in this noisy world. The Psalmist's advice to "be still" is timely. Words are and must be the normal method of communication, but it is right to remember the power of silence to convey great thoughts and to express deep feelings.

Silence is, for example, invaluable in prayer. Only by listening to "the still, small voice" can we discern the will of God. Silence in relation to people is an obligation of Christian love, Paul tells us, for "love finds nothing to be glad about when someone goes wrong, but is glad when truth is glad." Gossip and sensationalism are not part of the loving way.

The silence of awe and wonder, such a natural part of the spirituality of those in Bible days, is largely missing from contemporary attitudes. Many people are no longer even moved by the sheer holiness of God. Even within the church there is a need to recover "the sense of the numinous". It is however the silence of dignity on which I ask you to reflect in this Meditation.

Jesus has been called before his accusers – elders, priests, Herod. Insulting accusations are made against him and blasphemous things said. The Gospels record the situation succinctly. *Jesus answered them nothing*. That silence of dignity was the only appropriate response. It was, at the same time, a most effective contribution. There are some things in life which do not merit serious consideration. There are people to whom nothing relevant can be said. Verbal persecution is not dealt with best by counter-accusation. It is not words but silence that makes the point.

There is within us all a natural desire to offer eye for eye, argument for argument, accusation for accusation. That is understandably human and at times may even be appropriate. There may well arise situations, however, when the right answer is no answer; when strident argument is destructive and negative; when that which is potentially creative lies in "accentuating the positive" aspects of faith. Jesus offers us all the example of an attitude that he was able to show when under great pressure. It is an attitude to life and to people that is not easy to acquire, but it is one that it is indeed desirable to cultivate.

NO EASY WAY

"Prophecy, excellent! Impact, nil!" That was the damning divine report on the prophet Ezekiel's attempts to convey to God's people his word for today (Ezekiel, chapter 33, verses 30 to 32). The report is worth quoting.*

> The people say: "Let's go and hear what word has come from the Lord now." So my people crowd in to hear what you have to say, but they don't do what you tell them to do. Loving words are on their lips, but they continue their greedy ways. To them you are nothing more than an entertainer singing love-songs or playing a harp. They listen to all your words and don't obey a single one of them.

What a fascinating cameo! It throws into relief so dramatically a perennial problem of the faith – that of successful communication. How do you proclaim effectively *the unchanging Word to a rapidly changing world?* Yet the Bible remains contemporary, the teaching of Jesus is respected far outside the circle of his followers, the great verities of the faith – Incarnation, resurrection, the coming of the Spirit – continue to be the only ultimate answers to the human dilemma.

The problem is compounded by the generation gap – in lifestyles, attitudes, understanding. When I need help with any item of communication technology, I go to my grandson, for what is a mystery to me is child's play to him! Humbly I realise the differences that characterise the generations. Yet it is to such disparate groups, with all their infinite variations in standpoints and styles, that the unchanging Word has to be proclaimed.

Consider these two matters, related to this theme. The first concerns inner authority. This Jesus had. Indeed the people were "astonished ... for he taught them as one having authority, and not as the scribes". Successful communication depends on real inner authority.

The second issue asks the question: which is more likely to attract the seeker – a faith which accommodates its standards to make them less demanding, or one that tells its disciples there is no easy way to spiritual maturity? The facts provide the answer. The growing churches are those which demand profound commitment, continuing prayer and consecrated service. A faith which makes it too easy is a faith no one wants.

* *The Good News Bible* (HarperCollins).

A Giant of Faith

Nehemiah was a man of faith, courage, penetrating insight and profound spirituality. Called by God to rebuild the walls of Jerusalem, he carried out his task on principles and policies which, translated into the needs of contemporary mission, have much to say to today.

Nehemiah's prime purpose was to carry out the work through the people who were there. "The God of heaven, He will prosper us," he declared, "therefore *we* his servants will arise and build." It was "the locals" who must rebuild the walls. It is, similarly, Christ's people on the spot who are the agents of mission today. If the local church is not positively proclaiming the gospel, demonstrating the meaning of loving fellowship and offering care to the community in which it is set, it is effectively "null and void".

The second aim was to use everyone's diverse abilities in the operation and so some built, some fetched and carried, some acted as guards. What was important was that everyone should pool their gifts for the common cause. So must it be today. Some must preach, some teach, some sing, some administer. But there are also less public gifts which are important too – the capacity for friendship and healing relationship, a sense of humour, the ability to cater, for did not somebody lay the table for the Last Supper and so contribute mightily to Jesus' mission?

Nehemiah reminded them too of the danger of separation. "The work is great and large," he pointed out, "and we are separated upon the wall, one far from another." It is the same in evangelism. Mission and unity go together, for unnecessary disunity is damaging to the cause.

Above all, the task was encompassed in prayer. "I prayed to the God of heaven," says Nehemiah, and in doing so emphasises the truth which needs to be remembered today.

"Except the Lord build the house, they labour in vain that build it." God is the source, we are but channels.

WERE YOU THERE?

Holy Week begins with joy and ends with victory, but between Jesus' triumphal entry into Jerusalem and the triumph of his resurrection come the sombre events that culminate in his crucifixion. It is not clear that those who welcomed him when he arrived, "lowly and riding upon an ass", knew just why they were cheering. A similar reception, Professor J W Bowman tells us, was given to the pilgrim bands coming from the ends of the earth to worship at the Passover feast. Was it any more than that? Perhaps it does not matter greatly. Jesus knew what he was doing and why. He was presenting an acted parable in terms of Zechariah's prophecy about the humility of the coming King. "Rejoice greatly!" the prophet had said, and so they did with palms and loud hosannas.

Another prophet, Isaiah, in presenting his picture of "the suffering servant", had spoken of him as "despised and rejected of men, a man of sorrows and acquainted with grief". With that image of the Messiah, Jesus identified himself. And so, although the "the common people heard him gladly" because "he spoke with authority"; although he had intrigued many with his parables and amazed them with his miracles; although he "went about, doing good", by sharing people's pain and meeting their needs; although he had come, in Ezekiel's lovely words, to "search for the lost, recover the straggler and bandage the hurt", he was dragged before accusers, rejected by the people in favour of the robber Barabbas, made to wear a crown of thorns and compelled to carry his cross to his crucifixion. Why did they do such things to Jesus? What is it in human nature that wants to destroy the good and acclaim the evil? Why do we "crucify the Son of God afresh"? "Were you there when they crucified my Lord?" the old song asks. We were – and, forgive us, we did.

I turn in a perhaps unexpected direction for an insight into part of the answer. The late Kenny Everett, usually described as a "wacky" comedian, has – like other homosexual people – suffered abuse and violence because he is "different". A colleague pointed out that others – coloured (as he was), Jewish, the deformed, the ugly – suffer similarly. In a dramatic phrase, Everett commented: "We are receptacles for human hatred." Jesus, "different" because of his holiness and spirituality, was similarly persecuted, vilified, despised and rejected, an innocent receptacle for human hatred, a hatred that is blind, uninformed and wholly unacceptable.

Those who have experienced such abuse may well be comforted by the knowledge that there is a profound divine understanding of what it means and feels like to be acquainted with grief. Can they – and must not we all – be touched by Jesus' attitude to those who planned and executed his crucifixion? "Father, forgive them, for they know not what they do." This surely is the wonder of that love divine, all loves excelling, incarnate in Jesus. Such a capacity to forgive may feel to be far beyond our reach, but it remains the model for us all.

THE DIVINE JIGSAW

You cannot argue with a man born blind when he says categorically: "Whereas I was blind, now I see." Personal experience, as the Pharisees, critical of Jesus, had to accept, was the proof of a miracle. The interpretation of the event is another matter. For the recipient of the miracle there is the logical conclusion: "If this man were not of God, he could do nothing" and therefore the only possible reaction: "Lord, I believe." The Pharisees' not so logical conclusion was that "this man is not of God because he keepeth not the sabbath day." But they did not have his *personal* experience.

Experience is the ultimate ground of conviction. Robert Llewellyn, widely known for his spiritual writing and particularly as Chaplain of the Julian Cell in Norwich from 1976 to 1990, testifies to the doctrine of providence through his personal experience. At the age of 89, with a huge span of hindsight, he can say: "My life has been like a large jigsaw puzzle where it has often been impossible to see how this or that contributed to the picture, but as the whole has come together, the purpose has been made clear." Many will respond to that testimony and be ready to witness to their personal experiences of the Divine providence and their conviction that "all things work together for good to those who love God." Similarly, testimony will gladly be offered by those who, as a matter of personal experience, have known the extraordinary reach of the Divine forgiveness and the profound mystery of God's healing ways.

There is, however, a difference between the personal experience with which we began and the convictions about providence, forgiveness and healing just expressed. At the heart of the first incident is one objective fact that neither recipient or observer can deny. Eyes have been opened and a blind man can see. The latter experiences are not based on those sorts of facts but only on personal interpretations of events. In other words, in the first case there is an *objective* fact. In the second, apart from the possibility of a miracle of healing medically, conclusions are dependent on *subjective* factors. These may feel unquestionably reliable to the believer, but they are incapable of proof to the observer. Therein lies the problem of personal experience as a proof-text in matters of faith.

There is always the need for an objective standard by which to test convictions drawn from personal experience and it is the great Reformation emphasis on the Word of God as the supreme rule of faith and life that supplies this.

Only by testing experience against the Word of God can we be confirmed in our wonder at the way God deals with us through the divine forgiveness, providence and healing.

THE POWER TO CHANGE

Jesus understood the feeling of helplessness. However strange it may seem to say this of one to be called "Son of God", the Gospel records make clear his sense of impotence in certain situations. "O Jerusalem, Jerusalem," he cried to the city over which Luke tells us he shed tears, "how often would I have gathered your children together and you would not!" Human intransigence had made him helpless, as it had done in "his own country". "He did not many mighty works there because of their unbelief."

It is the unbearable sight of human suffering in so many places, where people seem to have descended into hell, that moves me to reflect on helplessness. How utterly impotent we can feel in the face of such pain! Thanks be to God for those who risk life and limb, health and future, to minister to the injured, sick and dying. For most of us, the sense of limitation can be overwhelming. We can pray, of course. We can give gifts. Beyond that, it is no more than a deep yearning ... if *only* we could really help. But we are not omnipotent. There are things we cannot do. Even our capacity to take so much suffering into our hearts is limited. Helpless ourselves, we cannot help the helpless.

To admit our limitations is not weakness, it is realism, It reminds us that there are unchangeable situations in life for which the only solace is in the doctrine of forgiveness. We must not feel guilty because we cannot ameliorate all the world's suffering. There *is* emotional pain for which we cannot find balm, illness we cannot cure, and death in relation to which we can arrange no resurrection. Yes, there are things we cannot do.

Such realism is however no excuse for despair. What is important in the life of Jesus is not the few things he could not do, but the record of what he did. His impact is in the signs and wonders he effected; in the changes in people which he wrought; in the new lives he created. It was the politics of Robert Louis Stevenson "to change what we can, to better what we can". It must also be our religion.

It is realistic and right to recognise our limitations. It is, however, much more important to be sensitive to the promised power of the Holy Spirit, that energy of God which turned weak and frightened disciples into world-changers. There is so much that can be different and better through the grace that is sufficient for all our weakness. It was people perceived as helpless who were given the power to be positive and productive in proclaiming the possibility of new life. Be encouraged by that!

SUSTAINING GRACE

Corruption is much more contagious than holiness. That is why the struggle to develop a spirituality, be it corporate or personal, is such a demanding one. It is not easy to live "life in the Spirit", to adhere to things that are "good and lovely and of good report" in the materialistic, competitive, even ruthless world we experience today.

The opening statement above was prompted by a curious and controversial passage in one of the minor prophets of the Old Testament, the prophecies of Haggai. The passage is in chapter 2, verses 10 to 14. There is much difference of view among scholars as to its correct interpretation. Here, only the central point of the passage can be considered. The priests are asked for a directive on the infectiousness of holiness in a certain sacrificial context. It is not possible, they say, for one holy object to spread holiness to other objects. But when uncleanness is involved, it is quite different. The contagiousness of uncleanness is real. The detail of the directive is unimportant here, but the general principle thrown up by the question is disturbing. Is it our experience that it is, in fact, much easier for us to be corrupted than to be sanctified? It is depressing to realise that it is indeed so.

There is a long established religious view that it is much simpler for humanity to choose evil rather than good, darkness rather than light; to be more vulnerable to the attraction of conforming to this world than being spiritually transformed within it. Both biblical testimony to the subtlety of sin and psychology's awareness of the dark, negative inner pressures coming from the shadow side of the unconscious bear this out. If it is true that we are more vulnerable to negative pressures than positive ones, more liable to temptation than able to resist it, then there is much in contemporary life and attitudes that inflates our problem. To be affluent can make us more vulnerable to greed than poverty. When money comes to be loved, and there is plenty in advertising to stimulate the desire for money, materialism can develop dangerously. Indeed, so weighted are the contrary factors that a sustained search for spirituality is a major task.

It would, however, be totally inconsistent with the religious spirit to lose heart or give up. It is of the very essence of the committed life to ask, seek, knock, search, struggle towards the light. And thanks are due to those outstanding people who, mostly unsung, encourage us on the spiritual way.

It is of the generosity of God that grace is given to those who are prepared to walk by faith; saving grace, sustaining grace, sanctifying grace. Those who use the means of grace that are provided – prayer, worship, sacraments, fellowship – will find that, on the road to a greater spirituality, they can make progress especially when they know they are not alone.

SENSE OF PURPOSE

One of the consequences of a bereavement, a broken relationship, a redundancy notice is the death of a sense of purpose. The sadness of the widow, bereft of the partner of a lifetime, proclaims, not through word but through expression, that "there is no point in going on". "A woman scorned" will, after the fury, feel the desperation of loneliness. Unemployment will lead to depression and despair, both through financial consequences and even more the loss of the dignity of work. The life that has lost its purpose and meaning can indeed become a desolate and derelict one.

The statistics of depression reflect such loss of purpose and meaning. It is an illness which is becoming one of the most prevalent of our time, nationally and internationally. It is not the clinical or endogenous depression that incapacitates so many people. It is the depression which is a reaction to circumstances. It is nevertheless real and, for many, devastating and debilitating. It follows serious disturbance of the equilibrium of life and is a response to changed and damaged physical circumstances (traumatic events brought about by war, natural disaster, famine, economic failure), emotional circumstances (bereavement, grief, loss, hurt, abuse, etc), spiritual circumstances (the crisis of "faith and doubt"). And it may be that the last is as serious as any other circumstance. As the "ancient landmarks" of belief and creed are removed; as the fundamental tenets of inherited faith are questioned – not only by those hostile to religious faith, but from within the church itself; as the traditional religious bases of ethics and behaviour are undermined, the faith itself becomes destabilised.

Nihilism is an expression of that movement from faith and morality, showing itself in cynicism, boredom, lack of concern, emptiness, meaninglessness. The spiritual dangers inherent in such loss of purpose are very much expressed in the corporate depression threatening to encompass society.

Religious faith ought to be showing through its preachers, and perhaps even more its pastors, that it is the realm in which purpose is nurtured and meaning developed; that the story of the Old Testament and the New is of people "called" to a purpose within a faith that provides insights into ultimate meaning and truth. "The life of faith is a continually renewed grasp of meaning in the midst of meaninglessness" wrote the late Lesslie Newbigin.

The sense of vocation, the conviction of being "called", the feeling of being chosen to serve, lies deeply in the hearts of all who are convinced their life-purpose is in service. It is that sense of purpose which drives men and women on, overcoming obstacles, riding crises, undeterred and undefeated.

"But what if I fail of my purpose here?" writes Robert Browning. "It is but to keep my nerves at strain, To dry one's eyes and laugh at a fall, And baffled, get up and begin again." Or in historic words: "To fight and fight and fight again."

A sense of purpose provides the ability to go on.

CALLED TO SERVICE

"To everything there is a season," declares The Preacher (Ecclesiastes). That applies, though he does not mention it, to "a time to retire". Churches now tend to lay down the age at which this must happen (partly for financial reasons). Such a trend is resisted by some and welcomed by many.

The concept of retirement from ministry does however give me a problem. The reason is stated dramatically by St Paul: "Woe is me," he cries "if I preach not the gospel!" I empathise with that. *Called* to the ministry by God and convinced of the imperative of preaching, how can I stop expounding the word?

The circumstances of my own call to the ministry may explain the strength of this feeling. The son of a clergyman, I spent my early years (apart from absence at boarding school) in manses. To the implicitly rhetorical question, "Will you follow in your father's footsteps?" I always offered a vehemently negative reply. I turned rather towards taking degrees in law at Edinburgh University. Poring one day over the *Institutes of Justinian*, suddenly and without forethought, I closed the book, returned it to the librarian, went home and announced that I would enter the ministry. Such an (as it was) irrational decision had serious lifelong implications for myself and my family, not least the abandonment of a potentially lucrative career in law for the stringent economics of the parish. I was convinced, however, that this was a divine call to service and could not be resisted. Many years on, I hold that view still. As a result, commitment to preach the gospel, in speech or written word, feels so mandatory that it cannot lightly be laid aside.

Such experiences of calling, as of conversion, are not always as instant as they seem. Paul's Damascus road experience demonstrates this. While the peak point in that story is the "hysterical" collapse which he suffered under the bright light, it seems clear (with hindsight) that the one who was "breathing out threatenings and slaughter against the disciples" was suffering inner conflict, touched off perhaps by the murder of the martyr, Stephen, to which he had consented. The conversion process had been under way, under the Spirit, for some time. It continued in his need to find the help of Ananias as his spiritual director. Now God's "chosen vessel", he was called to lifelong discipleship. It is something of that compulsion that creates the preacher.

It is not generally fashionable today to present preaching as the primary means of communication, but increasingly there is an awareness of the necessity for its return to that position. The spiritual needs of today require the exposition of the word, a positive biblical theology, an informed pastoral sense grounded in love, a recognition of the healing gifts of the Spirit and the authority of personal spiritual experience. It is the function of the ministry to bring these blessings to the world.

Preaching is the priority in making known the gospel to the world. What a privilege those have who are called to preach! What an opportunity to serve!

CONFLICT AND COMFORT

It was that true saint, George Johnstone Jeffrey, who insisted that every sermon must conclude with a message of comfort. William Barclay spoke similarly about worship. "Every act of worship," he wrote, "must include the note of comfort." With that, all will surely agree. But there is a problem, The gospel does not only bring comfort. It brings conflict.

That that is true is made clear in a saying of Jesus recorded in Matthew's Gospel: "Think not that I am come to send peace on earth; I came not to send peace, but a sword." He offers an explanation of this dramatic statement: "For I am come to set a man at variance against his father, and the daughter against her mother ... And a man's foes shall be they of his own household." Conflict indeed!

The point in this passage is the nature of commitment. "He that loveth father or mother more than me is not worthy of me," Jesus says. It is a daunting declaration. But is it a statement about intention, or rather about consequences? Loyalty to Christ can, as a matter of fact, bring extreme conflict to families. William Barclay's translation of the passage confirms this: "You must not suppose that the result of my coming will be peace for the world. The result of my coming will not be peace, but a sword. My coming is bound to result in a cleavage between a man and his father, between a daughter and her mother ..." Loyalty such as Christ demands can and does cause conflict. If comfort and conflict are associated with the gospel, should not every act of worship take account of both of them?

The role of the prophet, certainly in the Old Testament, includes the need to be a nuisance – to authority and those in whom authority is vested, to powers-that-be, both public and ecclesiastical. "Is that you, you troubler of Israel?" King Ahab asks the prophet Elijah, who replies that it is his duty to trouble not Israel, but Ahab and his house because of their wickedness. The modern preacher is not exempt from the prophet's responsibility, that is the need to subject policies and programmes to the scrutiny of God's will and declare God's judgement on them without fear or favour, especially if they harm people, endanger the social fabric or seek the interest not of all but of the few. The result of such denunciation may well be conflict.

Preaching is, however, but one element in a service, so William Barclay's dictum about worship needs to be fulfilled. Those who go from church must do so with a sense of comfort in both the sense of inner serenity and of spiritual encouragement.

"Comforter, where is your comforting?" asks Gerard Manley Hopkins as he agonisingly reflects on that tragedy of which "no worse, there is none". To provide comfort is of the essence of the gospel and every act of worship must represent the love of the Lord.

It takes skill and sensitivity to hold together, in one act of worship, the possibility of conflict and the necessity of comfort. Perhaps the key to achieving it is always to "speak the truth in love".

SPREAD THE WORD!

Broken relationships, at international or national levels, usually begin with a loss of communication. Equally, in personal relationships, it is a sure sign of potential marital breakdown when people can no longer talk to each other about elements that threaten their marriages. Such a loss of verbal communication is, moreover, symptomatic of a loss of contact at deeper levels. Words alone, however, cannot heal such broken relationships.

"Come, let us reason together," God says to his people about their relationships with him, damaged by their sin. "Let us argue it out," as the *New English Bible* translated that sentence in Isaiah.* The restoration of relationships is, however, much more than a matter of reasoning and discussion. For people or groups who have lost touch with one another (a significant phrase), verbal communication is just not enough.

How do we communicate the unchanging Word to a rapidly changing world? It is Paul who asks the relevant question: "How shall they hear without a preacher?"

Ordination is to the ministry of Word and Sacrament. The primacy of preaching is symbolically represented in some traditions by the centrality of the pulpit in churches. But for those traditions which make central the altar or communion table, there remains for all who are ordained a first commitment to preaching and proclamation.

Many today feel that preaching, as it is traditionally understood, is out-of-date and irrelevant; that "dialogue" is more important than "monologue"; that an experiential approach to communication is the only relevant way. But other forms of communication, however valuable in themselves, cannot be substitutes for that which Jesus specifically exhorted his disciples to do, that is to "go into all the world and preach the gospel to every creature."

The formation of the Christian community from the beginning was based on the command of Jesus to his followers to preach and heal. The disciples' response, as the book of Acts records, was to "speak the word of God with boldness". Down through the ages, the practice of preaching has been consistently maintained. Whatever additional forms of communication are needed to convey the wonder of the Word to a constantly changing world, evangelism will lose an essential tool if the proclamation of the Word ceases to be a priority today.

* See a fuller development of the point in the Meditation for November 9.

MINISTRY IN PRINT

I was 10 years old when my first journalistic effort appeared in *The Children's Newspaper*. The postal order for 2s 6d that came as a reward, while exciting, was less important than the encouragement I received to undertake a lifelong journey in "the ministry of print". The ministry of Word and Sacrament, expressed through preaching and teaching, has been and remains of prime importance; but the printed word, too, is an essential element in the communication of the gospel today.

"Letters mingle souls," wrote John Donne. Paul, from the beginning, used the "epistle" to proclaim the message, present his theology, proffer pastoral counsel to the young churches, offer a Christian apologetic. His letter to the Romans remains a formidable theological document. All kinds of pastoral concerns were dealt with in his epistles – sexual immorality in Corinth, confusion in Thessalonica over the second coming of Jesus, the meaning of humility in his epistle to the Philippians.

"The great art o' letter-writin'," (as Sam Weller described it) must not be sacrificed to the technological age, for it can be a medium of comfort and consolation to many. It also allows, to those who find face-to-face exchanges difficult, a way of expressing deep feelings. So important is the place of a letter that the instinctive urge to send one should rarely be resisted. How often we regret that, when we "meant to write", we failed to do so. We missed the opportunity to convey a blessing. That opportunity rarely returns.

It is the calling of evangelists to change people, but there are times when the best possible ministry is to recommend a book. How often there is a particular one that has the capacity to minister to the soul, stimulate the intellect, touch the emotions. John Ruskin, in another age, wrote: "What do we, as a nation, care about books? How much do you think we spend altogether on our libraries, public or private, compared with what we spend on our horses?" Change "horses" to "cars" and the question remains.

The need to feed minds, meet emotional needs and nourish souls is a primary concern of communication. The ministry of print, the writing of a letter, the publishing of a book, composing a poem – all these indeed can be tools of evangelism today, essential elements in communication.

A Sense of Destiny

"Hope is the future tense of faith," writes Bishop Richard Holloway.* It is hope that compels the Christian faith to be forward-looking, conscious of divine purpose, anticipating future glory, encouraging a sense of destiny.

That awareness of divine destiny manifested itself frequently in the Bible. "Speak unto the children of Israel that they go *forward*," God tells Moses. It is an invitation to reach out and fulfil their destiny within God's purpose.

Paul saw his destiny as the attainment of the spiritual goal. "I press toward the mark for the prize of the high calling of God in Christ Jesus," he told the Philippian church. It is a sense of destiny that helps to create the energy which makes us go on.

We have therefore four elements that provide a secure base from which we can face an unknown future in an uncertain world – a sense of direction, a sense of perspective, a sense of adventure and a sense of destiny. But what of security? Such is the potential violence of our modern world that not a day passes without a mention of that word. How ironic it is that this same world is psychologically, emotionally and spiritually gravely insecure! The loss of theological and ethical landmarks, the decreasing authority of the church, the constant erosion of traditional standards and values, the questioning of institutions, the revolution in attitudes to marriage and relationships, the obsession with possessions and gain – all these trends have combined to create in many people those negative characteristics already mentioned, rootlessness, alienation, meaninglessness and lostness. Inevitably, nervous and mental breakdown abound, while others increasingly find themselves unable to cope with the economic, psychological and social demands of life. It is, sadly, dis-ease rather than health that dominates our times.

It is part of our belief in a loving Providence to feel not only God is *with* us, but also that He goes *before* us. The Eastern shepherd who leads his sheep to ensure their safety is one biblical model for that truth. Another is the picture of the Israelites on their journey to the promised land as God "went before them by day in a pillar of cloud, to lead them the way".

"We love him because he *first* loved us," John writes in the New Testament. His, in Emil Brunner's phrase, is "the divine initiative". We have a sense of destiny because we know that he leads the way.

* *Anger, Sex, Doubt and Death* by Richard Holloway, (SPCK, 1992).

GENTLE SLEEP

"O sleep! O gentle sleep! Nature's soft nurse ..."* The ability to fall asleep, and sleep soundly, is a gift for which continual thanks should be offered. Sadly there are those, perhaps many, who just cannot sleep well and so have to endure dreaded "long night watches" with anxiety and indeed agony. The middle of the night is, for some, life's lowest point. The divine Presence can seem far away at 3am.

I remember well the text on which I was asked to preach in the "sermon class" when I was training for the ministry in Edinburgh University's Faculty of Divinity. It runs "When I awake, I am still with thee."

That statement is a glorious affirmation of a doctrine fundamental to faith, the belief in Providence. We may be unconscious in sleep but, as the Psalmist explains in "comfortable words": "Behold, he that keepeth Israel shall neither slumber nor sleep" (Psalm 121). We are, to put it in very human terms, in the care of an ever-wakeful and ever-watchful God, day and, even more importantly, night.

The Psalm from which my sermon class text comes (Psalm 139) describes dramatically the uniquely present Creator and, in New Testament language, Father. "Whither shall I flee from Thy presence?" the Psalmist asks. His answer is that there is nowhere, in heaven or hell, in "the uttermost parts of the sea", where God is not present. Nor is there any time when God is absent for "the darkness and the light are both alike to Thee". This is indeed the Psalmist's doctrine of providence worked out not by intellectual reasoning but out of living experience. The important part for those who cannot sleep is the assurance of God's presence *in the darkness as well as in daylight*. However hard it is to believe it, and even more to feel it, God shares our sleepless hell. The divine Presence is there even, and perhaps especially, at 3am.

It is, alas, much easier to affirm this spiritual truth than to apply it and immediately fall asleep. A night-time of physical, mental, emotional and/or spiritual restlessness takes away our sense of perspective. The worries associated with family, business, unemployment, illness, bereavement draw to themselves an exaggerated unreality. The facts with which we can courageously cope by day become ominously threatening by night. Is there any spiritual resource for this turmoil?

It would be much too facile to suggest that anxious sleeplessness can be spontaneously banished by spiritual reflection, but if the sense of God's providence is an active element in our faith, our spirituality should provide some solace. Recalling some "comfortable words" from the Psalms; repeating over and over again reassuring words from Jesus – "I will not leave you comfortless", "my peace I give to you", a silent prayer, perhaps to be able to "be still" – all these can be of benefit.

To fall asleep is an act of trust. How blessed are those who can take this step and awake to a lively sense of God's omnipresence. In the receiving of such blessings, remember at the same time those for whom, sadly, there is no gentle sleep.

* William Shakespeare, *Henry IV, part II*.

PERCHANCE TO DREAM

"To sleep; to sleep; perchance to dream," mused Hamlet. Dreams certainly feature in the Bible. The dreams in which the Old Testament Joseph became involved as an interpreter had a major prophetic element about them. In the New Testament, Mary's husband Joseph – a man of profound intuition, sensitive spirituality and religious awareness – experienced his dreams as divine warnings. The safety of the infant Jesus depended on his not only listening to his dreams but acting on them, in obedience to the divine will.

Modern psychology uses a different vocabulary in defining dreams. The Jungian therapist the late Carol Jeffrey (of The Open Way) saw the creative potential in dreams. "A dream," she once said, "is a photograph, *a snapshot of an area of the unconscious.*" Studying your dream "will lead to recognition and new perception of aspects, attitudes, functioning and knowledge. Revelation of this kind can provide guidance, wisdom, warning and stimulation, and lead to change and sometimes to the dynamic development of unused potential, hitherto unknown."

The unconscious is perhaps most simply described as a tape-recording of life's total experience from birth, possibly even before it. If our first contacts were warm, welcoming and loving, our emotional security in later life will be the greater. If, however, we suffered rejection and sensed no love, those negative experiences, recorded on life's tape, may well express themselves at some time in unacceptable attitudes and problem behaviour. Because the reasons for our unhappiness, pain and stress are beyond our conscious recollections we may find ourselves acting out our "shadow" feelings in unacceptable ways ... hurting people, damaging relationships. Yet in all truth, "we know not what we do" – nor why.

To fall asleep is an act of trust in which we deliberately lose consciousness but, like the ever-wakeful, ever-watchful God of Psalm 121, our *unconscious* "neither slumbers nor sleeps". With our defences down, material from that area may well express itself in dreams. If such material is positive, our creativity will be ultimately enhanced, but when negative material breaks through to give us uneasy feelings, our dreams may become nightmares. And because such "shadow" material is threatening, it will be expressed in complex symbolic forms.

In the dark hours of the night, when physical, nervous and spiritual energy is at a low ebb, how frightening our dreams can be! Fear and anxiety may well threaten our inner security while unresolved guilt,* especially of an inappropriate kind, can destroy our peace. There is no magic that can, in the twinkling of an eye, banish those threats but our spirituality, if real, should provide some solace. Outgoing love to others can help to disperse the fear that comes from anxiety about self (for, John tells us, "perfect love casts out fear").

For those struggling with guilt, our resource is the greatest of the articles of the faith, the doctrine of forgiveness. It is in the assurance of forgiveness as described by Jesus – infinite, repetitive, "full and free" – that the possibility of feeling something of that peace which "passeth understanding" can become authentic. The peace that "the world cannot give or take away" may even begin to be sensed as real in the dark hours of the night, telling us – as the life, death and resurrection of Jesus show – that the darkest hour is just before the dawn.

* See also Meditation for May 7.

RECONCILIATION

Reconciliation is a healing word. It has nothing to do with softness or appeasement. It refers to determined and costly effort to mend broken relationships. The Christian symbol, the cross, declares the cost of God's reconciling act in Jesus Christ. The Christian is, consequently, committed to the ministry of reconciliation.

In a war-torn world, bleeding to death because of broken relationships at so many levels, there is an obligation on us all to "take with us" the healing word, reconciliation, wherever we go. Across the divisions that fragment the world and violate the essential "one-ness" of humanity, the Bible exhorts us to be reconciled to one another.

When Paul speaks of reconciliation, he never talks of human beings reconciling men and women to God. He does speak of "God reconciling man to himself". In other words, as the late Professor William Barclay reminds us: "It was not God who needed to be pacified, but man who needed to be moved to surrender, penitence and love."

If this religious language feels foreign to the world of today, we can express it in contemporary terms. "Lostness", "alienation" and "meaninglessness" are very much part of our present experience. Negative feelings of that kind dominate the lives of many who find their way to psychiatric hospitals, psychotherapeutic agencies and counselling centres. Many more try to cope with such stressful feelings on their own. Alienation is the experience of being (metaphorically) a stranger in a foreign land, cut off from one's roots and out of relationships with people. It leaves life lacking in meaning and purpose.

But that is precisely the parable of the prodigal son in modern terms. It is a story that Jesus told about lostness ("for this my son was lost"), alienation ("in a far country") and meaninglessness (sharing with pigs while, at home, the board is spread). It is a parable about reconciliation – a waiting father, who is not there to rebuke, but to receive. It was not the father who "needed to be pacified". It was the son who was "moved to penitence and love". Significantly there follows a ministry of reconciliation towards the resentful elder brother. This is the way God acts, Jesus is telling us. He restores relationships. He effects reconciliation.

Take with you into this shattered world, the word of reconciliation. It is the healing word brought to us by and in Jesus.

A SENSE OF DISTANCE

There are two more healing words to "take with us". One is, not surprisingly, closeness. The other, perhaps surprisingly, is distance. Both are strikingly illustrated in Jesus' ministry.

John tells us in his Gospel that "Jesus knew what was in man" – and woman. It was his "divine intuition" which enabled him to enter into relationships with all kinds of people – like Nicodemus, who came to him secretly, by night; the woman from Samaria, whom he met at the well of Sychar; Zacchaeus, the despised tax gatherer; the woman "taken in adultery" by her self-righteous accusers. Jesus exercised his "ministry of closeness" to each one in whatever form they needed it and to whatever degree was appropriate. He gave people trust and, as a result, a sense of value. The followers of Jesus must reflect Jesus' sensitivity as they offer *their* ministry of closeness and, in so doing, help people to feel better.

There are times, however, when people need not closeness, but distance. The ministry of distance also requires great sensitivity. There is the Gospel story of the rich young ruler who could not meet the demands of discipleship because "he had great possessions". Jesus respected his decision. Looking at the young man as he slipped sorrowfully away, Jesus "loved him" – and let him go. He needed distance.

The prodigal son needed space to help him find right relationships. He went to "a far country" and, from that distance, learnt what home and values meant.

When his friend Lazarus died, Jesus stayed away from Bethany for two days. It seems extraordinary that, loving Lazarus' sisters Martha and Mary as he did, Jesus should deliberately remain at a distance from them, but the ministry of distance would contribute to the miracle of Lazarus' resurrection. There are times when closeness is inappropriate and distance is in the interests of all.

We return to the concept of closeness in order to note finally that Jesus often expressed that ministry by touch. He laid hands on the sick and the blind. He touched the leper. He took the children in his arms, laid his hands on them and blessed them. In return there were those who wanted to touch him – the woman who struggled to touch "the hem of his garment", Mary reaching out to touch him in the Garden of the Resurrection.

Touch, too, is a healing word.*

* See the development of this theme in The Ministry of Touch, the Meditation for May 26.

RIGHT RELATIONSHIPS

How sad it is when loving relationships break down. In that "love finds nothing to be glad about when someone goes wrong, but is glad when truth is glad",* dramatizing others' pain for satisfaction or profit is unacceptable. The reality is that love and relationship are both essential to human well-being. The primacy of love is written large in the Old Testament. To love God and our neighbour is the first and great commandment, says the New Testament. We shall come as close to inner health and spiritual wholeness as possible when all our relationships are in good order ... our relationship upward to God, downward to the earth, outward to others and inward to ourselves.

The Earth Summit has reminded us of the need for a positive, creative relationship to the ground. "The earth is the Lord's," proclaims the Psalmist. The Incarnation has demonstrated God's sharing in the life of the world, for it was on our earth that Jesus walked, preached and healed. The Creator committed his world into human hands and sought to be glorified through their stewardship of its resources. Human beings cannot therefore stand aside unaffected while the earth is abused, the atmosphere polluted, the living world destroyed. Our corporate failure in stewardship has damaged God's world and is destroying his creatures. How right it is that we are being compelled to re-assess our relationship to the earth.

If broken personal relationships are indeed hurtful, how increasingly awful are the consequences of fractured relationships in our national and international life? Look where you will in the world – here, where good men die on public duty, or to the world's troubled places where the innocent victims of wars, violence, aggression, racial prejudice, starvation (whether brought about by drought, aggression or selfish economics) – the dominating word is division, the missing word, reconciliation. Yet the biblical message is clear. You cannot hate your brother or sister and at the same time claim you love God.

The need for a right relationship with ourselves demands courageous self-understanding, especially in the obligation to accept the unacceptable side of our being. If we cannot learn to love our shadow selves, we will never be able fully to love our neighbour.

Loving our world, our neighbour and ourselves can grow only if that fourth, fundamental relationship is sound, our relationship "upward" to God. Loving relationships are founded, fed and forwarded by our love for God and, even more, his love for us.

* William Barclay's translation of 1 Corinthians, chapter 13, verse 6.

THE MINISTRY OF TOUCH

For wonderful language and dignity of expression, nothing surpasses the *Authorised Version* of the Bible. Other translations are, however, valuable as aids to understanding the Word.

Occasionally, one of the more recent versions touches great heights. In the *New English Bible* I find one such passage – Ephesians chapter 3, verses 14 to 19.* It offers a gloriously moving translation:**

> I kneel in prayer to the Father, from whom every family in heaven and on earth takes its name, that out of the treasures of his glory he may grant you strength and power through his Spirit in your inner being, that through faith Christ may dwell in your hearts in love. With deep roots and firm foundations, may you be strong to grasp, with all God's people, what is the breadth and length and height and depth of the love of Christ, and to know it, though it is beyond knowledge. So may you attain to fullness of being, the fullness of God himself.

Reflect quietly on these words and phrases: "deep roots and firm foundations"; "to know" that which is "beyond knowledge"; "strength and power through his Spirit in your inner being"; "the treasures of his glory". Language like this takes us into that realm in which it is the church's function to lead us ... the spiritual dimension. It is "communication" that reaches the deepest levels of the inner self. It touches a spiritual nerve and, when that happens, people are changed, converted, transformed, renewed.

In our reflecting on the responsibility we have for helping the unchanging Word to reach, touch and affect this changing world, we have pondered on the priority of preaching and the ministry of print in enlightening the mind; "being with" rather than "talking to" as ministry through healing relationships; music, poetry, art and other creative ways of stimulating the imagination. There must, however, also be ministry to the physical body. That involves the ministry of touch. It was something Jesus used frequently and effectively. It remains an essential element in communication today.

The ministry of healing unites all four elements. In the laying on of hands, we have the ministry of touch. The mind is stirred when the Word is proclaimed. Emotional serenity comes when hidden memories are healed. Prayer, which must always encompass healing work, feeds the soul. Healing ministry is then a most important means of communication, for it ministers to the whole person – body, soul, mind and spirit.

* See also the Meditations on The Healing Way, October 1-16.
** This passage is also quoted in the Meditation for August 23.

Back to the Roots

Jesus was a nonconformist (with a small 'n'). He did not speak and act as the kind of Messiah his contemporaries expected. He would not accept as binding legalistic interpretations of ecclesiastical rules and regulations. He was criticised for eating with "publicans and sinners". To engage a female stranger in conversation gave him no difficulty but – especially when the woman was a Samaritan – it puzzled his friends, the disciples. There were many factors involved in the process that led to his crucifixion, but included among them was his unacceptable nonconformity.

The attitude of Jesus to life and people led him into radical action. His radicalism was not however destructive of the law, something of which his detractors constantly accused him. He was in fact "going back to the roots" (which 'radical' means) and interpreting the spirit of the law. The meaning of "Sabbath observance" was an example of such an issue between Jesus and his critics. The way in which the scribes and Pharisees expressed the law was not only legalistic and inflexible. It damaged people. Jesus had therefore to go to the "root" understanding of the meaning of the Sabbath. "It was made for man's benefit," he told them in effect. "What you are doing is making the needs of man subservient to an institution, the Sabbath."

Where institutions, however worthy, however sacred, are made more important than people then religion, like the law, is demeaned rather than honoured.

The attitude and stance which Jesus took on such issues was based on his perception of the divine intention. Precisely because his insights were so clear, because he knew the will of the Father for his people, he never shirked the need to take a stand. His whole life and all his attitudes were determined by his obedience. There was only one thing to which he conformed and that was God's will. That obedience forced him so often to be nonconformist.

The disciple must be as the master who never flinched from the way of the cross, and who refused to conform to human expectations and attitudes in order to escape his inevitable death. It seems, from Acts (chapter 4), that the apostles learnt the lesson and made Jesus' attitude their own. Ordered by the magistrates not to speak in the name of Jesus they, too, had to become nonconformists. "We must obey God rather than men," they said. And did.

A SPIRITUAL BLAZE

God demands social justice and spiritual integrity. That theme is proclaimed through the Old Testament prophet, Micah, emphasised in the letter of James in the New Testament, and declared, both in Deuteronomy and by Jesus, to be the greatest commandment of all: namely that we must love God with heart, soul, mind and strength, and our neighbour as ourself.

Micah's words on this theme are memorable. God has a case against Israel. Despite the wonder of their deliverance, they were failing in righteousness. But their ultimate salvation depended not on any sacrificial rigmarole designed to placate God, be it thousands of lambs, 10,000 rivers of oil, or even the offering of one's firstborn. God asks not for the gift – but for the givers. Righteousness is expressed in doing justly, loving mercy and walking humbly with God.

James too speaks strongly on social responsibility. True religion, he says, consists of looking after widows and orphans *and* "keeping oneself from being polluted by the world"; in other words, social service and personal holiness. That is in fact summed up in the Bible's golden rule about the primacy of love.

The demand for social justice and spiritual integrity is relevant today. To do justly, love mercy and respect God are the bases of a healthy society. There are, however, allegations and accusations that threaten the foundations of public life. Political leaders rightly affirm their intention to banish "sleaze", but public unease will develop into cynicism unless doing justly is seen not as a theory, but as a reality. If confidence in social justice is to be re-established, injustice and deceit must be tackled now. Justice, as Benjamin Disraeli commented, is "truth in action".

The obligation to act mercifully is not in conflict with the need for justice. John Milton, like Micah, believes in tempering justice with mercy. This will prevent legalism. Compassion, caring, understanding and support depend on the element of mercy. There are deprived sections of society, the genuinely poor, the shockingly underpaid, the waiting ill, who will only believe in mercy when they experience it, and in compassion when they feel it.

Social justice and compassion by themselves fall short of constituting "true religion". The call to spiritual awareness must also be taken seriously. "If the world has not approached its end," writes Alexander Solzhenitsyn, "it has reached a major watershed in history ... It will demand from us a spiritual blaze; we shall have to rise to a new height of vision, a new kind of life." We need, indeed, a spiritual blaze!

Governments and oppositions can be pressed to do justly and love mercy, but can they be asked to walk humbly with God? Perhaps not – but individuals can. Democracy will become a different place through the influence of ordinary people demonstrating spiritual blaze.

It is the responsibility of the church to proclaim that message to the world, but it is bound by the same demand. We must always be seen to do justly, to love mercy and, however difficult it might be, to walk humbly with our God.

THE NEW CREATION

The disciples whose names are most familiar to many are, ironically, best known for their failures. Everyone is aware of Judas Iscariot and his betrayal of Jesus, as most would know Peter's denial of him. Thomas is associated with doubt, while James and his brother John publicly requested the most prestigious places when Jesus would come in his kingdom. The answer to this arrogance was, "You know not what you ask."

Peter, a great human being, had of course his successes too. So impressed was Jesus with Peter's confession of faith at Caesarea Philippi, that he said he would build his church on it; while Peter's spirit was willing, however, his flesh was weak. In the hour of crisis, Peter's instinct for self-preservation took over and the three-fold denial, foretold by Jesus, must have hurt. It is wounding to be publicly denied by those who love you. Peter knew that too. He wept bitterly.

Judas remains "one of the most enigmatic figures of the New Testament", wrote Professor Thomas Kepler. It seems unlikely that his motivation was money, more that it was some aspect of power. Trusted as treasurer of the group, and part of the intimate circle, he possibly had the opportunity to force Jesus' hand in the national interest or perhaps to betray him for his refusal to denounce their Roman overlords. That Judas did not foresee the result of his actions led him to remorse and suicide.

Thomas's doubt is to his credit, not discredit. A pragmatic man, he was also patently honest. If his disbelief was a failing, Jesus did not criticise him for it, but he did commend those who believed in his resurrection without visible proof.

James and John, asking Jesus to do for them whatever they wanted and looking for prime places in the pecking order of the kingdom, demonstrated a total failure to understand their Master's aims. They provide a cautionary tale. Neither length of service nor progress on the ecclesiastical ladder guarantees an understanding of "the things that are eternal".

From this analysis of failure, destructive themes emerge – greed, power, selfishness, arrogance, lack of faith. But the weakness of these disciples is our weakness today, individually and corporately. We too seem bent on destruction. The power-seekers choose war to gain territory. Speculators and financial entrepreneurs profit at the expense of ordinary people. Those who insist on further nuclear tests endanger the earth (as, for example, Jacques Cousteau, the distinguished marine expert, has made clear), even when experts say there is no military or scientific reason to have them. The loveliness of sea and land is defiled by oil pollution and the supposed needs of travel and speed. Newspaper magnates glorify the trivial and peddle the pornography which often masquerades as education. What deprivation and degradation are the result of the destructive instincts of human beings! Yet men and women were intended not to destroy but to share in creation.

"In the beginning God created the heavens and the earth" and God has never ceased to create, as miracles, signs and wonders show. To be co-operators with God in creativity is the divine purpose. Humanity working together with God in a relationship of love is the only sure way to the new creation.

GOD OF SURPRISES

It is almost impossible to take in the sheer scale of a catastrophic earthquake, so many thousands killed in such a short time, masses of people injured, the extent of the destruction, the many made homeless. Press photographs, painting in frightening colours the furious fires, present a picture that can only be described as sheer hell. On the scale of human suffering, this kind of natural disaster – added to, sometimes, by human failure – must rank high indeed.

There is an article in the Apostles' Creed which proclaims that Jesus "descended into hell". It is one that is not easy to understand or interpret. The scriptural references to the descent are in Peter's first letter where Jesus is described as "preaching to the spirits in prison", and then in Paul's letter to the Ephesians where, in a parenthesis, he comments on a verse from the Psalmist. These do not of themselves explain or clarify the credal statement. We are therefore left to interpret its meaning in terms of our understanding of the whole gospel.

That phrase speaks to me of the completeness of Christ's self-offering on the cross and in the resurrection. The divine love reaches down to and embraces every level of human experience, however awful. It becomes a great and glorious concept, perhaps pointing to Christ's ministering to those who died before his redeeming work was done, but certainly expressing the comprehensiveness of his saving acts. Paul puts the full impact of that belief into triumphant words: "Nothing shall be able to separate us from the love of God in Christ Jesus our Lord." Human beings never find themselves out of the reach of "love divine, all loves excelling".

John Greenleaf Whittier expresses that conviction superbly in well-known words:
> I know not what the future hath of marvel or surprise,
> Assured alone that, life or death, His mercy underlies.
> I know not where His islands lift their fronded palms to air;
> I only know I cannot drift beyond His love and care.

If this, the totality of divine love, is real then somewhere in the hell of an earthquake, God is reaching out to people in their dereliction.

Can such a claim be true? Can God really be present in such desolation? It is perhaps one of the divine surprises of faith that it is in "man's extremity" that God finds greatest opportunity.

"Surely the Lord is in this place and I knew it not." It was a surprised Jacob who said this in Bethel as he experienced the assurance of God's continuing presence. There, precisely where he was, the ladder, with angels descending to him and ascending to God, spoke to him of the One who keeps faith. "I will not leave you until I have done all I promised." There is no hesitation or reservation in that commitment.

Life brings its share of hell to many, possibly at some time to all. It is part of faith to believe in the God who is always there … sometimes to our great surprise.

A THEOLOGY FOR TODAY

"There is not and cannot be a *new* theology. There can only be a re-occupying of positions which had once been taken up and subsequently abandoned or forgotten." It was Alan Richardson, theologian and writer, who made that comment when he was referring to J R Campbell, minister early in this century at London's City Temple. Campbell was very much the focus of new ideas at the time and, in fact in 1907, wrote a book entitled *The New Theology*. The phrase has been used too of more recent endeavours to work out a relevant contemporary theology as the search goes on for ways to "conceptualise" God.

Today's preachers can find themselves facing a practical problem of communication, one which arises from the different ways in which people think of God. In any typical congregation there will be many, probably the majority, who are at ease with traditional descriptions of God such as "the Almighty" or "the Father" and with the familial language related to that latter concept. They are happy to express their faith, prayers and doctrinal beliefs in a vocabulary drawn from scripture, and often from words used by Jesus himself. Any threat to that loved and revered language will be resisted.

Congregations today, in my experience, also include those who feel that traditional concepts of God are irrelevant or limiting. Intellectually unacceptable, they are a barrier to faith. Having come of theological age and anxious to "put away childish things", they set them aside as unhelpful images drawn from the regal and military models that are exclusively male. They deeply desire concepts and images that are "meaningful" to them, that do not intellectually offend them and that are wider and therefore more embracing than they feel traditional terms to be. Perhaps to think of God as, in Paul Tillich's phrase, "the ground of our being" is much more comfortable for them with its emphasis on immanence rather than on the transcendent God "out there". Others have moved on from that phrase to newer models and images.

When the preacher proclaims the Word, he or she stands not in a theoretical or academic context but in a pastoral one. Be the worshippers traditional or radical Christians, all have much in common. Whatever intellectual differences and difficulties are represented among them, all believe in God, all bring some kind of faith, all are seeking the religious life in some form, all are sinners and *all need grace*. The offer of a right relationship with God, made possible by Jesus and sustained by the Holy Spirit, is there for all. The preacher's task is not to wallow in theological intricacies but to meet spiritual needs, personal and corporate.

"God cannot be expressed, only addressed," wrote Martin Buber in his seminal book, *I and Thou*. Wherever we are intellectually or devotionally, we all surely say in our need "Abba, Father." Faith is ultimately a relationship, however we try to explain it, with a personal God whose nature is love. This remains a theology for today.

PEOPLE MATTER

The life of Jesus demonstrated how to deal with people. At the heart of the gospel there lies a profound concern for human beings "made in the image of God". With sensitivity and understanding, Jesus acted out the essence of the message that he brought, namely that "God is love". He therefore made it clear that people matter.

The New Testament offers, in Christ, the opportunity for the restoration of a right relationship with God. If, deep in the divine heart, there is a yearning for relationship with created beings, it clearly means that people are of infinite importance in the economy of God.

When Paul wrote to the Philippians, he presented Jesus as our model. You must have "the mind of Jesus", he said. He was thinking primarily of the exemplary humility of Christ, but certainly in Professor William Barclay's translation of the New Testament, the advice seems to be widened. He says: "Try to have the same attitude to life that Jesus had." It is Jesus' attitude to life, to human situations and, especially to people that occupies our attention this month. He had a unique ability to be at ease with the rich and the poor, the intellectual and the uneducated, male and female, Jew and Samaritan. He brought to people sympathy and empathy, understanding and encouragement, appropriate words and gestures. As he himself said, he "knew what was in man" ... and woman, and child ... and he showed that he did.

It was therefore the sheer quality of his attitudes to life and people that enabled Jesus to offer comfort or criticism, to relate intimately or to know when to keep at a distance;* to challenge people to discipleship or to respect the decision of those who could not face his demands. As we look at these incidents we shall see how Jesus showed, by his attitudes, the unique importance of every individual, that indeed people matter.

In a world utterly overwhelmed by mass suffering on an unbelievable scale, it is important that we feel again the gospel emphasis on the value of each and every human being. It is after all (says Jesus) "not the will of your Father in heaven that *one* of these little ones should perish". Everybody matters.

* See the Meditation for May 24 for earlier comment on this point.

BE SENSITIVE!

So sensitive was Jesus to the suffering of people that he was constantly "moved to compassion". His was a loving concern for people in need. He expressed that concern in miracles of healing. It was, for example, his awareness of the inner turmoil in Zacchaeus that brought about the healing relationship that transformed the despised tax-gatherer. It was with similar perception that he used his encounters with Nicodemus* and "a woman of Samaria" as evangelical opportunities. Jesus showed these two people the deep needs they had, but of which they were unaware. Sensitivity and compassion were essential elements in the attitude to life and people that Jesus had.

Nicodemus visited Jesus secretly, "by night". That a Pharisee, "a master of Israel", should do something so risky testifies to the sincerity of his search for truth. The meeting with the woman of Samaria came about when Jesus was on his way back to Galilee. Going through Samaria, he stopped at a well to rest. The woman arrived to draw water, totally unaware that she was about to be involved in deeply spiritual conversation. These two incidents are recorded in John's Gospel, significantly close to each other in chapters 3 and 4. In each case the conversation seems, at first sight, to represent a failure in communication. To Jesus' statement about the necessity of being spiritually "born again", Nicodemus responds with a question about the possibility of *physical* re-birth. "Can one enter a second time into one's mother's womb and be born?" he asks. Jesus talks to the woman of Samaria about the "living water" which he offers. Her response is to raise the practical problem of drawing water from a deep well without proper equipment. Jesus leads both these conversations into deeply spiritual areas, declaring the essence of the gospel to Nicodemus and defining the meaning of true worship to the Samaritan woman.

The results of these exercises in evangelism are striking. That same Nicodemus was with Joseph of Arimathea when he asked to be given the body of Jesus after his crucifixion in order to tend it with care. It was the woman of Samaria who testified to her own people: "Is not this the Christ?" It is important that all who are involved in evangelical endeavour today reflect the sensitivity and compassion which Jesus showed to those whom he sought to lead towards the truth.

* See also Meditation Listen to the Wind dated April 24.

LOVE'S EXTRAVAGANCE

Jesus, probably to our great surprise and certainly that of the disciples who witnessed the event, once commended sheer extravagance! It is worth reflecting on that act of love, both graciously received and highly commended, an example of love's proper extravagance.

The story is well known. It is told, with differing details, in several Gospels, but the essence of the occasion is agreed by all. While Jesus was dining, a woman anointed his feet with a very "costly" and "precious" ointment and wiped them with her hair. It was the sincerity of that loving act that moved Jesus to say, in answer to "indignant" comments from the disciples about waste, that this story of extravagant love would be retold wherever the gospel was preached. That indicates Jesus' valuation of the gesture.

The word "extravagance" comes from two Latin words meaning to "wander beyond" the limits of the normal and the expected. It then takes on pejorative connotations – excess, immoderation, unnecessary lavishness and even (the disciples' word) waste. "Why was this ointment not sold for three hundred pence and given to the poor?" asks Judas Iscariot. Jesus did not question the need to minister to the poor; the gospel is concerned with the weak, whatever the reasons for their weakness. But poverty, he comments, is a perpetual problem. There will always be the need – and the opportunity to deal with it. What the woman had done was so special as to be unique, and that needed to be realised. The woman herself could not possibly see the gesture in the symbolic way that Jesus did – as a reference to his death and burial; for her, it was an offering of grateful love to someone she admired. Those with much to be forgiven (maybe she was in that category) want to give much. There is a time for love to be extravagant.

When, in Stainer's *Crucifixion*, the moving words "God so loved the world" are proclaimed, there is a notable emphasis on the word *so*, for it is the word that puts on record that God went "beyond the bounds" to ensure that "whosoever believeth in him should not perish but have everlasting life". It is that little word *so* which dramatically emphasises the extravagance of the divine love, forgiveness and compassion.

"Jesus, thy boundless love to me no thought can reach, no tongue declare." So runs John Wesley's translation of Gerhardt's hymn. The only response can be unconditional love to God and "our neighbour". But there are those who may feel that they have, in personal relationships, loved too much. The result has been rejection, betrayal, denial, pain. But can we ever love too much? Love such as this woman gave to Jesus is *never* wasted.

To love and not to count the cost can be a permissible and proper extravagance. It has its roots in the Incarnation which is indeed the extravagance of God.

CARING CONCERN

The capacity of Jesus to empathise with people in need was remarkable. It did not matter who they were or from what background they came. The common people heard him gladly, but so did an educated intellectual mind like Nicodemus. A blind beggar could cry from the roadside and be heard. The Syro-Phoenician woman, symbolically scrambling for the crumbs falling from the table of the privileged, could compel his interest and earn his commendation. He was equally at ease with a loathed tax-gatherer like Zacchaeus and an unknown woman of Samaria. His was indeed the divine empathy that characterised the attitude to life and people which Jesus had.

There was similarly the woman who, suffering from a long-standing haemorrhage, sought to "touch the hem of his garment", knowing that even that limited contact would heal her. It did, but not before Jesus had made sure he knew who had touched him. Healing is not magic. It takes place within a relationship. Jesus had to know her in order to heal her. In doing so, he did a significantly important thing. He showed she mattered. She had value.

The ability of Jesus to make people feel important was one of his outstanding contributions to caring ministry. So often then, and even more so now, too many people regard themselves as of no value, despising, rejecting and condemning themselves. The only way to a breakthrough with them is an act of love. It was, even more than his words, the loving *acts* of Jesus that showed his empathy. He understood and shared pain as he does the individual and corporate hells of people today. For, after all, he suffered the inner torment of Gethsemane and the physical agony of Calvary.

God does not send suffering. He sits "where we sit" whenever and wherever we suffer. He is the God who shares our pain – be it physical pain, the emotional pain of rejection, the spiritual pain of persistent failure, the hurt of redundancy and unemployment. God is not present in pious platitudes about "growing through suffering" (though people do). He is simply there, offering the divine empathy with human agony, individual or on the massive scale of modern times. This caring, loving concern is the attitude to life and people that Jesus had.

MITES, NOT MILLIONS

How difficult it is, in an economically ruthless world, to avoid becoming ruthless in order to survive. Greed is an infectious disease and desperately difficult to resist, even by religious people. The national lottery is breeding a new generation of millionaires, funded by ordinary and sometimes poor people, while a £15 million footballer earns £6 every second that he is on the pitch. Yet nurses and similar professions plead in vain for proper financial recognition, patients suffer because funds cannot be found for special treatments, unbelievably low wages are paid in some sectors of society and urgent research into cancer is limited by lack of funds. It really is time to turn away from the "temporal" purpose of making a million (and the kind of pay-offs and hand-outs that help some to do it) and rather reflect on the "eternal" importance of the widow's mite.

Let me offer a parable to help recover perspective and priorities, matters on which the New Testament has major things to say. It is a true story that I was told over 50 years ago. How I wish I could remember where this church is!

When the decision was taken to build a new church, everyone in the congregation, including the children, was asked to give sacrificially to help raise the funds needed. On a certain Sunday the children handed in their gifts, but one little boy looked very unhappy. "My father is always ill and never works," he told his teacher, "so I don't get a Saturday penny, or anything." Told not to worry, he nevertheless did so, and the following Sunday he handed in a spinning top and five marbles. "It's all I've got," he said, "but you can have it to help build the church."

When the teacher told the Sunday School Superintendent about the top and the marbles, he was so moved that he gave ten shillings in the boy's name. The minister was equally moved and increased the ten shillings into a larger gift.

An office-bearer called at the manse that week, was shown into the study, and saw the top and marbles on the desk. Overcome by curiosity, he asked how they came to be there. The minister gladly told him of the sacrificial gift the little boy had made. The office-bearer looked uncomfortable. "I have already given a large gift to help build the church," he said, "but you know I am wealthy and my gift has cost me very little. I will now, anonymously, give another £500 – on one condition: that when the church is built, this top and these marbles will be put on display so that when visitors come to our church they will see them and ask the question I asked you. Then they will be told of the little boy who brought his gift at a cost and, like me, they will learn the meaning of 'sacrificial giving'."

When "small is beautiful" once more, and sacrificial giving is truly valued, we shall feel that balance has come into the world again. Our perspective might be healthier and our priorities more sound if we concentrated less on millions and more on mites, less on gain and more on giving.

THE PRIMARY TASK

Jesus, as a Jew, found it natural to refer to, draw on and interpret "the Law and the Prophets". It is therefore not surprising that he found in the Old Testament a clear definition of his life's purpose.

It happened when he went into the synagogue in Nazareth. Rising to read from the scroll so that he might deliver the portion for the day, he found Isaiah's words staring him in the face. He had no doubt of their significance for him: "The Spirit of the Lord is upon me, because he hath sent me to heal the broken-hearted, to preach deliverance to the captives, and recovering of sight to the blind, to set at liberty them that are bruised, to preach the acceptable year of the Lord."

Jesus then sat down and said dramatically: "That scripture is fulfilled today." If the church is called to be, in a telling phrase (although not everyone feels theologically comfortable with it) an "extension of the Incarnation", there is no question as to what it has to do. There are three functions that Jesus saw as the prime reasons for his mission. He offered the world a preaching ministry, a pastoral ministry (healing the broken-hearted) and a healing ministry (recovery of sight to the blind).

The church must offer those same gifts to the world. In whatever other areas it is called to witness – politics, social service, public issues, pastoral psychology, industry, economics, ecology (for religion is concerned with the whole of life) – its primary responsibilities are crystal clear, namely to preach and teach a faith: to sustain and develop the spiritual life; to offer pastoral care to all; to exercise a ministry of healing and reconciliation to individuals and to society. The church is weakest when it forgets or sets aside the priorities of its Lord. The church is at its most dynamic when it applies his principles and reflects his practice.

It is fashionable to dismiss the church as irrelevant and ineffective, its clergy as answering questions no one is asking. The reality is different. What have I or any of its ministers, had to do over decades but engage with the facts of life – death and dying, depression and desolation, trauma and tribulation, pain and agony? All of these I have encountered today even as I write these words. To minister to people with understanding and empathy; to meet their deepest needs; to present to them, with sensitivity and strength, abiding truths; what can possibly be more relevant than this?

"Brother, Sister, let me serve you," wrote hymn-writer Richard Gillman, "let me be as Christ to you." That means being with people where they are. "I will weep when you are weeping, when you laugh, I'll laugh with you." Here surely is the truth of the Incarnation. Jesus is "God with us."

If the church properly represents Christ to the world, how can it possibly be irrelevant?

LOST AND FOUND

The death of a loved one can lead to despair, the death of a child to dereliction, but there are other forms of loss and they too can bring desolation: a breakdown in a loving relationship, the unhappiness of separation or divorce, the loss of a home through repossession, losing personal items in a burglary. Loss and pain inevitably go together.

One of the most moving cries of dereliction in the Bible surely comes from Mary Magdalene, gazing at the empty tomb. It is a heart-broken "They have taken away my Lord and I know not where they have laid him." To read that cry of desolation is to feel her grievous pain. It was the loss of the physical presence of one who had meant to so much to her that compelled her expression of desperation, but her cry can become the cry of any one of us, as the late Bishop George Appleton put it, dramatically, in a prayer he offered:

> O Christ, my Lord, again and again have I said with Mary Magdalene:
> "They have taken away my Lord and I know not where they have laid him."
> I have been desolate and alone.

Fortunate are those who never lost the sense of the transforming union which is at the heart of faith. Many there are, however, who have known that loss and been made desolate by it.

J B Phillips, describing the "darknesses and depressions" he knew so well in later life, felt that a key factor in their affecting him was the acceptance of "hundreds of demands made on my time which were out of all proportion to my real strength". Others may link their lost spirituality to their inability to overcome the "false self" formed in early years, and later to be the source of, in religious terms, temptation. Some too may feel that the rampant materialism and secularism so typical of life today is responsible for the development of a spiritual aridity that makes the pursuit of (as Jesus called them) the "other things" a priority rather than "seeking first the kingdom".

In our church life we may, like Martha, be "careful and troubled about many things" – meetings, organisations, activities – and obliterate attention to that "better part" to which Mary attended and which Jesus commended. Over-concentration on the correctness of liturgy or the intricacies of theology, both valuable disciplines, can obscure for some the essential simplicity of the gospel and hide the Jesus who is present in true worship. The genuine desire for contemporary ways of "conceptualising" God and the search for appropriate images in place of traditional but irrelevant ones can, as a by-product, create confusion for those with a simple faith. "Where is Jesus now?" they cry.

There is no need, however, for loss of hope. "I am desolate and alone," prayed Bishop Appleton, who then added triumphantly: "But you have found me again!" It is not on our grasp of God that the transforming union depends, but on God's grasp of us. The prodigal son found in a waiting, welcoming father the assurance that the relationship he thought he had lost was still there, strengthened through his desolation.

URGENT PERSUASION

There is a verse in Luke's Gospel that appears to authorise force to bring about religious commitment. St Augustine was one, and there were many others, who used it in this way. The reference is, of course, to the words spoken by a "certain man" in Jesus' parable about the great feast: "Compel them to come in."

The host, having received many apologies for declining his invitations to supper, asked his servant to ensure that every place at his table was occupied. A foray into the city streets and lanes was only partially successful although it produced a number of guests, some physically handicapped. The host, furious, sent his servant to search the highways and hedges outside the city to provide yet more guests. It was then that the crucial words were spoken: "Compel them to come in," he said (Luke chapter 14, verse 23).

I checked fifteen commentaries on the use of the word "compel". All were unanimous that it did not imply physical force. The translators confirmed this. Synonyms like "urge", "make", "strongly encourage", etc, were employed. The concept is much more that of (as one commentator summed it up) "urgent persuasion".

There are highly relevant contemporary issues relating to evangelistic methodology in those words. Response to the gospel is, of course, a matter of urgency. But are there boundaries which one has no right to cross in "evangelising" another person? Are there limits to what is acceptable in urgent persuasion?

Diversity is of the Spirit, Paul told the Corinthians. Every permissible form of communication must be used to meet the varied needs, temperaments, age-groupings and cultures of today. The gospel must be proclaimed and spirituality must be expressed in ways appropriate to contemporary youth culture. The challenge is to find the limits to what is acceptable.

Jesus, in his encounter with the rich young ruler, offers us a model for evangelistic endeavour, implicitly indicating the limits in persuasion permissible. He presented unequivocally to the rich young ruler the implications of a commitment to discipleship, but made no effort to force him to a decision. He loved him – and let him go.

The church must not be seduced by the need to attract thousands as some religious enterprises are. Recognising that small can be beautiful, that the glory of the Old Testament was not mass obedience but the reliability and faithfulness of the remnant, that Jesus set out to build the Kingdom of God with but twelve disciples (including one seriously flawed and others who were weak), it must adhere to its responsibility to present to the world a way of life grounded in Jesus Christ, to "preach the gospel", that is make known the offer of that gospel and leave the response to those challenged by it. What is also clear is that a caring, loving life, so grounded, may still be the most effective influence of all.

THE RISKS OF GIVING

Jesus left his followers with severe problems! Take, for example, the obligation to respond to human need. John deals in depth with this theme in his first epistle. "If a man has enough to live on and yet when he sees his brother [or sister] in need shuts up his heart against them, how can it be said that the divine love dwells in him?" (1 John 3:17), *New English Bible*. The logic of that cannot be gainsaid. "If God so loved us, we ought also to love one another."

Jesus' exhortations on compassionate response to another's needs are in the Sermon on the Mount. They are concise and specific. "Give to him [or her] that asketh thee and from him [or her] that would borrow of thee, turn thou not away." That statement, moreover, is made in proximity to his exposition of the principle of the "second mile". Compassion is expressed in a doubled generosity in response to pleas. But how do we apply these instructions, given in a simpler world, in our modern, complicated situations?

When I visited St Stephen's Cathedral in Vienna, I read among the rules applying to attitude, attire and behaviour "in this place of worship", a specific further injunction. It ran: "Do not give alms to professional beggars." That is indeed the rub – as was confirmed a few days earlier in a hotel in Budapest when an Irish teacher commented on this very problem. "I saw a man in Dublin with a poster round his neck," she said. "It proclaimed: 'I am hungry and homeless.' But I *knew* the bloke! He lives near me, in a normal house!"

The sense of helplessness over response to need can be very real. Yet moved to compassion we still must be – by the old Hungarian peasant, crouched on the pavement, outside the church in Pest; by the 11-year-old boy on crutches, waving his begging-tin before all the passengers on the Metro in Buda; by (although we have been officially warned) the young woman with the baby on the London Underground. Yet how difficult it is to turn away from such misery. And, in the corporate field, the appeals, three a day on average, roll in – Rwanda, Bosnia, multiple sclerosis, cancer, and so on. All are overwhelmingly urgent needs, but our capacity for practical compassion is so severely limited.

There is, at the heart of our faith, a belief in the infinite value of every human being, made in the image of God. That some turn out to be frauds is no reason to close down the innate compassion of the loving heart. The risks of giving are an integral part of the risks of loving – and there are many. It may be that, in the naïveté and innocence of our reaction, we become "fools for Christ's sake", but we dare not "shut up our hearts" against those in need.

There is a parable – about sheep and goats – which spells out the dangers of ignoring the needs of "one of the least of these", our brothers and sisters in Christ.

PASTORAL DILEMMA

When I read commentators who say, as William Barclay does, that "the best and most ancient (New Testament) manuscripts do not contain this story", I feel profoundly disappointed. In it Jesus speaks with his authority on one of the great dilemmas of today. How should religious people make judgements about the behaviour of others? The priest and pastor constantly face this problem. Is it their responsibility to condemn – on biblical, theological or ethical grounds – certain behaviour within personal relationships, or should they consider the issues in terms of "situation ethics"? The latter is, as David Edwards has written, "making a judgement that the right solution to any moral problem depends much more on the situation itself than on any moral code." And, he adds, "the key to the solution is always love." Contemporary attitudes are so often expressed either as sharply defined negative judgements or else in terms of Alan Richardson's definition: "The rightness of an action is to be judged in relation to the situation in which it takes place rather than with reference to laws or universally binding rules."

Issues at the heart of this tension include marriage, divorce, homosexuality, relationship situations of a triangular kind, living together, etc. Good people who feel bound by law can go through agony when they feel blessed by a love that is officially unacceptable. Pastors too can feel the pain of those who face them, struggling with the hurt of loving too much but bound by rules.

The story to which I referred is, of course, that of the woman taken in adultery in John's Gospel (chapter 7, verse 53 to chapter 8, verse 11) Its "ring of truth" feels so authentically "Jesus" that, as some commentators allow, it surely has (despite the technical textual difficulties) some foundation in fact.

The importance of the story lies in its demonstration of Jesus' attitude to human problems. Firstly, he rightly denounces, in the most subtle of ways, the judgementalism that forgets that no one is qualified by their own righteousness to condemn others. Secondly, he acts out the great statement that God "did not send his Son into the world to condemn the world but that the world through him might be saved." "Neither do I condemn you," he tells the woman. Thirdly, he says "Go and sin no more." That phrase is the answer to those who fear he has opened the door to moral licence and ethical irresponsibility.

Combining the need to give spiritual direction, with the obligation to love and accept the sinner while hating the sin, can create a traumatic tension for all who deal with personal problems. Always in the pastoral heart must be the awareness that "there but for the grace of God, go I."

Be the story technically dubious as some specialists suggest, or authentically Jesus as I sincerely feel, it is one that we should carry in both heart and mind when we attempt to deal creatively with human failure.

THE GOODNESS OF GOD

There is no doubt as to what the essence of the church is and what its priorities are. It is not primarily a building, an organisation or an institution – concepts with which it is legitimately associated in the public mind. It is "the people of God" through whom the Good News of the gospel is to be made known, and the "body of Christ" demonstrating the meaning of living, loving fellowship. It is moreover a servant people, committed to serve the world in love and without thought of return.

This statement of purpose is wholly founded on Jesus himself. He made clear what he had come to do, that is "proclaim the acceptable year of the Lord"; in more modern language that is to announce the nature and purpose of God towards people. The proclamation of the gospel is therefore committed to the church's hands. Ministry has as its chief aim making the goodness of God known through the exposition of the Word. The first task of the church today is to ensure that that obligation – to publicise the goodness of God – is at the centre of the church's life.

The second purpose of the church is pastoral responsibility. It is (Jesus said) to heal the broken-hearted, to comfort those who mourn, to send away in freedom those who are broken by life (William Barclay's translation of "to bring release to the captives"). The essence of the ministry is the fulfilling of the shepherd role so beloved as an image in the Old Testament and in Jesus himself. Just as it was the feeling that the church was not offering an adequate healing ministry that led to a proliferation of healing organisations in the early and mid-twentieth century, so it was a widespread perception that the church's pastoral ministry fell short of the standards of quality and specialism that led to the growth of counselling organisations in the last 40 years in this country. Theoretically, at least within the church, they should not be needed. The church is the specialist body in pastoral care because such ministry is fundamental to its very being.

It may be that the church's loss of influence and the misunderstandings that arise over ministry have arisen from a fundamental failure by "the people of God" to demonstrate to the world how clear its purpose is. The things at which the church by definition should be good are the power of the spoken word and the depth of its pastoral care. There are many marginal fields, serious and leisure, which are part of the church's life, but the church is nothing (and its ministry irrelevant) if it fails to declare God's will and demonstrate divine love in ministering to people. And it must always remember that it succeeds in these two primary aspects of ministry only through the presence and power of the Holy Spirit, for as Jesus himself said in declaring his purpose, "The Spirit of the Lord is upon me."

WITH RESPECT

"The heavens declare the glory of God and the firmament sheweth his handywork," exclaims the author of an Old Testament psalm. We all surely share a sense of wonder when we ponder creation, the grandeur of God. Yet that which was made so good is so spoiled that Wordsworth can say with sadness (in *Intimations of Immortality*): "But yet I know, where'er I go, there hath passed a glory from the earth." The headlines of yesterday, of today and no doubt of tomorrow witness to that decline.

In religious terms, sin is to blame for the descent from grandeur to departed glory. Adam and Eve wanted to be "as gods". That attitude is expressed in cultural terms as a process of secularisation with its denial of the spiritual dimension and the assumption of power by human beings.

This decline brings about a lack of respect which characterises many contemporary attitudes, personal and corporate. Many disability organisations feel that current legislation benefits not the service-user but the service-provider, denying respect to people with disabilities. Trivial pension increases withhold respect from people, who have contributed, often notably, to the welfare of the community and nation. All respect for the sacred intimacies of relationships has been jettisoned by a society that disconnects sex and love and in which "anything goes". And, while recognising that it is the sin of the few, not the many, widespread paedophilia in current society demonstrates a total lack of respect for the "little ones" who must not be offended. All this adds up to an arrogance that changes the Psalmist's words from "What is man that thou art mindful of him?" to: "What is God that we should be mindful of him?" The process of secularisation leads, as Thomas Oden, the American theologian and psychotherapist claims*, to "the reduction of human existence to spiritless body, sexuality to depersonalised orgasm, sciences to amoral data-gathering and politics to the manipulation of power, systematically ignoring the human capacity for transcendence, moral reasoning and self-sacrificial love."

Worship is essentially reverential adoration, in other words respect for God. "The idea of the holy" is a mystery that has been recognised down the ages by prophets and priests, saints and sinners. We simply do not live by bread alone. The human mind is forever reaching out for the knowledge which is beyond knowledge. The human spirit yearns for the divine embrace expressed in a love that will not let us go. To lose all awareness of the great mystery, to lack the imagination and the intuition that can sense the presence of the eternal, to miss the signs and wonders of the Spirit is to lose that "good part" which Mary of Bethany chose to learn as she sat at Jesus' feet.

* Quoted in *The Risks of Freedom*, published by The Pastoral Care Foundation in the Philippines, 1993.

DIVERSITY OF GIFTS

"There are diversities of gifts, but the same Spirit is the source of all of them." The laying down of that principle by Paul in his letter to the Corinthian church about errors in its life spelt out for them the important relationship between unity and variety. On the core of the faith every member of the Christian community must unite. That core he sums up as the confession "Jesus is Lord." With such a base, there is room for all kinds of difference in the ways individuals express their beliefs in action, in the gifts that they have, in the ways that they serve. Temperaments vary. The extrovert personality can express itself in a heartiness that the reserved find impossible. The intellectual will philosophise about belief and be articulate in doing so in a way different from the "simple faith" of many believers. But one is not "right" and the other "wrong". It is only a matter of legitimate variation.

The kind of worship that brings benefit to people varies from one church member to another. For some, the dignity of the ordered liturgy of the *Book of Common Prayer* is essential; for others informal, unstructured worship ministers to their spiritual life. Others may want the moving silence of the Quakers. Some will feel their worship needs cannot be met without participation in the Mass. Such variations are not unhealthy. What is unhealthy is any dogmatic attitude that arrogantly proclaims any approach other than its own to be unacceptable. Difference is not a threat where the bases of faith are sound.

It is for similar reasons that different forms of renewal should be welcomed. Movements for liturgical renewal can have profound effects on the spiritual life of worshippers. Forms of charismatic renewal with a proper emphasis on the renewing power of the Spirit have brought new inspiration to some people. Evangelistic crusades and missions aimed at a clear, direct offering of the grace of the gospel, have brought many to a lifelong commitment to discipleship. Whatever is done "decently and in good order" to renew spiritual life is to be welcomed rather than criticised.

Billy Graham's visit to Glasgow in the sixties had its effect on my congregation in the East End of the city. That influence was expressed not in an influx of new Christians who had "gone forward" at the Kelvin Hall, for I cannot remember even one such addition. What I do recall is that the effect on the young people already in the church was profound. They were noticeably drawn to a much deeper level of faith by the experience of the crusade. That was one factor in my Youth Fellowship producing three ordained ministers, two deaconesses, one (as it was then called) missionary to Africa, and several long-serving elders in their various congregations.

"Come, Holy Spirit, come," we pray in expectation. That coming may be in diverse forms. It is not however, the means through which that coming is expressed that is important, but the end result, namely growth in grace.

WHY ME?

The best of texts can become clichés if used excessively, inappropriately or irrelevantly. That could even happen to such moving words as "Well done, good and faithful servant. Enter into the joy of your Lord." At the funeral service I had to conduct last week, I had however no hesitation in using these words to sum up the life of a relative who had died, full of years and with a magnificent record of service to the church, to people, to good causes. Committed to her marriage and her family, to the members of the various organisations she served, to those allocated to her for pastoral care, she seemed, as much if not more than most, to deserve that "Well done!" But alongside such a positive life, well worthy of the thanksgiving offered, there was a shadowed side, expressed in disappointments, losses and personal tragedies. She felt herself almost singled out for misfortune and she had every right to be bitter for the family losses she suffered were enormous (both her son and her daughter, in their forties, died within a year). But though never herself blaming God, she was entitled to ask "Why me?"

Much has been said of the "curse of the Kennedys" following the deaths in an air crash of John F Kennedy Jnr, his wife and sister-in-law.* The inference has been made that there are individuals and families who seem to be chosen to suffer disproportionately in life. But the question "Why us?" hovers in the background wherever those professing a religious faith suffer grievously.

"What I feared has come upon me," he cried. "What I dreaded has happened to me. I have no peace, no quietness, no rest, but only turmoil," but "No one said a word to Job because they saw how great his suffering was." The "blameless and upright" Job was, according to this Old Testament story, through a catalogue of disasters, being tested by God.

"All these things are against me." Again the despairing cry against "outrageous fortune" comes from the heart of Jacob as he bewails the loss of his sons Simeon and Reuben and the impending loss of Benjamin.

The stories differ but the underlying question is the same. There is a mystery in suffering which is beyond our understanding. Is there nothing but a combination of circumstances in the appalling things that happen to people? Is there a purpose involved – with the divine role under scrutiny but beyond comprehension? Can a loving God be present when bad things happen to good people? "Why me?"

The mystery remains. How the Kennedys cope with their tragic history time will tell. Of Job, it is written that "the Lord blessed the latter part (of his life) more than the first." Jacob's feared losses would in due time lead to the dawning future of Israel. My relative's conjunction of triumphant discipleship and tragic experience combined to create a living faith and a life of service. Suffering remains a mystery which usually defies logic, but sometimes develops maturity. It is those who suffer most who sense that it can be a means of grace.

* This Meditation was written in 1997.

MISSED OPPORTUNITY

It can happen in pastoral ministry that a need is expressed and a response is not offered. Subsequent sorrow and remorse inevitably follow. The first is the visit that, for reasons of pressure, time, commitments, etc, is not made. The second is where a letter is not sent.

A letter is a pastoral tool of great importance. Paul used it to notable effect, to expound his theology to the various churches he had founded, but also (as the latter part of most of his letters demonstrate) to convey pastoral concern about people. Down through literary history, the letter has been a means of making needs known and meeting them, expressing feelings that could not be spoken, giving and receiving love, strengthening and encouraging someone in distress. The prompting of the inner spirit to "write" needs to be heeded too, because failure to respond to it may create a missed opportunity.

It is a failure in that latter field that is the reason for encouraging others to write when the spirit moves them. For it may be in a real sense a call to a ministry which is pastoral at heart.

The moment of disturbing truth came when I was shown a newspaper tribute to Professor Iain Dea, the distinguished scientist who specialised in polysaccharide chemistry. Scientists world-wide paid tribute to his work and the benefits it has brought to people. His death announced a missed opportunity.

I had not seen Iain in 45 years, that is since he had been in my Sunday School in Juniper Green, Edinburgh, and a playmate of my children, but I remember his parents well. They both died in 1996, one in January and the other in July. Between his mother's and his father's death, both his parents-in-law died. At Christmas time that same year Iain became ill. In the last three years Iain's cancer developed and became terminal.

I mention this sequence not because it is a further graphic example of the mystery of suffering, but because I regret so much the missed opportunity I was given when I met Iain's aunt soon after his parents' deaths. She asked me to re-establish contact with Iain and in some way to minister to him in his bereavements. At the height of his career, happily married and in mid-life, there seemed to be time to develop the connection. In the mass of correspondence, the piles and files of papers so typical of studies, church offices and even many a home, that necessary letter was never given the pastoral priority it deserved.

The experience underlines the importance of the written word in the personal, pastoral ministry which everyone can offer. It emphasises the need to catch the sound of, and listen to, the voice within, as messages from the unconscious seek to bring the urgent priority of meeting some personal need to our conscious notice. Sensitivity to need involves sensitivity to time and the organisation of our priorities not in terms of choice, but of commitment.

UNKNOWN DISCIPLES

If you advise someone unfamiliar with the New Testament to read it from beginning to end, it may be helpful to suggest that they start not with Matthew's Gospel, but with Mark's. Not only is that one of the sources on which both Matthew and Luke drew but it will save the uninitiated from an immediate confrontation with Matthew's daunting list of names, linked together by repeated "begats". Those interested in Joseph's family tree, and indeed Israel's history, will however, find that genealogy valuable; early in my ministry I found it important for other reasons, and took my text for one Sunday morning from it. The particular phrase I selected is in verse three and reads: "And Phares begat Esrom."

I could, of course, have taken other people from that long list and made the same points for I knew nothing of Phares and Esrom but their names. Truth to tell, there is not much more to know. And that precisely is the point. *It is their anonymity which is important.* How contrary is this to the current emphasis on "cult" figures, "personalities" and "celebrities", who, in popular press circles, are deemed to be so newsworthy. It is a shallow, superficial world that so glamorises the trivial. Those who make the biggest contribution to the things that matter most, such as creative living and unselfish loving, are often anonymous. Christianity certainly, and other religions equally, have reason to be grateful for their good, unknown disciples.

In many of our Meditations, because of awful events, there has been constantly before us that most profound of problems, human suffering. Here I take a lighter theme which some feel to be of no great significance or theological importance. It is, however, neither simplistic nor superficial for it relates to the privilege of being used by God for long-term purposes, the end results of which we cannot ever know.

Phares and Esrom were essential links in the chain which stretches backwards to Abraham and forward to (as Matthew puts it) "Joseph, the husband of Mary of whom was born Jesus, who is called Christ". In other words, they were – although they could not know it this side of heaven – participants in the process that culminated in the Incarnation, a privilege, indeed.

Unknown disciples are unlikely to feature in the headlines. In the field of human suffering, however, they are the people who often minister to the devastated, the disturbed, the poor, the aged, the terminally ill, the battered, the bereaved, the broken-hearted. The pages of religious history are gloriously illuminated by the goodness of unknown disciples, whose characteristics are love and anonymity.

When Christians come together to celebrate Holy Communion, they will remember, as they must, the one who is the focal point of the sacrament: "This do in remembrance of me." Perhaps too they should not forget those unknown and unnamed people who, with love and care, laid the table and provided the bread and wine for the Last Supper, for they too shared anonymously in helping to make known the whole gospel to the whole world.

FAITH, HOPE AND LOVE

The image of that Chechen girl, shell-shocked and "a mask of blood and dust", as the *Daily Telegraph* caption describes her,* will haunt us for a long time to come. She stands beside the Grozny building battered by an enemy tank. Six adults are dead and many children have been injured. She is desolate. Sadly it is an image that could equally come from Bosnia or Israel as it has done from war-zones of the past – and will in the future. What hopelessness she portrays, incarnating as she does the desolation of war.

Loss of hope is always destructive. That is what makes unemployment a curse and redundancy a disaster. And if the *fact* of redundancy hurts, how devastating is the running *fear* of the loss of one's job. It endangers financial security, family confidence, and quality of life. Young people too, with hard-earned degrees and qualifications, fear for the future. Apparently undervalued by the community, they lack the opportunity to earn and lose self-respect in the process. So prevalent is this sense of hopelessness that it is eating into the very fabric of society, creating in the collective unconscious emotional dis-ease and anxiety. The public fear of the Chechen girl and the private worries of ordinary people, are making this indeed a fear-full generation.

Selective text quotation and stock religious language do little to minister to such despair, being perceived as naive, superficial and unacceptably pious. It is no doubt true, as John says in his first New Testament letter, that "perfect love casts out fear", but the potential transformation implicit in the text is incredibly difficult to achieve. It is even worse in corporate situations ... family, national and international. What reality does such a statement have, or is it felt to have, where power politics and force of arms are the determining factors? It is the problem all too familiar to "moral man in an immoral society". Religious responses can seem academic, doctrinaire, unreal and irrelevant.

Yet the responsibility on people of faith to bring light into a dark world persists. If spiritual realities exist as religious people believe they do – and this the more so when Christians proclaim the energy of the Holy Spirit – they have to be brought to bear on human situations. "More things are wrought by prayer that this world dreams of," wrote Tennyson. "After Jesus lived and died," said J H Oldham (in his *Devotional Diary*), "new and spiritual energy entered into the process of human life." The great verities remain: *faith*, a personal relationship with God, the power of positive *hope* and the permanency of divine *love*. "And the greatest of these is love." "Love is the sublimest conception available to man" (Oldham again). It is the healing energy for the world.

No text, however profound, can meet the desolation of the Chechen girl or still the anxiety of the frightened unemployed, but all who believe in the spiritual dimension of life must strive to proclaim the wonder of faith, the necessity of hope and the power of love. Within these glorious concepts there is surely some response to despair and desolation.

* This Meditation was written in 1997. For fuller development of the themes of faith, hope and love, see the August sequence on Cords of Love.

LAW AND LOVE

For a definition of anarchy – political, moral or religious – turn to the Old Testament book of Judges where we are told that "every man did that which was right in his own eyes." Without a king in Israel, there was no external authority. The result was idolatry and immorality. That definition, where morality and religion are concerned, is not wholly inappropriate today, as recent public and ecclesiastical events demonstrate. The failure of a few does not condemn all but, given the declining influence of religion and a widespread cynicism over politics, external authority is weak. When this happens "things fall apart; the centre cannot hold," says W B Yeats. "Mere anarchy is loosed upon the world ... The best lack all conviction, while the worst are full of passionate intensity."

The historian Arnold Toynbee has noted that disintegrating societies are seldom simply over-run by another civilisation. They tend to commit a kind of cultural suicide. They fall into antinomianism as a substitute for creativeness. People stop believing in morality and yield to their impulses. Toynbee speaks of a consequent promiscuity, not in the sexual sense but in the indiscriminate acceptance of anything and everything, what Gene Edward Veith calls "An unfocused eclecticism and uncritical tolerance."* Toynbee's words touch a nerve today for we are caught in a dilemma. If the church is to be relevant, it is essential that it understands the culture of the times, but to take it too seriously may well lead to a watering-down of the faith and to a syncretism that inhibits effective witness to the gospel. Where truth is relative, values become relative too. Many will feel that this has already come about, but the alternative often offered is authoritarian fundamentalism of various kinds. Edmund Burke's comment is worth recording: "Freedom, not servitude, is the cure for anarchy." It must, however, be freedom with respect for law.

"When the foundations are being destroyed, what can the righteous man do?" asks the Psalmist. It may be that we should look to the relationship between law and love. In both the unhappy case of a bishop with his personal problems, and a political upset years ago, there was manifested a widespread willingness to forgive the human weakness part of the problem. Anger displaced that because of the public lies in both cases. The foundation of "law", which lays down the rules of behaviour and forbids lying for example, is essential for, without that, society will slide into anarchy. Then there can come into play the law of love with its compassion and forgiveness.

"Remove not the ancient landmarks," the Good Book says. The time may well have come for society and the church to put traditional markers back into place, markers that have disappeared into the haze created by the proponents not of liberty but of licence. These landmarks established, there is an enormous place in our attitudes and behaviour for the authority of love, the love which (according to Paul) "never fails". It is never conditioned by self-interest, real or imagined.

* Quoted and discussed in *Guide to Contemporary Culture* by Gene Edward Veith (Crossway Books, 1994).

UNITY IN DIVERSITY

The story of the Tower of Babel in Genesis 11, like the primal sin of Adam and Eve, relates to human pride. "Let us build a city with a tower that reaches up to heaven," said "the children of men" with inflated egocentricity. The arrogance was too much.* "Let us go down and confuse their language," said the Lord, "so that they will not understand each other." Compulsory diversity and the enforced dispersion of the people is an intriguing punishment for arrogance.

If the babble of many tongues was God's punishment for false pride, there is a different reaction to many languages in another story. The report of events at the first Pentecost, when the promised descent of the Holy Spirit on to the disciples took place, brought a sense of amazement and bewilderment. "How is it each one of us hears (the disciples) speaking in his own language?" It was a miracle. God was being praised in many tongues. This is surely the unity in diversity of which Paul spoke to the Corinthians. "The body," he said, "is not one part but many ... You are the body of Christ and each one is part of it."

The principle of unity in diversity is an important one in many fields. It is certainly a lesson that has been learnt in the development of ecumenism. The church is not best served by a dull uniformity, but benefits most by a true unity expressed in diversity. Every branch of the church, by its historic witness, underlines some element of truth. We need a corpus of belief shared enthusiastically by all who have one Lord and share one faith, but where contributions from different traditions are received graciously.

The same principle holds good in personal discipleship. Different temperaments need different ways of expressing spirituality. There was no more varied a group than the twelve disciples. Except for one, they were united in loyalty though very different in their attitudes. There is no place in healthy religion for the dogmatism of those who claim that their understanding of the faith is the only right way. People who describe everything that does not agree with their own interpretation as mistaken or, sometimes, even satanic are wholly out of consonance with the image of the free-flowing Spirit expressed in diversities of gifts.

We make our God too small if we suggest unity is weakened by a proper diversity. Faith, like love, is a many-splendour'd thing.

* For a further allusion to arrogance see, in particular, the Meditation for March 1.

DIVINE PARADOX

It is to the credit of those responsible for the National Health Service that the need for spiritual care is recognised. The Patient's Charter lays it down that "provider units, including NHS Trusts" should "make every effort to provide for the needs of patients and staff ... both Christian and non-Christian." Such public acknowledgement of the spiritual dimension of life is an encouragement to all who believe that coping with suffering and pain demands inner resources. It is therefore a part of modern care to nourish the spirit and so help people cope with the trauma and tragedy that life brings, especially when dreadful things damage and destroy children.

The strongest statement Jesus made was on that very theme: "Whosoever shall offend one of these little ones that believe in me, it is better for him that a millstone were hanged round his neck and he were cast into the sea." If only those who load the gun, prime the bomb or contemplate sexual abuse would "hear" these words, human lives, human hearts, human hopes and human faith would not be shattered by moments of evil madness. The scribbled word "Why?", lying among the flowers at Dunblane, testifies to that desolation.

Has there ever been such evil in the world as there is today? The answer must be "No" in terms of quantity (or is it that mass communication brings every human tragedy into our homes?), but "Yes" in terms of degree. Human beings have always, and often with great cruelty, hurt and harmed other human beings. So far as children are concerned, nothing more monstrous was ever ordained than that royal decree whereby every infant boy under two years old should be slain. The massacre of innocent children by King Herod following the birth of Jesus, is an enormity too awful to contemplate, yet its taking place makes a crucial point for us all in our utter despair over human evil. It was to a world which could perpetrate such an event that Jesus came, to preach, to heal and to love. Moreover, when he who "went about doing good" was himself the victim (though totally innocent) of an outrageous act of wickedness on Calvary, he left his disciples in no doubt as to their duty. "Go ye into all the world," he said "and preach the Good News to every creature." Here is the divine paradox that gives us hope today. It is when the world, in its freedom, can be so evil that there is the need to proclaim the way of love. The deeper the divisions, the greater is the need for reconciliation. The more serious the illness, the greater is the need for healing. When fear and hate pervade the atmosphere it is the more essential to encourage calm and to practise love.

If the National Health Service can recognise the need for spiritual sustenance, how much more should those of a religious faith strive to build up spiritual resources. The ability to survive in the world in which we live and move today depends on personal conviction, inner resources and true serenity. All who believe are under obligation to do all they can to create such strengths in others.

THE GIFT OF FREEDOM

What an excellent description of the work of the pastor, counsellor, spiritual director or just "friend in Christ" is the exhortation to "send away in freedom those who are broken by life". The phrase is William Barclay's translation of one of the items in Jesus' "mission statement", the one he took directly to the prophet Isaiah. His priorities as he saw them were clear. He had come to preach the gospel, to heal the broken-hearted, to comfort those who mourn and to offer healing ("open the eyes of the blind"). It is the commitment to (as Isaiah put it) "proclaim liberty to the captives and the opening of the prison to them that are bound" that is difficult to fit into our statement of purpose – what would it mean in practical terms today? – but when "to set at liberty them that are bruised" becomes "to send away in freedom those that are broken by life", a window of understanding opens. In these words lies the essence of the pastoral task.

Those who are depressed, fearful, anxious, guilty, possessive, jealous, prone to prejudice, tempted to violence, cannot enjoy true quality of life. They are in a real sense "imprisoned", restricted by an emotional or spiritual bondage which closes the door to healthy living. To loosen restrictions, remove obstructions, take away internal "blocks" and open up the possibility of positive living is the essential work of all called to the ministry of reconciliation and healing. It is a satisfaction and a joy to help someone to find that sense of freedom.

Take reactive depression for example (that is depression brought on by particular events or circumstances). How desperately restricted and indeed imprisoned someone feels when they do not want to get out of bed, cannot face another day, finds the thought of some normal undertaking a huge, threatening task. Life becomes a struggle to get anything done. That is a form of bondage from which it is desperately difficult to free oneself.

Guilt* is another imprisoning factor when it has become inappropriate guilt and is no longer linked to known failures. Guilt is a proper reaction to personal error, fault or sin, but once dealt with internally, through a consciousness of divine forgiveness, it has fulfilled its purpose. To continue to feel overwhelming guilt when it does not relate to anything that is happening and when it is wholly out of proportion, becomes a form of bondage that blights present and future living as well as denying the forgiveness received.

Jesus came to bring freedom to those who are broken by life and in doing so laid down the pattern for all who seek to follow him. It is of the very essence of the work of the church to offer real freedom to all who are in emotional and spiritual chains, to offer the grace that loosens bonds, to proclaim the truth that sets someone free.

* See also the Meditation for May 7.

NEED FOR GRACE

One of the most entertaining obituaries ever appeared in this newspaper, the *Daily Telegraph*, last week. I enjoyed it immensely. That seems surprising, for death is not a subject for enjoyment or entertainment. It is a time for sadness. It brings hurt and pain and tears. But it is this relationship between sadness and laughter which makes the obituary of Ambrose Appelbe noteworthy.

Ambrose was 95 when he died, "an inveterate founder of causes, some worthy, some eccentric". The "worthy" ones included his part in the creation of the National Marriage Guidance Council and War on Want; the eccentric, the Smell Society (which he founded in concert with George Bernard Shaw and H G Wells). It sought to eliminate foul odours from society!

It was in "worthy" causes that I met Ambrose when, as our solicitor, he was involved in the setting up of Highgate Counselling Centre in London, and later Westminster Pastoral Foundation. His generosity towards other causes in which I was involved was memorable.

Ambrose too would have read his obituary with a smile – the apparent contradictions in his life, the ironies, the delightful hint of the eccentric. The son of a Methodist minister, Ambrose in his professional work as a solicitor defended Mandy Rice-Davies (in the Christine Keeler case in the sixties). His clients included Ingrid Bergman and the murderer John Christie. He defended Bertrand Russell as a conscientious objector and, with John Profumo at Toynbee Hall, worried about poverty and need. He admired Gandhi and tried to reflect his simple life. He worked for women's rights and child-care support, housing, bereavement and counselling. He admired concise prose and wrote legal letters in longhand. A Co-Founder of the Anatomical Donors Association, his great age ironically prevented his own body being used for research! And there is so much more! He had personal power but used it well.

Abuse of power is a current theme, both in the European and national contexts. People in high places have a daunting responsibility for it is through the use or abuse of power that the destinies of people and nations are determined. The crucifixion is a story of power abused; ecclesiastical power by the chief priests and elders, temporal power by two rulers who, through their mutual abrogation of responsibility, became friends.

Jesus alone could make and sustain the claim that "all power" was given to him "in heaven and on earth" for divine grace was his. If the decision to crucify Jesus demonstrated the absence of grace in priests, rulers and the people of Jerusalem so long ago, may their memory bring back some grace to the world today. It, and those in it who wield power, need it.

A POSITIVE FAITH

"The strength of gentleness" is, Paul tells the Galatians, "one of the fruits of the Spirit." Other evidences of that same "harvest of the Spirit" (as William Barclay translates the phrase) are love, joy, peace, patience, goodness and faith.*

We need positive forces in a world dominated by negative, degrading and destructive attitudes. Relationships – be they individual, national, cultural, international and sometimes even ecclesiastical – are damaged by greed, violence, racial prejudice, the violation of creation and other modern obscenities. Starvation on the current vast scale is, in part, the product of wars, ruthlessness, selfishness and corruption. When so much that is negative is infecting the atmosphere, the churches dare not, by what they do or fail to do, add to the negative tone of our times. They must, on the contrary, enable people to find life in its fullness and wholeness.

Jesus underlines the positive nature of the divine intention in his own glorious statement in John's Gospel: "God send not his Son into the world to condemn the world; but that the world through him might be saved." God's concern is not with judgementalism and condemnation, but with salvation. Everything God does is intended to create, re-create, redeem and renew. How then can Christians be negative, arrogant, dogmatic or exclusive – yet still claim to be the mediums of the divine message to the world?

In his attitude to life and to people, Jesus always concentrated on seeking to make them whole. It was his sensitivity that helped people not only to feel better, but to be better. Those who saw him, met him, heard him and touched him became different people. All this he accomplished by his attitude to them. He not only listened to them but also heard them. He not only looked at them but also took notice of them. He not only recognised their pain but also ministered to them.

Christianity is positive or it is nothing. "Negative Christianity" is a self-contradictory phrase. If the church is to reflect the attitude to life and people which Jesus had, it must make known and available the divine grace which "makes all things new". Those who "have been with Jesus" will therefore radiate goodness and gentleness, understanding and encouragement, hope and love, to all. Such positive qualities are, indeed, "the harvest of the Spirit".

* The Harvest of the Spirit is the theme of the month of September.

GO FORWARD!

Dr Winifred Rushforth was a remarkably gifted doctor and psychotherapist. When I last saw her in her Edinburgh home, in the mid-nineties, she was 93, full of life and working hard. Still seeing her clients regularly, she was also interested in group work. Indeed, as I recall, she was in her seventies when she became involved in encounter groups and went on to lead them with skill and sensitivity. Dr Rushforth told me that she was also working on her next book but was finding progress difficult. "There is so much to do," she said, and then added, to my astonishment and delight, "and I have only ten working years left."

If life begins at 40, it is inspiring indeed to know it can still be productive at 90. What a thrilling experience it was to find such a wonderful commitment to life. Her *joie de vivre* is an encouragement to all of us.

"Speak to the children of Israel, that they go forward" was the divine exhortation to a downcast people. "Launch out into the deep" was Jesus' directive to very sceptical disciples. In the great Johannine statement on the meaning of the Incarnation, the divine purpose is shown to be not discouraging but encouraging: "God sent not his Son into the world to condemn the world." He came that it "might be saved". When the disciples trembled about the future without the Lord, they were encouraged by a promise: "You shall receive power." The Holy Spirit, which would be given to them, would in fact be "another Comforter" not only soothing their pain but bringing them fortitude, strength and encouragement.

Encouragement should be the hallmark of the caring community. Every member has the right to expect, in their times of wretchedness and dereliction, support and encouragement. Strangely, the church often fails in this ministry, perhaps because it finds it difficult to acknowledge weakness. Church members often find encountering human weakness a problem (as they do accepting the possibility of human weakness in their priest, pastor or minister) but how can caring begin if sharing is not allowed?

There is, second, a need to encourage ourselves. It is right to expect care from others but that does not take away the obligation on us to get up from our depths, go on and fight again. Too often we seek refuge in self-pity, defeatism and resentment when we are facing the darkness. While we cannot (as too many wrongly suggest) *will* ourselves out of our depression, we can consciously seek the strength to cope with it. Such self-encouragement is a necessary ministry to ourselves.

Third, King David deeply discouraged by defeat found strength in the resources of his faith. God, as his experience told him, would not let him down. We too have the tools of encouragement in the spiritual resources that are founded on the great sequence of the saving acts of God in Jesus, the crucifixion, the descent into the dark places, the resurrection, the ascension and the sending of the Comforter Spirit. It is a tale of triumph and of victory, a story of profound hope. Surely therein lies "encouragement in the Lord", the encouragement that sustained David.

Due Respect

We live at a time when, sadly, respect is a universal casualty. Respect for property and others' possessions diminishes as vandalism increases. Respect for old age is seriously lacking. Areas of life which are properly private and intensely intimate are subjects for public entertainment. Intrusion into private grief is all too common. The amount of violence and death on our television screens speaks of the contemporary lack of respect for human life. God is presented as a figure of fun in a society which is no longer in awe of the divine. Inevitably, respect for people is a casualty too in a world which is often ruthless and very de-humanising.

One of the attitudes to life and people which Jesus had was shown by the respect he had for people, irrespective of their social background or country of origin. It is an attitude much needed in our world today.

The Gospel story of the rich young ruler* is a declaration of the value which Jesus placed on another human being. It shows how the personality of another individual must be treated and honoured. Jesus gives the young man respect and even admiration. Indeed, Mark records that "Jesus, beholding him, loved him." The young ruler had lived a life according to the commandments. In only one thing was he lacking. That was the ability to make the total commitment which involved giving up his riches. He went away, "sorrowful", for he had great possessions.

Jesus let him go. The letting-go was very important. Jesus accepted his decision and rejoiced in his integrity. There are those who might act in a different way, running after him, pulling him back and "compelling him to come in". Others, filled with spiritual zeal, would insist on "praying him into the Kingdom". But such responses, *not* taken by the Lord, deny the respect which is due to those with whom we might disagree, but who have complete integrity. Jesus, by letting the young man go, was offering us all a lesson in how we are to treat each other. For though we may each travel our own way, we are all made in the image of God, and must respect each other.

If people really matter, our attitude to them must be of kind which Jesus had. A world based on that kind of due and loving respect would be a less intolerant place.

* I have mentioned the rich young ruler several times in these Meditations. It is a story that says a great deal. See in particular the note to the Meditation for April 4.

ACTS OF LOVE

The recorded words of Jesus include the most comforting invitation ever given: "Come unto me, all ye that labour and are heavy-laden, and I will give you rest." He was, however, confronting too, as those who experienced his anger learned when, by their dubious commercialism, they turned "a house of prayer" into "a den of thieves".

These two examples illustrate the attitude to life and people that Jesus had. His was the gentlest of ministries when he was face to face with human suffering. When, however, he encountered religious intolerance, blatant self-righteousness or, as in the Temple incident mentioned above, the prostitution of holy things, he was ready to confront whoever demonstrated wrong attitudes.

Even his disciples could not escape his anger when, by their spiritual blindness, they obstructed his mission. It was to Peter, conceivably his closest colleague, that he had to administer severe criticism: "Get thee behind me, Satan; for thou savourest not the things that be of God, but those that be of men."

Speaking the truth in love is, according to the New Testament, an obligation on Christians. Jesus did just that (as we have seen) to the rich young ruler, but he loved him in doing it. Confrontation as well as comfort is an act of love.

There are therefore times when it is one of the obligations of love to confront people ... perhaps within the family, where wrong policies are damaging the community, over cruelty to human beings and animals, or in face of commercial ruthlessness. If people really matter, those who harm and hurt them must be confronted.

Luke's Gospel contains a story to which I have referred in an earlier Meditation.* It illustrates dramatically that there is a time to comfort and a time to confront. It is in Luke, chapter 7, and it contains a glorious "divine surprise". It is the officially righteous Simon, the Pharisee, whom Jesus confronts with the damning words: "Simon, thou gavest me no water for my feet, but this woman hath washed my feet with her tears and wiped them with her hair." The comfort and the commendation go to the "woman of bad reputation" whose love will be spoken of for all time for "she loved much".

If people are truly important, we shall comfort them in their need and confront them with humility, when they are wrong. Either way, if we are to reflect the attitude to life that Jesus had, we must act in love.

* See also Acceptance, the Meditation for October 14.

INCLUSIVENESS

Jesus constantly produced "divine surprises" for both his enemies and friends by his answers, actions and reactions. Such incidents on which we have reflected in this series of Meditations* on "the attitude to life and people that Jesus had" illustrate that surprise element. The stories of "the woman taken in adultery", "a woman of bad reputation" who washed Jesus' feet with her tears in what he himself described as a never-to-be-forgotten gesture, Simon the Pharisee, whose meal she invaded to express her devotion to Jesus, the woman of Samaria – all these situations included elements of the unorthodox. It was the surprise factor in them that pointed up an aspect of the truth.

The ninth chapter of Mark's Gospel provides another example of the unexpected. Again, it was the disciples who were taken by surprise. They had encountered a man who was "casting out devils" in the name of Jesus and had no doubt as to how they should deal with him. "We forbade him," John reports, "because he does not follow us." There was however, no approving nod from Jesus for their action. "Forbid him not," he said, adding that anyone doing miracles in his name was unlikely to "speak evil" of him. "He that is not against us is on our part," he added.

The disciples' reactions and those of Jesus highlight the basic difference in their attitudes. His was one of inclusiveness, but theirs was one of exclusiveness. That flexibility "round the edges" of Jesus' stance is crucially important in determining the kind of attitude Christians should have to others.

There is a New Testament passage in which Peter declares that "there is no other name under heaven ... whereby we must be saved." This leads Christians to have a "Christ-centred" stance, but there is nothing in holding that conviction which needs to be translated into dogmatism, intolerance or exclusiveness. Since Paul reminds us that we "only see through a glass darkly", it is unwise to be inflexibly dogmatic about the truth.

Jesus' attitudes reflect the mind and heart of a God of love. The words to which we have been drawn in the way Jesus dealt with people are sensitivity, understanding empathy, inclusiveness and, of course, love itself. They sum up the attitudes to which disciples, now as then, are committed in everything they do and are.

* See, for example, the Meditation for April 29.

COMFORTABLE WORDS

"Comfort ye, comfort ye my people." "Comfortable words" as I understand them, are not only soothing, calming, restful words but – more importantly, as the Latin root *fortis* in the word "comfort" implies – fortifying, reassuring, encouraging words. The consequences of the proclamation of the gospel should be positive, enlivening and enhancing for the "Good News" it brings is not negative, discouraging or judgemental.

John's Gospel affirms the *positive* purpose of the Word: "God sent not his Son into the world to condemn the world, but that the world through him might be saved." The Incarnation was a positive action which offered the opportunity for relationships with God to be restored, an offer made to all who choose to receive it. It is not surprising that, in Jesus' farewell message to his disciples, he promised to send them "another Comforter". That was and is the Holy Spirit.

Be it in the older traditional vocabulary of justification and sanctification; in the biblical language of salvation and "fruits of the Spirit"; in contemporary words such as wholeness and growth, the thrust is the same. The divine initiatives in the scheme of redemption all seek to create purpose, meaning, reconciliation and peace. How beautifully the *Book of Common Prayer* sums it up: "Hear what comfortable words our Saviour Jesus Christ saith to all that truly turn to him."

The words that I have used so far are almost all from the New Testament, but the storehouse of encouraging words for the development of the spiritual and devotional life must surely be too the Old Testament Psalms. I find the practice, suggested by a spiritual director, of underlining in red particularly significant phrases and sentences very helpful. It may be a familiar phrase from Psalm 23 such as "He restoreth my soul" or the opening words of Psalm 46: "God is our refuge and strength, a very present help in trouble." It may be the anguished cry brought about by trial or tribulation: "Out of the depths have I cried to thee, O Lord: Lord, hear my voice" (Psalm 130), or the reminder of the ever-watchful Providence: "He that keepeth thee will not slumber" (Psalm 121). It may be the reassuring statement from Psalm 125 that recalls "the eternal verities": "They that trust in the Lord shall be as Mount Zion which cannot be removed but abideth for ever."

The Psalms persistently point to the Providence of God as a fundamental article of faith. It is not, however, a conviction reached primarily by intellectual endeavour. It is presented as the result of experience, both in the history of God's people and the stories of individual lives. The same conviction is classically stated in Paul's second letter to Timothy: "I know whom I have believed and am persuaded that he is able to keep that which I have committed unto him." With hindsight, as people of faith look back on life's aspects of joy, anguish or pain, they can begin both to see and say, as they could not at the time of their tragedies: "All things (can) work together for good" for those who serve and love their Lord.

It is the experience of God in creation and redemption which is reflected in the comfortable words that fortify and reassure the soul, strengthen the body, bring serenity to the mind and satisfy the heart.

MIRACLE OF GRACE

Don't expect miracles if you are over 40! That seems to be the message coming from Luke's report (in the Acts of the Apostles) of the disciples' healing of the lame man. The wonder of the miracle was even greater, Luke notes (and significantly he was a doctor by profession) because "the man was over 40 years old, on whom this miracle of healing was shewed". We now believe, of course, in the good news that "life begins at 40" – or, for that matter, 50 or 60. There is always the possibility of change and growth. Call the experience what you will – inner transformation, interior change, conversion, the turning–point – it can come at any age.

It is the second half of life which is the potentially creative half. The pressures arising from the making of a career, the securing of a home, the education and care of the family, dominate the first half of life. After 40, roughly speaking, there is more likely to be time available to explore undeveloped parts of our being and release the creative potential all too often dammed up by material pursuits.

Alas, in today's world, this is more a statement of the ideal than a reflection of reality for too many people. So many nowadays, both the young and the middle-aged, have no careers to create. There are few jobs for the redundant over-fifties. There is no relief from the pressures of the rat-race. We must not, however, allow the idea to fade away or the creative potential of life to be swamped. Indeed there are many still who find that in mid-life, crisis can be an opportunity. Life can be transformed. Gifts can be discovered. Creative self-awareness can develop. It is a time to grow. Those who do not proclaim a religious faith will see in such creativity indicators on the road to maturity or, as Jung called it, individuation. Those for whom faith is an essential part of life will see constructive inner change as evidence of the Spirit at work in the miracle of grace.

The conversion of Paul, formerly persecutor of the church, finally "the least of the apostles", is in terms of transformation experience, an interesting and helpful model. His Damascus road encounter must seem to many the prime example of a timed and dated conversion experience, whereas in fact the whole process took time. Outwardly aggressive, he "breathes out threatenings and slaughter against the disciples of the Lord". Inwardly the challenge to his conscience is taking place. Was it that he knew he was wrong to "consent" to the stoning of the martyr Stephen? In the words of William Barclay, Paul actually "thoroughly approved" of Stephen's murder. Did not unconscious feelings of guilt move him in the heat of the midday sun towards that hysterical collapse and blindness, the crisis in which he encountered the Jesus whom he persecuted? But more time was needed – three days – and then God sends to him a somewhat trembling but devout spiritual counsellor. Ananias laid hands on God's "chosen vessel". The gift of the Spirit was now Paul's.

Challenge, crisis, change . . . for some it happens in a minute, for others it may need months, perhaps even a lifetime. But the miracle of grace can come at any time. And it can certainly happen to the over-forties!

BE ENCOURAGED!

Nehemiah* was a cup-bearer in the palace of King Artaxerxes when God "put it into his heart" to do something for Jerusalem, the city of his forefathers and his spiritual home. He had heard, in exile, that it was broken down and desolate. With the king's permission, he set off for the holy city, obedient to the divine prompting that he must rebuild the walls of Jerusalem.

When Nehemiah reached the city, he found chaos. The walls were broken down and "the gates consumed with fire". He went out by night to survey the destruction and found he could not even find places for his ass to walk. The task was far greater than he had ever contemplated, but he refused to be discouraged by its magnitude. "The God of heaven, he will prosper us," he told his companions with conviction "and we his servants will arise and build."

It is part of the ministry of encouragement, laid on us all, to help people to accept whatever situation they face as Nehemiah did, and to ensure that they understand the realities of it. Whether we are dealing with our personal inner problems, contemplating the difficulties faced by the churches in engaging in evangelism in an excessively materialistic world or simply seeking to be (in Paul's words) "obedient to the heavenly vision", acceptance of the facts, positively not reluctantly, is the only valid launch-pad for "new creation".

I noticed that the piano tuner had only two stumps on his right hand. Six days before the end of his military service, an accident when working on a tank removed two fingers completely and half of each of the other two. The young professional pianist's playing days seemed to be over. He applied for a job as a piano tuner and was accepted, but was not satisfied. Refusing to pity himself, he took stock of the realities of his predicament, then determined to be a pianist again. He succeeded. Using the two stumps on his right hand skilfully and over-working his left, he learnt to play *his* way. The classics were out of the question, but pop music was not. He was a professional pianist once more, and has been ever since.

The pianist, like Nehemiah, accepted the things which could not be changed, but did wonders with what could! Be encouraged by their example to "go and do likewise"!

* See also on Nehemiah, the Meditation for May 10.

CHURCH WITHOUT WALLS

Bernard Braley, a Methodist layman whose expertise lay in exploring new ways of worship in the latter part of the twentieth century, would often employ exercises at conferences at which he was speaking to illustrate his themes. One of his favourites was to divide his audience into two sections, asking them to face each other across the hall where they were meeting. Those on the left wall would be the "church people", those on the right wall, "the world", that is people outside the church. He would then ask the "church people" to make contact with the "outsiders", but to do it non-verbally. The result was always the same. The church people would make beckoning gestures to the non-church folk inviting them to come over to them. This was exactly what Braley expected, thus giving him the opportunity to point out that therein lay the church's normal approach to mission and evangelism. Mission campaigns always focused on the expectation that people should join the church or go to its premises or locations and there hopefully find what they deeply sought. In fact, Braley stressed, the church's mission was essentially the reverse of that process. The church should go and meet people where they are and engage them there. This was the practice of the first disciples, "sent out" into the world. Indeed their being "apostles" expressed exactly that concept.

The current concept of a "church without walls" has evolved in protest against the static, moribund, introverted nature of much church life today. While there is within the Christian faith a need to "go to church" in order to be part of the Christian community, the process must never end there. Merely gathering together for worship and fellowship is but one of the essential elements of Christian life and work. We go *to* church in order to go *from* it in mission and evangelism. In the church without walls, the church is extrovert and outward looking. Its concern is not only a concern by individuals for their own salvation (though individual response to the gospel is a primary responsibility) but a concern in love for the world. Only when coming is followed by going is there a living church.

If the church is seen today by most people as irrelevant, out-of-date and ineffective, it may well be because of its cultivated insularity, its inability to change familiar ways and its failure to understand the vocabulary of the vastly changed world to which it is called to minister. The unyielding attachment to traditions that once were valuable needs to be loosened.

It is never too late for the gospel itself to be proclaimed in a new language and in relation to contemporary needs but the revolution required will be dramatic, radical and of necessity adventurous. It may however see the passing of much-loved buildings which can become no more than monuments to a departed age. It may be that the future lies much more in a church without walls, open to the world.

To do Justly

Widespread corruption, lust for power, rampant idolatry and the political arrogance that finds no place for God; is this a comment on our times? It is in fact a prophet's analysis of the profound faults he saw in his nation's life long ago. The prophet Micah had much to say to Judah about social injustice, sleaze and public hypocrisy. He also criticised the formality of ritual sacrifice. "Shall I come before him with burnt offerings . . . with thousands of rams . . . with ten thousand rivers of oil?" asks Micah with the irony of hyperbole, but it leads to a great statement about the true nature of personal, and indeed corporate, religion. What does the Lord really require? It is justice and fairness, mercy and compassion, humility and respect for God.

It would be insensitive to plead for *personal* commitment to justice and fairness. We are all surely committed to "doing justly". But in the public world, there are constant cries of "It's not fair!" Many very unhappy people are complaining fervently against present disability legislation and unfair cuts. Senior citizens' organisations are doing the same over pensions and there is much unease in some communities over the unjust ways in which different groups are treated.

The call to social righteousness in a world created by a God who (Jesus tells us) values each one is always before the church. Society must not only seek to do justly – but must be seen to do it.

The personal call to "love mercy" can again be taken as agreed. We may not always achieve it, but the standard is clear for compassion is integral to religion. The corporate call to mercy is more complicated. Can the state do justly *and* love mercy? Wherever the concept of mercy is related to justice, controversy is inevitable as is seen in high-profile issues which have divided society and caused major problems for the politicians who have to deal with them. This country is, however, widely seen as compassionate; it is a reputation not to be discarded lightly. And whatever further problems remain over debt, the cancellation of so-called Third World dues by this country in response to public and church pressure, is an act of corporate mercy that is to the credit of this nation.

The call to "walk humbly with God" is certainly made to individuals, and each one of us needs constantly to hear it. Living life without God comes too easily because of the pressures of contemporary materialism and secularism. Corporately the dispensing with any acknowledgement of and respect for God, which so troubled Micah, is all too clearly a mark of our time.

The prophets saw clearly what would happen as a result of living without any sense of the spiritual. It would be national disaster. The reminder to do justly and to love mercy, and the exhortation to walk humbly with God, is relevant prophecy today.

UNHEALTHY SOCIETY

It is with real affection that I remember the village doctor in my first parish many, many years ago. A highly respected member of the community, he was indeed the archetypal family doctor. He was always available in times of need. When our infant son was dangerously ill, he was there. When our daughter was knocked down on the busy road outside our manse, it was no unfamiliar member of a health centre team or an anonymous "locum" who happened to be on duty who turned up. It was the doctor himself.

The doctor was my senior by more than 40 years. Perhaps it was that fact and some immaturity or inexperience I had shown that led him to offer me a gentle homily on the theme of responsibility.

The doctor enjoyed his "dram" but always in his own home. He had, he told me, deliberately decided that however much he would have enjoyed socialising at the village inn, he would never drink there. The sight of him entering or leaving the public house might prove unhelpful to a "weaker brother" – or sister – among his patients. I admired his sense of responsibility.

Such a sense of overriding public duty has, sadly, been missing in the unhappy saga presently being played out across the Atlantic. Personal desires and needs have not been made properly subservient to public responsibility.* It is a significant omission. Benjamin Zander, the internationally renowned conductor, when leading a master-class in London recently, said to us with emphasis: "Never ask what's wrong; always ask what's missing." In other words, avoid the futility of concentration on purely negative elements in any situation. Rather contribute the positive missing elements.

If a satisfactory sense of responsibility is one factor too often missing today, another is the sense of reverence. In a depressingly materialistic world, reverence, with its components wonder, awe and respect, has become a casualty of our times. Widespread vandalism and destruction show a lack of respect for property, while old age and the wisdom it implies are dismissed as irrelevant. A total lack of respect for human life and fellow human beings is expressed in violence, terrorism, murder, mugging, rape and abuse. Any residual respect for the sacred intimacies of personal relationship has disappeared as every aspect of sexual behaviour, normal and abnormal, is openly paraded and, through modern technology, publicised internationally. Inevitably a similar disrespect is extended to the sacred and the holy. No sense of the numinous, the divine, can remain as minor satirists and comedians rubbish God and all things spiritual. A society that is losing all sense of reverence is an unhealthy society.

Tennyson offers a challenge not only to the world but to the churches when he asks that "more of reverence may dwell among us". To recover the sense of holy awe and wonder so important to prophets, priests and people of old, may do something to redeem a world which idolises wealth, glorifies the trivial and glamourises sin.

* A reference in 1998 to President Clinton's personal problems.

Rubbish!

Nehemiah's vision, his call to rebuild the walls of Jerusalem, was kept alive by his persistence in prayer. He believed "the gracious hand of God" was with him. He also needed courage to face the blatant scorn of his enemies. It was when faced with their hostility that he issued his clarion call: "The God of heaven, he will prosper us therefore we his servants will arise and build." And build they did, led by a great man whose construction policies, vital to the success of his project, can symbolically be interpreted to provide profound guidance for all involved in mission and evangelism. His insistence on using the people in the community where the walls needed to be rebuilt points to the role of the local community in mission. His need to use all the talents available recalls the need to use the diversities of gifts of different people as the unit of service. His instruction to work on the wall at the point nearest to home emphasises by implication the principle that evangelism is effected wherever the members of the church are: that is, at work, in leisure, at home, etc.

Nehemiah, however, encountered obstacles that held back God's work. These too can be helpful symbolically whenever we engage in spiritual self-analysis and increasing self-awareness. This exercise focuses on the rather unattractive word "rubbish". It is, nevertheless, a scriptural word. Nehemiah himself points out that "the strength of the labourers is giving out" because "there is so much rubbish" (Nehemiah chapter 4, verse 10). Just as literal rubbish was found to be getting in the way of the rebuilding process, so the negative effects of spiritual rubbish must be considered.

This theme is presently touching a nerve in a personal context! A house move after 30 years has underlined the accumulation of paper, possessions and books that a lack of discipline has encouraged. That sharp reminder recalls, uneasily, something similar in the spiritual field. Over-concentration on unnecessary, out-of-date, irrelevant matters can so easily inhibit spiritual tasks.

Now is an important word in the diary of salvation. Too often decisions of spiritual importance are pushed back, resisted, even rejected on the ground that time is always available. Awareness of our own mortality tells us consciously that this cannot be taken for granted. It is therefore necessary constantly to review our lives. It can come near to tragedy when concentration on the trivial, the topical and (remembering the rubbish) the tawdry so affects our perspective that we reverse St Paul's advice and fail to look at the things which are not seen, but which are eternal. What we can see all too easily becomes our "treasure".

The need to get rid of the rubbish accumulated in life – both material and spiritual – and restore the priority of "seeking the kingdom" is an exhortation related not to allocation of time, but to the understanding of priorities.

SHAFTS OF LIGHT

I have received an unusual gift. It is a table lamp with a shade which is open at the top, in a very heavy blue paper; the word *Light* is visible when it is not switched on. But switch on, and the change is dramatic. There, in white lettering, are the very first verses of the Bible: "*And darkness was on the face of the deep,*" it reads, but "*God said: 'Let there be light 'and there was light.*"

How one wishes that in real life it was so easy! Flick the switch and the darkness is dispelled! One touch and all around us is light. How wonderful it would be if the miracle – be it medical, psychological, emotional or spiritual – would follow at the flick of a switch. But in reality there is seldom a miracle for those for whom that darkness is all too real. Those feelings of darkness, depression, despair, doubt, even desperation can be all too persistent.

The world is, of course, not a wholly negative place with most of life lived out in the shadows. There are many good people, positive happenings, and creative developments in the world. But equally for many the darkness is all too real. Doctors' surgeries have many who are there not for physical reasons but because of anxiety and fear. Many hospital beds are occupied by those who are suffering nervous strain. In our own circles, many in our family, church or leisure groups, are victims of some illness. Darkness and despair seem to abound. Sometimes that leads at its worst to suicide, an increasing way of death, especially among young men. More often it is expressed in depression, that sense of being, as the word itself suggests, weighed down with anxiety, a fear of not being able to cope, a reluctance to face a new day. Are there shafts of light to help us to break up such darkness? Perhaps there are.

The first is the usefulness of healthy self-awareness, the effort to try to understand just why our moods can change and what particularly pulls us down. The second is the other side of that advice. Concern with self, if it is too continuous and concentrated, can create anxiety and fear. But fear is at the other end of the spectrum from love for (says St John), "perfect love casts out fear." The more we are involved in love for others, the less will be our unhealthy self-concern.

Thirdly, at the heart of faith, is the theme of death and resurrection, the ability to learn to live again. Let me not make this point by way of platitude or theory, but rather point you to people – you know them, as I do – who have faced, through accident or disability, a living death but who are examples of true resurrection, people who bring us a shaft of glorious light against the background of their own personal darkness. They are the ones who teach us how to learn to live again.

ONE-STEP DANCE

To have a grand aim is a proper part of creative living. St Paul spoke of his sense of purpose: "Forgetting those things which are behind and reaching forth to the things which are before," he said "I press toward the mark for the prize of the high calling of God in Christ Jesus." To have goals, set aims, pursue ideals is to have a positive attitude to life. It has often resulted in great achievements.

What is true in general may, however, bring problems in particular situations. Those who are lost in the darkness of depression and despair, for example, simply cannot cope with exhortations to "look forward". Those who have suffered a bereavement – especially if it be a tragic one like the death of a child, the suicide of a teenage son or daughter, the murder of a member of the family (all real situations) – just cannot contemplate the distant future. All they can do is try to cope with the dreadful present.

Ponder four statements which, broadly speaking, have a common theme. The first comes from Edmund Burke – *Nobody made a greater mistake than he (she) who did nothing because they could do only a little*. The second is attributed to Madame du Deffand – *The distance is nothing. It is only the first step that is difficult*. The third was the spontaneous reaction of astronaut Neil Armstrong to walking on the moon: *That is one small step for a man, but a giant leap for mankind*. The fourth comes from John Henry Newman's hymn 'Lead, kindly light': *I do not ask to see the distant scene, one step enough for me*. They all underline the importance of one step.

There are several contexts in which taking one step is extraordinarily difficult but extremely important. There is, for example, the counselling situation in which that step is the crucial one of lifting a telephone to say *I need help. Can I have an appointment?* There is the evangelical one in which resistance to the first necessary step in making a commitment obstructs the act of confession and faith. But it is in the field of bereavement, particularly, that progress (if it is possible at all) must be in the form of one step at a time. To take one pace towards coping, towards growth, can make severe demands on those so bereft that they cannot feel they have a future at all.

To become a partner with someone in grief or pain, darkness or despair, is to engage in that one-step dance which encourages healing. But the image needs qualification. A one-step dance is a rapid succession of quick steps. That could, alas, be well beyond the capacity of the wounded and the hurt. It is of the very essence of healing relationship to be acutely sensitive to the pace which the bereaved and the depressed can accept, and to recognise that the very most that can be faced is one step at a time.

HEALTHY HILARITY

It was exhilarating to read some words from Genesis this morning. "God has brought me laughter," said Abraham's wife, Sarah. And that laughter would be infectious, for "everyone who hears about this will laugh with me!" she added. The reason for such hilarity? That God had promised Sarah, "well-advanced in years" and "past the age of child-bearing", a son by her centenarian husband! So she laughed when the promise was made, and she laughed when Isaac was born.*

Sadly this world seems to be, for many, less a joyous journey, more a vale of tears. There has been human suffering beyond comprehension through the conflict in the Balkans.** To the cry: "Lord, how long?" there is no answer when starvation stalks the earth. The cruel hurricane, the devastating flood, the destructive earthquake are headlines for a day, only to be forced off the front pages – and therefore away from our attention – by the trivialities of celebrities' relationships and sporting controversies. So often it is ill-health and death which seem to dominate life as the telephone brings news of another cancer victim among our friends, an approaching death among our relatives, a crippling marital conflict. Against such a background, the God-given laughter of Sarah is indeed exhilarating. It reminds us of the wonder of the joy, the divine surprise, the new beginnings that brought her such glee.

In the splendid hymn by Richard Gillard, *Brother, sister, let me serve you* (quoted earlier), he writes:

> I will weep when you are weeping,
> when you laugh, I'll laugh with you;
> I will share your joy and sorrow
> till we've seen this journey through.

Pastoral responsibility for those for whom life is bleak and blighted, tense and tragic is deeply embedded in religious faith. But it is equally important that Christianity proclaims the wonder inherent in being human. Within the divine creation, there was provided the capacity for goodness, creativity, inspiration, wonder, love. The Spirit of God which, in the creation story "hovered over the waters", becomes, in the Christian story, the energising Holy Spirit at work in the world and in human beings.

So where that Spirit is at work, "fruits of the Spirit" will evolve in glorious splendour – love, joy, peace, patience, kindness, goodness, faithfulness, gentle-ness and self-control. Against these things (Paul writes to the Galatians), "there is no law". Indeed, there is everything to be said for them!***

There is a time to weep and weep we will – with others, for others, alone. But thanks to Sarah, and her joyous glee, we are reminded that there is a time to laugh and laugh we must. Health is helped by genuine hilarity. It is, as Sarah said, a gift from God.

* This incident is also referred to in the Meditations for February 20 and October 30.
** July 1999.
*** The Meditations for September are devoted to The Harvest of the Spirit.

THE DAYSPRING

"The day sprynge or dawnynge of the days giveth a certeine lyght before the rysinge of the sonne," writes a sixteenth-century author speaking of the "dayspring", a word used in the books of Job and St Luke. That image became reality for us one late September morning.

Due to a meeting in north London in the evening, Jillian and I had to leave the lovely, car-less island of Tresco in the Scillies at 6am. It needed seven forms of transport to get us to the church on time! First, from the hotel, was the tractor-drawn trailer with its two bench-seats and a rail to grab, then a specially provided boat to ferry us to St Mary's, the main island. An airport coach was waiting to take us to catch the first helicopter of the day to Penzance; from there by minibus to Penzance station and a five-hour train journey to London Paddington. Finally, a taxi took an hour struggling through traffic to complete the half-hour run to north London and remind us of the worst aspects of city life.

It was between Tresco and St Mary's that dawn began to break over St Martin's (another island in the Scillies), exactly as the writer of long ago described it. The experience was a moving, indeed thrilling one, as that "certeine lyght" appeared just before sunrise. It spoke of a new day, a new beginning, new opportunities, and it underlined an image so strongly present in the Gospels where it speaks of the coming of Christ as a light shining in the darkness. How beautifully Zechariah, the father of John the Baptist, spoke with prophetic insight of the coming of the Messiah. "You will be the Lord's forerunner," he said (as Luke reports in William Barclay's translation) "to prepare the road which he will travel" and to tell of "the deep compassion of our God which has graciously sent heaven's dawn to break upon us, to shine on those who sit in darkness and in the shadow of death, and to direct our steps in the roads that lead to peace."

"The people that walked in darkness have seen a great light," Isaiah had prophesied. "The light" continues to shine in the darkness, "and the darkness has never extinguished it." In that lies our hope.

"The heavenly Jerusalem is not in some dream of the future. It is now. One only needs to open one's eyes." That encouraging statement was made by a holy Indian man on his deathbed. Too often, the sheer weight of the world's evil overwhelms us, its materialism blinds us, its pain and suffering desensitise us. Look then towards "the dayspring from on high who has visited us", to sense the dawn with its "certeine lyght", to find around us so much that is good – marvellous gifts of creation, inspiration in the creative arts. Look at the multitude of good and loving people who, stimulated by their faith, whatever their religion, pour compassion into a needy world. Jerusalem, heaven, the Kingdom of God *is* now. We need to open our eyes, minds, hearts, souls, and gladly embrace it.

THE UNITY OF LIGHT

It was cold indeed that night, with a biting chill wind that spoke of the depths of winter. It was very dark too for the hundreds of people gathered in the grounds of our local hospice.* But there was expectation also. Just as long as it takes to press a switch, and in one movement, hundreds of bulbs on the huge horse chestnut tree in the grounds of the hospice would burst into light to proclaim the need to "light up a life".

"God is light and in him is no darkness at all" proclaimed one voice in the darkness. "Light represents the attributes of God" said another. A third added: "Physical light is but a true reflection of the true light in the world of reality, and that true light is God." "Then God said: 'Let there be light' and there was light" added a fourth. But from whom and where did these four statements come? The last one was spoken by a Jewish rabbi, quoting the Old Testament. The first came from the Gospel of St John and the Christian tradition. The second is an Upanishads message and was conveyed by a Hindu. The third was offered by a Muslim, quoting the Quran. That such differing traditions could unite to declare that God is light was a moving symbol of a unity which is compulsory in matters of life and death. In that the hospice offers a multi-faith approach to care, and acknowledges too that patients may have no religious faith or belief at all, the sole concern was to unite everyone from wherever they came in "lighting up a life".

There is today a creative contribution coming from caring organisations which specifically and deliberately operate on a non-religious basis (The Compassionate Friends, in the bereavement field, for example**). Such organisations are able to create unity in caring at a highly practical level while acknowledging the right of members to have, or not to have, religious beliefs. It is an exercise in tolerance that – far from being criticised, as it sometimes is within the churches – deserves commendation. To allow religious rights to others does not in any way diminish one's own beliefs and convictions, nor does it prevent anyone from witnessing to the things which they most surely believe. To listen and learn need never be interpreted as a sign of weakness. Only by such attitudes can an understanding of others' views become possible. Only with understanding can that which is wrong be refuted. It is precisely those who stand on solid ground in their own beliefs who can most safely seek to understand and assess other approaches to faith.

Jesus, as Luke records, saw his ministry in terms of preaching, healing and liberty. Freedom in Christ is positive and energising. It is not licence. There is no New Testament warrant for behaviour with no bounds, or belief with no boundaries. True freedom is a mature and living faith which can engage confidently with a hostile world.

* The North London Hospice, 47 Woodside Avenue, London N12 8TF.
** This bereavement support organisation, following the death of a son or daughter of any age, is also referred to in the Meditations for February 15, March 19 and December 10.

THE CENTRE-MAN

It was early in 1918, seven months before the end of the First World War, that twelve men of the 2/1 Wessex Field Ambulance Unit asked the Padre, appropriately named Donald Standfast, to form an association for various small groups meeting under his leadership at the Soldiers' Club in Bethune, France, a base behind the front line. "*Our essential idea is to form a Fellowship in which we may assist each other to live the Christian life,*" they said. They often met under fire. "Living or dying", they felt fellowship with Christ to be their greatest need. Standfast intended this "league of fellowship" to close down at the Armistice. It didn't. Appeals led him to make it into the Regnal League in March 1919 in Rouen. In 1999, it was 80 years old.

I thought my experience in ecumenical organisations and interdenominational journalism had made me aware of all the national bodies whose purpose, like the Regnal League, is to explore wholeness of life. I have to confess that up to a month or two ago, I had never heard of the Regnal League. It does not seem to have made an effective public impact. Having addressed Regnal's 69th annual conference and learned of their existence and history, I feel that it is a great pity that the movement is not better known. It has something to offer.

Its vow is worth recording. The Commitments of Membership involve "*the endeavour to be a true friend to all, not allowing myself by word or deed to do injury to anyone, to take care of my body and seek to develop my mental gifts for the sake of others. With the help of God, I will seek Wholeness of Life.*" It is not narrow in outlook but encourages tolerance, openness and sharing in friendship. It is earthed in the real world in that it is committed to seek wholeness for society too. Its belief is not in rule, but in love. "*A rule can never be enough for a Christian. It has to be a love springing from the individual heart towards God.*"

The quest for wholeness, health, healing, maturity, individuation, eternal life, whichever term is your particular choice, is in effect the journey of life. The achievement of it in Christian terms is dependent on the gift of grace and the energy of the Holy Spirit. The process is not however a purely personal one. Changed people change situations. The Incarnation compels active involvement in the health and healing of society.

I am glad to have come upon the Regnal League. Broad-based, open, non-directive, non-judgemental, creative, it is not a substitute for the church, but is a bridge to it. Its local groups are, appropriately given their emphasis on wholeness, "circles". The focus throughout the Regnal League is on the One who "reigns", that is Christ. Indeed they have a name for Jesus that sums up their faith. They say he is "the Centre-man".

GRATITUDE AND HOPE

The world is saturated with words; millions of them each day, of the making of books there is certainly no end. The same is true of magazines, journals, learned papers, etc. Newspapers grow bigger and bigger to encompass every aspect of life in numerous 'sections' and colour magazines.

The same is true in the religious field. One of the biggest classifications in the trade journal that deals with bookselling is the category 'religious'. Be it inspirational anecdotes or heavy theology, many millions of words are offered to us to shape and guide our thinking. Is it all necessary to cope with life and its needs? Are intellectuals better at handling life's problems than, as the New Testament would describe them, "the common people", who (we are told) "heard Jesus gladly". He gave them not the theological minutiae so valued by the official teachers of religion in his time, but the truth in a form they could understand.

Professor Noam Chomsky, in a BBC Radio 3 interview, described the three revolutions which had changed the world as: the computer revolution and the microchip, the genetic code, and the fundamental change in the way we understand the mind and language. But for many, especially of an older generation, the computer remains a mystery beyond understanding, while discussions of matters in the field of genetics can be too technical for average people. Being illiterate in computers and trying hard to understand genetic mysteries, I had to struggle too to comprehend Professor Chomsky and his broadcast! It is easy to feel decidedly deficient in one's ability to cope with the complexities of the contemporary world!

Of course we need to study philosophy, psychology, sociology and theology if we are to understand and deal with the issues of our time – and especially to preach about them – but sometimes the very simplicity of statements from, for example, aged saints or profoundly spiritual writers with a capacity for turning profundity into simplicity, take us further along the road to coping with life and its problems.

Jillian and I visited a lady in her nineties recently. She gave herself "one out of ten for her physical state" but she deserves a very much higher rating for her mental ability and memory. She is widely read and very much in touch with world affairs, but lives her life now in terms of a philosophy summed up in a simple phrase, passed on to her by an archbishop friend quoting a lady whom he had met. "I goes to bed thankful, and I wakes up hopeful," she told him. Gratitude and hope are essential to a happy life.

We need the academic, the intellectual, the philosopher, the sage and the scholar with their contributions to the world's thinking. Long may they make them! But how welcome too is the simplicity of the saints who, with gratitude and hope, leave and live their lives "in the hands of God". To meet such people is a blessing indeed. They witness to their faith – without any words.

True Compassion

The most plaintive question asked in the Old Testament is surely that in the Lamentations of Jeremiah. Reflecting on the destruction, desolation and despair in Jerusalem, Jeremiah cries out: "Is it nothing to you, all ye that pass by?" In other words, does anybody care?

The sermon I heard at a famous Glasgow church did not make any great impression at the time, but looking back over some 40 years I realise its central message did register on me. It was a simple one, but an important one. Commenting on Jesus' visit to the house where Peter's mother-in-law had taken ill, the preacher (Dr Ernest Jarvis of Wellington Church) was at pains to stress the sensitivity of Jesus. He did not only see her there. He did something more, he "took notice" of her and acted to heal her. It is a factor which is equally important in caring relationships, professional or personal. It is imperative that those who care do not simply listen to words that are used, but "hear" what is being said. It is the point made in Stevie Smith's poem: "He's not waving, but drowning."

The same question might have been asked as Jesus hung from the cross on Calvary. For some it was a very distressing experience. Not unnaturally, Mary sadly stood near the cross with other women. But to others it was nothing, a familiar sight where crucifixion was a public punishment. Like Pilate, passers-by could wash their hands of it.

The question might well be asked of us all in times of great suffering. Do we only see it – but fail to take notice of it? Do we listen to – but fail to hear – the cries that come from those in despair? Are we actually moved to action?

It is right to recognise what we cannot do. But there still remains the call, especially in painful personal situations, to reach a level of sensitivity greater than we normally show as part of our attempt to "try always to have the same attitude to life as Jesus had."*

If in our attitude to others' need, we seek to express the mind of Christ, we must have a compassionate heart, an active mind, sensitive intuition, a dedicated imagination, a disciplined will and a soul with sincere desire. Then we will take note of needs, hear desperate cries and find physical strength to respond as far as we can.

Our capacity to serve is confined by the limitations we have, both physical and emotional, but these have often been shown to be capable of expansion through "the grace which is sufficient." "She has done what she could," said Jesus of the woman who had washed his feet with her tears and dried them with her hair. To make whatever effort we can carries the approval of the Lord.

* Philippians, chapter 2, verse 5, (William Barclay's translation).

GIFTS OF CREATION

The shape and structure of the church is temporary, but its faith is permanent. The primary concern of believers is with the content of faith, not the form of the church needed for a particular time. Today's world and its needs require major organisational change. However hard it is to leave behind familiar and loved ways of working, the statistics relating to the church are shouting ever more loudly that change in outward form must come. What is changeless is the validity and vitality of the things which we most surely believe and there is no need for despondency about them. Our convictions about creation, Incarnation and resurrection still provide excitement and encouragement.

It was the late Erik Routley, theologian and musician of rare distinction, who said that "although humanity was not born Christian, it was born singing." A hymn of praise was indeed appropriate to the wonder of the creation story. But creation did not end after Genesis' "seven days". God is always creating. Both the Bible and religious history record the creating work of God through the Spirit which in the beginning hovered over chaos, inspired prophets, rested on Jesus at his baptism and was present in Pentecostal power to celebrate the birthday of the church. As the Spirit (so Jesus told Nicodemus) gives birth to spirit, so human beings participate in creation especially in the birth of a child. That same Spirit is present in the creative arts and many other fields of human activity, so providing the glorious gifts of creation. It is exciting indeed.

The Incarnation, similarly, brings profound joy. The false distinction between material and spiritual is taken away as the Word becomes flesh. The sharing of Jesus in the life of the world sanctifies the whole of life. The wonder of the Incarnation is good news to everyone. God shares human suffering because Jesus suffered like as we do – and more.

Resurrection is the declaration that new life is possible through grace, that triumph not defeat is at the heart of the gospel. It is not easy to believe that statement in a world where natural disasters bring death and suffering on an unimaginable scale, but it remains the hope at the heart of faith.

There is no need for despondency about the faith itself, but we must never pretend that present structures are the "decisive component of the heavenly host". The form of the church, as we know it, has served the church in the times when it was appropriate, met needs, forwarded the cause. Having served its time, new forms are called for – something which will inevitably cause major ecclesiastical problems. But the deep-down things go forward, encouraging faith and hope. If humanity was born singing, let it continue to offer praise in celebration of an unchanging but excitingly relevant faith, grounded in creation, Incarnation and resurrection.

WHEN WORDS FAIL

Words fail us. There are none that can describe our feelings following the crime in Omagh.* In the presence of shattered bodies, shattered lives, shattered minds, shattered faith, words seem totally irrelevant. What can be said in the face of such evil, such grief, such pain? And so Omagh is added to the agonising roll-call of places which will be forever associated with death, destruction and despair – and it feels in such a short period of time – Bradford, Hillsborough, Lockerbie, Zeebrugge, King's Cross, *The Marchioness*, Dunblane. How can human beings blow other human beings out of the sky? fire randomly at innocent school-children? and have destroyed, in the most callous and cruel way the children, the parents, the people of Omagh? Words fail . . .

History is strewn with unspeakable situations: the hell of the Holocaust, the horror of Hiroshima. They are there too in the Bible – the slaughter of the innocents at the command of King Herod with the agonising cry: *Rachel weeping for her children and refusing to be comforted, because they are no more*; the distress of King David and his men after finding their wives and daughters taken captive at Ziklag: *so David and his men wept aloud until they had no strength left to weep*.

There will never be a time when life will "get back to normal" in Omagh, nor can families bereaved by such a monstrous evil event be expected to cope with that experience. Yet somehow living goes on . . . as it has done after Dunblane. It is only those in the very midst of the suffering who will learn how to do this. It will come not through theory but of necessity. For some the resources will lie within their families, through the bond of shared pain; others will find them with friends and neighbours, themselves victims of the blast, or shocked spectators of it; some will find it in the fellowship of their church or club or community activity. Some will find it in compassion from friends and strangers. Some may find it in their faith. But it will not be in theories about suffering. It will be in the knowledge that the Jesus who wept over the death of a friend and over the desolation of Jerusalem, is the one who himself suffered at the hands of wicked people, who endured agony in Gethsemane and cruelty on Calvary, who was despised and rejected of men, who was acquainted with grief.

There is no answer to the problem of suffering, nor any explanation as to how human beings can be capable of the cruelty that crucified Omagh. There will, however, in due course, come from the people in that community some witness to their belief that, in the darkest hour of their lives, the suffering God was there with them, not to explain the inexplicable, but to weep with them in their desolation. As it was said at Dunblane, the first tears would be God's tears.

* The bomb planted in August 1998.

CAREFUL WORDS

The evidence for the presence of reporters following Jesus during his ministry, it has been jocularly said, is the third verse of St Luke's Gospel, chapter 19, in the *Authorised Version*. Zacchaeus, anxious to see Jesus but being a little man, "could not (see him) for the press". This somewhat archaic way of referring to crowd problems has nothing, of course, to do with journalists, but it may serve to introduce a discussion of the responsibilities of those who work with words.

The issue is a relevant one, especially as we approach the anniversary of the death of Diana, Princess of Wales.* There is an art in remembering that must be nourished as the time of remembrance comes, but it really does involve care with words.

Oliver Tomkins, formerly the Bishop of Bristol, has written a very searching prayer, in his book, *Asking God*. It is relevant to those who work with words: "O God, deliver us from the abstract words that hide men and women behind a cloud; deliver us from the untrue words that value sensation more than the facts; deliver us from the emotive words that rouse our feelings at the expense of our minds; and guard, through the Word himself, all those who follow the dangerous trade of dealing in words." These are wise words indeed.

When St Paul wrote in his Hymn of Love in 1 Corinthians, chapter 13, that "love rejoiceth not in iniquity but rejoiceth in the truth," he touched a nerve relating to human weakness. William Barclay in his translation of the same passage makes the thrust of that statement even stronger. He puts it: "Love finds nothing to be glad about when things go wrong, but is glad when truth is glad." That statement, of course, describes the ideal more than actuality for there is something in human nature – it is surely part of our fallen nature – that is (to put it at its best) interested in the things which go wrong for others. The media is therefore often accused of publishing mainly bad news. And as newspapers need high sales, and radio and television require good figures, one can only conclude that the media is providing what the public wants, namely sensation. Gossip is a human weakness. Circulation is built on the suffering of others. We hopefully fall short of being glad when someone goes wrong, but we are, alas, all too interested in such events.

"Take with you words ... take away all iniquity; accept that which is good and we will render the fruit of our lips" – and pens, word processors and the internet. The words of Hosea are taken out of context, but they underline for each one of us our responsibility for what we say, write, broadcast, publish, read. If it is true that "to every thing there is a time and a season," now is a time for particular care with words.

* The Princess of Wales died on 31 August 1997, so this Meditation was in August 1998.

THE SILENCE OF THE TONGUE

Careless talk costs lives. Those who remember the Second World War will recall well the campaign to compel people to think before they spoke, lest they carelessly conveyed information that might help the enemy. Careless talk has, this week, done a great deal of damage, causing bitter hurt to people with disabilities,* provoking a monumental row that, even though it was in the context of sport, involved government ministers, even the Prime Minister. It has blighted a brilliant professional career. "It's very easy to talk," said Mrs Mantalini in Dickens' *Nicholas Nickleby*, but if you "chance to talk a little wild" as Henry VIII (in Shakespeare's play of that name) commented and do it as a so-called celebrity in a media-conscious age, the consequences can be, and often are, serious.

The reading at our ministry of healing service on Sunday – from St James's letter in the New Testament – happened to be on the theme of what Mother Teresa calls "the silence of the tongue". This letter is surely the most down-to-earth among the epistles in the New Testament. James soars to no theological heights such as Paul did in the intricacies of his letter to the Romans. But he is extremely practical. He hates sham ("Faith without works is dead"). It is James who has most to say about the power for good and evil of the tongue. "What a huge forest fire can be set ablaze by the tiniest spark," he writes, underlining its inherent power.

Mother Teresa's similar emphasis on the importance of the silence of the tongue re-echoes James's point, that is the need to recognise that the tongue can be "an unruly evil" or the medium through which we praise God. The choice is ours! We can (Mother Teresa says) "refrain from every word that causes darkness, turmoil, and death". We must use it for "praising God and speaking the life-giving word of truth, that is the truth which enlightens and inspires, brings peace, hope and joy".

It is towards 2000 years since James spoke with fervour about careless talk. It is within our times that Mother Teresa has encouraged the silence of the tongue. Both James and Mother Teresa need to be heard today.

In the field of disability, it has been shown how a careless, thoughtless statement can hurt and offend people with disabilities.* That is an obvious error for which a heavy price has been paid. It is the subtler ways in which we all talk carelessly about people with disability that create pain and grief. Many commentators have described people with disabilities as "the disabled", "the handicapped", "people of that kind" etc. Nor is it right to describe people with disabilities as "invalids". It is too near "in-valids", that is second-class citizens. That demonstrates the lack of awareness and sensitivity which hurts so much.

It is important to speak the truth, but it must be done in love. It is that qualification which will help us to avoid the careless talk that so damages lives.

* The reference is to the England football manager, Glenn Hoddle, who lost his position as a result of his relating disability to punishment.

SHARING IN CREATION

It is intriguing to read in Genesis that the task of giving the birds and animals their names was allocated to Adam. "And out of the ground, the Lord God formed every beast of the field, and every fowl of the air, and brought them unto Adam to see what he would call them: and whatsoever Adam called every living creature, that was the name thereof." The incident is delightful, its significance is profound. *Human beings share in the creativity of God.* What a glorious, hopeful message this conveys! What a vision, not least for the creative arts!

The Creation did not end after seven days, or any specific number of years. God is the Creator still – as miracles, signs and wonders demonstrate. If (as, again Genesis records) "God saw everything he had made, and behold it was very good," the same is true of God's on-going creativity. It is our responsibility, as sharers in creation, to do everything we can to ensure that what we create is good too. Then, as St Paul exhorted the Thessalonians, we can "hold fast that which is good". That surely is the criterion for assessing the products of the creative arts.

What is, in fact, "good" requires further definition, for sometimes it is necessary to portray evil in order to demonstrate good. Here, having brought the faith and the arts together, let us consider a quality related to both, that of beauty. "Worship the Lord in the beauty of holiness," we sing in J S B Monsell's hymn, but there is also the holiness of beauty, with its capacity to move and excite the inner being. To appreciate beauty requires more than that on which, in religious exercises, we so often focus, namely the intellect. We need to involve the imagination, a creative faculty often undervalued today. "We believe that imagination is stronger than knowledge," runs a prayer, the source of which I do not know. It continues: "We believe that myth is more potent than history, that dreams are more powerful than facts. We believe that hope triumphs over experience, that laughter is the only cure for grief. And we believe that love is stronger than death."

This is not the kind of material on which the tabloid press survives nor is it the diet of politicians, big business and public relations. It will not be regarded as reality in a world in which the trivial is glorified, the irrelevant over-publicised, greed glamourised and possessions celebrated. It is, nevertheless, for those who have the inner eyes to see it, an intimation of reality that takes us beyond the material to the spiritual, that enables us "to touch and handle things unseen". It affirms the truth of the Pauline declaration that it is not "the things that are temporal" that represent ultimate reality, but "the things which are eternal".

Let us here rejoice in our call to share in creation and, in so doing, forward the things that are good and lovely.

TRIVIAL PURSUITS

"Live at the Church on Sunday" the poster proclaimed. Was this some important religious event – a choral concert? the presence of a great evangelist? a modern group presenting new forms of musical communication? an inter-faith dialogue?

The full announcement in fact read: "Live at the Church on Sunday – Arsenal v Manchester United."

The location, still popularly known as "The Church" is in fact a very large public house (the other church in a local union being selected as the place of worship). A "listed building", surplus to needs, its exterior had to remain unaltered, but the sanctuary area was transformed into a very large modern pub. It was in that building that the live football match would be available on screen. A large congregation no doubt attended that act of worship, for "act of worship" in some sense it was. Sport has become a popular religion. Its leading lights are worshipped (not only in words, but gestures) as god-like beings. Some well-known managers have been said (in an oblique reference to the one who came as Messiah) to "walk on water". And the liberality is huge. It has to be to pay wages to its most outstanding participants of figures like £40,000 a week. That poster symbolised the superficiality of so much at the heart of contemporary society, the modern search for a substitute religion and the sheer triviality of many contemporary pursuits.

It is frightening to realise that in the real world, the number who actually attended that match is not dissimilar to the number who are believed to have died in the appalling earthquake in Turkey. When a geological fault and human failure combine to destroy the lives and livelihoods of thousands upon thousands of people, we are staring the realities of life in the face. It is here that the mystery of suffering tears at faith, delves deeply into doubt, and frames the questions that cannot be answered but seem to question the integrity of a God of love.

There is no good purpose served by the church berating society for its trivial pursuits and tawdry ways. Far better that it should proclaim positively the truths it has received from the One who was listened to gladly in his time because he spoke with authority. The rediscovery of the authority of the Word, and the finding of ways to proclaim it "with boldness" in today's world remains a millennium priority.

There is no practical purpose served by the academic discussion of "the problem of suffering". Theological intricacies are of no immediate comfort to the distraught parent, the despairing partner or the crushed family. The need is for the understanding that reflects the loving heart of God.

The foundations of faith lie in the experiences which teach and train the soul in faith and trust – the wonder of the divine forgiveness and an unwavering conviction in the desire of God to bring wholeness and healing to the world.

GREATER GLORY

A large collection of photographs, perhaps, or the accumulated sermons of a lifetime's ministry; a large file of press-cuttings; box after box of correspondence, much of it personal; the heaped-up copies of the journal containing editorials and articles emanating from a long time in journalism – the words of The Preacher in the Old Testament (known to us as Ecclesiastes) force us to make difficult decisions. "There is," he says, "a time to keep and a time to throw away." But the decision to do the latter can create something like emotional paralysis. To throw away can feel like throwing a large part of yourself out to waste.

It was, if I may again be personal, the last of the categories I mentioned that brought about the need for my decision. Over 500 issues of the religious newspaper for which I had had responsibility for 13 years had to be destroyed. The alternative meant that they would continue to lie, respected but unlooked at as they had been for years, for a further period of time.

Not only practical reasons came into that difficult decision. In that one felt as if one was throwing away a large part of oneself – and that would apply in all the other categories, like photographs and letters, too – emotional aspects are involved. And because the material to be cast away was religious, spiritual aspects came into it too. There is a time to look at what really matters in life and what does not; a time to re-evaluate the past and make decisions about the future.

It is right to hold to the past so long as it is done with proper proportion. It is right to "keep" memories that are inspirational and comforting. There is however a point where nostalgic attachment to the past can affect future development. This was explained by the Old Testament prophet, Haggai, in his rebuke to those who glorified the past temple and said a future one would never equal it. "The glory of the latter house," he said "shall be greater than the former." In other words, when God is present in events "the best is yet to be". It is a reminder that God is still creating, that Jesus is the same tomorrow as he was yesterday, that the Holy Spirit, like the freely blowing wind, is active in this world. Thus that which is still to be done is more important than that which is past, however memorable.

There is too a specifically spiritual aspect to this matter that is for our blessing. Too often the unhappy past is "kept" and becomes overwhelming guilt. The Christian doctrine of forgiveness stresses that there is a time to "throw away". The spiritual energy made available by the acceptance of forgiveness is the greatest possible contribution to inner peace.

MOTHERS' PAIN

Jonathan Sacks, the Chief Rabbi of Britain and the Commonwealth, speaks of his mother as a living role-model for celebrating life in her enhancing the lives of others. In her eighties, she is "still visiting the sick, doing acts of kindness and finding happiness in unexpected places".* It is a tribute that encourages us all to give thanks for motherhood, mothers and the gentle graces associated with so many of them. It is a time too to be aware of the sensitivity of mothers to suffering.

Ministry to those who are bereaved means sharing grief, when injury or death has made tears flow from parents overwhelmed by their loss. For a mother, facing the loss of – literally – her own flesh and blood, how can she hold back those tears? Nor should she, for it is right to cry. Can there be anything more painful than to see her child suffer pain or death?

When Simeon, described in St Luke's Gospel as a "righteous and devout man", received the baby Jesus into his arms, his gratitude overflowed. Having seen God's act of salvation – he described it as the "consolation of Israel" – Simeon was ready to "depart in peace". But in his prayer – a eulogy in praise of the Messiah – there is an important parenthesis. To Jesus' mother Mary, he addressed a significant prophecy. "A sword," he says, "will pierce your soul." His saving work would bring suffering not only to her son but to her. Mary, it is certain, "heard" these words and pondered them in her heart.

"Life, sadly, is inescapably unfair." So wrote Minette Martin in this newspaper.** How dramatically true this is in the life of Jesus. He encountered injustice at so many points in his life – that he, described as "the King of the Jews", should be born in a stable, there being no room for him elsewhere; that he, from the time of his birth, should be a target for Herod's terrorism, having to be taken hastily to Egypt to escape the slaughter of the innocent children; that he, the very Incarnation of goodness, should be hounded by soldiers in Gethsemane's garden, harangued by rulers and priests, hustled along the road to Calvary for crucifixion between two robbers; what justice is this? Yet it was all ominously present in the picture of the suffering servant in Isaiah, an interpretation of the Messianic role on which Jesus clearly drew. Despised, rejected, a man of sorrows, acquainted with grief, oppressed, afflicted, wounded, non-violent and utterly truthful, yet "it pleased the Lord to bruise him." Simeon seemed to have this very picture in mind when he prophesied Mary's grief and pain.

Somewhere within the pain lie the seeds of growth. It is appropriate to give grateful thanks for that gift too.

* *Celebrating Life*, Jonathan Sacks, Fount (HarperCollins 2000).
** *Daily Telegraph*, 17 March 2001.

REJOICE AND SIGN!

Rejoice and sign! No, it is not a misprint for "sing". Signing is the way in which deaf and deaf-blind people offer their praise to God – as they did at their annual Service of Lessons and Carols* in St Margaret's Church in Westminster, London, before Christmas. To share in such an occasion is moving and encouraging, for the pleasure shown by people with disabilities in so worshipping God is both manifest and infectious. Because each word has to be made visual, and the words of worship – at least on this occasion – are joyful, there is a radiance demonstrated by hands, eyes and faces not often seen in "normal" verbal worship.

If those who have a disability can so *en*courage us, why do we do so many things to *dis*courage them? If it is part of religious belief to say that every person is of equal value to God who is "no respecter of persons"; if we believe that every human being is unique and has the right to develop his or her full potential; if it is a fundamental obligation to have compassion for those whose lives are beset with difficulties, why can we not do more to meet the needs of those with physical limitations? If *we* were to spend just one day in a wheelchair, trying to enter shops, libraries, banks, cinemas, swimming-pools, and coping with domestic duties such as cooking, bathing, cleaning we might empathise much more with the frustration and desperation engendered in such situations.

Lin, my multi-handicapped friend to whom I have referred before,** has struggled magnificently with the difficulties created for her by insensitive people and unsympathetic organisations. Writer, lecturer, preacher, therapist, she is also the first multi-handicapped – cerebral-palsied, blind and in a wheelchair – student to complete successfully a basic course in homoeopathy. Eleven years ago she initiated a trust to deal with something she has often faced – the lack of holiday accommodation equipped to meet the needs of people like herself. £170,000 was raised so that a holiday cottage, fully equipped, could be built in East Harling in Norfolk. It has now been in full use for several years. What a vision! What an achievement!

Much has been done to create public awareness of the needs of people with disability. Toilets, parking, lifts, ramps, doorways and, in some hotels, baths have been provided. Football stadia, following the Taylor Report, have acted positively, as they must, in this matter. The disabled sign is known and recognised. But personal and public blinkers remain, and we create discouragement and distress for those who, though they have disabilities, are due the human rights that belong to all God's creatures.

If that implies money, so be it! It is no credit to a country with a religious background to (in Jesus' word) offend, as it so often does, any of those little – or older – ones who happen to have to cope with a disability.

* Arranged by RAD, the Royal Association in aid of Deaf people, 27 Old Oak Road, London W3.

** See also the Meditations for January 16, October 26 and December 6. The Lin Berwick Trust is at 4 Chaucer Road, Sudbury, Suffolk CO10 1LN.

Note: Readers may like to know that over £7,000 was sent to Lin by readers of *The Daily Telegraph* to help her to reach her £170,000 target. A second cottage will be built at Dirleton in East Lothian as soon as £300,000 is raised. The ultimate cost will be £400,000.

THE ART OF REMEMBERING

Fifty-three memorial works had been sensitively distributed among the trees, lawns, gardens and grounds of Blickling Hall near Aylsham in Norfolk, an eight-month exhibition designed to stimulate *The Art of Remembering*. To visit it was a memorable and moving experience.

Its purpose is not related directly to the anniversary this weekend* of the deaths of Diana, Princess of Wales, and of Mother Teresa, but its theme cannot but impinge on us all. It has proved difficult for many people to discover the art of remembering "the People's Princess" who has been spoken about as much in her death as in her life. Not a day has passed without press attention focussing on her, her sons, her family, her friends. Disagreements over the forms of memorial, profiteering in tacky souvenirs, insensitive criticism and sincere devotion have all played a part in a country unwilling to let its most loved woman go. She radiated affection and compassion. The proper of way of remembering her is an art still to be found.

At the heart of both the Jewish religion and of the Christian faith the importance of remembering in an appropriate way is underlined. Because Jesus was a Jew, the essence of the former is carried over into the latter. It was at a Passover meal that Jesus instituted the great Christian act of remembrance, the last supper. The Jewish table-ceremony began with the blessing of the bread and ended with the common cup. To these elements of blessing and thanksgiving, taken into the last supper, Jesus added his instruction that the action would become a commemoration "for as often as you eat this bread and drink this cup, you do show the Lord's death until he come." Can we, in this, find the basic elements in the art of remembering?

There is first simplicity. Strip away all that has been added liturgically to Jesus' commemoration – be it described as Mass, Eucharist, Lord's Supper or Holy Communion – and the ritual is simple indeed. Take bread, take wine, give thanks and share. Remembering needs to be profound in its simplicity. Then there is sincerity, a factor emphasised by St Paul in his instructions about motivation in his guidance to the Corinthians on communion. Thirdly, grief must be personal. All will mourn, but each must do it in their own way. For some, the public demonstration of emotion will ease the strain. Others will line no routes, shed no public tears, but cry their hearts out alone. For some, ritual will be needed, but the temperaments of others may have no such need, for each one's grieving is unique in circumstance, tone and depth of feeling.

The anniversary of Diana's death, affecting each one of us in its own way, may bless us by helping us to find something of the art of remembering, and the invitation to commitment and compassion implicit in any true memorial.

* This Meditation was published in August 1998.

A GOOD THING SPOILED

Sue Barker, tennis player turned television commentator, was interviewed on *Sport on 4* by the Welsh rugby legend, now a radio presenter, Cliff Morgan. Monica Seles had been stabbed on court at a major tournament that week and the conversation turned to the need for security. Finally the unthinkable was mentioned as a future possibility – Wimbledon fenced in. With great feeling and profound sadness, Cliff Morgan said (if I recall his words exactly), "It really is a lousy world we're living in!"

I hesitate as I quote the word "lousy". When a child, I was taught that it was a word which was not quite "drawing-room". The inhibition remains. But the synonyms I find in my thesaurus – nauseating, sickening, revolting, shocking, detestable, etc – do not as accurately express just what Cliff Morgan felt. Reluctantly but realistically, I accept his word. The world of today feels an increasingly "lousy" world.

A brick was hurled through my car window recently, for no reason but vandalism. But that incident, compared with other things, is utterly trivial. Monstrous things are constantly happening today – the murder of children, the mugging of the frail, the violent rape of women, so much spilt blood in Bosnia (and many other places), bereavement in Belfast (and many other places), starvation in the Sudan, terror in Somalia.* We can go on and on in this vein as each day brings news of large-scale pain and suffering. Cliff Morgan's plaintive cry reflects the despair now so prevalent in the world. We may even be tempted to cry, "Stop the world! I want to get off!"

But people of faith cannot contract out of life, however desperate they feel it to be, for this is the world created by God in love, the world "God so loved that he gave his only-begotten Son" for it. This is the world in which Jesus lived, taught and healed, the world on which he set such a value that he died for it. This is the world in which that "living energy of a loving God", the Holy Spirit, moves and, like the wind, blows where that Spirit chooses. The world may, in John Baillie's phrase, be "a good thing spoiled", but it is still God's world; the world with which in forgiveness and redemption he has a relationship of love; the world he longs to change.

The vocabulary of faith is full of words about change – renewal, regeneration, redemption, transformation, sanctification. Fundamental to faith is the conviction that "amazing grace" can bring about change in individuals and, through them, in society. To surrender belief in the possibility of change is to deny the power promised by God to his world. To succumb to despair is to destroy the future.

* This Meditation was written in 1997.

MANY WAYS TO FAITH

It is part of the wonder of religious faith that God reveals himself in many-splendoured ways. Variety, rather than uniformity, characterises the Divine activity. In speaking of the gifts of the Spirit, Paul confirms this: "There are different kinds of gifts, but the same Spirit gives them all." What is important is that the mark of the Spirit is not sameness, but difference.

Because of this, it is intolerant for anyone to claim that what they assert or do is alone "the will of God". A true spirituality never claims that (adapting some words from Isaiah) "my ways must be God's ways and my thoughts God's thoughts". The Holy Spirit, Jesus tells us, like the wind, "blows wherever it wishes". The Spirit cannot and must not be imprisoned within human concepts. Faith is therefore more expressed in freedom than in limitation, in inclusiveness rather than exclusiveness. This does not mean that inclusiveness has no boundaries, that it is open to anything and everything. To be "conformed to this world" would end up as licence rather than responsible liberty in Christ.

While Christians must be united on the great foundational verities of the faith, there should be ample opportunity for varying expression of it. In worship, for example, it is a privilege to share varieties of religious experience – emphasis on preaching as in my own Church of Scotland tradition, the glorious programmes of music related to worship in Anglican cathedrals, the singing of the Methodists, the silence of the Quakers, the "enthusiasm" of a congregation charismatically renewed, whether Roman Catholic or Protestant, the elaborate liturgy of the Eastern Orthodox churches, the evangelical simplicity of some small independent group. The variety and diversity characteristic of the Spirit's activity, provide what human beings need, the opportunity for different kinds of people to share worship, liturgy and fellowship appropriate to their temperaments.

Communication is too often aimed at the intellect and forgets the imagination. Music, art, poetry and indeed the whole range of the creative arts offer profound ways of reaching the needs of the soul and spirit. Meditation, contemplation and (to those so gifted) mysticism are means through which, as the Psalmist says, "deep speaks to deep".

So many-splendoured are love, worship, the gifts of the Spirit and even God that there must be an infinite variety of ways in which we communicate the faith to the changing world of today.

WEALTH AND MORALITY

Poverty is a gift and a grace, but only in one context, the self-chosen commitment of good people. Those who maintain vows of poverty deserve unstinted admiration. But poverty unsought, especially in the horrendous examples of it in certain parts of the world, is not only damaging to bodies. It also destroys minds and souls. It must therefore be as contrary to the will of God as anything can be. So also is the fear of poverty that stalks so many people today. The reduction of poverty by half by 2015, an internationally agreed aim, is, as Clare Short (the Secretary of State for International Development) has said "a moral and environmental imperative".

Wealth, too, can be threatening. The Psalmist puts it succinctly: "Though your riches increase, set not your heart upon them" (Psalm 62 verse 10). It is not money as such that is the root of evil. It is the *love* of money which is so subtly dangerous. Wealth can fundamentally change attitudes. Having much becomes wanting more. It is not surprising that Jesus said that it is not easy for a rich man to enter the kingdom.

That wealth and morality have worrying connections is borne witness to by commentators from another age. Seneca, the Roman writer, notes that "money is the ruin of the true honour of things. We ask not what a thing truly is, but what it costs." Juvenal, the satirical poet, describes money as "the nurse of debauchery". He goes on: "No guilt or deed of lust is wanting since Roman poverty disappeared." Paul wrote a withering criticism, in devastating detail, about that "age of shame" in his letter to the Romans, calling it "a situation of degeneracy of morals almost without parallel in human history" (William Barclay). That this was not simply the view of an hysterical preacher is confirmed by his secular contemporaries.

There is much talk these days of the irrelevance of personal morality to political ability; of personal failure to political judgement. That question will continue to be debated. But the danger is that a belief is nourished that morality in public life does not matter at all. There follows the inevitable corollary that in an enlightened world, spiritual attitudes are of no importance. If, however, both morality and spirituality are set aside, standards and values lose their traditional platforms. That then becomes a climate in which uncertainty and confusion grow. In some branches of the church, indeed, anxiety and division are arising over particular pastoral problems in the field of sexuality. Many believe this to be the consequence of the erosion of biblical authority and traditional beliefs.

Degeneracy in Rome was countered by the proclamation of the gospel. The unique contribution of the church is still its knowledge of the transforming power of God through grace. Its primary role today therefore remains the need to help the nation to flourish through the preaching of the Word. Changed people change situations. They did then. They can do today.

SEVEN SOCIAL SINS

How perceptive, profound and stimulating is Mahatma Gandhi's identification of the "seven social sins". Each one is so devastatingly relevant in relation to all we encounter in personal and public life today. If church groups need an agenda for their study of today's weaknesses and problems, let them look closely at these seven sins that affect society now as much as they ever did.

Gandhi's seven social sins are:

> Politics without principle
> Wealth without work
> Commerce without morality
> Pleasure without conscience
> Education without character
> Science without humanity
> Worship without sacrifice*

The more I read and re-read these words, the more I want to say "Amen" to them. Not everyone will necessarily acknowledge the truth of each. It would indeed be illuminating to know of possible alternatives. The chosen seven do seem to me, however, to probe deeply into contemporary business, political and ecclesiastical life.

At the heart of religion is a personal commitment, and that is certainly true of the Christian faith. The question put to Simon Peter – "Who do you say I am?" – produced the great confession of faith which led to Peter being described as a "rock". But emphasis on the need for individual response to the call to discipleship must never hide the corporate responsibilities which are built into being "the church". So many words in the vocabulary of faith in the New Testament are "social" words ... fellowship, community, body, flock and the word church itself. Nor are these cosy words of comfort only. The dynamics of fellowship are expressed in service.

Added to the responsibilities of the church is the prophetic role, the need to assess and criticise all human institutions, including political ones. The Old Testament prophets set a glorious example of how essential it is to bring the will of God to bear on human programmes and policies, especially when they affect people's welfare.

If the judgement of God on royal behaviour in Old Testament times was one of support and approval, that affirmation was given to kings and rulers. If they disobeyed the divine will, then a resounding "Thus saith the Lord" would issue forth in a denunciation of self-centredness and self-interest, blatant greed, sexual misbehaviour, sleaze and any policy that was not acceptable to "the King of Kings and Lord of Lords". Those who repeatedly refused to "return to the Lord" encountered the dramatic command: "Prepare to meet thy God."

The church today must exercise that prophetic role, encouraging and supporting every policy that makes for goodness and the blessing of people, but bringing the divine perspective to bear on those who commit the social sins.

THE WAY TO RENEWAL

The church dare not try to demonstrate its need to be "relevant" by reducing its standards, lowering its personal demands or accommodating its beliefs to contemporary criticisms. In other words, it will not fulfil its purposes by, in Paul's words to the Romans, being "conformed to this world". Its function is exactly the opposite. It is to "transform" the world.

The *presentation* of the church's beliefs is a different matter. Of course it must avail itself of technological advance and modern methods of communication, accepting that many people (and most children) are used to visual aids in their education. Where the medium of the message is concerned, the church must be contemporary indeed. But the message itself – that remains constant. Jesus Christ *is* "the same yesterday, today and for ever". All that is needed for salvation and wholeness is in the gospel. Christianity is best served when it presents itself as it is, stressing its call to commitment and personal sacrifice. Significantly, those churches which underline the demands of discipleship are the growing churches. Those that do not tend to wither away.

I had some time ago the privilege of leading a weekend retreat for a village parish church. It was a "family weekend" held at a conference centre some distance from the congregation's home base. For various reasons, that church had had lean years and its work and witness had decreased. Morale in the congregation was low. Then arrived their dedicated and gifted young minister and his wife, and a remarkable renewal had taken place, quantitatively and qualitatively. The gathering was made up of young couples, families, young people, older people. All were enthusiastic about the church and its purpose and unanimous about the minister's part in the church's growth and the deepening of its spiritual life.

After the event, I found myself reflecting on the underlying reasons for this impressive development and identified three crucial elements in it. They were the emphases placed on *preaching, prayer* and *pastoral concern*. Yet there was no off-putting over-earnestness involved and no false piety. There was real fellowship and plenty of fun. The core of the renewal process did however clearly lie in a sound preaching and teaching ministry, a commitment to personal and corporate prayer and real *koinonia*, that is fellowship expressed in mutual pastoral concern.

The church must be the church. It must do the things to which it is primarily called. The gospel must be proclaimed. Prayer must be offered. The love of God must be made incarnate in pastoral care. There is in that congregation much activity of other kinds – social concern, shared leisure activities, local outreach, etc – but the three identified factors are now and will always be their priorities.

There are, of course, many churches across the country equally relevant and showing similar growth. I focus on this one example because I was there to see what can happen where it is accepted that there is the word to be preached, a corporate spiritual life to be developed and a fellowship of love to be actively demonstrated; where, in fact, the church is the church.

THE TORPOR OF INDIFFERENCE

Repetition, when properly used, can be very effective. In the book of the Old Testament prophet, Amos, there is a good example of repetition used for emphasis. Five times the God of Israel says: "Yet have you not returned unto me." "Yet" is the crucial word. Though judgements have been "sent" by God, one after another – famine, drought, destruction, pestilence, defeat – Israel just will not respond and repent. Words of inevitable doom follow: "Prepare to meet thy God, O Israel."

I once asked a colleague to read this passage from Amos at morning worship. She flatly refused, on the grounds that any God "sending" such punishments was not the God she knew in Jesus. I respected her feelings and changed the reading, but the responses to the judgements recorded in this passage point to something important to the spiritual life. It is the phenomenon of the hardening heart.

"A wicked man hardeneth his face," says the writer of the Proverbs. The hardening face (male, female or group) is the exterior expression of the hardening heart, so graphically illustrated in the case of Pharaoh, king of Egypt. After each new plague sent in judgement, he "hardened his heart" and still refused, as Moses said, to "let my people go".

If the language sounds old-fashioned, the phenomenon itself is wholly contemporary. There is today an over-acceptance of, and indifference to, wrong-doing. It is another form of the hardening heart expressed in insensitivity to evil. The violence, featured so much in the media, is seen as a "normal" part of society, a fact we acknowledge as we avoid the fear-full streets and create our fortress homes. Language once banned from radio and television is now a regular part of, especially, late-night programmes. "When I was a young man," said the late Professor Jack Perry, the authority on trading with China, responding to eightieth birthday tributes, "I did not know anyone who was divorced." Recalling his seven-year courtship of his wife, Kate, he contrasted such a practice with the instant relationships of today and the reduced stability they bring. In so many fields, standards have deteriorated, values have been undermined and the gentle graces discouraged. What we would have denounced yesterday is acceptable today. That is the subtle deterioration evident in our society. It is this insensitivity to grace and goodness which, in this widespread unawareness of them, is the contemporary expression of the hardened heart. We are indifferent to that process at our peril.

Indifference is a dangerous and an infectious disease. Untreated, it develops into something worse. "There is nothing so fatal to religion as indifference," wrote Edmund Burke in 1795. "It is, at least, half infidelity." It is not open hostility that the faith has to fight today. It is (in the words of John of Salisbury) "the torpor of indifference". It is that which leads to the hardening of the spiritual arteries today.

"I know thy works that they are neither cold nor hot," was the judgement made on the church of the Laodiceans (in the book of Revelation). "Thou art merely lukewarm." Apathy, indifference, insensitivity, the hardened heart – these are the current symptoms of estrangement and alienation from spiritual resources. It is time to "make all things new".

TIME TO MAKE PEACE

"Some people think reconciliation is a soft option, that it means papering over the cracks. But the biblical meaning involves looking facts in the face. Reconciliation can be very costly." The cost implicit in the ministry of reconciliation was well known to the author of these words, Desmond Tutu.

To be concerned with reconciliation is not one of the options religious people can select or reject. It is a commitment that is grounded in the very essence of the faith. In his second letter to the Corinthians, Paul spoke of the need to be "Christ's ambassadors", carrying "the message of reconciliation" as a prime responsibility because it flows from the very heart of the gospel. Because of our experience of God's reconciling love in Jesus, there is an obligation upon us to exercise a ministry of reconciliation to others. The ministry of reconciliation is rooted in the Incarnation. It is an obligation arising from the relationship restored by the saving acts of God.

Desmond Tutu's emphasis on the need to face the facts of any situation involving deep division must always be the first practical step in the ministry of reconciliation. The second must be the willingness of one party to the quarrel to take the first step in a reconciling endeavour. And moreover – and it is here that the element of cost is certainly present – to take that step while believing that the responsibility for that action should be on the other side.

A door with a hole cut out of it, on display in a church in Ireland, offers historic testimony to the potential fruitfulness of such an action. The hole was cut in the door by the head of one of two families locked in near-mortal combat, when the pursued leader found "sanctuary" in the church. It was the pursuer who cried to his enemy within the church to "take his sword, cut a hole in the door and extend the hand of reconciliation". It was the pursued leader who, questioning the integrity of the invitation, declined to take the suggested action. It was the pursuer who then cried out that, in those circumstances, he himself would cut the hole in the door and extend his hand in reconciliation to end the conflict. The hole in the door on display testifies to the action that was taken and the reconciliation that ensued, brought about by, perhaps, the one less obliged to do it, taking the first step.

There is no easy way to heal the hurt of family or domestic division; to bring healing to society; to lead the church to a greater unity. Facile as it may seem to some, it needs to be remembered that Paul expounded his call to the ministry of reconciliation having just borne testimony to the fact that "if anyone is in Christ, he/she is a new creation. The old has gone, the new has come." Those who seek to reconcile the irreconcilable will always be believers in prayer and the transforming power of grace to bring new relationships into being.

COMMON GROUND

I find it difficult to think of noise as the medium of the divine message. I felt that problem acutely when I attended a Mission to London meeting in the Earl's Court arena. Thousands came each night to hear Morris Cerullo's preaching. It was a proclamation of the gospel that declared the faith, sought conversions, demanded commitment and encouraged the Christian life. The core message was the wonder of God's love, the transformation brought about by encountering Jesus and the power of the Holy Spirit. To all that, I offer an enthusiastic "Amen". It is not, however, the message which creates difficulties. It is the method.

The mission offered traditional evangelistic endeavour accompanied by the usual components of mass evangelism – music, choir, soloist, confrontational preaching, "going forward", the appeal for money, etc. What was new to me was the setting of the exercise in a pop concert genre. That meant three hours (one of "build-up", two of meeting) of unremitting noise – voices, music, the solo trumpet used (skilfully) by the associate evangelist (who preached the night I was there) to emphasise his message, all efficiently amplified. There was, too, the response of the thousands present, a singing, swaying addition to the total volume of sound.

It was patently clear that the whole experience brought to many of the young people around me, inspiration, affirmation and genuine spiritual joy. God, it seemed, was present in the incessant noise and flashing lights. Yet somehow, deep down, I felt the lesson Elijah learned was an important one. He did not, as he expected, find God's presence in the drama of earthquake, wind and fire. It was in the silence that he had to listen to the still, small voice.

There has always been a gulf between older and younger generations, but that gulf has never been greater than it is now. Technologically confused grandparents seem to inhabit a different world from their computer-literate grandchildren who move serenely through the maze of information technology and enter easily (though not without the danger of addiction) into the world of the internet. While traditional religious language meets the needs of many (but not all) older people, young people need to express their spirituality through their own culture and vocabulary. There is however, in terms of faith, common ground. Jesus is the same "yesterday, today and for ever". For older and younger, the crucial question is the same. It is the one put to Peter by Jesus: "What do you make of Christ?"

The response can only be offered individually and will be expressed in concepts and language belonging to the generation to which each belongs and within the milieu in which they are at ease. For some that will be the silence of the desert place, for others it will be amid the noise of so-called "rave culture" services.

It is, I believe, in the quiet moment that the wonder of the divine love is revealed. Following the miracle of grace there is, of course, every reason to shout "Hallelujah!"

MORAL PROGRESS?

Morality is prominent in public discussion as we approach the Millennium. On the political agenda, it is also the focus of religious writing. Bishop Richard Holloway in his most recent book, *Godless Morality*,* making the case for "a morality without God", describes his book as "an attempt to offer a human-centred justification" for morality.

When the late Sir Malcolm Sargent was asked by a nonconformist minister and author, Frank Jennings (popularly know as "The Tramps' Parson"), "In your opinion is our nation progressing morally and spiritually?" he rather tartly replied that "England today must surely be at its most immoral period in history." That strong response was not reflected in the replies of other "leading people". Dame Sybil Thorndike wrote in her own hand (all these quotations are from personal, but not private letters in front of me) an enthusiastic "Yes! Yes! Yes!" and saw progress in the attitudes and activities of the younger generation. "We are progressing," agreed Sir Richard Acland. "The vast majority of English men and women have retained the moral and spiritual sense which has long been a national characteristic," wrote Christina Foyle. Others were less sure: Beverley Baxter was not confident: "There has undoubtedly been a lowering of moral values since the end of the war . . . In political life, all the parties have concentrated almost solely on the material aspect of life and neglected the spiritual." Vera Brittain wrote strongly: "Morally and spiritually there has been a great deterioration in the higher places of our country. On the other hand there has been a great change for the better among ordinary people." Lord Vansittart was definite: "No, of course we are not progressing morally or spiritually. We are going backward – and how!"

That was 1949. Fifty years and more on, what would the responses to that same question be? Varied, no doubt, but many would probably feel that deterioration in both the moral and spiritual areas had increased. The two world wars and the ability of mankind to continue to inflict mutual suffering through conflict, the love of power, the strength of selfishness and greed, the obsessive desire to acquire and possess, the abuse of the world's resources, the accumulation of the "haves" and the poverty of the "have-nots", have done much to erase beliefs in continuous progress, and re-emphasise the realities of the power of evil, latent and real, within humanity.

The coming of the Millennium can serve a purpose if it compels in us a personal spiritual stock-taking and in the world a fresh look at the need for a true morality, godless or God-inspired. What we take into the new millennium are the traditions that are of lasting value: an openness to new ideas in every part of life, not least theological and ecclesiastical, and a determination to forward the things that are good and lovely.

The new millennium points to new opportunities. Many will therefore say 'Let the renewing Spirit come!'

* Canongate Books, Edinburgh 1999.
This Meditation was written in October 1999.

THE PRIMACY OF LOVE

"Love is the keystone in the arch that joins the soul to God." So wrote Martin Israel in his first book, *Summons to Life*.* That definition is spelt out in the most glorious way in St Paul's great "Hymn of Love" in 1 Corinthians, chapter 13. That such a man, with his history of violence and persecution towards Christians, a man who "approved" the stoning of Stephen the martyr, should reach such heights of sensitivity and understanding of the nature of love, is nothing short of miraculous. That such a man could be transformed and become "the chief of the apostles" is a miracle of grace. Paul was so changed, so inwardly renewed, that he was able to touch and handle, with such spiritual delicacy, the concept of divine love as possibly no one else has. If we can follow St Paul to the heights of his vision of the nature of love, we will draw as near to the heart of God as human beings can. Preacher, prophet, poet, the many facets of Paul come together to proclaim the nature of that love which is divine and which excels all human love.

There is a difficulty over the word "love" in that the English word has to be used to translate four different Greek words. There is first the word *eros* (which is used mainly in the context of human love, "love between the sexes" as William Barclay describes it in his book *New Testament Words*).** There is *storge* which means family affection, the love of a people for their monarch, etc. There is *philia*, the love typical of true friendship as in, for example, "the disciple whom Jesus loved" or Jesus' love for Lazarus. There is, finally and importantly, the word used in the New Testament for Christian love because it is all-embracing: it involves the whole person. That word is *agape*. It is, William Barclay tells us, "a deliberate principle of the mind and a deliberate conquest of the will. It is in part the power to love the unlovable ... It takes everything to achieve Christian love ... it takes not only the heart, it takes the mind and the will as well."

It is *agape,* this Christian love, which is the basis of (to use a phrase I have used before) "the eternal triangle" which is at the heart of the gospel, the love that flows first from God to our neighbour as it does to us, then from our neighbour and us to God, and consequently from us to our neighbour and *vice versa*. Only when the three points in the triangle are joined up by the love that flows in every direction is God's will fully expressed and his way made incarnate.

So "love is of God" John tells us in his first epistle and "God is love." No wonder the "more excellent way" in the Hymn of Love, is, as the *New English Bible* puts it, "the best way of all".

* Hodder, 1974.
** SCM, 1980.

LOVE, THE WORD THAT HEALS

St Paul's exposition of the nature of love in the New Testament sense shows it to be the rock on which relationships are built. Love means treating people as God treats them – and us. Love is therefore the foundation on which the Christian life and the ideal of service are built.

In our reflections on Christian love, it is important to remember, all the time, the sense in which we are using that word. The word "love" is much mis-used today in a sex-obsessed society. Romantic love, physical love, erotic love are spoken of as if, altogether or singly, they mean the same as *agape*, the New Testament concept of love. So love, in our society is glamourised, trivialised, misrepresented, misunderstood, commercialised and prostituted. "Making love" is translated so often as "having sex". But while the sexual element, properly understood and placed in context in profound and loving relationships has its place – for human beings have not only hearts, minds and souls but bodies (as the Incarnation underlines) – love loses its real meaning if one element in wholeness is extracted, separated off, taken out of context and made all-important. Love is the word that heals only if we mean love in its fullness, truly human and related to the divine. Anything less than that falls short of the understanding of the love St Paul describes so wonderfully in his Hymn of Love.

The initiator of loving relationships expressed in "the eternal triangle" is always God. "We love Him because He first loved us." The vertical element in the symbol of the cross is that initiating divine love made real in the One who came to be "God with us". The horizontal arms of the cross symbolise the outstretched arms of Jesus in love for mankind, ourselves and our neighbours. The fullness of love involves both elements, thus making the cross a mystical symbol of the great reality of life, the primacy of love expressed in relationship between God, us and our neighbour.

Life in the Spirit, the life dominated by love, is both a "one-to-one" relationship with God and its expression in service to the world. There is no gap or void between personal or individual spirituality and social Christianity. Personal devotion is only a false piety if it does not engage with the world. Equally, social involvement, if it does not ground itself in worship, becomes no more than social service. This is not to downgrade social service, a wholly important discipline in the world, but Christian service is more than just social outreach.

The exposition of Christian love in 1 Corinthians 13 "joins the soul to God". God in his divine initiative has drawn us to him and to each other through the "cords of love that cannot be broken". That binding together in love is, I repeat, the solid foundation on which Christian life and service is built. Love is of God, for God *is* love.

THE LOVE THAT IS PATIENT

It might be thought risky to try and break love up into the elements of which it is composed. Just as with magic, analysis only succeeds in destroying that which we are examining. But St Paul has, with inspired sensitivity, attempted (as the great Henry Drummond did much later in his classic little book *The Greatest Thing in the World*) to examine various aspects of it. His Hymn of Love in 1 Corinthians 13 is the result. He begins with the love that is patient.*

Patience, proverbially, is a virtue, but a virtue expressed in different ways by different people. In some it is the capacity to cope with difficult situations calmly, and at times with difficult people. In others, we see it as a degree of consistency, solidity, the ability to withstand pressure. It is a quality not at all typical of our hurried, harassed world. Lack of patience leads to unpleasantness, anger (as in road rage), frustration and division. The result is that it creates broken relationships and unreconciled conflicts. Patience is a gift that enables admirable people to undertake the education of, or caring for, those who are in special need, those who are physically handicapped or mentally limited, the socially deprived, the psychologically disturbed. Love is – or ought to be – patient. Blessed indeed are those who have the gift of patience.

In the use of the word "patient" in the New Testament, there is another and very profound element. It is the way in which God is seen to demonstrate patience in his dealing with recalcitrant people. It may be the stubbornness of "the children of Israel" in the Old Testament or reluctant potential disciples (like the rich young ruler) in the New Testament. But the divine patience is there.

The word "patient" is linked, by derivation, with suffering. The Bible extends this link by moving to the concept of (as the *Authorised Version* renders it) long-suffering. So the patience of God is expressed dramatically in St Paul's hymn of love: "Love suffers long ..." William Barclay translates it: "Love is patient with people."

The Greek word for long-suffering is *makrothumia*. It means "a long-holding out of the mind before it gives room to action or passion." It witnesses to "the steadfast spirit which will never give in" according to William Barclay. It is used by Paul in his letter to the Romans (chapter 2, verse 4) to describe "the goodness and forbearance and long-suffering of God."

In popular parlance, long-suffering has a negative sound to it, but it is not at all negative when applied, as it is here, to the patience of God. Indeed the cross symbolises that patience. "God so loved the world" in Jesus.

The disciple must reflect his or her master in attitude and action. We can be so impatient with the over-persistent, so irritated with the perpetual invader of our privacy, so provoked by our critics. But the demand of love is clear. Love is patient with people. Love suffers long.

* This theme was introduced in the Meditation for January 27.

THE LOVE THAT IS KIND

"Be kind to each other." So Paul writes in his letter to the church at Ephesus (in J B Phillips' translation). The *New English Bible* renders "kind" as "generous". That is helpful for kindness is a quality that has within it the desire to bless someone with good. Consult the dictionary, and you will almost certainly find that this element – the disposition to do good to another – is at the heart of the concept of kindness. Kindness involves understanding. Kindness wants to do what it can to bring about well-being. Love then, according to Paul, is kind.

J B Phillips in his *Letters to Young Churches* draws attention to the creative aspect of kindness. He translates the phrase "Love is kind" in this way: "love looks for a way of being constructive." Kindness is never possessiveness, nor does it seek to deny freedom of personality. It does not take people over. It is an offering, in compassion, of whatever we can give and which we hope, if it is accepted, will bring a blessing to another human being. That compassionate element in kindness is in effect its capacity to enable someone to grow. In particular, it releases the potential within people. It brings out the good and the beautiful, sometimes where such qualities are very hidden. It therefore reflects the attitude of compassion, goodwill and patience that characterises the heart of God. His only aim is to do us good.

"Love does not dominate: it cultivates." So runs a poster on my wall. How true this is of the divine kindness! How true it must be of ours! Love as kindness is never a smothering process. It is a creative one. It never seeks to bind, only to liberate. It is not presented as an order to be obeyed but as a gift to be received. The model for this attitude is in Jesus himself who watched with sadness as the rich young ruler walked away. He let him go and he did that with kindness. We dare not try to browbeat anyone into the kingdom of God. We dare not do, as Simon Magus sought to do, as related in the Acts of the Apostles, and that is seek to manipulate the Holy Spirit. The prodigal son was free to go to "the far country". His father would yearn for him and pray for him, but he did not go and fetch him back. "Selfhood begins" says the poet C Day Lewis, "in a walking away, and love is known in the letting go."

And so the divine kindness is revealed. Salvation is not a magic potion to be applied: it is a gift to be offered and received – or rejected. In this, the divine way, "be kind to one another."

THE LOVE THAT DOES NOT ENVY

Envy is the antithesis of Christian love. It is linked in the New Testament with strife, division, hatred, even murder. These are all denials of love. Pilate, we learn from St Matthew's Gospel, knew that "for *envy* they had delivered Jesus to him". Paul, writing to the Romans, describes people *full of envy* as "ungodly" and "unrighteous". And he has other comments about envy to make in his letters to the churches with which he was associated: "Let us walk ... not in strife or *envying*", "the works of the flesh are ... *envyings*". James in his letter tells us that "where *envying* and strife is, there is confusion and every evil work."

Envy is "an attribute of the Devil" according to Francis Bacon in his essay on this subject. Through it relationships are threatened, poisoned and, often, broken. Examples of this connection can be seen in the relationships of Cain and Abel, Esau and Jacob, Joseph and his brothers, King Saul and David, and the touchy relationship between "the elder brother" and "the prodigal son". It was not wholly absent from the relationship of Peter and Paul. Envy is indeed one of the deadly sins. It has no place in the way of love.

The *Authorised Version* of the Bible and the *New English Bible* keep to the word envy, but the *Jerusalem Bible* prefers the word "jealous". J B Phillips interprets this sin as "possessiveness". The dictionary definition of envy focuses on that element too, adding that an essential point of envy is that of "grudging", a "grudging ill-will at another's superiority" or, as it might be, over another's possessions.

It is worth recording that envy was part of the primal sin of the Garden of Eden. There it was expressed as the desire to "be as God" and have total knowledge as he did. So envy played its part in the downfall of humanity. Envy is an unwelcome aspect of life. It is expressed in so many ways to the detriment of human welfare and the welfare of the individual.

While envy is wrong because of its begrudging element, we should note too the proper and positive side of legitimate envy. We should long for and yearn for the ability to reach standards of spiritual living that we see in others who are so much further along the way than we are. A genuine envy that aims at that which is good and lovely is different from those unacceptable envious feelings we so dislike. It is perhaps best expressed in St Paul's statement of his own struggle to reach the highest levels of spiritual desire: "I press toward the mark," he said, "for the prize of the high calling of God in Jesus Christ" (Philippians, chapter 3, verse 13). Such reaching forward in humble faith can only be good. But in relation to that negative, grudging attitude which in fact diminishes us we need to say: "Love envies not."

THE LOVE THAT IS HUMBLE

The translations may vary and the descriptive phrases used differ in detail, but there is no doubt at all what St Paul is saying. Humility is the essence of the loving-ness of God. So "Love vaunteth not itself, is not puffed up," or as William Barclay puts it: "Love makes no proud claims, there is no conceit in love." All this means that love is not boastful. It does not set out to impress others. It has no inflated idea of its own importance.

Humility is often presented as unhealthily self-effacing and self-deprecating. It is, as a result, associated with weakness. The wringing hands of a Uriah Heep in no way represent true humility. Cringing before superior power, creeping surreptitiously onwards in the pursuit of favours, crawling in feigned self-abasement in the hope of acceptance – none of this has anything to do with humility.

As will be constantly necessary, it is to the idea that is so fundamental to Christian thought that we must first go. Love is *of God*. God *is* love. The garment of humility that we must wear is in the image of the humility shown by Jesus. That humility is expressed memorably in another magnificent passage from one of Paul's letters, the letter to the Philippians. I cannot do other than quote that marvellous section (chapter 2, verses 5 to 11):

> Jesus shared the very being of God, but he did not regard his equality with God as something to be clutched to himself. So far from that, he emptied himself and really and truly became a servant. He was made for a time exactly like man. In a human form that all could see, he accepted such a depth of humiliation that he was prepared to die, and to die on a cross. That is why God has given him the highest place and has conferred on him the name that is greater than any name so that, at the name of Jesus, every creature in heaven and on earth and beneath the earth should kneel in reverence and submission, and so that everything which has a voice should openly declare that Jesus Christ is Lord and thus bring glory to God the Father.*

Humility is not a denial of our worth. It is an affirmation of it. As the *New English Bible* renders that passage, it stresses that "the divine nature was his from the start." Jesus did not lack worth; he possessed it uniquely. It is precisely because Jesus "shared the very being of God" yet "did not regard his equality as something to be clutched to himself" that his humility is so movingly splendid. He voluntarily, freely and deliberately "humbled himself" in accepting, obediently, his death, even though it was death on a cross. This was not weakness. It was true humility.

But there is more to be said on this great theme.

* William Barclay's translation.

TRUE HUMILITY

"Try to have the same attitude to life that Jesus had." So William Barclay translates Philippians chapter 2, verses 1-4. "If there is such a thing as Christian encouragement," Paul says, "if there is such a thing as love's comforting power, if you and I are really sharing in the partnership which only the Holy Spirit can make possible, if you wish to show me a heartfelt sympathy which is like the mercy of God, make my joy complete by being in perfect harmony of mind, by joining in a common love for God and for each other, by sharing in a common life, by taking every decision in unity of mind, by never acting from motives of competitive rivalry or in the conceited desire for empty prestige. If you want to make my joy complete, instead of that each of you must humbly think the other better than himself. Each of you must concentrate, not on his own interest, but on the interests of others also."

True humility is the mark of Christian love. It will always "increase" us rather than "decrease" us if we can find the secret of it. It is when we set out to boast and impress that we decline in spiritual stature, for love "vaunteth not itself, is not puffed up". It is when we make it our purpose to grow in the grace of humility in our inner being that we begin to be truly great. This is growth that we cannot plan or manufacture. It simply evolves in the soul of the truly humble. Humility is an integral part of "the best way of all".

The saints of God have always demonstrated this great quality. Indeed its absence or presence is the test of true spirituality. Arrogance is wholly foreign to authentic Christian character. There is simply no place for the exalted claims of the arrogant in a faith which has the divine humility at the centre of it. To give and not to count the cost, to accept participation in the human lot rather than abuse the power available to him, to share our suffering and pain and temptation as a demonstration of the true humanity of the Son of God – these are foundation stones of the edifice of love of which Christ is the corner-stone.

This is, perhaps, the hardest part of the gospel to accept, yet it is an essential part. "Nothing in my hands I bring. Simply to the cross I cling." Of ourselves we can do nothing. The miracle is that through "the grace which is sufficient for us" all things, spiritually, become possible. It is indeed "the Lord's doing and it is marvellous in our eyes". How can the disciple, aware of the wonder of the divine initiative and the totality of God's unconditional gift of love to the world, be other than moved to humility?

Listen to love . . . and be humble.

The Love that does no Graceless Thing

"Love does not behave itself unseemly." So runs the verse in the *Authorised Version*. What does that phrase convey today to those who read it and hear it? Most might well say that has a *moral* feel to it, that it would probably mean: "Love is not guilty of immoral behaviour." That kind of behaviour for most people probably means primarily sexual behaviour for it is, in church circles particularly, that area of life which comes to mind first of all as sin. Perhaps that should not be, but it is a very prevalent view. Jesus constantly pointed to other areas which are equally immoral. Indeed he might suggest they are *more* immoral, things like spiritual pride, self-righteousness, envy, intolerance, hypocrisy, the treating of people as means, not ends. There are particular instances where he made strong points on precisely this matter. The woman "of bad reputation" who wept tears over his feet and dried them with her hair, was praised very highly (what she had done, he said, would be told wherever the gospel is proclaimed) whereas Simon the Pharisee was rebuked for his lack of care of any kind. Whatever "unseemly behaviour" is, it is much more than immoral behaviour as it is commonly understood. It has something to say about a person's whole attitude to life and to people.

For the *Authorised Version*'s "unseemly", the *New English Bible* uses the word "rude". But that word is too ambiguous. It can mean insulting, insolent and offensive, but its primary meaning is simply unsophisticated and genuine in a primitive sort of way (as in the Christmas carol which describes the stable at Bethlehem as "rude and bare"). Once again, both William Barclay and J B Phillips provide illumination. Phillips' *New Testament in Modern English* interprets the phrase like this: "Love has good manners," bringing an element of courtesy and consideration into the "seemliness" of behaviour, but Barclay provides the most helpful alternative of all. "Love never does the graceless thing," he writes. Unseemly behaviour is behaviour that lacks grace.

Grace is a word of various shades of meaning. As I have already said, in its New Testament sense, it has the very specific meanings of goodwill, favour and undeserved benefit at the hands of a loving God. It speaks of that which blesses spiritually, uplifts, transforms and renews the inner spirit. Grace contributes, through its capacity as the gift of the Holy Spirit, to re-create, re-generate and invigorate. All that is good. Gracelessness however is its opposite. It degrades, diminishes, distorts and damages our inner life, our soul, our spiritual welfare. It must belong to evil.

Gracelessness is then the characteristic of everything that pulls down rather than builds up, degrades rather than refines, brings deterioration in the spiritual life rather than improvement. Love must never do the graceless thing.

There is more to be said on this theme, however.

AWAY WITH GRACELESSNESS!

Love never does the graceless thing. That means, as we have seen, that love can have no association with attitudes or behaviour that degrade mankind, that draw people away from the spiritual life, that influence or afflict human beings in a deleterious or a destructive way. This is important in personal life but it also has major implications for the welfare of the community.

Policies that diminish the quality of life cannot have Christian support. There is a real guideline here to test out policies of many kinds – political, educational, medical and economic. Love cannot be party to proposals, no matter where they come from or out of which political philosophy, that reduce the quality of people's lives. Pornography, pollution or prejudice in a racial or social context are graceless things. They act against the things that are "good and lovely and of good report".

The same test must be applied to other public issues – the stewardship of the earth's resources, abortion, euthanasia, media permissiveness, industrial relations, etc. Is what is being offered, provided, proposed, developed, proclaimed an addition to the good which God wills for all people, or does it subtract from it and, in the process, add to the sum of evil? If the latter is the case, then these are graceless things that are no part of love.

This is a theme that touches the very roots of salvation and spiritual growth as well as ethical discussion. We are dealing with much more than moral peccadilloes, bad manners or social indiscretion. We are, in fact, discussing all that we do or are in relation to its effect on our own and others' spiritual wholeness. These are the things with which God is concerned. He has made salvation, wholeness, spiritual maturity, health possible through Christ by the sanctifying power of the Holy Spirit. In the process of conversion, justification, "turn-around", redemption – call it what you will – he offers the opportunity for "life abundant", that is true, authentic life. The process of sanctification, that is spiritual growth, develops from that moment of conversion, enriched by the Spirit, helped by the means of grace, stimulated by prayer. Graceless things hold back growth into the fullness of the stature of the Lord Jesus Christ, in other words our progress in the spiritual life.

This is one of the most important themes with respect to life in the world of today. St Paul spoke with feeling about the powers of darkness that hover over life. These powers are real. Life in the twenty-first century is engaged in a constant struggle with gracelessness in entertainment, in the media, in ruthless commercialism and subtle secularism. Materialism, again a graceless concept when made a dominating influence in life, is untouched by grace. Greed and possessions, promoted by the hidden persuaders, have little connection with grace. The battle against gracelessness in all its forms needs to go on, out there in the world of course, but also internally, in ourselves. Away with gracelessness!

THE LOVE THAT DOES NOT SEEK ITS OWN

"Love does not seek its own." Jesus said, when he made a pertinent comment on the way the human mind thinks and human beings behave: "Where your treasure is, there will your heart be also." If we are going to live creatively, we need to have the right "centre". That right centre can never be self. Love is not "selfish", as the *New English Bible* renders this verse. "Love does not pursue selfish advantage" is J B Phillips' translation. In other words, love can never be self-centred. It does not make its own interests a primary concern.

It is worth reflecting a little on the danger of self-centredness which so conflicts with a proper understanding of relationship. We also need to think about the need, as beings made in the image of God, to secure our proper "centredness". Such reflection takes us to such themes as balance, perspective and proportion, concepts embedded in the New Testament.

Let us look a little more at balance in the context of faith because balance is a sound relationship of the parts to the centre. In terms of that, Jesus was surely the most balanced person ever. He functioned from a calm, inner centre and reflected the perfect relationship between the physical, emotional, mental and spiritual aspects of his life. He was truly balanced.

Perhaps the concept of balance, like the exhortation to someone to be "ordered" in their ways, sounds dull and unadventurous, but balance and order, in a Christian context, are far from that. Sometimes we do have to be fools for Christ's sake! That certainly sounds anything but a discouragement of adventure for it speaks rather of risk of various kinds. But basically, disciples are *disciplined* people. However adventurous they are, it is still true that the presence and power of the Holy Spirit is expressed, not in disorder but in order. Indeed we should question whether the Spirit is in fact present, as is often claimed, in situations of disorder, emotional or otherwise. The fundamental point is that it is the balanced person who is best equipped to take risks. Jesus demonstrated that fact in his own life of action. It was because he was so balanced that he felt it necessary to say and do things that upset "authority", secular and religious. It was the ordered, disciplined man of Nazareth, totally "centred" in faith, hope and love who could accept the risky road that led to crucifixion. The cross was a *skandalon*, a scandal to Greeks and to Jews, to the former "foolishness" and to the latter "a stumbling-block", but it was in no sense, when it is looked at *sub specie aeternitatis*, that is in the context of eternity, an act of eccentricity. It was "the power of God unto salvation" and represented the balanced, ordered will of God who risked sending his Son to share the life of the world in order to save it.

The Love that Flows out . . .

There is no place in the Christian community for the self-centred man or woman. That goes without saying. If we place ourselves at the centre of everything and see life as that in which *our* needs are primary and *our* ways are always right, then we are creating a world in which we "seek our own". *We* determine what matters. *We* control and manipulate the means to *our* own ends. *We* use other people as pawns in *our* own game. To get ourselves into this self-centred position is to live a life which is anything but "the best way of all". For love is not concerned with the control of everyone for our purposes. It is the opposite of that. It is the outflowing of love and compassion in the service of others. There is a fundamental difference in the two philosophies of life. It is imperative for our wholeness that we choose the right one.

If any evidence is needed of the danger of self-centredness and what can follow from "off-centre" attitudes, consider the case of someone I have mentioned briefly earlier, Simon Magus.* The book of the Acts of the Apostles portrays him as a sorcerer all too ready to try to manipulate the Holy Spirit in his own selfish interests. We are told in Acts chapter 8 that he "believed" and had been baptised (verse 13) but he showed that that spiritual experience was not authentic when he asked (verses 18-19) if he could buy the power of the Holy Spirit. In his self-centredness he would even seek to manipulate God. (It recalls that primal sin in the Garden of Eden again.) No wonder the other Simon, that is Simon Peter, had to say to him: "Your heart is not right in the sight of God." Here indeed was an imbalance to be corrected, a perspective to be changed and proportion to be created.

So we return to the emphasis with which we began. If the disciple is to model himself or herself on the God whose very nature is love, selfishness can have no place in our lives. It is not the nature of divine love to keep, control, or manipulate. It is the way of God to give.

> Love ever gives, forgives, outlives
> Ever stands with open hands.
> And while it lives, it gives
> For this is love's prerogative
> To give and give and give.

"God so loved the world that he gave ..." This verse, already quoted and no doubt to be quoted again, is definitive so far as the nature of God is concerned. Christ "emptied himself". It was a total self-giving for the sake of humanity. Our lives must reflect the "givingness" of God. If it is of the essence of divine love to flow out in compassion towards others and to ourselves, then it is of the essence of the disciplined life to flow out in love to the world too. How can we ever, against such a background, have a love that "seeks its own"?

* Acts 4.

THE LOVE THAT IS NOT EASILY PROVOKED

There is an incident recorded in St Mark's Gospel which incarnates the concept of the "love that is not easily provoked". The occasion is the inquisition by the high priest, chief priests, elders and scribes (Mark chapter 14, verse 53). Mark records how various witnesses for and against Jesus were called by the council and the subsequent confusion due to contradictions within their statements. Jesus' response to this is both impressive and moving. To all the false statements which would have provoked in most people an angry reaction, Jesus, we are told, "held his peace and answered them nothing". That demonstration of inner strength and unwavering patience in the face of supreme provocation is an example of the love that is not easily provoked.

It is interesting to note that the name of one particular disciple occurs in that passage. He was a distant observer and a man who is almost notorious for being provoked! I refer, of course, to Peter who "followed him from afar off even to the palace of the high priest", Peter who was easily provoked to protest when Jesus insisted on washing his feet; Peter who was easily provoked by Jesus' repeated question "Do you really love me?" and who showed his irritation in his anxiety to know what would happen to favoured John, "the disciple whom Jesus loved". Perhaps by looking at these reactions to provocative situations we can find the clue to the nature of the love that is not easily provoked.

Irritation, frustration, quickness to take offence often arises not so much from conscious dislikes but more often from unconscious feelings. In filing away memories from the very early years of our lives, or dismissing unpleasant associations (the process called "repression") those memories do not cease to be active or potentially active. An encounter with someone who, unknown to ourselves, reminds us of an unhappy relationship in the past can trigger these negative feelings. Peter's attitude to John, as the quotation above shows, was quite strong. Normally it would be hidden, consciously controlled, but under pressure it came to the surface. Peter's irritation with Jesus for his three-fold question, the answer to which he felt was not in doubt, was all the more real just because such love for his Lord was not an assumption he could sustain. He had failed, significantly three times, in his denial of Jesus after defiant assurances that such a failure could not happen. It did, so the area was a touchy one for him.

All this throws into relief the difference between Peter and Jesus. Just imagine the reaction of a man like Peter to the impertinence and indeed blasphemy directed at Jesus by his accusers. The man who unsheathed his sword in Gethsemane would certainly have reacted strongly to such an inquisition. But Jesus had a calm and a dignity that illustrated so effectively how to deal with such matters. He was not easily provoked.

THE LOVE THAT THINKS NO EVIL

The Hymn of Love is so familiar in the words of the *Authorised Version* that we tend to accept each phrase or verse without question or deeper analysis. The verse "Love thinks no evil" falls into that category, so it may be worthwhile pausing for a moment over it and trying to understand just what St Paul is saying to us.

The word "think" has cerebral and cognitive connections. May it not rather be depth of feeling, rather than thinking, that Paul is getting at? That possibility seems to be supported by the various ways the statement is translated in other versions. The *Jerusalem Bible* and the *Revised Standard Version* both use a "feeling" word here, the word "resentful". The *New English Bible* and William Barclay go further in their efforts to interpret what "thinking evil" means. From a spiritual point of view, the state of mind represented by such a negative attitude is an unhealthy one. The *NEB* says "Love keeps no score of wrongs" while Barclay offers an illuminating statement: "Love never nurses its wrath to keep it warm."

Let us look more closely at this clearly negative element in "thinking evil". Resentment is "cherishing bitter feelings towards someone or about some situation." Ponder the word "cherishing", the *New English Bible*'s rendering of the same phrase, "keeping a score" and Barclay's "nursing our wrath to keep it warm". They speak of an attitude which refuses to let accusation or criticism go. It is surely that holding-on element in resentment that is so negative and destructive.

In some ways this cherishing, nursing, holding-on process points towards that strange and disturbing concept mentioned by Jesus, "blasphemy against the Holy Spirit". In pastoral ministry, we meet people who strongly believe that they have committed the unforgivable sin against the Holy Spirit. They therefore suffer perhaps a lifetime of pain and misery, fear and dread which is out of proportion to anything that they have actually done. The fact is that if they have a real awareness of such sin, they are proving that they have not committed it. The whole point about the sin which Jesus called near unforgivable* is that it relates to a condition in which you cannot be spiritually aware. Jesus was indicating a group of people whose perceptions were so skewed that they could no longer distinguish between good and evil. As a result your spiritual state is so degraded that you will not realise what you are doing and so never repent of it. If repentance is impossible, by definition so is forgiveness.

"Thinking evil" and the so-called unforgivable sin are not the same thing. Refusing to let evil thoughts go, indeed cherishing them, nursing them to keep them active, that is the beginning of a process that moves inexorably towards that darkness of mind and attitude that becomes completely destructive.

Thinking evil and refusing to change that attitude can well become a stage in a downward journey that endangers the soul. It is therefore of the essence of love not to "think evil".

* See also the Meditations for February 14 and March 15.

THE LOVE THAT REJOICES IN THE TRUTH

"Love is not glad when things go wrong for others." So James Moffatt long ago translated this verse from 1 Corinthians, chapter 13. William Barclay translated thus: "Love finds nothing to be glad about when someone goes wrong, but is glad when truth is glad." "Love does not gloat over other men's sins, but delights in the truth" is the *New English Bible*'s version. "Love takes no pleasure in other people's sins," the *Jerusalem Bible* has it, "but delights in the truth."

The first part of Paul's statement is a condemnation of something that is far too prevalent today, that is media failings. While one cannot help but recognise that newspapers depend on bad news to fill their columns – this is, sadly, a fact of life – many newspapers today, especially those in tabloid form, depend for their circulation and therefore survival on gossip and scandal. Some of the papers with the highest circulations are those which concentrate on the things that go wrong for others, especially in their marriages, their relationships and their associations. Nowadays, in a climate where every aspect of life is out in the open, be it deviation or perversion, wrong conduct or corruption, the things that go wrong for so-called celebrities are used to titillate readers who, by "rejoicing in the things that go wrong for others" derive their pleasure from the faults and failings of other people.

As all who are involved in pastoral work know, human failure affects the saint as well as the sinner, the educated as well as the simple, the religious as well as the non-religious, the distinguished as well as the unknown, the cleric as well as the lay man or woman, the devout as well as the apathetic, the strong as well as the weak. "There is none righteous, no, not one. All" (if they are honest) "have sinned and come short of the glory of God." The kingdom of heaven will be populated not by perfect people who had no contact with evil and who don't actually exist, not by saints who had no contact with sin, but by those with a long list of failures who, knowing their need of grace agonised over "the law in their members" and prayed for release. "There but for the grace of God go I" is especially to be remembered when we gloat over others' failures.

It is the same with gossip. It would be wonderful if we could all "speak the truth in love" at all times, but it does not happen. We are all prone to find pleasure in gossip, however apparently innocent, and are not wholly free from finding some pleasure in other people's misfortunes. If we are scrupulously honest, we may find that we too often get pleasure out of others' failures, that is we "rejoice in iniquity". What is it in us that leads us to so revel in human unhappiness?

To look at that question is a necessary act of spiritual discipline, so that is our next task.

INNER PRESSURES

What is it in us all (let those who feel they can exclude themselves from this generalisation) that prompts us to "rejoice in iniquity"?

It may help to put the matter first in psychological terms. The term "the unconscious"* describes an area of our being where all kinds of memories of early life are stored. (Some therapists would claim that even ante-natal memories should be included in this statement.) That personal "unconscious" is, to use a modern analogy, rather like a tape-recording of all we experienced in our earliest days. Those memories may be pleasant if we were received into the world with loving care and affection. If we were unfortunate perhaps because we were unwanted babies, we may have "registered" unhappy experiences and the feelings that go with them. The point is that these events and the feelings they created are beyond our ability to remember. They are there but we are not conscious of them. They are nevertheless real and they can have an influence on us all through our life.

These feelings are either positive or negative. If positive as a result of a happy first part of life, they may show themselves later in outgoing love to others, but if they were negative and belong to the "shadow" side of the unconscious, they may produce very major psychological consequences. Feelings of rejection in our earliest years, registered but unremembered, may result in inability to relate to others, fear of close contact or a sense of being threatened by other people. This, of course, may lead to unhappy marriages or partnerships, a severe lack of self-worth, etc. These negative feelings are below the surface of consciousness but, under pressure, or in unhappy and stressful circumstances, they may not be able to be "contained" and so unacceptable behaviour, perhaps sexual, perhaps violent, will occur. Those inner negative pressures can lead us to very negative feelings. We may find ourselves to be glad over other people's misfortunes, especially if we do not like them.

Let us now put that into religious language. The word we use in this context is "temptation" by which we mean the sense of pressure coming from within, caused, some would say, by Satan. St Paul has himself put into words, and from his own experience, just how strong these pressures are and the awful things to which they can lead. He is conscious of his dilemma: "The good which I would do, I do not," he says and "the evil that I would not, that I do. There is a law within me." Does Paul's statement of his spiritual dilemma touch a nerve with you?

This then is where some of the negative attitudes we have, but which surprise us by their very existence, have their source. Nevertheless the degree to which we rejoice less and less in others' failures and failings and the measure by which we long for their good, will testify to our "growing up" in Christ and demonstrate the reality of our progress towards spiritual maturity.

* There are a number of references to this concept in these Meditations; see, for example, those for January 13, March 15, May 2, August 31.

The Love that Bears, Believes, hopes, Endures all Things

The four words that make up this statement about love divide themselves into two categories. One is positive and the other negative. That love "believes" all and "hopes" all is the positive side. That love "bears" all and "endures" all has a more negative sound.

We talk about bearing burdens and enduring hardship, and so speak of responses like "resolute acceptance", "stolid submission" and even "brave resignation" over such situations. As love is a wholly positive word, I cannot think that Paul intended to speak in a negative way. There is nothing negative about the God who *is* love.

It may be useful to look, at this point, at another passage where Paul seems to be using negative, not positive, words, and yet his aim is to put a positive point. This is the occasion on which he wrote: "I have learned in whatsoever state I am, therewith to be content" (Philippians chapter 4, verse 11). Again there is a negative feel to it. "Make the best of it. Grin and bear it. Soldier on." The more I read Paul's words, the more convinced I am that it was not his intention to give this impression. What Paul is, in fact, saying is very creative. He says: "In every situation in which I have been" (he then gives a list of very dramatic events and experiences) "I have found a creative opportunity. I have found within the limitations of any given set of circumstances, however intolerable, a way to use these circumstances to good effect. So I accept these limits as reality, as the things which cannot be changed, but I try to find, in them and through them, satisfaction, contentment and true fulfilment."

That example helps us to see the words bear and endure in a more positive light. But there is still more help for us in this matter if we turn to the *New English Bible* translation of the sentence "I have learnt in whatsoever state I am therewith to be content." It reads: "I have learned to find resources in myself whatever the circumstances." Limitation, hostility and adversity can be learning situations. If opposition and disappointment can be looked at in this way, they can be part of the growth process.

It is essential for growing Christians that they should develop the capacity to learn in such a way. It is desirable too that we should help others to see suffering in this context … easy to say, but in practice very hard. It has been said that "man's extremity is God's opportunity." To bear and to endure, in terms of love, means taking and accepting, even eagerly grasping what is apparently to our hurt, and redeeming it so that it becomes a spiritually beneficial experience. If adversity can be handled in that way, bearing and enduring can contribute to our growth.

"Love bears all things": we must look at that next.

THE LOVE THAT BEARS ALL THINGS

The sentence "Love bears all things" has an interesting variation that was known as far back as St Cyprian (he died in AD 259). It was the use of the Greek word *stergei* instead of *stegei*. *Stergei* means "cherishing", "holding dear". It might, however, be the heart ruling the head to pursue that interpretation too far! "Bears" seems to be the correct word. I emphasise the point, however, that I have already made, namely that it must not be thought of as "quiet, brave endurance" (to quote, would you believe, from a *wedding* hymn!). It must be seen as a positive and active word. The motto of the Royal Air Force is *Per ardua ad astra;* it is through hardship that we reach the stars. It is "through dying we live" (2 Corinthians chapter 6, verse 9). All that we have to bear in life is in the end, a gateway to growth. Hardship is an educational process if we allow it to be so.

The various translations add colour to the concept of bearing all things. Take, for instance, the *New English Bible*. "There is nothing love cannot face", an example of "accentuating the positive" as a song of yesteryear said, by duplicating the negative. The *Jerusalem Bible* chooses the rendering: "Love is always ready to excuse" while William Barclay says: "Love can stand any kind of treatment." What then does it means to say "Love bears all things"?

The essential elements are those that we have noted on our journey into and through love as Paul proclaims it. There is the divine patience with which the long-suffering God waits and waits for the prodigal son to return, drawn by "cords of love". There is the divine kindness which, desiring our good, will never stampede us into the kingdom, but rather, respecting our personalities, will lead us gently towards the "living water".

It is on the capacity of divine love to bear all things in order to win the hearts of human beings that we draw in our own effort to bear the burdens others have put on us. We have, with the help of grace, to bear the unbearable, be patient with those who try our patience, be kind to those who make themselves intolerable, be loving to those whom we find it hard to love, "forbearing one another in love" (Ephesians chapter 4, verse 2), and always "for Christ's sake". This is not a demand of a romantic or idealistic kind. It is not a plea for patience that is weakness, a kindness that is soft, a sympathy that is sentimental or a forgiveness that is meek and mild. The divine love was seen in a man of courage who, in the hour of his ultimate suffering, could cry: "Father, forgive them for they know not what they do" (Luke chapter 23, verse 34). This surely was to "bear all things", to "stand any kind of treatment". There was "nothing love did not face".

THE LOVE THAT BELIEVES ALL THINGS

"Love believes all things, hopes all things." While we look specifically at the word "believes", we keep an eye too on the very positive word "hopes". With belief and hope united, we are in the realm of *faith* and *trust* and *promise*. To say anything about our beliefs is to touch a very fundamental part of us, for our belief determines what we do. Without belief, we will do nothing. With belief, all things begin to become possible.

This aspect of faith and trust is reflected in the way "Love believeth all things" is translated in some of the other versions. "Love is ready to trust" runs the *Jerusalem Bible*. William Barclay puts it in a very dramatic sentence: "Love's first instinct is to believe in people." First instinct? The reference is to very basic attitudes.

As has been the case all through this month's Meditations, I apply the phrase first to the divine love and ask just what William Barclay is saying. He is, in fact, claiming that the "first instinct of God, in his love, is to believe in people." The whole of God's redemptive activity is based on the assumption that, no matter what happens, no matter how appallingly men or women, in their freedom, behave, the purpose is to enable the prodigal son or daughter to "come to themselves" and make for home. "Love suffers long" indeed. Love is also "kind". Love seeks our good without ever denying our freedom. Love is prepared to wait, and to wait at great cost, to show that it "believes in people". It sticks to that belief whatever happens.

The union of love and hope in this matter is no accident. They always belong together. There is a divine optimism at the heart of the universe that sees the end of everything as redemption, renewal and integration. This is the direction and aim of the divine activity always. Love will never lose that first instinct to believe in people made in the image of God.

We live at a time of ever-increasing gracelessness and it is often hard to keep believing in people. But we must keep things in perspective. As Roman chapter 1 makes clear, it has all happened before. It is not however the way of divine love to give humanity up. The divine love holds to its primary instinct, which is to have faith in people. It acts on that principle. There is therefore no choice in the matter. If our love is to reflect the divine love, we must work and pray on the premise that there is the possibility of good in every man and woman, and in every situation. Love does "believe all things". This is not an invitation to fantasy, nor is it false piety. It is the way in which God acts so it must be the way for disciples too.

THE LOVE THAT HOPES ALL THINGS

"Three things last for ever ... faith, hope and love," Paul writes (in William Barclay's translation). He then goes on to declare that "the greatest of these is love." No one will, I think, disagree with that. The fact that love is so categorised as "the greatest" of all does not diminish in any way the importance of "faith" and "hope". It is then a matter for joy that in this great Hymn of Love, there is a phrase that demands that we consider the wonderful concept of hope. "Love hopes all things."

Hope is related to the view of life which takes in the spiritual dimension, the "eternal" dimension and regards it as a matter of prime importance. It is a true optimism that is based on energies and powers that belong to that spiritual dimension. If our view of life only takes in this world and all that goes on in it, there is comparatively little ground for hope. Hope comes when faith projects the dimension that is spiritual into our perspective on life and makes it not an extra element but an essential one.

This is borne out by the relationship that hope has, in the New Testament, to life after death (for example in 1 Corinthians chapter 15, verse 19). Hope is based on the reality of the risen Christ as the church experienced him. If there is no resurrection, Paul tells us, we are "a people to be pitied"! We have no *hope*. The church is the company of people with hope. They have a proper perspective on life, on its events and on its history. In the most profound sense they can feel that, convinced of the presence of the risen Christ and the power of the Holy Spirit, all will be truly well. That is Christian hope.

In analysing the love that bears all things and believes all things, the principle I have been emphasising is the one fundamental to the Hymn of Love, namely the *divine* attitude to people. The divine patience is to bear all that man, in the hardness of his heart, will produce. God believes in people. So love "hopes all things" too. Again it is William Barclay who brings out the full meaning of that hope in his magnificent translation of the verse under discussion, "Love never regards anyone or anything as hopeless." It has been said that there is a road that leads to hell from the very gate of heaven. That may be true. But there is also a road that leads to heaven from the very gates of hell. Love never regards anyone as beyond hope.

We are, Paul says to the Romans (chapter 8, verse 24) "saved by hope". Hope lifts our eyes from the immediate and the material to a perspective divinely conditioned. From that perspective "Love never fails ... love hopes all things." Neither love divine nor its human reflection, however, frail, can ever regard anyone or anything as hopeless.

THE LOVE THAT ENDURES ALL THINGS

Once again it is in William Barclay's translation that I find illumination of the verse "Love endures everything." While other versions confine themselves to variations on the form we have in the *Authorised Version* (see, for example, the *New English Bible*'s "There is no limit to love's endurance" and the *Jerusalem Bible*'s "Love endures what comes"), Professor Barclay somehow gives the text another dimension when he writes: "Nothing can happen that can break love's spirit." That is a fine version indeed.

In this form, the verse gives assurance and security. If God is one who, no matter what happens, extends his arms in love and welcome – which is just what the parable of the prodigal son suggests – then there is no need for so much of the guilt that people feel. The divine forgiveness is real. The capacity of God to accept us is beyond our understanding because it goes so much further than human beings do in the face of wrong. And yet so often people fail to *feel* forgiven when forgiveness has surely been given. Acceptance of the intellectual proposition "God forgives" is just not the same as *knowing that statement to be true for oneself* in specific situations. Because the *refusal* to *feel* forgiven is present in the personality, the possibility that that sense will express itself in psychosomatic illness is very real. Guilt persisting in someone's troubled soul may actually begin to show itself in dis-ease of the body.

It is part of the healing ministry to find a way to ease away the memories of mistakes made long ago. On-going guilt situations need to be resolved. Unresolved conflicts and tensions need to be released. Continuous anxiety can lead, not only to desperation but suicide. Repressed and pushed deeper into the unconscious, it will express itself in physical illness and symptoms.

This is an area where ministers, teachers, pastors, carers have to learn to express the principle of love expounded in these Meditations. All who minister to people must be sensitive to the possible presence of unresolved guilt in people presenting problems. So many lives of great potential have been destroyed or nearly so when those who are emotionally or spiritually down and out have encountered unforgiving condemnation and judgementalism from fellow Christians and the church from which they expected understanding and forgiving love. There is nothing that can break love's spirit if there is sincere repentance. Forgiveness is promised and always on offer, but it must be graciously accepted.

Jesus came not to condemn but to save. That statement is specific and absolutely fundamental for our understanding of the gospel. The message of Jesus should never be turned into any kind of discouragement. It is foreign to the purpose of God in the Incarnation. The gospel is one of encouragement and no preacher, pastor or teacher should ever forget that primary fact. There is no situation so bad, no crisis so overwhelming, that it can break love's spirit.

THE LOVE THAT LASTS FOR EVER

Loved with everlasting love
Led by grace that love to know

So wrote George Wade Robinson in his well-known hymn. It is the word "everlasting" on which I want to concentrate as we turn to the reassuring words in verse 8 of the Hymn of Love, "Love never fails".

Reaching this phrase is rather like breaking through the clouds as the plane in which you are flying ascends into the bright sunshine above. We seem to be moving into a realm of knowledge – perhaps the knowledge which, St Paul tells the Ephesians, is a "knowledge beyond knowledge" – not cognitively acquired. It comes by intuition. Although that knowledge is expressed in lyrical terms, it still deals with reality, the reality of "the things which are eternal". "Love never fails." In human weakness it does, over and over again, but the divine love does not fail ... ever.

The word "ever" takes us back to this key concept of "everlasting". Paul sees love as something which goes beyond "the present age", an age which will ultimately pass away. That end of the present age was considered by Paul, as it was by the early church as a whole, as imminent. Christians then lived as if the world they knew would soon come to an end, and a "new age" be born.

In such circumstances, all that belongs to the present, including prophecy and tongues, will pass away but "Love does not come to an end" (*New English Bible*), "Love lasts for ever" (William Barclay). It is in that sense of "everlasting" that "love never fails". It is love which "abides". That which is only "in part" shall be "done away" when "that which is perfect is come". Love is present always, constant and unchangeable. When we see not "through a glass darkly" but "face to face", love remains. Love is everlasting love. "Love lasts for ever."

I have repeatedly referred to 1 Corinthians 13 as a *Hymn* of Love. By so doing, I am emphasising the lyrical nature of the passage. Paul's ability, when inspired, to rise to extraordinary levels of insight and true knowledge is expressed in as sublime a way as he ever attained. The fullness of the divine love is therefore presented truly poetically. It could only be written "under the Spirit". But is such poetic vision and enlightened awareness so lyrical that it feels unrelated to the real lives we have to live?

It is the reality of that "great event of faith", the Incarnation of Jesus, "born of the Virgin Mary, crucified under Pontius Pilate" (an "event of fact" too) that ensures that the Hymn of Love is not mere fantasy but is the sound and solid base on which all faith and life are founded. We are called to love God and our neighbour in this world just because we belong, in spiritual terms, to that other eternal world.

CREATIVE TENSION

One of Paul Tillich's books is called *On the Boundary*. It is, like others he has written, autobiographical in that it contains reflections on his life. It is a statement of the stance he found himself compelled to take in life. He said he lived "on the frontier", that is on the boundaries between, for example, city and country, theology and philosophy, native land and foreign land, religion and culture, idealism and Marxism, etc. The Christian has the same kind of thing to do. Here (that is, in this world) we have "no permanent home" (Hebrews chapter 13, verse 14, *New English Bible*) but we seek "one to come". We have to be, as Jesus says when praying for his disciples (John chapter 17, verses 15-16) "in" the world but not "of" it. We live on the boundary between them. We are on the frontier between the physical and the spiritual but must be related to both.

This means a life in which there is constant tension. As the two realms impinge on each other, it is easy to slip off, as it were, on to one side or the other, and so to lose a proper balance between them. This affects creative living. To reduce the physical aspect and so prevent it playing a proper part in life's equation is to deny the Incarnation and to diminish the value of life in the here and now. To fail to give the spiritual element its proper place is to lose the vital factor that determines the right direction on our journey. That element has a "priority among equals". The balance is illustrated in our basic convictions about Jesus who was truly human and truly divine (according to our creeds). No view of Christ makes sense if either description is weakened, but similarly in that "priority among equals", paradoxically, it must be said the divine must be seen to have first place. Jesus was the eternal Christ ("before Abraham was I am" he says in John's Gospel) and he returned through resurrection and ascension to be with God the Father. Yet the Incarnation means that the Christian's base in the eternal dimension demands a real and total involvement in this world, a world where Jesus was tempted "like as we are" and suffered in a way that none of us has had to experience. He was "in" the world indeed! But he could not and would not be "of" it.

The nature, quality and depth of love to which we are called is a response in gratitude to the love that never fails. Though heaven and earth may pass away, that love "lasts for ever". We cannot, knowing our human weakness and limitations, begin to pretend that our love has the divine everlasting quality about it that it should have. But the standard is set. Our constant desire must be the gift of more of that unfailing love to be within us, for it is unfailing love we are to offer in his name.

LISTEN TO LOVE

Verses 8 to 12 of the Hymn of Love are about knowledge, the full knowledge that will come when the whole picture, in the divine perspective, is revealed. There is knowledge that is partial and knowledge that is whole and complete. "My knowledge now is partial," Paul writes, "then it will be whole like God's knowledge of me" (verse 12, *New English Bible*). I would like to look at the two kinds of knowledge of which Paul speaks.

For help with this I turn to another of his letters, that written to the Ephesians. One of the reasons many want to adhere to the *Authorised Version* of the Bible is the sheer beauty and dignity of its language, especially for public reading. The *New English Bible* has done much to clarify difficult passages in the older translation, but seldom does it equal the high levels of poetic expression so long associated with the *King James Version* (as the *Authorised Version* is often known). There is one passage however, that may have reached equality with its predecessor and perhaps even surpassed it in terms of beauty of language and effectiveness of words and phrase. It is the section to which I now turn – Ephesians chapter 3, verses 14 to 21.

As the passage may not be familiar to all, I again reproduce it in full.* It is the statement on knowledge to which, particularly, I want to draw attention. The passage reads:

> With this in mind, then I kneel in prayer to the Father from whom every family in heaven and on earth takes its name, that out of the treasures of his glory he may grant you strength and power through his Spirit in our inner being, that through faith Christ may dwell in your hearts in love. With deep roots and firm foundations may you be strong to grasp, with all God's people, what is the breadth and length and height and depth of the love of Christ, and *to know it, though it is beyond knowledge*. So may you be filled with all the fullness of being, the fullness of God himself.
>
> Now to him who is able to do immeasurably more than all we can ask or conceive, by the power which is at work among us, to him be glory in the church and in Christ Jesus from generation to generation evermore!

"*To know* (the love of Christ) *though it is beyond knowledge*." This is paradox indeed ... the exhortation to know what cannot be known! There can be only one conclusion. Paul is indeed talking about two kinds of knowledge. There is knowledge of a rational, intellectual, cognitive kind, and there is a knowledge that comes to us in a totally different way. That way must be an intuitive way, a way related to attributes like feeling, sensitivity and imagination. That means it comes through the antennae of the soul.

We must listen further to love.

* See the Meditation for May 26.

KNOWLEDGE BEYOND KNOWLEDGE

Though I have the gift of all knowledge, without love, Paul says, it means nothing. Within the Hymn of Love the distinction that has been made between two kinds of knowledge has been registered. We can reach the heights of cognitive knowledge in this earthly life, but that kind of knowledge is not that of which Paul speaks in verse 19. We are now talking of that kind of knowledge that is peculiar to the soul. It is not the product of a rational process. Something of that kind of knowledge can be ours in this life, but it can only be "in part". Only in the life of eternity can that knowledge be complete, for in that life we shall know and be known. This is knowledge in that more profound sense. It is the knowledge that is beyond knowledge. That level of knowledge is impossible without love.

It is from such knowledge that the ability to reflect the divine love in life comes. It is the source of the patience, kindness and forgiveness of love. We cannot be in touch with "the fullness of God himself" (of which Paul wrote to the Ephesians) unless we have been "strong to grasp" the divine love. It can only be attained through experience of the length, depth, breadth and height of the love of Christ. That love having been received, in terms of our eternal triangle, it goes out to our neighbour and the community in Christ's name.

It is, alas, ever more difficult in this distracting world "to hear the angels sing", to be aware of the still, small voice within. Driven by the ruthlessness of a very materialistic society, influenced by the media and its essentially self-centred approach (that is circulation figures, viewing numbers and shareholders' interests), it becomes increasingly difficult to "seek first the kingdom and his righteousness". The "other things" dominate life. There is too the deep anxiety which now affects life, especially after what has come to be known as "September 11th" events. The strain on the emotions that comes from the breakdown of society as we have known it, the financial pressures that are part of a competitive and threatening economic order bringing ever-rising costs, the problems of poverty and deprivation ... all this adds up to an atmosphere hostile to the development of a spiritual life. There is therefore all the more need to escape into "the desert place" to meditate on the wonder of divine and human love. Listen to love, for such listening leads towards faith, hope and peace.

The Hymn of Love is not just a lyrical song in praise of love. It is a statement about the very basis on which we must found our lives, personal and corporate. The more we know and understand at the level of the knowledge which is beyond knowledge, the more we will love.

PUT LOVE FIRST

The phrase "first among equals" is not unknown in church circles. It is certainly familiar in Presbyterian church polity where, in its Latin form, *primus inter pares*, it describes the essential parity of its clergy. When one of them is deliberately chosen to be "Moderator" to preside over the annual General Assembly, it does not destroy the essential parity of its ministry. Love is in a similar relationship in the triumvirate of the words "faith", "hope" and "love". The greatest of these great qualities of equal value is love. Love will last for ever (William Barclay) or abide for ever (*Authorised Version*), but the greatest of them must be love.

The phrase "the best way of all" or, in the *Authorised Version*, "the more excellent way" comes not in the thirteenth chapter of 1 Corinthians, but from the previous chapter (chapter 12, verse 31). It is the *New English Bible*'s rendering of that verse. Similarly, the phrase which I now discuss comes from the next chapter, chapter 14. "Follow after love" begins that fourteenth chapter. This, in the *New English Bible* is translated "Put love first." This is the natural consequence to the presentation of the primacy of love so far made. "Spare no effort to possess love," William Barclay's version runs. "You must want love more than anything else," the *Jerusalem Bible* tells us.

So, wondrously, the gift of love is given, but there is always effort involved in spiritual achievement. "You must want love more than anything else" and therefore accept the discipline required. It is not that love has to be earned. It does not require that for it is a gift of grace. But the struggle to reflect it is always present. How can I love spontaneously? How can I love those whom I dislike? Those who drive me to frustration and despair? Those who set out to destroy me? Those who represent everything I dislike? Still the command remains ... put love first.

Again I remind that our human love must be based on the divine pattern of love. That is a love that accepted betrayal for 30 pieces of silver, denial three times by Jesus' right-hand man, and the insensitive cruelty of crucifixion by people who did not know what they were doing. To have the grace to reach heights of love was a gift from God but that does not deny the strength he showed in coping with such events. In Gethsemane, "being in agony, he prayed more earnestly", evidence surely of the struggle taking place within his soul and the sheer spiritual effort he had to make.

To walk the way of love demands faith; to continue walking that way, whatever happens, demands hope. So faith and hope are essential components in the process which leads to life abundant.

The best way of all is love.

Spare no effort to possess love.

Love lasts for ever.

LOVE, THE HEALING WORD (1)

God is love. Jesus is the love of God incarnate, the Word made flesh. He is the source of healing. It is therefore the Word, Jesus Christ, God incarnate that is the healing Word. He brings love for he is love. Love is the Word that heals.

There is here a play on the word "word". It is being used in two senses, first as itself a healing word, and secondly to describe, as John's Gospel does, the healing "Word made flesh". The great passage in which John expounds the idea of Christ as the Word is at the beginning of his Gospel. He sets out his theme as Jesus, the *Logos*, the Word. The passage becomes awkward for two reasons: first the difficulty the Greek word (and concept) creates for us all, and secondly the limitations of the word *word* in English. Clearly the various translators have found problems in conveying the full meaning of the word *Logos*, but they have tried to do it! J B Phillips in his *New Testament in Modern English* offers the paraphrase (for it is rather a paraphrase than a literal translation)

> At the beginning, God expressed himself. That personal expression, that Word, was with God and was God, and he existed from the beginning.

The healing Word is Christ himself, but John's use of this concept is special (though not unique to him. I say "special" rather than "unique" because both in Paul's letters, and the Letter to the Hebrews there are allusions to the kind of ideas John is expressing). We therefore have to try to understand the ideas with which John is working and the thoughts he is seeking to convey through this particular description of the cosmic Christ.

Logos, classically, means "reason". The New Testament use of the term is more related to its other use (also classical) meaning "word". As used by John, however, *Logos* takes on a specifically religious, theological and spiritual character which, though almost indefinable, nevertheless feels real and authentic. *Logos* now becomes the declaration of the divine Word and so of the divine will. It is both Christ himself and the Word of God. The whole is "the divine plan of salvation" so gloriously expressed in the Incarnation. So the *Word*, the *Logos*, was made flesh – for our salvation – and "dwelt among us".

This is a wonderful way of presenting the essence of the gospel in another form. It adds a new insight of depth to the Gospel's combined witness to "Emmanuel", "God with us", Christ. The real Christ of the roads of Palestine was the healing Word in action. The living Christ of the Christian faith is the healing Word today. So the concept of the *Logos* or *Word* is used by John to proclaim two great purposes. The first is that Christ is the "revealer" of God and second, the saviour of men and women. He is the healing Word.

LOVE, THE HEALING WORD (2)

As we look further at *Logos*, the healing Word which is the theme of the introduction to St John's Gospel, there are three things in particular that need to be said:

i) the *Logos*, the *Word*, is not only concerned with speech but with *power*. We can listen to all that the Word, Jesus Christ, has to say and be greatly blessed by it – as people have been for 2000 years, but what is more important is the realisation that he came to be "God with us" and to do something for us that we could not do for ourselves. So the great plan of salvation, revealed by the healing Word, Jesus, is the demonstration in power, in history, of the mighty acts of God in Christ, the Word who was "with him at the beginning and through whom all things come to be". The Word is the power within both creation and re-creation that is the means of the redemption of mankind. There was, we are told, light in him, and that life is the light of men and women.

ii) I draw from William Barclay's comments on St John's Gospel this important statement: "Both Jew and Greek possessed the conception of the *Logos* of God." That knowledge would help them understand that Christ had come in the fullness of time, that is at the right moment, to be the medium of both healing and salvation (two words with a common root). So not only for the individual but for the world ("God so loved the world ...") Jesus, the Logos, is the healing Word. He is relevant to, and can be welcomed by, men and women of every nation, culture, vocabulary or intellectual background, Jew or Greek (as Paul says), Roman, Galatian, Ephesian, Corinthian and many more. In him lies the power to redeem, re-create and transform, universally.

iii) The third comment I take from Henry Drummond and his classic little book to which I have referred before, *The Greatest Thing in the World*. In response to questions as to both his orthodoxy and his integrity, after *Natural Law in the Spiritual World* and especially *The Ascent of Man* had been published, he wrote to the great evangelist Ira D Sankey that what he had written "represented both my words and my deepest convictions". What he said to Sankey is a tremendous affirmation of the healing Word:

> The power to set the heart right, to renew the springs of affection, comes from Christ. The sense of the infinite worth of a single soul and the recoverableness of man at his worst are the gifts of Christ. Freedom from guilt, the forgiveness of sins come from Christ's cross; the hope of immortality springs from Christ's grave ..."

In this sense, Christ, the divine *Logos*, is the healing Word.

LOOKING TO JESUS

In this Meditation we are going to keep "looking unto Jesus" who is "the author and finisher of our faith" (Hebrews chapter 12, verse 2) for he is, as we have seen, the healing Word himself, *Logos*, the Word made flesh, incarnate Son of God, Jesus the Christ. In the Barclay translation, those words read: "All the time we must concentrate on nothing but Jesus in whom our faith had its beginning and must have its end."

In this and forthcoming Meditations we shall indeed "concentrate" on Jesus, the healing Word, on his attributes and attitudes. Jesus is the truth about God. His attributes and attitudes are therefore those of the Father.

One of the attributes of him who is "the Word that heals", "love divine, love incarnate" is that he *understands* the pain and problems of human beings. That is stated very simply and directly in John's Gospel (chapter 2, verses 24 and 25): "He knew what was in man ... because he knew all men." (The New Testament in the *Authorised Version* was published so long ago that it does not use inclusive language! He knew what was in women too!) Again Barclay's version is helpful: "He did not need anyone to tell him about human nature because he was well aware what it is like."

The feeling of disillusionment and sometimes, after persistent failure, despair can be very strong. We just do not reach the standards of life and the levels of love that properly reflect Christ. If the truth about us were known, if people knew what we were really like, our faults, secret sins, hidden thoughts, our unacceptable desires, how awful it would be. Why even Paul saw himself as "the chief of sinners" (1 Timothy chapter 1, verse 15) and hated it so much that that description was apt for him.

If that feeling is genuine, it is in fact a good sign. It suggests that we are, spiritually, on the move, for it is an awareness only possible to those who sense where true goodness lies and where we are in relation to it. The cry of confession and the longing for forgiveness "full and free" are signs of progress towards the life of the Spirit.

This attribute of self-understanding and repentance is one that makes for healing. We may hide our faults and failings from our friends because we fear the disillusionment that such revelation must surely bring. God is "well aware of what human nature is like". It is out of his understanding of us in our totality, "warts and all", that he can bring healing. As the comedienne, the late Hylda Baker, used to say: "He knows, you know!"

Healing begins with the knowledge that all we are and do is accepted in the divine understanding. What goes wrong for us and causes us such distress and pain, God can put into the perspective of forgiveness and even use it to contribute to the new being for which we yearn.

LOVE'S SENSITIVITY

Very close to the theme of God's understanding love is his sensitivity to our needs. That sensitivity is, again, an attribute seen so clearly in the healing Word, the *Logos*, Jesus Christ. And that sensitivity to the needs of all is very present in the Gospels. "Sheep without a shepherd", lost and forlorn, attracted his attention, even when he had retired, as he needed to do at times, to a quiet place. Children and their parents, the latter rebuked by the disciples, had the comfort of hearing him say: "Suffer the little children to come to me and forbid them not." Perhaps that sensitivity is exemplified in his re-assuring statement: "He knows our needs *before* we ask."

Sensitivity is a requirement for all who seek to offer healing ministry of any kind. It is a word which speaks of an understanding of the need for (in the best sense) subtlety in dealing with human relationships. It implies sureness of touch, sympathy, and intuition. Sensitivity is founded on respect for personality so there will never be invasion of privacy but it also has a prophetic or at least an anticipatory quality that enables the healing agent to sense, before it is verbalised, need, depression, fear, guilt, etc. Sensitivity is a concept that places importance on intuition and empathy. It is simply not possible for us fully to empathise with an experience we have not had (like, for example, the death of a child), but experienced sensitivity can help us to (as the prophet Ezekiel said in another context) "sit where they sit". All this will make possible care-full concern in providing the appropriate response to need, a response which will not be turned into actions or even words until the right moment has come.

Can there be an attribute of the *Logos*, the healing Word, that offers us more comfort and assurance than the divine sensitivity so demonstrated as a reality in the life of Christ? Ask the rich young ruler who was, in love, allowed to go away, unharassed, unpursued, when he could not meet the standards of discipleship! Ask "the woman of bad reputation" who, with tears and hair, spontaneously demonstrated love for the Lord and who, for that, was hugely praised? Ask Nicodemus who came to talk to Jesus by night and learned the meaning of being "born again"!

Our sins are no surprise to God! As a result of his foreknowledge of our spiritual condition, our attitude in prayer is completely changed. When we "take it to the Lord in prayer," we know we shall not be rejected, judged, condemned. We are there knowing that God will not end our relationship with him because of what he knows about us. Rather, in forgiveness, he will strengthen that relationship. No wonder Frederick William Faber wrote:

> For the love of God is broader
> than the measures of man's mind;
> and the love of the Eternal
> is most wonderfully kind.

LOVE'S EMPATHY

"Jesus the Son of God ... is not a high priest who is unable to sympathise with the weakness we possess ... In every respect (he) has gone through the same ordeal of temptation as we have to go through ..." This quotation from the letter to the Hebrews, again in William Barclay's translation, is a statement about the divine empathy in all its wonder. What a healing attribute the *Logos*, the healing Word, presents! This is indeed love in action. That our weaknesses and failures should touch such a chord in Jesus' experience is good news indeed. There must be a sense of joy in every human heart when our ways, though not God's ways, are understood and dealt with sympathetically. God "feels" as well as knows.

To put things in this way may seem to tend towards being anthropomorphic in attitude and possibly naïve intellectually. I grant this but my purpose is essentially pastoral, that is seeking to help people spiritually at whatever level they function and particularly to enable them to sense the great theological truths behind the language.. The relationship we have with God in Christ through the Holy Spirit is one marked by the divine empathy. That is theological reality, confirmed by Christian experience.

Every pastor knows how easily people undergo temptation, accede to temptation and therefore feel guilty to a point that brings agony to the soul. May I quote again John Donne's moving poem but with the second verse included:

> Wilt thou forgive that sinne where I begunne
> which is my sin, though it were done before?
> wilt thou forgive those sinnes through which I runne
> and do run still; though still I do deplore?
> When thou hast done, thou hast not done,
> for I have more.
>
> Wilt thou forgive that sinne by which I've wonne
> others to sinne? And made my sin their door?
> Wilt thou forgive the sinne which I did shunne
> a year, or two; but wallowed in a score?
> When thou hast done, thou hast not done,
> for I have more.

It is easy indeed to empathise with John Donne's words as he looks at his life and into his soul for there, in his words, is every one of us! Guilt hounds many people.* And guilt there should be. It is a proper response to wrongdoing. Appropriate guilt is indeed wholly right. What ought to concern the pastor is guilt which is out of all proportion to the sin and more importantly persists, unhealed, long after the failure, *even when forgiveness has been asked for and given.* That guilt is inappropriate and unhealthy. It cries out for understanding and help. "Wave upon wave of grace" (John chapter 1, verse 16, William Barclay) is necessary to get us through it, as John Donne has still to confirm – tomorrow.

* See Meditation for May 7.

LOVE'S "WAVES OF GRACE"

Sin is not peculiar to any one of us. It is common to all human beings. "All have sinned," as I quoted earlier "and come short of the glory of God." The point being made yesterday and today is that – yes, it can be said – temptation was also part of the divine experience. The temptations felt and faced by God-made-man were not the ones that most trouble men and women, such as behavioural sins, possibly of a sexual kind or, it may be, unholy bitterness, greed, unrighteous anger, etc. The focal point of Satan's attack on Jesus was in relation to the use of power, the special divine power he recognised as God's gift to him, the "beloved Son in whom I am well pleased" (Matthew chapter 3, verse 17). Should he use it for selfish, material ends such as turning stones into bread? Should he perform divine conjuring tricks such as jumping off the tower of the temple? Should he be a military Messiah, powerfully conquering all to gain for himself "the kingdoms of this world"? Nor was that attack temporary for St Luke tells us that "the devil left him *for a season*" (chapter 4, verse 13). That meant he would return to the attack on Jesus at many points in his life. There was temptation in the Garden of Gethsemane ("Let this cup pass from me"). Jesus was under severe pressure on Calvary ("My God, my God, why hast thou forsaken me?"). Temptation went on until life was ended. Whether we see temptation from a personal negative power called Satan or the devil, or whether, as others would prefer it, as a build-up of inner pressures coming from the negative or shadow side of the personality of our personal and collective unconscious, is a matter of personal preference. It may even be there is something of both involved. Paul testified to the "law in his members" that made him choose evil rather than good but, at the same time, he spoke of the cosmic principalities and powers, the rulers of darkness of which he was so aware. Either way, or both ways, the ultimate experience is the same. There is the pressure from within to give in to the promptings coming from our dark side. There is the struggle during the sinning, the regret and remorse afterwards. The agony of remorse drove Peter to tears and Judas to suicide. How easily the awful realisation that comes after the temptation has passed and sin has been committed can drive the troubled soul to agony and despair. Go further then, with John Donne, but *go right to the end:*

> I have a sinne of fear that when I have spunne
> my last thread, I shall perish on the shore;
> sweare by thy selfe, that at my death thy sonne
> shall shine as he shines now, and heretofore.
> And having done that, Thou hast done.
> I feare no more.

DEATH HURTS

"Death hurts," I wrote in a Meditation last year.* "Death brings a deep sense of loss, whether it comes as a release from long suffering, as the climax of a fruitful life, in war, by murder, as sudden accident." A sudden and, in this case, dreadful, dreadful road crash has brought universal hurt this week.

"In the midst of life we are in death," reads a burial service in the *Book of Common Prayer*. From a religious perspective, as the empty Cross proclaims, "in the midst of death we are in life." But how difficult to grasp that truth when we are faced by a road crash such as that which has killed the Princess of Wales; by the deaths of two children, strangled when playing a game; by the suffering of loved ones struck down by cancer, AIDS, motor neurone or Alzheimer's diseases.

The questions that flow from such circumstances are not easily met by some philosophical theory or theological dogma. "Where is God in the circumstances that took the life of the Princess?" "How can a compassionate God allow two children to fall victim to such an awful combination of circumstances?" If God has given human beings the freedom to do wrong, make mistakes, hurt others, can that same God intervene to overrule the results of our freedom? But surely divine intervention must be possible for an omnipotent God? There are those who have seen miracles who would testify that this is so. But why in some cases and not in others? Why are some healed physically and others not?

God does not will such suffering. Of the children, Jesus said clearly and with great feeling, "It is **not** the will of your Father that one of these little ones should perish." We each have to find our own answers to these impossible questions. While deep in tragedy is not, however, the time to do it. Bereavement needs prayer rather than propositions, silence rather than words, presence rather than action, touch rather than texts.

Those who cannot take a religious view will find their solace, certainly in the case of the Princess of Wales, in the healing influence of someone never to be forgotten, someone with whose own pain they could empathise, and by whose sensitive compassion they have been blessed. Those holding faiths other than Christian will find their strength in the spirituality they know and the beliefs they trust. As one Muslim leader said of the divine compassion: "He will caress their souls." Christians, believing in the Incarnation, find there the assurance that, in Jesus, God shared in human pain, pain that reached its climax in awful suffering on a cross. It may be just possible to believe – but only on a long-term view – that "all things work together for good," through sensing the blessings that can come from human tragedies.

In the midst of the death which hurts, may we glimpse light and life.

* In this volume, the reference is in the Meditation for December 9.
This Meditation was published on the Saturday after Princess Diana died, on the day of her funeral (September 6). By chance, it was placed as the only other item on the full-page obituary to Mother Teresa who had died the night before (on Friday 5 September, 1997).

THE HARVEST OF THE SPIRIT

The Harvest of the Spirit is the wonderful phrase used in the *New English Bible* to describe what the *Authorised Version* calls "the fruit of the Spirit" (Galatians chapter 5, verse 22). That harvest is, according to St Paul, "love, joy, peace, patience, kindness, goodness, fidelity, gentleness and self-control". And all these qualities are the product of the life nourished by meditation, contemplation and silence, and developed in the power of the Spirit. This is where we reap what the Spirit has sown.

The letter to the Galatians was, possibly, the first letter Paul wrote to the new Christian communities he had initiated on his missionary journeys. He felt a real responsibility for these churches. The letter contains, even in its short compass, the essence of his teaching. It is personal, passionate and pointed, yet pastoral through and through. The pastor who loves his people will pull no punches over the fundamentals of the faith but he will always, nevertheless, speak the truth in love. Paul did this to the Galatians.

The letter embraces several great Pauline themes. It has, for example, a spirited defence of his apostolate. Paul, always honest, had no qualms about admitting his past. "You have heard of my former career when the religion of the Jews was my religion," he writes in chapter 1, verses 13 and 14 in William Barclay's translation. "You are well aware that there were no bounds to my persecution of God's church and that I tried to blast it out of existence. In my fanatical enthusiasm for my ancestral traditions, I outstripped most of my contemporaries and my compatriots in the Jewish way of life and belief." But he had no doubt about the validity of his apostleship or the source of his message. "I owe my knowledge to no human institution and to no man's teaching. No! It came to me by direct revelation from Jesus Christ." Then he goes to the very centre of his position, the belief that was a direct product of his experience. There is only one way to "get it right with God". That way is "by faith alone".

Paul's letter to the Galatians was intended to establish clearly and for ever, the essential message of the gospel. "No one can get into a right relationship with God," he says "by doing the things which the law prescribes. The only way to get into a right relationship with God is through faith in Christ Jesus" (Galatians chapter 2, verse 16). We are not saved by works but by grace. It is by faith alone that we are "justified". "In Christ's school, we are made right with God through faith." So the great Reformation emphasis on "justification by faith" has built itself into our view of how we attain to life.

The harvest of the Spirit is not the merit through which we gain salvation. It is the product of the salvation we already have. It comes through the miracle of grace.

In Step with the Spirit

"Are you simply going to write off the *facts* of your faith?" Paul asks the Galatians (chapter 3, verse 4). He is determined that the church in Galatia should fully understand the message which for him is the heart of the gospel. To talk about "justification by faith" may well to modern ears sound old fashioned and out of tune with modern speech, but it is, in the end, not the terms used that are important but the facts they describe. And it was the facts of faith that he had put so strongly to them that they must not "write off". Use your own language to try to describe the experience about which Paul felt so strongly. It is essentially that experience of realising the wonderful truth that we do not have to win the divine approval or (if you want to so put it) secure your salvation by your own effort. That is given as a gift of grace. This should take away the sense of sheer despair brought about by trying to be good enough to get into a right relationship with God. Paul had learnt the sheer awfulness of that effort and struggle. Share with Paul then the joy of the discovery that "getting right with God" is about acceptance and receiving.

The agent in our reconciliation with God on his initiative is the Holy Spirit. "It is," says Paul to the Galatian church, "by the help of the Spirit that we eagerly await the hoped-for right relationship with God which comes from faith." Such is the miracle of new creation, the turning-point (which conversion by derivation means) that leads to new life.

"If the Spirit is the ruling principle of our lives," Paul goes on with enthusiasm, "let us march in step with the Spirit." Again, what a wonderful translation William Barclay has produced! What an image – marching in step with the Spirit! Our growth in grace and in the likeness of Jesus Christ will come slowly but surely until we reap the harvest of the Spirit and begin to produce the fruit that bears testimony to the miracle within. "I am not going to treat the grace of God as if it did not exist."

We have then laid down the fundamentals of our faith and we dare not treat them as if they were not true. We cannot hope to produce the harvest of the Spirit unless the grace of God is real *and* felt to be real. The production in our lives of love, joy and peace and all those other great elements that constitute the harvest of the Spirit, depend on that amazing grace. That harvest will come not because we set ourselves moral standards, not because we resolve but because we receive, not because we increase our good works' target, but because we allow the Spirit to flow through us in abundance.

GRACE ABOUNDING

We look now at some of the most important statements from Paul's letter to the Galatians to give light to our understanding of grace abounding. They are all taken from William Barclay's translation of the letter to the Galatians. First, one we have already quoted: "I am not going to treat the grace of Christ as if it did not exist."

> "God called me by his grace and he chose to reveal his Son to me, and through me to others." (chapter 1, verses 15 and 16)

> "No man can get into a right relationships with God by means of doing the things which the law prescribes. The only way to get into a right relationship with God is through faith in Christ Jesus." (chapter 2, verse 16)

> "The law was therefore the servant who brought us to the door of the school for Christ, so that in Christ's school we might be made right with God through faith." (chapter 3, verse 24)

All this adds up to our view that Paul's *experience*, allied to his *intuitional* understanding of the essence of faith – a matter of revelation, not rational argument – plus his *intellectual* ability to "theologise" the content of his experience and the revelation that he had received, left him in no doubt at all where the crux of the gospel lay. It was in the opportunity, through grace alone, to attain to the stature and fullness of Christ.

The "school of Christ" is an important one for us all. Paul saw an education for life element in the law. Its function was to bring us to the gateway to faith and show us the need for something more than law if we would find salvation and wholeness. In that preparatory school, Paul had been thoroughly educated. He could see clearly that the law was the schoolmaster (chapter 3, verse 24) that prepared him for Christ. In that school he had been an outstanding scholar and had built up an excellent pedigree. "As far as the goodness which the law prescribes and demands are concerned," he says, "I was beyond criticism. But whatever I achieved in life and in my career, achievements I would at one time regard as the profit of life, I have written off as a dead loss for the sake of Christ. Yes, and more than that, I am prepared to write off everything as a dead loss for the sake of getting to know Christ Jesus, our Lord."

It is a strong case that Paul makes for grace abounding.

CALLED BY GRACE

The glory of the doctrine of justification by faith alone is the anxiety it takes away from us all for it divorces salvation from meritorious effort and grounds us in grace alone. The danger it carries with it is a confusion between liberty and licence. Liberty and freedom in Christ is a positive privilege. Licence is liberty abused. Let us look at both these points, drawing comfort from the first and taking caution from the second.

In relation to the first, we need to go back to a point I made earlier, that the doorway to the new liberty and freedom which Paul began to discover on the road to Damascus lay in his personal experience. "The gospel which I preach," he said, "is no human affair. I owe my knowledge to no man's instruction and to no man's teaching. No! It came to me by direct revelation from Jesus Christ!" (Galatians chapter 1, verses 11 and 12, WB). Paul had experienced real agony in his efforts to please God by obedience to the law and by moral achievements. But the law could not *cure* sin. It was there that the dilemma thrown up in his preparatory school, the school of law, lay. Only in the school of grace could he find his peace.

Paul's conversion is not a psychological phenomenon to be explained away in terms of a guilt or other complex. It was a life-changing experience that, examined by that highly competent mind, attributed it all to that knowledge beyond knowledge revealed to him, and this he saw as the action of Christ. The man who was in bondage to the law became the man who through grace was made free. Relationship to God, obscured by the impossible pressure to attain to perfection by works, found illumination in the realisation that, to those with faith, grace was freely given, unearned and undeserved. The strains of striving to attain victory over the inner forces of sin belonged to the past.

The second point, the danger of liberty descending into licence, has always been present where there is immaturity in religious experience and understanding. It is always possible to argue that if salvation is so free, we can sin more so that grace may the more abound – precisely what was said within the churches at that time. But this is a misunderstanding of the responsibilities of true liberty. Freedom means not anarchy but discipline. Grace does not allow us to do what we like. It enables us to do as God likes in a way we could not do it before. The doctrine of justification by faith is not a passport to licence. It is a demand that, knowing a new freedom, we become the more disciplined and responsible. It is then the fruits of the Spirit are developed in abundance – love, joy, peace and all those lovely things against which there is no law.

In the next Meditation we shall begin to look at these.

JOY...

The first three elements in the harvest of the Spirit are listed by St Paul as "love", "joy" and "peace". I do not propose to say more on "love" as I have devoted a month's Meditations to that theme (August). It is desirable however to reflect on "joy" and "peace".

Joy is the product of a healthy relationship with God. There is a passage in the Psalms (Psalm 1, verses 1 to 3a) that has something of that flavour. It reads: "Blessed is the man that walketh not in the counsel of the ungodly, nor standeth in the way of sinners, nor sitteth in the seat of the scornful, but his delight is in the law of the Lord; and in his law doth meditate day and night. He shall be like a tree planted by the water that bringeth forth fruit in his season." That sense of delight is joy in the Lord.

The dictionary definitions of joy fall short of the full measure given to "joy" in the Bible. Joy is, the dictionary says, "the emotion produced by gratified desire, success, happy fortune". It is mirth, gaiety and so on. Only when it goes on to speak of gladness, happiness, delight and exultation does it begin to reach something of the biblical understanding of joy.

"Gratified desire" has very physical connotations. If that phrase has to have any relevance at all, it must be to biblical joy. That concept needs to be spiritualised. Joy in Christian terms is related to the gratification of (to use a phrase from the writer Glenn Clark) "the soul's sincere desire". It is related to a "healthy" relationship to God, that is a relationship of the whole being to God, body, soul, mind and spirit. It is a relationship on the physical level, the mental level, the emotional level and the spiritual level. "Gratified desire" at any level short of the needs of the soul will not produce the joy of which the Bible speaks. "Man does not live by bread alone." People who marry mainly to satisfy physical desire almost always discover, and that not so far along the road of life, that flesh satisfied and passion spent, the search for real joy and meaning begins.

Joy as a fruit of the Spirit is, then, no superficial emotion, no noisy expression of amusement, no passing involvement in pleasure-providing play. It is a quality, deep in our inner being, of smiling radiance, a product of the presence of the peace that passes understanding, a reflection of reconciliation experienced through the redemptive activity of God. Joy is, in its depth, a real fruit of the Spirit. *It is a joy related to our wholeness which cannot be felt unless our spiritual needs are met,* but which is rightly felt in the experience of delight through the senses, so long as it is dedicated to the glory of God.

...AND PEACE

There is a little more that needs to be said about joy as a gift of the Spirit before we speak about "peace", so this Meditation looks at a particular aspect of joy and that is the way in which it is related to reconciliation. You have only to recall the parable of the prodigal son to see how connected these concepts are.

The particular example of the prodigal son is only one of a number of references Jesus made to the "joy" that there is "among the angels over one sinner who repents" (Luke chapter 15, verse 10). Similarly the divine joy is expounded and explained in a second verse from that chapter, verse 7: "There will be greater joy in heaven over one sinner who repents than over ninety and nine who do not need to repent." Consider too what Jesus said to his disciples about joy: "I have spoken this to you" (that is about God's love) "so that my joy may be in you and your joy complete" (John chapter 15, verse 11).

St Paul too brings joy to the centre of the gospel that he proclaims. The Christian is to "rejoice always" – that he says to the Thessalonian Christian community (1 Thessalonians chapter 5, verse 16). That joy must be retained in adversity (Romans chapter 5, verses 3 to 11; also Colossians chapter 1, verse 24). St Peter too wrote on the theme of joy in his first letter (1 Peter chapter 1, verses 6 to 9). Triumphant victory over adversity is evidence of the all-embracing joy that is to come. And so, the book of Revelation tells us in typical symbolic language, there will be the joyous singing of "a new song" when the powers of darkness are defeated.

We turn now to the theme of "peace".

There is a touching reference to the importance of inner peace in one of the Psalms (Psalm 55). In verses 16 to 18, in the *New English Bible* translation, we read: "He has heard my cry ... and gave me back my peace." The blessing lay in the restoration of something valuable that he had lost, his sense of peace. Of all the fruits of the Spirit, peace is one of the most important. "Our hearts are restless till they rest in Thee." The heart cries out for relationship restored. The soul yearns for reunion with God where our waywardness has broken our relationship to God. The whole of our being "groans" (the Psalmist uses the word as well as St Paul who speaks of "the whole creation" groaning until the final redemption comes) to be at one with God and at peace with him; and by implication, with our neighbours. Relationship is restored by grace alone and so in reconciliation our peace is "given back". It means the Spirit is at work. The harvest is peace.

THE PEACE THAT PASSES UNDERSTANDING

Peace, we saw in yesterday's Meditation, is the recovery of something lost. "He gave me back my peace." In the traditional devotional language of Christianity, the divine-human relationship has been broken by sin. Mankind lost the right to that relationship through the sin (set out in the story of Genesis) of arrogance.* Adam and Eve, symbols of every man and woman, wanted to be "as God". In more contemporary psychological terms, the cumulative shadow of the personal and collective unconscious (to use Jung's terms) stimulates negative psychic influences that create a barrier between men, women and God. God's initiative in love, breaks down the blocks. That is the reconciliation that comes where faith responds to grace. Choose whichever term feels right – conversion, redemption, salvation, new birth, eternal life, individuation, integration, meaning. It is from the platform of justification that "sanctification", "regeneration", "life abundant" evolve through the presence and power of the Holy Spirit. The ultimate product of the miracle of grace is a deep, inner peace, a peace that in truth "passes understanding".

The presence of such peace has profound practical effects on life. One of them is an ability to cope with criticism in such a way that we are able to continue creatively, despite opposition, hostility, even ridicule (as Jesus did in his trials before Caiaphas and Pilate). We are the better equipped to handle pressure without breakdown. The strength of inner peace can be enough to bring perspective where there might be panic. It can also help us to see that each day, as Jesus said, brings enough of its own troubles; we need to live a day at a time. Inner peace can provide an unruffled calm in the face of decisions that must be made. It can bring the blessing of sleep where others have sleepless nights. The fruit of peace is a true serenity.

Another consequence of peace within is a sense of purpose in relation to God's providence. It is sometimes hard, in the kind of world in which we live, to feel sure about the purpose of life, what it means, where it is going; to be convinced that good will triumph over evil, that "the kingdoms of this world" can become "the kingdom of our Lord Jesus Christ". Peace brings perspective, a perspective that sees more clearly the implications of time and enables us to look at life, as I said before, *sub specie aeternitatis*, that is in the context of timelessness, that is eternity. There cannot be confidence and tranquillity if we always look at history and "the news" from floor level. Only by taking a standpoint outside daily happenings can we begin to see the purpose of God within human history, the possibilities for good amid so much evil and the certainty of the ultimate triumph of grace in the world. "Thou wilt keep him in perfect peace whose mind is stayed on Thee."

* This theme was developed in the Meditation for March 1.

MEEKNESS

The next three fruits of the Spirit are patience, meekness and goodness. Patience I have already discussed in my Meditation on August 3 but meekness and goodness are qualities into which we need to look.

The word "meekness" is a word that creates difficulties for us. It has a certain "feel" about it in English and that sense is not wholly acceptable to us. It suggests something somewhat weak when what we need is strength.

Meekness, in dictionary terms, suggests such adjectives as mild, submissive, humble, tame (Cassell's Dictionary). This is not however the biblical understanding of the word so another translation must be found for it. Certainly meekness in the Bible is not of the "gentle Jesus, meek and mild" kind. It has to do with different concepts, concepts such as lowliness, humility, distress, poverty (in material terms) and a status described as "of low estate". These are words which describe people in need of help and they are seen by God as in such need. "The poor man cried and the Lord heard him and saved him out of all his troubles" (Psalm 34, verse 6).

"The meek shall inherit the earth" indeed and God has special blessings for them. They have, in worldly terms, little going for them but, given that they have – and often did have – a trusting, humble attitude of mind, "all will be well" for them "all will be truly well". So to be "meek" is to submit oneself willingly to the will of God at all times. It is a quality typical of the truly devoted person. Meekness is the attitude of those devout souls who "waited for the consolation of Israel" (Luke chapter 2, verse 25).

Jesus had no hesitation in identifying himself with meekness in that biblical sense. It was a characteristic of his kingly and messianic role. He entered Jerusalem on his final journey there "meek and sitting on an ass" (Matthew chapter 21, verse 5) just as the prophet Zechariah had prophesied (Zechariah chapter 9, verse 9).

St Paul, in the great Philippians passage on the humility of Christ (Philippians chapter 2) underlines the true meekness of Christ. His true poverty, his trust in God, his genuine humility. The Christ who is cosmic in that he existed "in the beginning with God", who was incarnate and lived a truly human life, who rose again after "becoming obedient unto death, even death on a cross" is, in his acceptance of the whole spectrum of suffering, truly meek.

Meekness, therefore, incarnate in Jesus is a hugely impressive quality. To read and reread that Philippians passage is to sense just what greatness there is in meekness. There is no weakness, submissiveness, tameness in that wonderful picture. There is only an example of the kind of attitudes we should seek to express. It is a fruit of the Spirit to be coveted and valued.

But there is more to be said tomorrow about the meaning of true meekness.

THE STRENGTH OF GENTLENESS

What word can we substitute for meekness? As always, the different versions of the Bible offer possible help in finding the right word or phrase. "Gentleness" is chosen by the *New English Bible*, the *Jerusalem Bible* and the *Revised Standard Version*. J B Phillips suggests "tolerance", but once again it is William Barclay who gets it absolutely right with his wonderful suggestion, "the strength of gentleness". I am sure that it is in the paradoxical relationship of strength to gentleness that the real meaning of this fruit of the Spirit lies. This is confirmed by the use of the Greek word for meek which means "under control". But whichever translation we use, the fundamental biblical emphasis in meekness is humble obedience to the divine will.

The strength of gentleness! What a glorious concept this is! How truly it describes the Jesus who walked this earth. It is even true of God himself! "He shall feed his flock like a shepherd. He shall gather the lambs with his arms and carry them in his bosom and shall gently lead those that are with young" (Isaiah chapter 40, verse 11). This is a picture of the combination of tenderness and strength. To this we add yet another remarkable picture of the God who is like a good shepherd. It comes from the *New English Bible*'s rendering of Ezekiel chapter 34, verses 15 and 16. "I will search for the lost, recover the straggler, bandage the hurt, strengthen the sick, leave the healthy and strong to play and give them their proper food." There in the Old Testament is yet another picture of gentle strength in action! The New Testament incarnates that strength of gentleness in the image of the Good Shepherd used to portray the nature of Jesus, Son of God. This then is a gift of the Spirit for which we must have real desire. The true Christian *is* the gentle man, the gentle woman. There is a tenderness about the way they do things that is strangely powerful both in relationship and in healing. There is, as Rupert Brooke tells us, "gentleness in hearts at peace".

There is perhaps something of importance in that last quotation on which we need to reflect. The more we dig deeply into the meaning of the gifts of the Spirit, the more they impinge on each other. It is out of inner peace that the capacity to be both strong and gentle comes. It is out of love that patience evolves. The developed Christian life is a rounded life, a balanced life, an ordered life. The Holy Spirit brings order and balance. The symbol of wholeness is a circle, love in the round.

Perhaps the last word on the strength of gentleness comes not from the Bible but from William Shakespeare's *As You Like It*:

"Let gentleness my strong enforcement be."

GOODNESS...

What is goodness? To ask that is to raise one of the great questions that have occupied philosophers from time immemorial, yet surprisingly, when I looked up my *Dictionary of the Bible* (Hastings, revised by Grant and Rowley) there was no entry for "goodness" at all. The other fruits of the Spirit are there – love, joy, peace, patience (long-suffering) and kindness all had entries, but not goodness. I wonder why, for it is one of the great, if indefinable, concepts. It is worth noticing too that there are variations for other words in other translations of the Bible (as we have seen*). There is no significant variation in relation to goodness.

Goodness feels as if it had a direct connection with "God-ness". It is certainly related to things divine. It must therefore relate to love, for God is love. Goodness is essentially an expression of God-ness and so is love. For that reason, goodness is more an attribute than an achievement or an attainment, more related to values than morals.

This brings me to one of the most important comments that can be made about goodness, because it takes us down to the very foundations perhaps even the corner-stone of our life system. As with so much that is spiritual, goodness becomes less attainable the more we *try* to attain it. It shows itself naturally if the Spirit is at work within us.

This great truth lies at the very heart of the witness of the Protestant Reformers. It is the theological lynch-pin of the Reformation. So much did the Reformers emphasise it that it became, as the doctrine of justification by faith, one of the rocks on which the Reformed churches were based. Goodness is not the merit we create and offer to God as a claim for recognition. It is that which is created in us in the process of sanctification, through what I have called the miracle of grace. So if goodness is seen to be part of our offering to the world, the credit goes not to us, but to the Spirit which works in us. That makes the possession of goodness a matter for profound humility. Goodness comes from the God-ness we meet in the incarnate Christ. It is evidence of "the Christ within".

Jesus brought many blessings into life when "the Word became flesh and dwelt among us." The demonstration in Jesus of true goodness was one of the greatest of them. When that rich young ruler addressed Jesus as "good master", Jesus deliberately pointed him to the source of all goodness, that is God, but the young man was undoubtedly expressing, spontaneously and in admiration and respect, what he and others felt when they met the man from Galilee. The centurion at Jesus' crucifixion thought similarly when he, also spontaneously, said: "Truly this was the son of God." The divine goodness was self-evident in Jesus.

* See, for example, Meditations for August 1, 10, 13, 14, 17; September 1 and 9.

Faith...

There are three products of the harvest of the Spirit that we have not yet looked at in these Meditations. They are faith, kindness and temperance. As we have done with other words in this series of reflections, we will draw on alternative translations of each word in other versions of the Bible. We begin with the word "faith".

Faith is like the word love in that it has many meanings, and many shades of meaning. It is a very important word biblically and, as we have seen in yesterday's Meditation, it stands at the centre of Reformation theology, with its emphasis on faith alone as the road to salvation. Is it that meaning of "faith" that is in St Paul's mind when he lists it as one of the fruits of the Spirit?

William Barclay finds four shades of meaning in the New Testament use of the word "faith". *Pistis*, the Greek word for faith, has as its main meaning the characteristically Pauline notion of *total commitment to Jesus*. This commitment involves accepting Christ at his word both in relation to his demands and his promises. Secondly it may mean "unshakeable hope". Thirdly it stands for the "acceptance of certain propositions" in an intellectual way. Fourthly it can be used as it is in the phrase "the Christian faith". In Galatians chapter 5, verses 22 to 24, our theme passage for the harvest of the Spirit, it is used to mean "fidelity" or "keeping faith".

This is confirmed by the variations in translations in some of the other versions of the Bible. The *New English Bible* has "fidelity" and Dr Barclay uses that term too. The *Revised Standard Version* prefers "faithfulness" and the *Jerusalem Bible* "trustfulness".

Once again I underline the point made repeatedly in these Meditations. The quality that *we* must have as evidence of the presence of the Spirit in our lives is a reflection of an attribute of God. The call to "love" arises because "God is love" and "God first loved us". The divine joy precedes our human joy. The peace we seek and need will be, in some way, a reflection of the divine peace. The demand for patience presupposes the patience of a long-suffering God. The need to be kind is founded on the divine kindness. The life of goodness is a reflection, on a very human scale, of the goodness of God, and something which, remembering the lasting associations with "September 11th", is to be promoted.

When we come to "faith" in the sense of "fidelity" we touch once more a fundamental attribute of God. "O Thou that changest not ..."; "the same yesterday, today and forever." When David, in great distress over defeat and the loss of family and friends, "encouraged himself in the Lord his God," he was trusting in the certainty that God, by his very nature, could never let his servants down and would not do it now. He had solid grounds for his faith.

But the study of "faith" needs to go further.

...KINDNESS

There is an innate constancy and consistency about God that does not allow any kind of unreliability. The God of Abraham, Isaac and Jacob is a God of loyalty and that was the point at which we ended yesterday's Meditation. The God and Father of our Lord Jesus Christ will never leave us "comfortless"! Is it not this "faith" that we are asked to express as part of the harvest of the Spirit? It would be a quality in us that reflects the divine consistency, something that might be suitably summed up in the modern word "commitment". And commitment? The poet Robert Frost points the direction for us when he writes:

> And I have promises to keep . . . and miles to go before I sleep.

Commitment ignores applause or criticism. It sets aside money as a determinant of behaviour. It dismisses prestige and status as irrelevancies when duty calls. Commitment means what Paul put so strikingly, "pressing towards the mark for the prize of the high calling of God in Christ Jesus." That involves "forgetting the things which are behind and reaching forth to the things which are before (Philippians chapter 3, verses 13 and 14). It means (St Paul again), "counting all things but loss" in the search for inner consistency and wholeness.

The faith, the fidelity which God asks of us is obedience to the Light we have. That is commitment.

"I expect to pass through this world but once. Any good therefore that I can do, or any kindness that I can show to my fellow-creature, let me do it now. Let me not defer or neglect it, for I shall not pass this way again." There is apparently some uncertainty over who the author of this quotation is – was it Emerson or Edward Courtney or someone else? – but there is no doubt about its validity. Kindness must be shown where and when it can be shown. Kindness is a product in the harvest of the Spirit.

In our Meditation for August 4 we discussed the meaning of kindness. "Love is kindness," we said. It is. But it may be helpful to say a little more about it within our current theme of the fruits of the Spirit.

Kindness is, according to the dictionary definition, a "disposition to do good to others". Kindness is "kin-ness". It is part of the attitude required within the brotherhood of man and the sisterhood of woman. It is bound up with the Fatherhood of God. Its essential element is compassion. "Any kindness that I can show . . . let me do it now."

"The heart of the eternal is most wonderfully kind," writes Frederick William Faber. It is the kindness of God that insists on our participation in the practical life of the world. Compassion is born out of the kindness of God. The "disposition to do good" is a fruit of the Spirit.

Temperance

The last of the list of qualities included in St Paul's harvest of the Spirit is temperance. This is the word used in the *Authorised Version*, but it is a word with certain associations which do not help it to be the best word for us. "Self-control" is the word favoured by several translators – certainly including J B Phillips, the *Jerusalem Bible*, the *Revised Standard Version*, the *New English Bible* and William Barclay.

To try and understand the words Paul particularly and deliberately uses, it is necessary to consider the local problems he was addressing in his letter. He was especially concerned about the tension between "flesh" and "spirit", that is between what he calls our "lower nature" (the sensual or physical part of our being) and our spiritual aspirations.

Gnosticism was a prevailing philosophy in areas where Paul had established new Christian communities. One of the characteristic Gnostic theories was that of "duality". This held that the soul is "good" and the body "evil". The soul suffers then because it is imprisoned in an evil body. At death, the body will be destroyed and the soul will be freed to go back to God to whom it belongs. In our Christian vocabulary, some of these ideas sometimes creep in. We can see that in such phrases as "saving souls" and "the immortality of the soul". These are not mainstream Christian concepts but go back to Gnostic ideas, ideas incidentally present in much contemporary esoteric thinking. That sort of approach had led, in extreme cases in Paul's experience, to ascetic excesses. It also sometimes turned into a form of antinomianism which Paul felt he had to oppose because it led to licence – if the body is evil and to be destroyed, nothing matters any more, so gratify it as much as you like. This was licence that was unhealthy and misguided.

In Paul's concept of salvation the *whole* person matters, body, soul, mind, spirit. We, not a part of us, live on. So in the resurrection the body is included. The body is not therefore, as Gnosticism claimed, wholly evil. Christians believe in the resurrection of the *body*, as the Creeds say. What Paul did see is the conflict *within* us. That so-called lower nature creates demands that culminate in sexual sins and perversions, idolatry and involvement in the occult, violence and hostility, heresy, alcohol, etc (Galatians, chapter 5, verses 20 and 21). It is in contrast to this that he spells out the "things against which there is no law", love, joy, peace and all the other "good fruits" we have been considering. The last of these is "temperance" or "self-control". The "flesh" is not inherently evil but it needs proper control, that is self-control. And it is that important element, self-control, that is rightly one of the fruits of the Spirit.

ENCOURAGEMENT

Paul has given us a comprehensive list of the fruits and gifts of the Spirit. It might however be a useful exercise for us to add to that list some qualities, virtues or attitudes that we see or meet in others that could provide helpful addenda to that list.

There are three that come to mind as I write. The first of these is *encouragement*.

This is the theme of another Meditation in this collection of daily reflections. It was centred on King David's positive statement following defeat in battle and the death and destruction it had brought. It is said of David (1 Samuel chapter 30, verse 6) that he "encouraged himself in the Lord his God". But the theme is an important one and is worth extended reflection.

The gospel is concerned not to *discourage* but to *encourage*. The keynote text on this subject, one I have already referred to in this context, is John chapter 3, verse 17. "God so loved the world that he sent not his Son into the world to condemn the world but that the world through him might be saved." The gospel is one that "accentuates the positive" rather than the negative. Salvation is God's purpose, not condemnation.

Sadly within the history of the church the negative, judgemental, condemnatory aspect has too often been emphasised. It has, in past days rather than now, shaped its discipline to bring people to be judged (as was the case with the woman taken in adultery in the New Testament) inevitably bringing a self-righteousness to the forefront of church life. The stress has been too often on "Thou shalt not . . .", too little on the encouragement of the fruits of the Spirit. What was so typical of the attitude that Jesus had to people was his sensitivity to their needs and understanding of their problems. Stage caricatures of ecclesiastical figures almost always focus on believed negative essentials like no smoking, no drinking and no sensual failures, in other words on what clergy and other church representatives are expected not to do. That often meant that really serious sins like greed, materialism, judgementalism, hypocrisy and insensitivity were not shown to be the sinful attitudes they really are. And in the more public sphere obscenities like violence (verbal and otherwise) and exploitation, arms-dealing for profit, profiteering from slave labour (still a feature of contemporary international business), have failed to attract the condemnation they merited. One of the perceptions of the church in the eyes of "the public" is its failure to lead opinion on the serious abuses prevalent in economics and business all too common today.

A J Gossip, a great Scottish preacher of former years, insisted that whatever a sermon had to say and however challenging it had to be, it should always end with words of encouragement. The soothing of the troubled and the strengthening of the weak was a prime purpose in preaching. Those who have the gift of encouraging others display a mark of the Spirit.

FRIENDSHIP

The next fruit of the Spirit to be added to St Paul's harvest of the Spirit is that of friendship. It may sound an everyday sort of quality, but it is much more than that. It is in some people a very special attribute.

When Paul talks of the diversity of gifts, he is enunciating the great principle of variety, something that is very much an expression of the presence of the Spirit's energy at work in people. Too often, in church life and practice, we have laid emphasis, at least implicitly, on the importance of "public" gifts, that is those expressed in holding named offices in the church, taking leadership roles, acting as accountant or property convener, etc. These are not gifts to be devalued, quite the reverse. The organisation "church" could not function if there were not people able and willing to take on such positions. But the proper value we put on these public gifts must not prevent our recognising that there are other perhaps more private gifts, gifts which result in no publicity or votes of thanks, but which are very valuable indeed in the life of the church.

Another principle Paul laid down was the peculiarity of gifts to people. The Spirit manifests itself in different ways in different individuals. One person has the gift of wisdom, another has faith by the same Spirit. Some, and therefore not all, have the gift of tongues, while yet another has the ability to discern true spirits from false. Some can interpret tongues, some have the gift of healing, some demonstrate the gift of prophecy, others have miraculous powers. But all these gifts are the work of the same Holy Spirit distributing them to individuals in whatever way that Spirit chooses (1 Corinthians chapter 12, verses 7 to 11). It is not in any way a criticism of us if we do not have certain gifts. It will be our privilege to demonstrate some other gifts. This is simply the way God, in his wisdom, deals with people.

This brings an egalitarianism into the distribution of gifts that is salutary. Ecclesiastical status may be important to men and women but "status symbols mean nothing to God" (Galatians chapter 2, verse 6, William Barclay). The more public gifts seen in churches are as important as, but ultimately no more important than, more private gifts like the ability to offer friendship. This is seen in the composition of the apostolic band. There was the extrovert Peter, inevitably taking on a leadership role and the introvert Andrew, the enabler.* It was the quiet friendliness of Andrew that drew them to him as the gateway to Jesus.

The capacity to make friends and to offer real friendship is not everybody's gift. Some who seem otherwise confident may simply not have the ability to relate at deeper levels. It is indeed the comparatively unknown and unnoticed who may most truly have this talent. When it has been discovered, the church has found an asset indeed.

* See further on the this theme in the Meditation for November 30.

COMPASSION

The third additional fruit of the Spirit to be listed, extra to St Paul's sound selection, is *compassion*, a word that has cropped up many times in the course of these Meditations (and rightly so) but on which there may be more to reflect.

It is possibly unfair to suggest that this great quality should be "added" to Paul's list simply because love is in that list and compassion is love in action. But a moment or two's further reflection is, I feel, still called for.

First let us recall some verses from Mark's Gospel:

> And Jesus, moved with compassion for him, put forth his hand . . .
> When Jesus saw the multitudes, he was moved with compassion.

As we shall see in the month that we spend on "the healing way" (October), compassion is the force that lies behind motivation for healing. This was certainly so in the case of Jesus as the lovely phrase "he was moved to compassion" shows. The God and Father of Jesus Christ is a God of compassion.

Translators of versions other than the *Authorised Version*, often give the impression that they feel they must use alternative phrases for familiar ones and, in the case of the words "moved to compassion", do just that. "Moved to pity", which is for me less telling. "Moved with warm indignation" is the phrase used by the *New English Bible* for the first of the Marcan quotations above. The *Revised Standard Version* opts for simply "he had compassion" and "he felt sorry" is the *Jerusalem Bible*'s choice. "Deeply moved with pity" is the way in which J B Phillips renders it. I still feel that "moved to compassion" remains the right contribution. It seems to say everything that needs to be said about the nature of God.

Compassion, by derivation a "suffering with", is more than sympathy (also by derivation "suffering with"), and empathy because of the "action" element within it. Compassion results in an action of some kind, a touch, an embrace, a kiss, a decision. The heart has been "moved" and that inner sense of wanting to do something if it is at all possible is the result.

The feeling of compassion is a distinctive one and a recognisable one. It wells up in situations when for some reason, but not one necessarily definable, the soul is grazed and love is stimulated. The feelings are subjective but the characteristic of compassion turns that inner sense of loving response into objective reality, namely action. This is not the love that identifies in the sense of emotional involvement, nor is it the love that develops into a deeper relationship, shorter or longer. It is a love that carries no implications beyond the compassion it feels. It is the outflow of the moment in response to need or pain or grief or hurt. Sincerely offered, it brings the blessing of the moment.

Be glad to be "moved to compassion". It is a sign of the healing spirit within you.

EMPATHY

Sympathy is a very creditable quality. As we noted yesterday it is a sense of "suffering with". But the gift I would add to the products of the harvest of the Spirit is *empathy*. It is part of a relationship of understanding that enables us to enter into another's suffering.

The nature of the divine energy is stated in the letter to the Hebrews chapter 4, verses 14 to 15. In William Barclay's translation that verse reads:

> Jesus the Son of God . . . is not a high priest who is unable to
> sympathise with the weakness that we possess . . . In every
> respect (he) has gone through the same ordeal of temptation
> as we have to go through . . .

That verse encapsulates the meaning of sympathy but even more the essence of empathy of which God is capable. That should touch us deeply and at the same time make us glad.

The reality of the divine empathy is an encouragement to healing. Even in purely human terms, the knowledge that our sin or our suffering is not unique to us can be greatly comforting. When we are told that temptation and suffering are part of the experience of the Son of God, what adds to the sense of comfort is the divine consistency that underlines the divine empathy. Forgiveness, the result of the empathy of God with us, is given "seventy times seven". It is not a once-only action. It is ongoing understanding and love.

To have the ability truly to empathise with another's need is indeed a gift of the Spirit.

By way of epilogue, I add two further fruits of the Spirit. One is the ability to make a good cup of tea (perhaps a surprise there!), and the other is a sense of humour. On the latter I need add no more as it is dealt with in other Meditations.*

In every church there are those who can do no more than make a good cup of tea. But should we use a phrase like "no more than" in this context? I think not! The "tea-makers" take us back to the heart of Christianity.

There was an evening on which Jesus and his friends gathered in an upper room to share the Passover meal. It was in fact to become The Lord's Supper. "When the even was come," we read, "he sat down with the twelve disciples ... and they did eat." But who made the meal, set out the food and wine, and served them? Who washed up? The answer is, of course, that we just do not know. But whoever did it, they had played a crucial part in the creation of a mission that has brought us into the church of today. To "such a man" who had been asked to give the use of his room, and to those who served the meal, was given the privilege of participating in the creation of a glorious movement, one which he had a huge influence on the life of the world.

*See Meditation for October 30 and December 1.

THE PILGRIMAGE OF GRACE

In our September Meditations thus far, our stance has been within a perspective which gives a primary place to the spiritual aspect of life and the initiative God takes in first loving us, the process of growth and development towards wholeness expressed in the harvest of the Spirit. The Christian journey is a pilgrimage in grace. The miracle of grace is demonstrated in the fruits that come from seeds planted by God and nurtured by the presence and power of the Holy Spirit.

Also emphasised as we have journeyed on has been the reality and strength of the "opposing forces" within us, something which every honest believer will acknowledge. Indeed it is part of the experience of the pilgrim that pressure from evil grows stronger as we grow in grace. Put in symbolic terms, Satan has to fight all the harder as the favourable influence of God is seen to be at work in those whom the devil seeks to seduce. But our ground of hope is that God is in the struggle with us and this not passively but actively.

Our Christian "map" is theocentric, as the Nicene Creed makes clear. "I believe in God, the Father Almighty, Maker of heaven and earth and of all things visible and invisible": God is at the centre. The power of creation and re-creation is in the divine care just as is the initiative in redemption and the giving of new life. It is because God "first loved us" that we respond in love in our worship.

Our stance is "Christ-centred". This is not a statement about "exclusivity" but simply saying that, as we interpret life, it is to Jesus we look as we "run the race". It is in accord with Peter's confession: "Thou art the Son of the living God."

"I believe in "the Holy Spirit"…the Giver of Life," promised in the words of Christ about the "other Comforter" who would in due time come. That time was Pentecost when the disciples were transformed, renewed and stimulated to "take on" the world in Jesus' name.

The experience of faith, that is of the meeting with God in Christ, through the Spirit is the experience of the ages, authenticated by the church in "the Word of God". It is the experience of followers today and every day if they are receptive to the Spirit. The harvest of the Spirit is evidence of the Triune God working to integrate believers and to make them whole.

The pilgrimage of grace involves a constant waiting on God in the silence in order to hear "the still, small voice" which is God's means of communication in the desert place. The symbols of "earthquake, wind and fire," familiar to the prophet Elijah, needed to be changed, as symbols do. It was to that "sound of a faint whisper" (to use Professor Robert Davidson's rendering of "the still, small voice") that Elijah was directed. So must it be today for all determined to journey forwards on the pilgrimage of grace.

CONTEMPLATIVE MEDITATION

"Meditation" as the word has been used in this book refers to short reflections on matters of faith and life, the sense in which it is used in the *Daily Telegraph* "Saturday Meditation" to which I have contributed over 300 weekly contributions, 26 a year, over the past 12 years. It is primarily a "thinking" process based on biblical themes. The next 11 Meditations (specially written to complete the 366 making up a year) are Meditations in a slightly different sense. They are Meditations used in a meditation group where some 45 minutes are spent in silence. As some members of the group may find complete silence difficult, or are new to the method, a theme or just several sentences are used to help "guide" the meditation.

The amount of words or guidelines in the first Meditation on "Wings" is considerable and the spaces (for silent reflection) much smaller and more numerous. If that is compared with the Meditation on Love (see September 30) the differences will be clear. The latter is predominantly silence, the words or guidelines very few.

Another reason for the spaces (every two or three minutes in the earlier Meditations but tending to become longer spaces in the later ones) is to help the inexperienced to stop "mind-wandering" which so easily happens in silent reflection. An additional aid against that danger is to have a visible focal point to which the attention can be brought back whenever it starts to drift away. This might be a lit candle, a flower, a shell, or a simple symbol like a cross, in the centre of the group.

A further difficulty may be the danger of deep reflection "opening up" the unconscious. In that case some of those who meditate may find discomfort over material that is surfacing from the deep inner places ... unhappy but so far unremembered memories, associations, etc. Unidentifiable feelings of a negative kind may also cease to be "contained" (as they normally are by our "defences") and produce fear, even panic symptoms. For this reason, meditation should be (unless the participant is long experienced) in a sharing, caring group so that support is available if discomfort arises.

This type of meditation is a valuable devotional exercise and should lead to a deepening of the spiritual life. It is not, I should perhaps add, "transcendental meditation" (which always needs to be cautiously entered into) but a form of contemplative meditation used over the centuries by pilgrims on the way.

It should be said too that mysticism comes at another level, and involves experiences that require great awareness of the things of the Spirit. It should also be stressed that it is a gift that is given, not something we can strive to create or train to achieve. Those given this gift are greatly blessed in having it.

WINGS

They that wait upon the Lord . . .
    shall mount up with wings . . .
THE WINGS OF DIVINE INSPIRATION

I will make my refuge in the shadow of thy wings
THE WINGS OF DIVINE PROVIDENCE

How often would I have gathered thy children together,
    as a hen doth gather her brood under her wings
THE WINGS OF DIVINE COMPASSION

The sun of righteousness shall arise
    with healing in his wings
THE WINGS OF DIVINE HEALING

Come as the dove and spread thy wings,
    the wings of peaceful love

Amen

WASHED . . .

(based on Psalm 51 verse 7, *New English Bible*; John chapter 13, verses 1 to 7, *New English Bible*; Luke chapter 7, verses 36 to 50, *Authorised Version*; Revelation chapter 7, verse 14, *Authorised Version*)

Wash me, that I may become whiter than snow
Our Prayer for Cleansing

If I your Lord and Master have washed your feet,
you also ought to wash one another's feet
Our Prayer for Humility

But she hath washed my feet with her tears
Our Prayer for Greater Love

These are they which have come out of great tribulation
and have washed their robes and made them white . . .
Our Prayer for those who suffer

Amen

DEEP ROOTS

(based on Ephesians chapter 3, verse 18, *New English Bible*)

Let your focal point be A TREE
      growing . . .
          living . . .
It has leaves . . . branches . . . trunk . . .
But its life comes from its ROOTS

That life will be more secure with DEEP ROOTS

Its life is fed by rain . . . sun . . . wind . . .
      resources from outside, given to enable growth

We are as TREES
We need resources from outside of us . . .
      the warmth of people, the wind of the Spirit

Then we can push down DEEP ROOTS

From these roots we
      GROW . . . into Faith
          REACH UP . . . in Hope
              SPREAD OUT . . . in Love

Amen

THE DAYSPRING

(based on Luke chapter 1, verses 78 and 79, *Authorised Version* and *New English Bible*)

The Dayspring from on high hath visited us
THE DAWN HAS BROKEN

In the tender compassion of our God
IT IS GOD'S GIFT

To shine on those who live in darkness
TO THOSE IN NEED

To give light to those in the shadow of death
AND IN DESPAIR

To guide our feet into the way of peace
AND TO ALL WHO SEEK

Amen

THE GLORY OF LIFE

The Glory of Life
      is
           to love . . .
                to give . . .

To be a strong hand in the dark to another in time of need . . .

To be a cup of strength to any soul in a crisis of weakness . . .

This is to know
THE GLORY OF LIFE

Amen

   This Meditation is based on an anonymous poem on the wall of Alida Bosshardt's room in the Goodwill Centre in Amsterdam's red light district. It is the room from which Major Bosshardt of the Salvation Army has exercised her ministry in that area for the past 26 years. Her story is told in *Here is my Hand* (by Denis Duncan, paperback, Hodder & Stoughton) and referred to in the Meditation for February 24.

THE RIVER OF LIFE

(based on Revelation chapter 22, verses 1 and 2)

And he showed me a pure river of
WATER OF LIFE

On either side of the river was the
TREE OF LIFE

The river of the water of life had its
SOURCE IN GOD HIMSELF
Proceeding out of the throne of God and of the Lamb

And the leaves of the tree were for the
HEALING OF THE NATIONS

Amen

Life Renewed

(based on Psalm 23, *New English Bible*)

The Lord is my shepherd

He makes me lie down in green pastures
HE GIVES TO MY BODY

He leads me beside the waters of peace
HE GIVES TO MY MIND

He renews life within me
HE GIVES TO MY SOUL

And so He leads me in the right path

Goodness and Love unfailing . . . will follow me all the days of my life

I shall want nothing

And these, the Shepherd's blessings, I ask

FOR ALL

Amen

A New Song

(based on Psalm 40 verses 1 to 3, *New English Bible)*

I waited, waited for the Lord . . .

He bent down to me . . .

He heard my cry . . .

He brought me up . . .

He set my feet on a rock . . .

He gave me a firm footing . . .

On my lips, he put a new song . . .
Thanks be to God who giveth us the victory through our Lord, Jesus Christ

Amen

THE VINE

(based on John chapter 15, verses 1 to 7)

I am the vine

You are the branches

Without me, you can do nothing

Abide in me

If you abide in me
    You shall ask what you will
        And it shall be done unto you

Amen

JESUS, LORD

Jesus is LORD

Jesus IS Lord

JESUS is Lord

LORD JESUS

Amen

LOVE

(based on I John chapter 4, verses 7 and 16)

Love is of God

God is Love

Amen

THE HEALING MINISTRY

There has been a remarkable recovery of the healing ministry in virtually all the mainstream churches in the last twenty years. Those who sought a service of blessing by the laying on of hands used to have to search assiduously to find such a ministry, but now "Healing Services" are held in a great number of churches of many kinds. The restoration of the ministry of healing to a prominent place in contemporary worship is one of the significant signs of the times.

The word "recovery" is important. Such a ministry dare not be used as a gimmick that might attract more people into church. It is simply that the recovery of what the late Cameron Peddie called "the forgotten talent"* is now seen by so many to be a move "back to basics". When Jesus commissioned his disciples, he told them to "preach the gospel" and "heal the sick". The instructions appear to be of equal importance. The ministry of healing is not, therefore, just the province of eccentrics or extremists. It is a normal and crucial part of the church's life.

It is important to do everything to ensure that the ministry of healing is carried out responsibly and in a spirit of humility (for arrogance and healing ministry simply do not go together). Three spiritual principles should always be applied where ministry is undertaken. They are:

i) it must be encompassed in prayer
ii) it must be founded on, and grounded in, the Word of God
iii) it must be the subject of constant reflection under the guidance of the Holy Spirit.

The ambience of prayer is crucially important. Those who minister by laying on of hands are not the sources of healing. Christ is the healer and his ministering servants (whether they be individuals or, as was emphasised in healing services in Iona Abbey, the whole congregation) are but channels of grace. For that reason corporate prayer is of the utmost importance when the ministry is being offered "in Jesus' name".

While a distinction between the aim of the healing ministry (that is the wholeness of each seeker) and physical cure needs to be maintained, it is important to remember that Jesus interpreted his miracles of physical healing as "signs of the presence of the Kingdom". While the purpose of the ministry of healing is to make people whole in soul, mind and spirit, that wholeness includes too the blessing of the body. Jesus did restore sight and hearing. He dealt with epilepsy. The dumb spoke and the lame walked. When John the Baptist (as I mentioned in an earlier Meditation **) seemed to question the authenticity of Jesus' Messianic role, he was directed to those very miracles as evidence of Jesus' claims. It is therefore right and proper that while those in need should be pointed towards wholeness of being as the desirable aim, they should feel wholly free to ask for physical healing. Many asked Jesus in his lifetime for that blessing, and they were granted their prayer.

* *The Forgotten Talent* by Cameron Peddie, published by Arthur James.
** See Go Forward!, the Meditation for June 24.

HEALING POWER

One of the most exciting developments in the life of the church over the last two decades is the recovery of the healing ministry as a fundamental part of the presentation of the gospel. In so many churches across the denominations, services offering blessing by the laying on of hands are a normal part of the church's worship programme. Many would see this development as a work of the Holy Spirit.

Most such services are liturgical in their emphasis, and rightly so. All services should of course be healing, but to have a particular context in which the ministry to wholeness is visibly expressed in symbolic action is certainly another means of grace. Laying on of hands, a prominent biblical practice associated with the giving of power in both the Old and New Testaments, can be an energising sign and seal of the promise of God to seek wholeness in body, soul, mind and spirit for all people.

In some churches, a counselling component is introduced into healing ministry services, but not happily. To have spiritual counselling available after the service itself in an appropriate place is proper but, for both personal and practical reasons, it is not helpful in a public situation. Confining the action to a purely liturgical one is more appropriate. It is a proclamation to all, recipients and congregation, of the healing power of Jesus. The word "power" is important. It was this healing power that Jesus used in whatever method he applied to individual needs. As the doctor-evangelist Luke noted: "The power of the Lord was present to heal." The question then arises: "Is healing power actually transmitted in the act of laying on of hands?" In Jesus' time it was. That it still is where people minister *in his name* is the conviction of many.

There are those who think that being able to touch holy things, a relic, an icon or other religious symbol can bring about a healing miracle. There was certainly a belief that being able to touch Jesus could have such an effect. Is this belief or superstition? The authoritative answer is given by Jesus himself in the incident where a woman with a long-standing uterine haemorrhage ("an issue of blood for twelve years") succeeded in touching one of the tassels of his cloak. It was for her not superstition but an act of faith (as Jesus recognised when saying "Your faith has made you whole"). Still more important is the fact that Jesus confirms that power (*dunamis*) has gone out of him. "The woman was healed by the power of God which was available in Jesus," writes John Wilkinson, a medical doctor. He continues: "This was the power which Jesus used in every method he used for healing."*

Medicine and healing ministry are both God-given and complementary to each other. I suspect that many a doctor or surgeon would testify that where healing power unites with medical or surgical skill, the possibilities of a miracle are considerable. There are certainly those who have so benefited who would testify to the wonder of such co-operation.

* *Health and Healing, Studies in New Testament Principles and Practice* (Handsel Press, 1980).

THE SPECTRUM OF HEALING

When Paul said that there were "diversities of gifts" but that they all had their source in that "selfsame Spirit", he laid down a spiritual principle of great importance. It puts paid to the kind of intolerance that claims "my ways", and only "my ways" accord with the will of God. There is an infinite variety in the way God deals with people and there are infinite manifestations of his presence in the gifts that people demonstrate. Let us reflect on the varied gifts offered for our healing. Sometimes one or more disciplines will meet the need. At other times, a different discipline will become the chosen resource.

i) "Honour the doctor for his services", we read in Ecclesiasticus. "The doctor's knowledge gives him high standing and wins him the admiration of the great ... His skill comes from the Most High ..." (see chapter 38, verses 1 to 15)

No responsible ministry of healing denies or diminishes the place of medicine among God's gifts of creation. All who seek pastoral advice and help will not only be encouraged to see their GP, but exhorted to do so. Co-operation between medicine and religion is a primary concern in the field of healing ministry, and that co-operation is constantly growing. The truth is clear and simple: doctors, surgeons, nurses and all involved with them in medical and associated disciplines are part of the spectrum of healing.

ii) Turn to the fields of psychiatry, psychotherapy, counselling and other varieties of therapeutic relationship and the same principle applies. Ministry to mental and emotional needs can be found in these disciplines. They too are in the spectrum of healing.

iii) God uses people to minister to people. Through personal relations, whether it is informally as friends, more formally in pastoral care, or professionally through pastoral counselling and other forms of therapeutic relationships, people can be helped not only to feel better but to be better.

iv) Music is another of God's gifts for our healing. For those unable to cope with verbal methods of help, music therapy can have a very important part to play.

v) There are also valuable resources available in complementary medicines. That is a field which is much too wide, with unhelpful and unacceptable approaches within it, but there are, for example, "natural healing" methods within the field that are undoubtedly God's gifts of creation.

vi) Supremely there is the church's contribution, the gifts of redemption, without which wholeness cannot be complete. Grace is conveyed through prayer, intercession, laying on of hands and, in some traditions, anointing. It is also the church's role to minister to the healing of the memories.

What a glorious spectrum of healing gifts, given in grace by the God whom we meet in variety and diversity rather than in exclusiveness and limitation!

FIRM FOUNDATIONS

Some of the most important insights into healing ministry come not from the Gospel records of the miracles of Jesus but from the report of a healing miracle effected by the disciples. It is, significantly, the doctor among the evangelists who tells us of the miracle of the lame man healed by Peter "in the name of Jesus Christ of Nazareth", and also of the public consequences of that action.

The miracle is described in Acts chapter 3, and the consequences of it in Acts chapter 4. Within that latter chapter are four matters on which reflection will usefully be made.

First to be noticed is the number of times the world "boldness" comes into the story. The authorities saw their boldness, the disciples' prayer was that they should "speak the word with boldness", and Luke's report is that they did "speak the word with boldness". This fearlessness (to use William Barclay's translation of the same word) is necessary if the gospel is to be proclaimed today. To speak of signs, wonders and the possibility of healing miracles to a scientifically conditioned and materialistic world requires boldness; not the boldness of arrogance but the fearlessness of conviction. To be involved in healing ministry and indeed true proclamation "in Jesus' name" today requires such boldness.

Secondly, the ministry the disciples were trying to effect was, as they testified, the work of the Holy Spirit. And so must all such ministry be. Those who feel called to the Christian ministry of healing do not speak of themselves as "healers" as some others do. It is the risen Christ who is the agent of miracle. He seeks those who will be channels for his healing power but the power, like the glory, belongs to him alone.

Thirdly, look at the reference made to the apostles by those who observed them. "They took knowledge of them that they had been with Jesus." The disciples would almost certainly be surprised to realise that they had – by what they did and said, by what they were – proclaimed their allegiance. That message had certainly come through. All who seek to serve as disciples should have a similar effect. If they do, it will be demonstrated by the attitudes they show. There is no place for arrogance in those who engage in the ministry of healing, only humility. To have such an influence without realising it is discipleship indeed.

Fourthly, and most significantly of all, the report reveals how totally the disciples had understood the message of their leader. "Now, Lord," they prayed, "grant unto thy servants that with all boldness they may speak thy word, by stretching out thine hand to heal." Miracles, signs and wonders are the symbols, signs and seals of the truth of the gospel.

Jesus, in sending out the disciples, said: "Preach the gospel, heal the sick." Preaching and healing are but two sides of the same coin, the miracles of healing being demonstrations in action of the love the gospel proclaims. Preaching and healing together constitute the firm foundations of the faith.

HOLY HARMONY

Health is "a state of complete physical, mental and social well-being and not merely the absence of disease or infirmity". This definition of health, offered by the World Health Organisation in 1948, remains a satisfactory one. Those with a religious background may feel, however, that it is less than an ideal definition because of its lack of reference to a spiritual component.

The Old Testament always sees good health as including a happy relationship with God. The New Testament makes use of several words in this context. There is, for example, the Greek word for peace (*eirene*), the one that comes nearest to that almost indefinable but extraordinarily expressive Hebrew word, *shalom*. Then there is the word *teleios* meaning "maturity" and, in the New Testament sense, "perfection". Another word is *soteria* of which the root meaning is "safe and sound". In Greek translations of the Old Testament, it came to mean deliverance (for example the deliverance of the children of Israel at the Red Sea) and further developed its meaning in the New Testament as the word for "spiritual safety", namely salvation. That association between health and salvation is interesting.

If there is any definition of health in the New Testament, Paul's first letter to the Thessalonians (chapter 5, verse 23, *New English Bible*) provides it: "May God himself, the God of peace, make you holy in every part and keep you sound in spirit, soul and body, without fault when our Lord Jesus Christ comes." Wholeness and holiness come close together in this benediction.

Are there any contemporary concepts or images that help us further to define the meaning of health? There are two possibilities, of which the first is *balance*.

Those who seek healing are usually yearning for physical restoration. There is nothing wrong in that. The majority of Jesus' healing miracles involved physical healing. That acknowledged, it is essential to recognise that we are not just bodies. We have also mental, emotional and spiritual aspects to our being. Conscious as we are today of psychosomatic factors in illness, we can see the interdependence between those four aspects. Dis-ease in our emotional or spiritual life may well contribute to disease in our bodies. To see health, therefore, as the achievement of balance in the inter-relationship of the physical, mental, emotional and spiritual aspects of our being may well point us towards a significant understanding of what good health means.

The other image which may be of help is *harmony*,* "the pleasing interaction or an appropriate combination of the elements in a whole". And, if wholeness and holiness are indeed close in meaning, we can helpfully and happily describe good health as "holy harmony".

* See further comment on this theme in the Meditation for October 25.

THE HEALING RELATIONSHIP

There is no doubt that in the past two weeks* the nation has undergone a profound spiritual experience, something no national mission could have achieved or evangelistic effort created. Hearts have been touched, minds have been changed, souls have been stirred, perhaps even restored by the contemplation in one person of the wonder of healing relationship. For this is the essence of a ministry of compassion. Caring sensitivity and loving touch offered to someone in need brings profound healing.

This will be at the heart of the memories of Diana, Princess of Wales.* And how gloriously that ministry of compassion was underlined in the coincidence of the death of Mother Teresa. That two people from such different backgrounds who knew, respected and loved each other, who were givers of life, should be united in death was surely a divine synchronicity of prophetic significance. It seemed to compel us all to be involved in the creation of a more compassionate society.

The classic presentation of the meaning of healing relationship in the Bible is the encounter of Jesus with the unpopular tax-gatherer Zacchaeus.** In what becomes an acted-out parable, Jesus makes clear the key elements in healing relationship, namely a *moving towards*, a *being with* and the resultant *going on*. The "moving towards" comes from compassion. The "being with" is expressed in sensitivity to need and empathy with suffering (outer or inner), the "moving on" is the growth that comes from such a healing relationship. It is hard to think of two people who, in one brief week, so illuminated our understanding of healing relationship.

But there is more to the spiritual experience that has touched virtually everyone. How many have said they could not have believed they could feel and act as they did? What they have seen and shared has created a self-awareness that has manifested itself in vibrant emotion, a readiness to cry, an enthusiasm to express feelings in flowers, written words, applause.

When Jesus met, talked to and befriended a Samaritan woman, the effect on her was dramatic. "He told me all about myself," she said to her friends. A totally unplanned meeting, breaking religious protocol – for "the Jews had no dealings with the Samaritans" (the woman said) – touched the depths of her being to the point of a conversion. So is it for us all. The experiences that transform us are so often seemingly accidental but with hindsight providential – an encounter with someone special, a combination of unusual circumstances, an involvement in tragedy. A dreadful happening two weeks ago has done something to a nation which means it will never be the same again.

Millions watched a service in a church. Thousands sang hymns and said prayers on city streets. Those who might well have denied they were in any way interested in the spiritual dimension were caught up in prayer, praise and dedication. And all because someone showed the meaning of healing relationship. Within a dreadful tragedy there has been given a glorious gift for which we must all be grateful to God.

* Published just after the death of Diana, Princess of Wales, in August 1997.
** Zacchaeus is also referred to in the Meditations for January 16, February 21, April 5, June 2 and 4, July 15, October 23 and December 12.

A HEALING MIRACLE

For weeks the patient lay in the intensive care ward, holding on to life by a thread – or rather the wires that led to the support machines around his bed. Under heavy sedation for further weeks, he remained to all intents unconscious. I was there when the consultant said the position was "desperate". It was underlined by the expressed need to move towards a decision to withdraw such life support.

It is always dangerous to discuss a patient's problems round the bed in such circumstances. The hearing faculty, it has been suggested, is the last one to go. Patients, though deeply unconscious, may hear what is being said about them – as happened in this case. As my friend told me after his astonishing return from death to life – a product of superb medical care and, perhaps, the bedside service suggested to his wife by one of the nurses – of his hearing a member of the medical team say to colleagues as they studied his "desperate" situation: "If I were him, I would just let go." His inner response was immediate and clear as he heard himself saying: "No, I am going to live."

There are miraculous recoveries from near-death to new life and this is one of them. Three factors seemed to be involved in the miracle. First there was the extraordinary level of medical expertise and technology. That is in itself part of the miracle of modern medicine. The second was the presence of the faith and prayers of believing family and friends. The third was the patient's will to win. The miracle lies, surely, in a combination of all three. The spontaneous joy and admiration of the medical staff seemed to testify to the miracle too.

It is unwise to be over-simplistic in talking about healing miracles, but in this still-evolving story there lies encouragement to those who wrestle with illness and feel fatalistic forces at work. Medicine, faith and will make a potent treatment.

That Jesus recognised the causes of illness included emotional or spiritual factors seems clear from the miracles he worked on the man who was "sick of the palsy" let down through the roof and the "impotent" man who had waited a long time to get into the pool by the temple, to be the first to get there when an angel stirred the waters. In both cases Jesus effected the physical cure, but he also stressed the need for something in addition to physical healing. In the case of the palsied young man, he not only cured his condition but emphasised his need for forgiveness. To the impotent man he issued a stern warning: "If you don't change your lifestyle," he said in effect, "your illness will return and next time it will be worse."

It is not only disease of the body that needs treatment. It is the dis-ease that affects mind, heart and spirit that also needs the healing touch.

BY WORD AND TOUCH

The teaching of Jesus has had an immeasurable impact on the life of the world. The wonder of his wisdom and insight has fascinated people far beyond the confines of the church. And rightly so. He brought together a profound spirituality that leads the pilgrim into the realm of "the eternal" and yet no teacher was more practical and down-to-earth than he was.

For some, Jesus' healing ministry is even more fascinating than his teaching ministry. It certainly must have intrigued St Luke, a physician, as much as it impressed him. There are many miracles of healing recorded in Luke's Gospel. Equally interesting is the variety Jesus showed in his approach to healing. Sometimes he healed by word alone, sometimes by touch, sometimes by word *and* touch.

When Jesus healed by word alone, the key element seemed to be his authority. This was especially so in his casting out of demons. He never laid hands on the demon-possessed. Cases in which he used words of command, usually addressed to the demon, are those of the demoniac in the synagogue, the Gadarene demoniac and an epileptic boy who had "a foul spirit".

What is impressive in all these cases is the *authority* of his words. Whether Jesus is casting out demons or carrying out physical healings (as in one case of a paralysed man), he is issuing orders with the power of the kingdom as the background to what he is doing. This is the same in the other category of miracles, attested by word alone, the raising of the dead. To Lazarus he said: "Lazarus, come out." The dead cannot hear commands, but the issuing of the order is in terms of the authority and power which Jesus says comes from the Father.

If authority is the key concept in healing by word alone, compassion is at the heart of healing by touch alone. The ministry of touch is expressed as laying on of hands (as in the case of the man with dropsy, or that of Malchus, whose ear was cut off by Peter – according to John's Gospel) and is always an act of compassion. So far as a combination of word *and* touch is concerned, authority and compassion are welded together. In the case of Peter's mother-in-law, he "rebuked the fever" and "he touched her hand".

So are word and/or touch essential in healing? No, for on three occasions certainly Jesus healed people at a distance from him. There was, for example, the Roman centurion who pleaded with Jesus for his servant. Jesus immediately offered to go and heal him. The centurion, however, appealed to Jesus whom he saw as a man in authority. "Just speak the word only, and my servant shall be healed," he said. He was.

What a marvellously moving statement of belief in the authority and compassion of Jesus! No wonder he commented that he had not found "so great faith, no, not in Israel".

THE HEALING OF THE MEMORIES

O wad some Pow'r the giftie gie us
To see oursels as ithers see us

It was Robert Burns, in his poem *To a Louse*, who penned this important sentiment. There are things that others know about us of which we ourselves are not aware. We should pay heed both to what they see in us and the way in which we present ourselves, and learn from it. We do not need to accept their impressions without question but we should, at least, carefully consider this new knowledge of ourselves.

Robert Burns' reminder that there is knowledge others have of us which we do not have recalls other aspects of our self-knowledge. There is, for example, that knowledge we have of ourselves which others share, a superficial knowledge but real. There is that darker area of our being of which *we* are aware, but of which , happily, others are not. Beyond that there is a further area of knowledge of which others do not have cognisance and of which we ourselves are unaware. It contains our hidden, unconscious memories. And some of these may well be unhealed.

This record of early experiences and the feelings associated with them (known in analytical psychology as "the unconscious") very much determines our behaviour, attitudes and the quality of our relationships in later life. It is part of the healing ministry to try to heal those hidden memories.

"Deep speaks to deep" says the Psalmist. Was he perhaps suggesting that the depth of the divine love can reach right down to the ultimate depths of human need? The image of Jesus' descent into hell perhaps sheds light on the divine intention. There is no level of need that the grace which is "sufficient for all our needs" cannot reach.

There are various healing ministries directed toward the healing of the memories. First there is the patient, long-term approach of orthodox therapeutic relationship expressed in counselling, psychotherapy or analysis. Through a process of interaction between the therapist and the person in need, memories may be brought into consciousness, faced and healed. Others, in a different tradition, will perhaps suggest (and use) some form of prayer counselling to attack the negative and, as they are believed to be, evil memories, and bring about inner reconciliation and peace. A third method, particularly practised by Esmond Jefferies at his Pin Mill healing centre,* is that of hypnosis within a prayerful context. As in psychotherapy, the approach is gentle, but the reaching of the hidden memories is much quicker. With the defences of the conscious mind removed, the hurtful, hidden memories are uncovered and released within an ambience of prayer and love.

To know oneself is an important aim. To attempt the fulfilment of this aim will be by the way that is felt to be safe and secure. However the healing of the memories is to be accomplished, it will be a process of pain and the suffering that ultimately contributes to our peace, ensuring that we can "Be still and know ..."

* The Pin Mill Fellowship, Corner House, Hollesley, Woodbridge, Suffolk IP12 3RH. The story of Esmond Jefferies' healing work is told in *The Power and The Glory* (Arthur James, 1991).

ABSENT HEALING

One of the most illuminating comments Jesus made in relation to his work of healing was his response to the woman who, famously, "touched the hem of his garment" in the hope of a cure for her uterine haemorrhage, a condition from which she had suffered for twelve years. Clearly the woman believed that any contact with Jesus, be it only the tassel of his cloak, constituted the possibility of cure. The extraordinary aspect of the incident was the awareness that Jesus had of her touch. After all, he was surrounded by a crowd of people pressing in upon him, yet he sensed that he had been touched by someone in particular need. "Who touched my clothes?" he asked. Helpfully he gave the reason for his awareness of what had happened. He knew "in himself that power had gone out of him".

This is a clear indication that Jesus believed power was in some way transmitted in the act of healing where faith was present. "Your faith has made you whole." This surely has implications for those called to the healing ministry and to minister "in his name". The laying on of hands is not only a symbolic act, but the means whereby the power of the risen Lord, present in this ministry, is conveyed to those who, in faith, seek it. Laying on of hands is more than a liturgical symbol. It is an act of transformation; an act which testifies not to the healing power of the minister involved, but to the eternal Christ at work in the world where those who believe in him minister "in his name".

Sometimes Jesus uses one method in healing, sometimes another. It is however clear that none of these methods – for example, words, touch, saliva – was essential for the transmission of divine power to those who needed it, for there were occasions when he healed people who were not in his presence. Three examples come to mind. There was John's report of the healing of the nobleman's son. There was Mark's story of the Syrophoenician woman who pleaded for her daughter's cure. There was the centurion's servant referred to in St Matthew's Gospel. Word, touch, word *and* touch, were not essential components in miracles. Healing took place too when there was no contact at all. There is then a place for what some would call "absent healing" in the ministry of the church. It may be that someone brings another's need to the altar rail as the centurion brought his servant's need to Jesus. Intercession specifically focused and supported by group prayer is a vital part of healing ministry. What matters is not technique or method, word, touch, saliva, essential presence or accepted absence. The great and glorious truth is that Jesus heals today; that "his touch has not lost its ancient power"; that, while God offers healing through the gifts of creation – medicine, psychotherapy, music, healing relationships and some (but not all) of the complementary therapies – there is available to all the transmission of power in response to prayer, pleading and faith. The result is changed lives. Those in need are made more whole.

UNCONDITIONAL LOVE

Evangelism and preaching should not concentrate on condemnation and judgement. The gospel in fact proclaims the unconditional love of God. At the heart of reality is the divine compassion expressed in a longing "to seek and to save that which is lost".

The parable in Jesus' teaching method was used to indicate the attributes of God, to provide pictures illustrating the nature of the divine. The statement with which we began is founded not only on the specific Johannine words making clear that God did not send his son into the world to condemn the world but to bring it salvation, but also on stories Jesus told about, for example, a lost sheep and a lost son. The first points to the divine initiative, the God who in compassion seeks the lost. The second demonstrates the welcome, love and grace which is expressed in unconditional joy over one who was lost and is found.

The prodigal son is a young man in the depths of misery. His money is spent. His dignity is destroyed. He longs, in his hunger, to share the pods put out for the pigs. Dispirited, devastated, desperate, he "comes to himself" and sincerely and honestly prepares his confession. His sin is both against God and against his father. He no longer has the right to be considered a son. He must ask to be treated like one of the servants.

It is easy to picture the lost son rehearsing his speech on the journey back from the far country. He must take the initiative and pour out his confession. What happened was quite different! There was his father, already outside the house, waiting for him. And it was the latter who took the initiative, running to meet his son, throwing his arms around him in a warm embrace, kissing him rapturously. Did Jesus perhaps smile as he painted the picture of the lost son, trying to emerge from his father's embrace to pour out his planned words, almost to have them ignored? It is the father who takes the lead, sends for the best robe to put on his son, calls for sandals for his feet and a ring for his finger, and orders an immediate celebration. No doubt the confession, muffled by the embrace and drowned by the words of welcome, was heard, but far more important was the demonstration of unconditional welcome, unconditional grace and unconditional love offered by a father to his son. It is Jesus' picture of the love of God.

Repentance is a right, proper and necessary element in the restoring of the divine-human relationship, but the impact of the stories Jesus told lies in his demonstration of the divine initiative in reconciliation and the yearning love of God for those who have chosen to go away. What a positive message lies at the centre of the gospel! What a marvellous insight is given into the nature of God!

FAILURE IN FAITH

He was a kindly man, a devoted pastor and a thoughtful preacher. A senior minister when I was just entering the ministry many years ago, I recall him still as a man of grace and goodness. In later years this minister had a life-threatening condition. In addition to orthodox medical help, he sought healing through the hands of the saintly author of *The Forgotten Talent,* Cameron Peddie, so great an influence in my own ministry. His condition, far from improving, deteriorated and, despite repeatedly praying for the miracle he believed would happen, he became increasingly ill. He died a bitter man. He had 'asked, believing' and had Jesus' assurance that 'he would receive'. He didn't and he was very angry about it.

This is a dilemma which those who take the healing ministry seriously feel very deeply. On one hand there is a lot about faith in the Gospels, praise from Jesus for those who had it, rebuke for the disciples who failed to heal because of their 'unbelief', that is lack of faith. Jesus' message is clear. Have faith, 'even as a grain of mustard seed.' To be 'of little faith' is to prevent a miracle. On the other hand, as has been demonstrated so often in public healing services or missions, the building up of huge expectation followed by failures in healing results in real anguish. The resulting state may even be worse than the one which led to the search for a miracle.

The problem is not whether healing miracles occur or not. From my observation of others' experience, as from my own, they do. God is the God of surprises and 'wonder-full' things happen. Sometimes it will be through a combination of medical expertise and faith (for medicine is one of the gifts of creation for our healing); sometimes it will be more 'directly' in mysterious ways beyond our understanding. The problem comes when miracles prayerfully sought do not take place. The result can be devastation and bitterness.

There is a huge gap between what Jesus commands and what we achieve. Is it lack of faith? Or is it the low level of our spirituality? Jesus certainly seemed critical of his disciples' failure to learn from him. The miracle of the epileptic boy is placed by each Gospel author immediately after the transfiguration and followed by Jesus' intimation of his coming death. But time is running out. 'How long shall I stay with you?' he asks. 'How long will I put up with you?' There is both disappointment and frustration because the disciples have so little faith. It only needs faith 'as a grain of mustard seed.' But just there is the continuing gap.

The church involves itself rightly with the problems of the world, be they political, economic or social. The primary task of the church remains the obligation to deepen the spiritual power of people through bringing them into a closer relationship with Christ. It is through contact with him that spiritual power increases.

THE GIFT OF WHOLENESS

"Do you really want to be well?" This penetrating question was asked by Jesus of a man who had been ill for 38 years. In the *Authorised Version* of the Bible it reads: "Wilt thou be made whole?" (John, chapter 5, verse 6), but the form of the question in a modern version increases its relevance. It is a question to be taken seriously by all who have to deal with personal and pastoral problems. Do those who seek help really *want* to be made well, or do they – for whatever reason, conscious or unconscious – need to hold on to their illnesses?

The question seems at first sight, to be a rhetorical one. "Who wants to be ill?" most people would ask. The truth is, however, different. Illness can be a weapon in unhappy lives. It is used in some situations for manipulative purposes. It may also become a desperate method for attracting "tender, loving care" by those who, overwhelmed by lifelong loneliness, never manage to attract love from anybody. Illness can be a crutch which we dare not let go. Both carers and the cared-for need to be aware of the subtleties of this question put to the "impotent" (that is, the powerless or paralysed) man who was never able to get into the healing pool at Bethesda.

Jesus' attitude to life and people in relation to their "health" meant that he did not only heal bodies; he mended broken hearts. He offered people peace of mind. He went even further and gave them forgiveness where it was needed. In other words, he sought to make people *whole*. It is in the offered gift of wholeness that we sense the profundity of his loving attitude to people and their needs. He offered them life with all its creative potential.

The church's pastoral ministry must be based on the attitudes of its Lord. Caring, loving concern, expressed in a longing to bring wholeness to all people, needs to be at the heart of contemporary ministry. This is the Word *in action*.

If we take seriously the attitude to life and people which Jesus had, we will make proclamation and pastoral care central to evangelism today. He not only preached the gospel with boldness, but made it real and relevant in his loving compassion for a suffering world. His disciples must "go and do likewise".

ACCEPTANCE

Acceptance is a contemporary word. It occurs once in the Bible, but it is used there in another sense. "Being accepted" reflects a particular experience, well understood by most people today. That experience is wholly biblical. Acceptance, then, is one of the healing words needed by the world. Accepting love is the gospel in action.

We have reflected on the healing word "reconciliation" and in doing so thought about the parable of the prodigal son. Recall again that image of the father as he runs, arms outstretched in potential embrace, to meet his lost son. That image incarnates the words "accepting love". No criticism, rebuke or condemnation (which he expected) met that son. What he unexpectedly received was unconditional acceptance. That element of unexpectedness characterises the biblical understanding of acceptance.

Consider the story of "the woman taken in adultery" (John, chapter 8, verses 1-11). This story has been questioned as to its authenticity because it is not in some important manuscripts, but it has (in J B Phillips' phrase) "a ring of truth" about it. The woman was taken to Jesus by her accusers, the scribes and Pharisees. They reminded Jesus that the punishment laid down in the law of Moses for adultery was stoning. Then the unexpected happened. Jesus suggested that anyone who was without sin should administer the punishment. One by one her accusers slipped away in total discomfort. The woman, however, received accepting love from Jesus who did not condone her sin (he told her not to do it again) but offered her no condemnation. The unexpectedness of his acceptance of her must have touched her deeply.

Then there was "the woman of bad reputation" who, in the house of Simon the Pharisee, washed the feet of Jesus with her tears and wiped them dry with her hair (Luke, chapter 7, verses 36 to 50). Again the tables are turned by Jesus' accepting love. The technically religious Simon is "told off".* The woman who was technically a sinner was, with her sincere and genuine love, totally accepted.

If the receiving of mercy compels us to show mercy – as it does; if being forgiven commits us to forgive others – as it does; if we find ourselves the recipients of the accepting love of God – which we do; we are bound to offer acceptance to others, whatever their situation.

Acceptance is indeed a healing word.

* See also Acts of Love, the Meditation for June 26.

HEALING MUSIC

"Music alone with sudden charms can bind the wandering sense, and calm the troubled mind." So wrote William Congreve, who died in 1729, but many centuries before that a demented king of Israel sensed the truth of that claim. When "an evil spirit tormented him," King Saul's attendants suggested that he ask for "someone who can play on the harp" and "you will feel better." One of the servants specifically suggested David, "a son of Jesse of Bethlehem who knows how to play the harp ... and the Lord is with him." The story (in 1 Samuel chapter 16, *New International Version*) is an intriguing testimony to the healing power of music.

When the remarkable Healing and Counselling Centre in the crypt of St Marylebone Parish Church in London was envisaged and effected by the then Rector, Christopher Hamel Cooke, the grand vision was of an agency incorporating four disciplines that would, under one roof, minister to the needs that people brought, be they physical, mental, emotional or spiritual. The four agencies were (i) that church's healing and counselling ministry; (ii) a National Health Service practice; (iii) healing organisations and (iv) a music therapy unit. In that plan, the place of music in healing was significantly recognised. Unfortunately that fourth element had, for practical reasons, to cease but the concept incarnated in that centre proclaimed the place of church, medicine, healing organisations and music therapy in co-operative ministry to wholeness.

The spoken word and the written word will continue to be crucial in the proclamation of the gospel. In healing the sick – so linked with preaching in Jesus' instructions to the disciples – pastoral care, counselling, psychotherapy, spiritual direction, etc, will play their part, as will healing relationships, for God uses people to help people in ministering to emotional and spiritual dis-ease. But all who are involved in healing ministry constantly agonise over the difficulties which are encountered when mental limitation makes words of little use and customary pastoral practices largely irrelevant. What a healing gift music can be in that situation. Dr Glen Wilson, a distinguished music therapist, puts it clearly: "Music plugs more directly into feelings than words. Words have to go through intermediate stages for construction, such as dealing with pictures and synthesising memory. Music goes straight in." The results are often dramatic.

Beethoven's capacity to compose while profoundly deaf, Katharine Hadley notes, "is well documented, but he also used it to comfort himself. While he was dying, he chose one piece, the String Quartet in Bb, opus 130 (Cavatina), perhaps the music he wanted the world to recognise as his personal signature tune. He read the score repeatedly, and wrote: 'I leave my music to heal the world.'"*

The music that heals is surely one of God's gracious gifts to the world.

* An article on "Music on the Mind" was published in *Classic FM Magazine* in May 1996.

LOVE IN ACTION

The attitude to life and people that Jesus had was grounded in the scriptures of the Old Testament. Appointed to read the lesson in his home town synagogue in Nazareth, Jesus found himself saying: "The Spirit of the Lord is upon me, because he hath anointed me to preach the gospel to the poor; he hath sent me to heal the broken-hearted, to preach deliverance to the captives, and recovering of sight to the blind, to set at liberty them that are bruised, to preach the acceptable year of the Lord."

With a genuine sense of drama, he told the congregation that those very words were being fulfilled that day in him. It is, then, not surprising that when he was ready to "send out" his disciples he should tell them, quite specifically to "preach the gospel" *and* "heal the sick".

A large number of healing miracles are recorded in the Gospels. These acts of compassion represent the divine love in action. Preaching the gospel and healing the sick are, in effect, but two sides of a coin. The latter is the former "acted out".

Jesus put the greatest possible value on the physical healings that he carried out. As he told John the Baptist, in response to John's message from prison that seemed to question Jesus' Messiahship, miracles (such as those which enabled the blind to see and the deaf to hear) authenticated his divine calling. They witnessed to "the power of the Kingdom" present in him.

But human beings need more than physical cures. They need to be healed emotionally, mentally and spiritually. When a man who was "sick of the palsy" was healed by Jesus he was told: "Arise, take up thy bed and walk!" But, as the spectator scribes confirmed by their questioning of his right to say it, Jesus also said: "Thy sins be forgiven thee." In other words, there were spiritual factors contributing to that illness. He needed the ministry of forgiveness with all its healing power too.

As those who study illness today can confirm, emotional and spiritual dis-ease may well express themselves in physical ill-health. It was of the essence of the attitude of Jesus to people and their needs to want not only to make them physically well, but also to mend their broken hearts. Jesus, in his compassion for people, sought to make them *whole*. That was love in action.

MANIPULATION

Jacob, the son of Isaac and Rebekah, younger brother of Esau and grandson of Abraham, is not a very attractive character. To be frank, he was something of a "con-man" who might well have felt at home in the spin and manipulation of our times.

Two incidents in the Old Testament story make such a negative judgement of Jacob inevitable. He was a man who sought position and power, and was determined to get it. The balance in the family helped him in this. Isaac loved Esau, the hunter, but Rebekah loved Jacob, "a quiet man". That he might have been, but within him was a lust for power and position that would make him ruthless in pursuit of them. Sadly, Rebekah encouraged him in this and comes out of the story with little credit.

The first instance tells the story of Jacob's bargaining with his brother to get his birthright from him. Esau came home hungry and exhausted from a day's hunting. Jacob was not slow to see the possibilities of personal gain in this everyday situation. The reward for supplying the meal was the acquisition of Esau's birthright. Jacob got what he wanted, deliberately and cynically. Esau lost his birthright.

In the second example of Jacob's trickery, it must sadly be said that Rebekah played a major part. The deceiving of the aged and now blind Isaac by Jacob with Rebekah's help is a stain on the character of both of them. Rebekah provided the skins to cover Jacob's hands for Isaac knew Esau "was a hairy man" and cooked the meal for Jacob to serve. Esau returned to find the lying and deception had worked and deprived him of the blessing which was the right of the elder son. The action taken was, in Isaac's eyes, irrevocable. Tears followed, then threats. Esau would, he said, in due time after Isaac's death, kill his brother. Rebekah, hearing that threat, encouraged Jacob to flee until his brother's wrath had abated. It was a sorry story of deception, ruthlessness and blatant manipulation. It is not to the credit of the power-seeking Jacob.

But Jacob is not finished. His concern was to strike a bargain with God. "If you will be with me," he said to God, "if you will give me bread to eat and clothes to wear, then will the Lord be my God!" Even God had to be willing to serve Jacob's needs to gain his loyalty and devotion. It is a failing that has demonstrated its presence in ages past and will, human nature being what it is, in years to come. We determine the kind of God we want as a condition of devotion and worship.

Later in life, thankfully, Jacob would change, the change sealed by a new name. In future he will be "Israel" which means "God perseveres". It is a great truth and a comforting one. The divine patience perseveres with recalcitrant and stubborn people.

THE TRANSCENDENCE OF GOD

"Tenderly, He watches over you ..." The old mission song about the loving God who is with us "every step of the way" may seem far from the rigorous demands of a contemporary theology, but it always strikes a chord for me. Not skilled or trained musically, it was one of the few songs I was ever able to accompany publicly with ease and satisfaction and, because it was in those circumstances, always sung by the same person, Betty.

Betty, from my earliest recollection of her, always had a simple and at the same time profound faith. It lasted all her life. A choir member each Sunday for over 50 years, the lead soprano in our "operatic society" (she was Yum-Yum in The Mikado for example), she was the ever-willing soloist in services, women's meetings, "lodging house missions" (as they were called in Glasgow) etc. Her background would be regarded as ordinary, but she was very special. I played for her this one song because it was a ministry not only to many but to me.

Betty was my first bride after I went to Glasgow in 1950. Her husband – a professional carpenter – was the leader in transforming our surplus church building into a hall/theatre. He died a long time ago. Their children were adopted. Betty had several family sorrows, rejection by relations among them. She died from cancer in March 2001. The last time I played "Tenderly, He watches over you" for her was 50 years on, when she sang it at a reunion of the group that had become a lifelong fellowship. At her cremation, the present minister paid fulsome tribute to her life, faith and ministry of music. So affected was he by her devoted life and courage in illness and death that he felt unable to join the post-funeral lunch.

The image of the tenderness of God encircling us on life's journey may not be felt sophisticated enough to be used to define God in a climate that demands new metaphors to "explain" God to an unsympathetic world. That effort must go on as contemporary evangelism must convince those who are products of modern philosophies, contemporary ethics and post-modern theological needs. The simple sentiments of an old-fashioned sacred song may carry little weight or make any intellectual impact. But to speak of the tenderness of God is not to be dismissed as merely the application of anthropomorphic language to the task of defining God. Such a concept of a long-suffering, compassionate God who first loved us in fact reflects the view of God that Jesus himself had and preached. It is all there in the image of the good shepherd who carries the lambs in his arms. Jesus spoke of the relationship of sheep and shepherd as intimate and loving,

As an insight into the nature of God, perhaps the old song is not far away. The tenderness of God is real.

IF GOOD PEOPLE DO NOTHING

It is difficult to avoid feelings of utter helplessness in terms of our individual ability to end wars, feed the hungry, deal with the AIDS epidemic, bring peace between Palestine and Israel, solve the problems of the National Health Service, stop trafficking in drugs, in arms, in pornography and many other issues. But evil prospers, it is said, when "good people do nothing". No sense of despair, however present, dare lead us into passive acceptance of destructive policies, diminishing standards, unnecessary distress and suffering. Glorious it is that however awful the events that take place in this world, there are always and without fail, organisations which exist solely to deal with suffering wherever and however it occurs, individuals who dedicate their lives to the alleviation of pain, starvation, disease and death, researchers who forever probe the causes of cancer, multiple sclerosis, Parkinson's Disease, Alzheimer's Disease and so many other causes of human distress. The world can be an evil place, but within it there are so many "good people" who wrestle with that evil. For those who do this, there must be eternal gratitude. In the end, however, a time of reassessment such as a new year, imposes on all whose philosophy of life is based on loving God and our neighbour the need to examine our priorities, assess our abilities (for these will vary with age, physical strength, strength of will and degree of conviction) with a view to greater active involvement with "good people" who "do something".

In public terms, influence on life depends on using fully the processes of democracy in a society which wavers over the value given to people because power seems more centralised in government. The privileges and powers of democracy must never be allowed to fail through apathy or default. Individuals must ask how seriously the needs of others actually affect the way we think, act, live. The response too can only be individual. A personal confession is that however much one does for others, the causes of peace, poverty, justice have not loomed large enough in the allocation of time, energy and talent. That needs to be changed.

The call to a ministry of reconciliation is set solidly in the New Testament. It is a ministry which, given the problems of the world, nations and people, demands re-assessment now. "To love one another as sisters and brothers should be to have a profound respect for each other," said St Paul to the Romans.* The crucial action is taking the first step to change situations. "If good people do nothing ..."

* See tomorrow's Meditation for an exposition of this text.

MUTUAL LOVE, PROFOUND RESPECT

When St Paul wrote, in words of exhortation "Love one another as sisters and brothers should, and have respect for one another" he was of course addressing a Christian community, namely the church in Rome. That he gave such an instruction implies that it was needed. It is no less relevant advice today. Anyone who has spent their lives involved in the service of the church knows only too well, from unhappy experience, that as well as extraordinary service and exemplary commitment by so many people, there is much in church circles that is anything but loving, forgiving, reconciling and healing. The church at local as well as denominational level can display small-mindedness, petty jealousy, envy, self-righteousness and many other weaknesses that are part of the human condition but which, within the fellowship of the church of Jesus Christ, deny by their existence the very nature of true religion. All too often the church can be a place where the love of power obscures the power of love.

These same positive attributes are not however the private property of Christianity or any other religion in which they would be regarded as primary qualities. In any healthy society, attitudes based on mutual love and respect for others which is a by-product of such mutuality may not be the norm but certainly should be. If it were the norm, there would be no racial discrimination, no arrogant intolerance of ways of living other than our own, no abuse of child, woman or man, no social injustice or selfish competitiveness, no prostitution or adult pornography (at present a growing, multi-million pound industry), no sale of arms for profit or any of the economic ruthlessness that characterises contemporary society, no homophobic attitudes, no media harassment of those whose weaknesses have led them into public trouble. "We don't treat people like you," said a dental consultant in a London hospital recently to a young man of integrity and public achievement, who had the misfortune to become HIV positive. Does this constitute "profound respect" for another human being? "Kill Jews" proclaimed a poster on a billboard in a British city. That such a suggestion should be made in our so-called civilised society beggars belief.

"You cannot govern without convictions," said a distinguished public figure commenting on the unexpected strength of the Jean-Marie le Pen election success in France (in April 2002). That was his view of the failure of the Jospin socialist administration and a suggested contributory factor to such major support for the "far right" in French politics. The need for uplift and improvement in our common life demands a passion for social justice, social integration and persistent reconciliation that merits a public crusade. It needs convictions.

The church can take a lead in such a cause, but only if it too, within its own domain, prizes mutual love and profound respect as aims *and* puts them into practice.

UNCONSCIOUS INFLUENCE

Lunch was being taken in the gracious home of a distinguished lady and gentleman noted for, among other things, giving of their time, talents and money to a very caring and worthwhile charity. I had been asked to conduct and preach at a service in an institution which provides homes and careers for orphaned children. These were days when affluent people of some distinction had a staff to serve the meal and a maid to wait at the table. Halfway through the meal, the maid entered the room. "You wanted something?" she said to my hostess. "No," said my hostess, "but thank you." The maid left. Ten minutes later the scenario was repeated. The maid again returned, not needed. A few minutes later it all happened yet again; once again she left. Quietly my hostess said to me: "Mr Duncan, there is a bell in the floor under the dining table which we use to call the maid when we need her. I think you must be accidentally pressing it for it is ringing in the kitchen." Such was the unconscious influence I had been exerting, totally unaware of the results of what I was doing.

The event is trivial but the wider implication of the anecdote are of considerable importance. "Father, forgive us for we know not what we do" sometimes. Hopefully at others it might just be: "Father bless him or her, for they know not what they do."

In the fourth chapter of the Book of the Acts of the Apostles, there is a moving record of the power of influence unrealised by those who have it. The disciples have performed a miracle of healing. This led to Peter and John being summoned to appear before the rulers, elders and teachers of the law along with Annas and Caiaphas and other members of the high priest's family. The latter were concerned to find out from the disciples "by what power or in what name" they had performed this miracle. Peter immediately, with typical vigour, defended their mission and explained the uniqueness of their leader, Jesus Christ of Nazareth who had been raised from the dead. "There is no other name under heaven whereby we must be saved," he declared. The gathered officials were impressed and let them go, at least temporarily. But St Luke's report of the incident contains a moving reference to the influence they had had. "They took note that these men had been with Jesus." The effect of Peter's words was valuable but there was something about them that bore testimony to their faith. It is that unrealised radiance that perhaps more than words bears testimony to "whose we are and whom we serve".

It is not only a valuable individual contribution that comes from the influence we have, but do not know. It is a lesson for the church too. "It is simply by being the church and living its own supernatural life," wrote Eric Mascall,* "that the church performs its greatest service to the world." How true!

* In *Corpus Christi*.

COMPENDIUM OF GRACE

The older one grows the greater becomes the gratitude that Jesus was a Jew for, whatever else he brought from that particular mature religious background, to give us the Old Testament scriptures was a huge blessing. What an extraordinary record of a people growing in their understanding of God and his ways! How penetrating is the insight therein contained of the depth of human sin and the wonder of "divine grace". Here is a record of real people, however different their circumstances and environment to ours, who wrestled with the problems of sin and suffering, providence and prayer, temptation and repentance, grace and forgiveness.

Jesus drew on those, his scriptures, for an understanding of himself, and his place in the divine plan. He was buoyed up by the Spirit promised by prophets long before his time and clear that it was his responsibility to fulfil the hopes and promises given to his forebears. That we have "the Law and the Prophets", that our lectionaries provide Old Testament as well as New Testament readings when the Christian community gathers for worship, is a matter for profound thanksgiving. The compendium of grace that is the Old Testament has blessed two areas of enormous value in it. One is the collection of Psalms and the other the proclamation of the prophets.

The first contributes more than almost any other literature to devotional life. Within the Psalms as we have them we find our thoughts and feelings, fears and hopes, sorrows and joys, desolation and ecstasy reflected in songs from a far distant age. Yet the Psalmist's experience seems to reflect ours accurately. How brilliantly the wonder of worship is expressed in Psalms of celebration and joy with nature joining in the hymn of praise! It is all outstanding devotional literature and yet it comes from so long ago!

When it comes to the prophets, we can only wish that such men and women (remembering Anna) were the spokespeople of the church today. Under the guidance of the Spirit, their insights were searching and indeed searing, their authority clear, their understanding of spiritual laws profound. It was in that last category that their true calling as prophets lay. They were not soothsayers or magicians foretelling the future in that kind of way. It was in their understanding of the relationship of obedience to the ways of God and the consequences of disobedience, individual or (as so often in their case, nationally) that their power and influence lay.

Their prophecies were not trumpets with uncertain sounds, but analyses of the life and behaviour of those who broke their covenant relationship with God. Well could we do with the impact of those prophets of long ago to help us see much more clearly, in terms of behaviour, church and national life, what is right and what is wrong today.

A Holy Place

An interesting assignment has reached me. Entitled *Five Gold Rings*, its editor asks me, with a selection of others in the devotional field, to write tome 500 words on each of five topics, the *person* who has most influenced your life, the *book* that has served the same purpose, the *poem* that has had the same effect. The fourth "gold ring" is a similarly short essay on one's *philosophy of life*.

It is the fifth element or gold ring that has set me thinking. What is the *place* that has most influenced your life? That does raise intriguing questions.

First thought (and possibly this is the editor's intention) is simply to choose a geographic location that evokes not merely memories but inspiration. If thinking of places at which spiritual stimulation has been received, Taizé and Iona certainly come to mind. Then there are places which, for often unidentifiable reasons, are remembered not only for their physical beauty or benefits, but are in some way deeply symbolic. The tiny village of Amulree in Perthshire at, geographically, the very centre of Scotland has something to say about roots.

Another candidate would be the lovely island of Tresco in the Scillies, a place of beauty (the Abbey gardens are famous), quietness (cars are not allowed on the island) and peace (it is famous for its birds and flowers). These are candidates indeed for that most influential place, but places of importance may be of a different sort, not so much geographical locations as symbolic ones. There are two of these which come to mind, "the desert place" is one and "the holy place" is another.

The desert place is simply the sanctuary, be it literally in the wilderness or just a corner of one room set aside as the place to meet with God. Within that broad band of possibilities, each will have their own sanctuary dressed perhaps with symbols that focus attention on "the things which are eternal" or signs that recall the memory of those who are, in Christian language, within "the communion of saints".

"The holy place" in the sense in which I use it here, is the place of encounter with God and with others. It may be the holy place of intimacy within a loving relationship. It may be the intimacy of the pastoral encounter, a holy place where secret sins may be faced and cast off. It may be the holy place where awareness of God makes it possible to face ourselves in all our frailty, misery and sinfulness and, through that encounter use our weakness to help us to become strong. And so the holy place may be a place of influence for all time, be it the first sight of the Sea of Galilee from a hill above Tiberias or that closed and confidential place where Jesus met Zacchaeus. Closed doors confine the details of such encounter to each other but for both, surely it was a holy and a healing place.

A COVENANT OF LOVE

It was part of very early life, long, long ago, but the memory of it is still disturbing. The picture given to me of God was of a Divine Recorder who had a large book about each of us and, at the end of each day, he put down black marks for every fault, failing and sin committed. Hopefully there was a "credit" column too, but no memory of that is retained. "It is a terrifying thing to fall into the hands of the living God" said the writer of the letter to the Hebrews. It felt rather like that to a child's mind! What a dreadful image of God to have had, however it was acquired.

The biblical testimony to the nature of the divine-human relationship is gloriously encapsulated in two images. From the Old Testament there comes the "covenant" relationship of God with his chosen people. From the New Testament, on the authority of Jesus, comes the picture of the Father and his children. Both "covenant" and "family" are based on love which is mutual, commitment which is a gift on both sides of the relationship, and trust that God will not fail, that human beings will be obedient.

In college days, a fellow-student was engaged to a young lady eminently suitable to be a future minister's wife. She was down-to-earth, coming as she did from a working family, bright and intelligent, domestically equipped and pleasantly round and jolly. But she would not have passed the first round in a beauty contest. Her husband-to-be was fulsome in his praise of her, summing up his opinion in a homely phrase: "She's maybe no' bonnie, but she's mine." That very human picture may not be felt by theologians and academics to serve as a comment on covenant, but it does say something about the essence of that relationship. "There is none righteous, no not one" (in other words we are spiritually "no' bonnie") but "God so loved the world", in other words "but you are mine". That is indeed a covenant relationship.

The story of the prophet Hosea underlines this theme. Hosea married Gomer and had three children by her, but she was guilty of serious marital infidelity. Reading between the lines of the story, Gomer left Hosea for a period and pursued a life of adultery and fornication. But Hosea never ceased to love her. This experience spoke to Hosea of the passionate longsuffering of God. Hosea's utter desire was that wayward Israel might be saved and return to its love of the God who had made that covenant relationship with her.

There are other Old Testament witnesses to that covenant and its power in the Old Testament but Hosea beyond all others, because of his own trials and troubles, is able to hold up the vision of the love, trust and commitment such a right relationship with God demands. The New Testament picture of the Fatherhood of God simply underlines, with Jesus' authority, the reality and strength of the divine love. It is the love that heals.

POSITIVE HEALTH

"Length of days, fitness of body, joy of heart, radiance of spirit"; as a definition of "health" this fourfold statement is not unattractive. Surprisingly, it comes from somewhere about 727 to 705 BC. It constituted, in fact, a prayer to the gods offered by (it is said) Sargon II, ruler of Assyria. Since then the effort to define "health" has continued down the ages and is regularly repeated today. In healing organisation after healing guild or group, time has been given at the outset of conferences on health and healing, to try to create a proper definition of health.

In other Meditations in this book, there are reflections on words or concepts that help to describe health. A useful one is for example that of harmony (see Holy Harmony, October 5). A second concept is balance. The latter is in fact the meaning of the earliest of Greek words used for health (isonomia). Dr John Wilkinson, both medical doctor and theologian, writing a paper submitted to the Standing Committee on Health and Healing of the Church of Scotland, says: "The earliest Greek word used for health in a technical sense is isonomia which means balance or equilibrium. This referred to a proper balance of the four elements which were believed to make up the body, that is blood, phlegm, black bile and yellow bile."

In the Old Testament, emphasis is laid on a right relationship with God as the basis of health, that is the righteousness that grows out of faith in God and obedience to his law. The product of such righteousness is shalom, that fine Hebrew word which is almost untranslatable. It means "peace" but much more than that. It implies wholeness, serenity and fulfilment.

The New Testament is primarily concerned with putting wrong situations right, that is the way in which our relationship with God, damaged by sin, is made good in Jesus. There is therefore in the New Testament an emphasis on healing rather than just health. Jesus offers a way back to God. Jesus heals.

The most recent well-known definition was composed by the World Health Organisation in 1948. It may perhaps be taken as definitive and runs:

> Health is a state of complete physical, mental and social well-being
> and not merely the absence of illness.

We can, I think, feel at ease with that definition although in Christian terms we might want to go a little further, but the WHO definition makes two points which resonate within a Christian view of health and healing. The first is the linking of physical and mental aspects of being in a way that takes note of their interdependence. This is a connection more and more recognised in contemporary medicine under the description "psychosomatic".

The second point made by the WHO definition which relates too to New Testament ways of understanding is the link between individual and community factors in health. Christianity is a social religion, as words like fellowship, congregation, church make clear. The community too needs healing.

Disability with Dignity

Later this month,* Suffolk College in association with the University of East Anglia, will confer the honorary degree of DCL (Doctor of Civil Law) on Lin Berwick. The name will be known to many readers for, in the twelve years in which I have had the privilege of contributing these weekly Meditations, I have mentioned her twice. Those references are so long ago, however, that a word about this extraordinary woman is necessary.

Lin weighed 2lb at her birth. She was twelve weeks premature. She is now in her early fifties. Lin is however, and always has been, severely disabled, cerebral palsied and totally blind. The removal of her eyes early in her life was almost as great a bereavement as the loss of her life. She has to spend her life in a wheelchair, looked after day and night by her husband, Ralph. Getting up, lying down, turning over – the physical strain on him is great and ever present.

When Lin's parents took her home from hospital, they were told that she would be able to do little or more likely nothing. How wrong that prognosis was, as her record of achievement shows!

Lin trained as a counsellor, is the official counsellor for *Disability Now*, the journal of Scope, has taken diplomas in homoeopathy, is a member of the Chartered Institute of Journalists, has broadcast nationally many times, lectures on disability issues and is a fully accredited Methodist Local Preacher. She is a Braillist and earns part of her living providing that service.

The award of the Doctorate is however not only a recognition of such amazing achievement. It honours her vision in forming a Trust to build fully equipped holiday homes for severely disabled people and their families or carers. Her own region of East Anglia (she lives at 4 Chaucer Road, Sudbury, Suffolk) is the first to have a fully operative holiday cottage. It opened in 1997, having cost £170,000 to build and equip it with every possible disability aid. The second house is being set up now, and the £400,000 required to complete the project in East Lothian is being raised by this small Trust.

In Lin's life there is constant pain, physical of course (she has had several serious operations) but emotional too. Ralph has developed Parkinson's Disease. Additionally two knee joint operations take place this year. Lin's care, while he is in hospital and after, is a costly problem.

When, all being well, we go to see Lin publicly honoured for her living example of disability with dignity, undergirded by determination, courage and faith, it will be to wonder again at the ability of anyone to offer to the world such a life of service, and to be reminded of how wrong those have been proved to be who said she would "be able to do little or nothing".

* 2002.

LIGHT IN THE DARKNESS

Autumn brings its annual beauty. The evening sun lights up the changing leaves. Holidays are taken. Children return to school. The normal activities go on as they must – work and play, eating and drinking, social leisure, sport. The awful irony is that it does so this year under a dark cloud, a sense of foreboding, apprehension over an unknown future. The felt certainty of retaliation for the attack on America itself creates the uncertainty so prevalent in a world under threat, for the implications of such a development are beyond knowledge.* The noise of planes overhead, the sirens coming from the emergency services rushing down some nearby road, sounds which are a normal part of city life, now seem to be ominous and threatening in the context of the massive security operation in place today. There ought to be a feeling of bliss "this (and each) morn to be alive" but with the present overwhelming sense of catastrophe, there is everywhere, and despite conscious attempts to overcome it, a profound un-ease and fear. A new day only reinforces it.

Darkness is a much-used symbol in the biblical tradition.** It relates to times of disaster, tragedy and confusion. "Darkness shall cover the earth and gross darkness the people," Isaiah prophesied. In the Genesis story of creation we are told that "darkness lay over the surface of the deep," which was a formless void, empty, chaotic. As the moment of Jesus' death on the cross approached "there was darkness over all the earth". What is so gloriously encouraging is that it was precisely in those dark situations that shafts of light appeared. Out of the darkness of which Isaiah spoke, there comes the promise: "The Lord shall arise and over you his glory will appear." "The Spirit of God was hovering over the waters," Genesis tells us and then creation began as into the darkness there came light: "God said 'Let there be light' and there was light." From the dereliction of the cross there followed the wonder of the resurrection. In each situation light shines through the darkness.

This is a time to delve deeply into the resources of a personal faith, and to sense anew the essential beliefs that create faith, hope and love. The first is a belief in the omnipotence of God expressed in the divine ability to bring light out of darkness. The second is the profound conviction enshrined in the doctrine of the Incarnation which declares that God will share whatever people suffer in whatever circumstances they find themselves. The third is the conviction that the Holy Spirit is active in the world, initiating change in people and through changed people, changed society.

"A weak faith," wrote Viktor Frankl (in *The Unconscious God*) "is weakened by predicaments and catastrophes whereas a strong faith is strengthened by them." The light that shines in the darkness may lead us, through awful experience, to deeper faith. But only hindsight will confirm the validity of that life-enhancing experience.

* This Meditation was published on 29 September 2002.
** See also Darkness, my Friend, the Meditation for January 19.

PASTORAL PASSION

The location is not Palestine but Northumberland. The two lost sheep are real. The livestock farmer and his wife, already battling against foot-and-mouth disease, find themselves facing atrocious weather conditions. Lights flicker, snowdrifts form, icicles hang from the roof of the house. The farmer digs his way through three feet of snow to check that all his cattle are safe. But two of his sheep cannot be accounted for. "The search for the lost sheep has begun" the farmer's wife reports. It is the story of a typical shepherd.

In the pastoral parable which Jesus told to focus attention on the unique importance of one animal and, by implication, one human, one sheep was lost and must be found. It is the attitude of the good shepherd and so of the passionate pastor. Jesus, the story tells us, was passionate about people.

Jesus' passion, in the sense of his suffering, is a demonstration of his passion, in the sense of his overwhelming concern for people. "He died that we might be forgiven, he died to make us good; that we might go at last to heaven . . . " So runs the familiar hymn, but the language will feel irrelevant. Other concepts must therefore be found to express the core thought behind these words. In the passion of Jesus, something happened that is profoundly important to us all. The life, death and resurrection of Jesus are the expression of the grace-full love of God in making it possible for us to achieve what we cannot do for ourselves, and that is return to a right relationship with God. Call it what you will in the language and images with which you feel comfortable – salvation, justification, redemption, entering the kingdom, attaining to eternal life, being reconciled, finding what is meaningful, attaining spiritual satisfaction – the cornerstone is that "it was for us he hung and suffered there." It is God's initiative that brings us back into a right relationship.

It is right that spirituality and faith should be rooted in reality – as the Incarnation demonstrated. But whatever matters occupy our attention, it remains essential to keep "looking unto Jesus" to ensure that we do not miss the passion of his passion, his overwhelming love for the needy people.

> I will search for the lost, recover the straggler, bandage the hurt, strengthen the sick, leave the healthy and strong to play and give them their proper food.*

These are God's words in the book of the prophet Ezekiel.* They encapsulate the passion of the shepherd for his sheep and at the same time the level of love expected of the pastor for his or her people.

* Ezekiel, chapter 34, verse 16, *New English Bible*.

O, JERUSALEM

"Pray for the peace of Jerusalem." The Psalmist's heartfelt plea was pertinent in his time. It is equally relevant today. Jerusalem is, as it has so often been, a city in need of prayer. Nehemiah, sensitive to God's call to rebuild the city's shattered walls, "prayed to the God of heaven" for help in his work of restoration. Jesus, much later, looking at Jerusalem, shed tears for it. "O Jerusalem, Jerusalem! Killer of the prophets! Stoners of those who were sent to you by God!" he said, in anguish, "how often have I wanted to gather your children together as a bird gathers her nestlings under the shelter of her wings – and you refused! God no longer has his home among you."* Still today, the world grieves for Jerusalem,** sorely divided, deeply despairing, physically and emotionally damaged by conflict and violence. That "peace be within its walls" is surely a universal prayer.

It was in that city that Jesus of Nazareth was crucified. That event changed the world, determining its chronology, shaping its history, challenging its thinking. "What do you think of Christ?" Jesus had once asked his disciple, Peter. The question becomes a universal one on which everyone needs to reflect. The name of Jesus will compel admiration in many and respect in others. For some it will only be used when taken in vain. Be the church strong or weak, respected or ignored, the world is still faced by the challenge of Jesus

If Jesus was, as the Creeds affirm, "Son of God", then the enormity of his violent death in Jerusalem begins to make its presence felt. When "God became man" (a phrase so much loved and used by the late J B Phillips) or as John's Gospel puts it, when "the Word became flesh and dwelt among us," the human response of the day was rejection. Given the choice, as is so dramatically illustrated in the one word cry in Bach's *St Matthew Passion*, they all preferred Barabbas. And so the Son of God endures the agony of crucifixion. But then there comes the resurrection. In astonishment and in faith, those who were there at the time began to see in the sequence – incarnate, crucified and risen – a divine redemptive act, that made possible the restoration of loving relationship with God.

This act of faith lies at the very heart of the Christian message. Those, however, who cannot make that leap of faith still have a relationship with Jesus for did he not say: "And I, if I be lifted up from the earth, will draw *everyone* to me"? St John certainly understood that to refer to the magnetism of the crucifixion.

It is right – despite the divided Jerusalem of today – to proclaim the unifying power of Jesus. The world may reject him, but it cannot ignore him.

* Matthew, chapter 23, verses 37 and 38, William Barclay's translation.
** This Meditation was published in March 2001.

SAVED BY LAUGHTER

Mothers bring important gifts to the world. The so-called "macho" marks of masculinity are all too prominent in the culture of violence which, frighteningly, grips our society. Jesus – a man's man in his ability to attract, lead and inspire that varied group of men of the world who would become the apostolic band – also showed his respect for femininity in the intimate relations he had with, among others, practical Martha and spiritual Mary, Mary Magdalene where deep affection was expressed in that moving exchange of names in the garden of the resurrection and his mother, Mary, a model of spirituality and sensitivity.

There are of course, other biblical mothers to respect and value. Hannah, the mother of Samuel, was so grateful for his birth that she said: "As long as he lives, he shall be lent to the Lord." Then there was Sarah, Abraham's wife, who became pregnant in her old age. The situation was so ludicrous that Sarah burst out laughing. "God has brought me laughter," she said, "and everyone who hears about this will laugh with me." A mother with a sense of humour, indeed!

The healing power of humour manifests itself in various ways, for example the ability to be aware of personal idiosyncracies, the willingness to analyse our eccentricities, and a lively ability to see the funny side of life. Patrick Forbes who, says Gerald Priestland, "may pretend to be a clown but actually is a wise and wily priest," writes in his book, *The Gospel of Folly,** "I've been saved by laughter." He also tells of a brother priest who went to see a friend who had had a coronary brought on by jogging to keep fit. Sitting on his friend's bed, priest and patient had laughed together at the incongruity of the whole situation. "To laugh you have to believe in God: to believe in God you also have to laugh," they agreed. Not all will find themselves wholly in agreement with that statement, but it is true that the capacity to laugh can be lifesaving.

A sense of humour can, of course, be misused. Turned into flippancy it can destroy confidence in those who treat superficially that which should be serious. In the eternal joker, turning everything into a quip or jest may well be a defence against difficult situations or a diverting tactic to lead the conversation into safer places. The perpetual smiler may turn humour into a defence against a threatening closeness or a tactic to hide the negative side of their personality. Alternatively, it may be a protection against insecurity and the inability to cope with life.

If there are gifts of the Spirit to be added to St Paul's list, one should be a sense of humour. It exists for our healing. So gratitude to Sarah who chose to call her son Isaac. It means: "He laughs."

* Angel Press, 1988.

PROFOUND SIMPLICITY

To be able to convey profound truths in simple ways is an outstanding gift, one fully demonstrated by the greatest exponents in communication. It is a particularly important talent in preaching. Supremely skilful in this way was Jesus himself. The content was deep, the form of expression simple, the tone one of authority.

There is a story told of the great Swiss theologian, Karl Barth, whose *Church Dogmatics* is one of the most profound theological works ever written. Hardly could it be said of him that he combined profundity with simplicity! The impact of his theology on generations of mid- and late-twentieth century theological students was, however, immense. Yet in one brief moment he demonstrated a simplicity that took everyone by surprise. Famed for his massive theological system, he was once asked by a journalist what the heart of his message was. Barth thought for a moment then began to hum quietly the lines of a familiar children's hymn:

> Jesus loves me, this I know
> for the Bible tells me so.

Here again in another form profundity and simplicity intertwine. When it happens it is moving indeed.

The greatest of men and women are essentially humble by nature. This humility adds weight to effective proclamation. Take, for example, William Barclay whose translation of the New Testament I have quoted above (as I regularly do) and who was one of the greatest communicators of religion in the twentieth century. He was a very humble man. His range of books, many deliberately written for, as he describes it, the "plain man" – and woman – is one of the biggest ever. His *Daily Study Bible* series is world famous. Recently reissued under the guidance of his son, Ronald, it is the highest selling series of commentaries on the New Testament ever published. Allied to his gifts of profound simplicity in writing, he had the same ability in preaching, teaching and lecturing. A giant among communicators, William Barclay was most generous, kind and available to us all and, despite his unique abilities, exceedingly humble. He summed up in the best possible way the wonder of profound simplicity.

Different in style but similar in gifts was another friend, the late James S Stewart, whom I have already described as "a prince of preachers". *His capacity for conveying the deepest aspects of the gospel, in a comprehensible way all through his ministries in Aberdeen and Edinburgh, drew crowds of worshippers to his churches and wherever he preached after he took over a chair in New Testament studies at Edinburgh University. As with Barclay, his ability to illustrate his preaching with relevant stories and modern parables gave him a gift of communication wholly dedicated to his Lord. Yet this truly great man, outstanding in any catalogue of great beings, was so shy that, while he excelled in pastoral care, visiting was a worry and a strain to him.

Profundity with simplicity, in humility; it is always a privilege to encounter such greatness.

* In the Meditation for January 21.

THINGS NEW AND OLD

"Ordination is not a licence to do violence to a congregation." That statement, made in 1980 by the Church of Scotland's Panel on Worship in a publication called *New Ways of Worship*, merits careful reflection by anyone called to ministry. The responsibilities of ordination are not to be taken lightly.

When I was at boarding school we were sent each Sunday morning to a local church. I recall clearly the sweat on the brow of that minister and his nervous fiddling with the corners of the pages of his pulpit Bible as he strove to cope with the demands of his office. The responsibility of leading a group of people in worship (be it 1000 or "two or three" gathered together) and proclaiming the will of God to them is, as it was for the prophets of old, nerve-racking.

Preaching is a function which is not for the private advantage of the preacher, but for the blessing of the hearers. The pulpit must not be used to expound personal prejudices or political views, nor should its hidden purpose be to meet one's own inner needs or satisfy individual interests. The proclamation must, of course, be channelled through the personality of the preacher. So long as the content is safe-guarded by reference to "the supreme rule of faith and life", the Bible, freedom in the Spirit is real. The living word can never be imprisoned within inflexible dogma or formal creeds. The Spirit, Jesus tells us, blows where it chooses. So long as the preacher is consciously dependent on that Spirit, given to prayer and concerned to build up the faith of the people, he or she has freedom. The preacher's calling is onerous indeed, but it is privileged. It is, after all, about the cure of souls.

The same degree of responsibility exists in relation to the conduct of worship. The desire to be freed from rigid, fixed orders of service, so as to make worship relevant, is a proper aim. It should not, however, become as it sometimes does, directed to amusement and entertainment rather than glorifying God and blessing people. The words of the Panel of Worship of the Church of Scotland are wise indeed: "The recurring task of those who conduct worship may be seen as similar to that of the householder in the parable (Matthew chapter 13, verse 52) who was expected to 'produce from this store things new and old.' In worship, it is the old which provides continuity with the past and allows one generation to speak to another. But to turn to another parable (Matthew chapter 11, verse 17) we must also pipe to this generation in airs it recognises and with music to which it has grown accustomed, if people today are to join in the dance of the divine service." How true!

Those called to ministry have a responsibility from which they cannot abdicate. The reactions of "my" early minister were perhaps exaggerated, but completely understandable – and right. It is demanding to be called to be the bearer of the good tidings of the gospel.

A TIME FOR TEARS

If Jesus came back to Jerusalem, he would weep. Were he to go to Bethlehem, the tears would roll again. "Jesus wept" when he learnt that his friend Lazarus was dead. Bereavement made it a time for tears.

There was another occasion when Jesus wept. It was when, in his lifetime, he came near to Jerusalem that, looking down on the holy city, he felt an overwhelming sense of tragedy. "If only . . . ," he cried. But he knew what surely must happen: "The time will come when your enemies . . . will attack you ... they will level the city to the ground, and you and your children in it. They will not leave one stone standing on another."* It was indeed a time for tears.

It is important to know that Jesus wept.** The verse may be the shortest in the Bible, but is a profound theological statement, for it tells us of the humanity of God. If Jesus is, as the Nicene Creed says, "God of God", then we can see in the way that Jesus responds to both people and situations, the way God himself reacts. It is therefore with confidence that we can say, for our comfort and using human terms, that God's heart bleeds whenever his children suffer. Be it then the death of a friend, the destruction of a city, the death of children on a ferry, the murder of a young mother in Wimbledon, bombs in Belfast, or starvation in Somalia, we can be sure that God feels the pain of his people.

Academic analysis of "the problem of suffering" is fraught with danger. It can so easily lead to the promulgation of pious platitudes that are totally irrelevant at a time when people are shattered by tragedy. Of course it is possible with hindsight to see how God can bring blessing out of hurt and so to believe sincerely that "all things work together for good to them that love God." That is, however, the result of experience over a long time. It is not a text for the day for distraught parents and grieving families. In the hour of desolation it is not words, however well-intentioned, that minister to grief. It is all-embracing love.

The "problem of suffering" remains the greatest of all human issues, and there is much to say on that question. In this world of ever-present and overwhelming suffering, however, the appropriate reaction is not analysis but tears. That is why "Jesus wept."

* Luke, chapter 19, verses 43 and 44, in William Barclay's translation.
**See also the Meditation for December 14 and several references to Jesus' tears for Lazarus and Jerusalem.

WALKING WITH GOD

We know little about Enoch, listed in Genesis in "the generations of Adam", but we do know his moving epitaph: "Enoch walked with God."

It was during the Second World War that I had to find an address in an unfamiliar city. Lighting, street names and careless talk were all forbidden. Directions followed by the inevitable "You can't miss it" failed completely. I could and did. I asked for help a third time and was about to receive yet another set of instructions when the stranger halted: "To be sure you get there safely," he said, "I will go with you."

This story, in itself trivial, is nevertheless a cameo of our spiritual pilgrimage. If, as travellers on life's journey, we feel safe and secure in our destination, it is because (like Enoch) we are "walking with God". The Divine Companion will honour the faith of those who, at his word, "launch out into the deep".

Lent, in particular, is a time of "commitment to humility and growth in holiness . . . an exercise in penitential spiritual renewal," writes David Tripp.* It is a time of spiritual combat . . . characterised by confidence in spiritual victory through grace . . . It will be a struggle (but) it represents an opportunity for personal growth." The sense of the presence of God on the stormy journey of life is vital to the development of spiritual maturity.

Growth in holiness involves self-examination, but there is no need for morbid introspection or a surfeit of inappropriate guilt (as distinct from a proper sense of guilt over wrong done). Consciousness of that perhaps over-dramatic phrase (in the letter to the Hebrews) "crucifying the Son of God afresh", may, however, lead to feelings of anxiety over our part, even if it is only by association, in bringing about Jesus' death. What tension there was at the Last Supper when Jesus said to the disciples: "One of you shall betray me"! We are told that, "one after another" the disciples mumbled, "Lord, is it I?" Did Peter wonder about his past gaffes and coming denial? Did Thomas sense his inner doubt? And so on, round the table, representing perhaps our own failings and sins.

There is, hidden behind each individual persona, that side of us which it is hard to acknowledge, our unconscious shadow. Reflection on that part of us is essential and right, even though it may lead us towards despair (as it did Paul). But we need never be overwhelmed. Lent is, as Tripp tells us, "characterised by confidence in spiritual victory through grace".

"O for a closer walk with God," wrote William Cowper. Penitential exercise is a spiritual obligation but it takes place within the assurance of the gospel promises. Those who walk with God on life's journey are guaranteed forgiveness, renewal and life.

* Taken from 'Lent' in *A Dictionary of Christian Spirituality*, edited Gordon S Wakefield (SCM Press).

THE GENTLE STRONG

"Meekness," according to Paul, is – like love, joy and peace – evidence of "the fruit of the Spirit" in the Christian life. It is not, however, a word which relates comfortably to the world as we know it. The meek obviously do not "inherit the earth".*

It is the word, not the concept, that poses problems. In the Old Testament, the meek are the poor and lowly, a theme which both the New Testament and Jesus continue. "The Son of man has nowhere to lay his head," Jesus said. In Paul's great passage on humility in his letter to the Philippians, the stress on self-effacement is added.

In English, meekness is more associated with mildness, and suggests weakness. The "gentle-Jesus-meek-and-mild" image has, however, done little to portray effectively the character of Christ or indeed the true ethos of the faith he presented. It is not surprising, therefore, that several translators have looked for words other than meekness in listing evidences of (in William Barclay's phrase) "the harvest of the Spirit". J B Phillips suggests "tolerance" and several versions – for example, the *New English Bible* and the *Jerusalem Bible* – offer "gentleness".

The latter is an improvement, for sensitivity is a valuable and creative quality, but Barclay goes further. Meekness is, rather "the strength of gentleness". What a marvellous phrase that is, expressing superbly the paradoxical relationship between strength and gentleness! That concept does feel relevant to modern needs.

It is always risky to apply the vocabulary of faith to the somewhat ruthless world of which are a part. The result may be sentimental or doctrinaire. Reinhold Niebuhr, expounding the theme of his book, *Moral Man and Immoral Society*, pointed to this danger as he emphasised the dominance of power, political, economic and material, in human and especially group relationships.

It is a danger to be taken seriously, but it is not a reason for setting aside spiritual concepts. Change takes place, God declares through the prophet Zechariah, "not by might nor by power, but by my spirit". Jesus, seeking in his religious tradition for a model through which to explain his divine purpose, chose not the warrior king but the suffering servant. It was a choice that set him on the way of the cross. When, therefore, he entered Jerusalem not on a charger but on an ass, he presented an acted parable about the strength of gentleness.

* This theme is dealt with in the Meditation for September 8. See also the Meditation for September 9, The Strength of Gentleness.

A Time to Die

"There is a time to die," wrote the Preacher (Ecclesiastes) in the Old Testament. It is a truth on which organisations, not least religious ones, should sometimes reflect.

Too often, bodies – much respected and greatly loved – when moving into decline, redouble their efforts to continue their existence. Those who fight hardest to "keep going" are usually older people who, having seen and known the benefits of belonging to a group with a particular purpose, believe new generations should receive similar blessings from it.

The reality is different. Times move on. Needs change. What one generation feels is essential may have little or no relevance to another generation. The trouble is that when the members of an organisation feel the need to keep the group alive all the available energy is drawn into maintaining the organisation while leaving too little time or thought for the aims and purposes for which the body was originally created. Perspective and priorities become victims of the overriding desire to continue "at all costs". It should sometimes be recognised that there is a time to die, and that, paradoxically, death, if accepted gracefully, can lead to the possibility of new life.

One respected organisation in the field of health and healing has faced this issue and is hoping that its action will open the door to new life and positive gain in the field it has served for 54 years. The interdenominational, interdisciplinary Churches' Council for Health and Healing died on 31 December 1999. Founded by William Temple to forward co-operation between medicine and religion, it sought to fulfil that purpose by bringing together all the mainstream denominations, the healing organisations, the royal colleges of medicine and related disciplines. To fulfil this co-ordinating role, a structure evolved over the years that was necessary to meet the responsibilities the Council had in relation to health and healing. The sheer weight and complexity of that increasingly irrelevant structure was one of the core factors in persuading those responsible for its work to decide to recommend closure.

But there is dramatic irony in this situation! The field of health and healing is one of the growth points in the life of the church. More churches are holding regular healing services than ever before. A major report on health and healing will be presented to the Anglican church by its working party in the near future. Meetings have recently taken place between senior clergy and doctors to encourage co-operation in the area of health and wholeness. Healing homes continue to develop their ministries. The Churches' Council for Health and Healing has fulfilled its brief by making such developments possible.

When a purpose is accomplished, the time to die may have arrived. But in its freeing of energy and resources, human and financial, it will be a death that leads to life. That theme of death and resurrection belongs to essential Christianity.

DIVINE ARITHMETIC

Multiplication is an important factor in the divine arithmetic. The spiritual law to which it relates is perhaps seen at its simplest in Jesus' statement that "where two or three are gathered together in my name, there am I in the midst of them." There is something about community that increases spiritual energy.

The Christian faith is, on one hand, a highly individualistic religion in that the ultimate questions it poses must be resolved in a one-to-one encounter with God. On the other hand, as I mentioned earlier,* there is a considerable emphasis on fellowship and community in Christianity. It is indeed a corporate religion. Both elements in that paradoxical relationship merit our reflection.

"Whom do you say that I am?" It is the question addressed to the disciples which produces Peter's personal confession. It is the question which confronts each one of us and no one else can answer it for us. When God asks for someone to speak to the people on his behalf, Isaiah answers: "Here am *I*, *send me*." Doubting Thomas's response to Jesus, who had proved the reality of his resurrection, was intensely personal: "*My* Lord and *my* God." The question put to Jesus by the rich young ruler was equally personal: "What must *I* do to inherit eternal life?" The response was addressed to that individual. "Sell all that *you* have and give it to the poor and . . . come, follow *me*." God deals with us individually in matters of salvation. We alone are responsible for our reaction to the offer of grace.

In religion, however, as in life, as John Donne tells us, "no man is an island". Nor is a woman. The vocabulary of the faith is therefore sprinkled with words and concepts that establish its corporate nature – *koinonia* or fellowship, church and community, congregation and flock, the body and its parts, the *people* of God.* Of course it is possible to worship God "on the hills" in solitude, but that is a limited discipleship. Response to the miracle of grace involves a commitment to become part of the worshipping, believing fellowship which is committed to the expansion of the kingdom and to serving the world. Robert Herrick in describing Lent underlines our true responsibility. He sees it as a positive giving rather than a negative concern with self:

> Is it to fast an hour
> Or ragg'd to go
> Or show
> A downcast look and sour?
> No: 'tis a fast
> To dole thy sheaf of wheat
> And meat
> Unto the hungry soul

It is part of the spiritual law of multiplication to understand that while (according to James) "the effectual fervent prayer of a righteous man availeth much," there is a yet greater power in the prayers of a group, two or three – or more – gathered in Christ's name. For in the divine arithmetic, the power of the prayers of such a group, meeting with one accord, is far greater than that of its individual members each on their own.

* In Absolute Demand, Meditation for February 12 which similarly refers to the corporate nature of Christianity.

RURAL NEEDS

Jesus died in the city but lived in the country. His pulpit was the hillside and the lakeside. His sermon illustrations were so often about nature . . . sheep and shepherds, the lilies which he asked an attentive open-air congregation to "consider", fig-trees, the "fowls of the air", sowers and seed, reapers and harvest.

When he looked for an analogy to try to explain to a puzzled Nicodemus the nature of the Spirit, he asked him to listen to the wind blowing through the olive trees. His relationship to God was profound. His relationship to others was extraordinarily compassionate. His understanding of himself and his purpose was acute. His relationship to the earth was part of his rural heritage.

The plight of the farming community, because of the world's trauma since last September, has had too little public attention. Ravaged by floods earlier last year, the outbreak of foot-and-mouth disease, in such intensity and over such an area, devastated the farming industry. It has created severe problems, financial and other, for the people of the land. That part of our fourfold relationship at the centre of faith which binds us to the land should compel our active concern for the suffering of those who farm and the many other groups of people dependent on that industry.

Money, as the psychotherapeutic profession is constantly reminding us, is an important element in expressing the level of value put on the service one person renders to another or to the community. Many professions, such as nursing, teaching, the ministry, do not emphasise money in this way. "Part of the farming community is prepared to accept low returns," says a report prepared for a major supermarket, "because for them farming is a way of life as much as it is a commercial activity." Commerce may ease its conscience by this kind of statement, but figures provided recently in a tabloid newspaper indicate the monstrosity of our current sense of values in the materialistic world of today. A television presenter on a popular programme is reported to earn £750 a minute; a noted actor in a highly successful 128-minute film £60,546 a minute, a pop star £189,873 a minute of an album's playing time, a world class footballer £1,203 for each minute on the pitch, while a nurse (based on a 40-hour week) receives about 18p a minute. The average farmer, in the first half of last year, earned 4p a minute. The figures, assuming their relative accuracy, tell the contemporary valuation story.

The tribulations of the farmers have brought some blessings. It is said that co-operation between farmers has increased and farmers' markets are developing to their advantage. But the needs of the rural community who live close to the earth deserve to reside much more in the awareness of those who live in cities. There is surely a place on intercessory lists for farmers and others who, like Jesus, live near to nature.

THE DIVIDED SELF

Internal division is the harbinger of self-destruction, as Jesus made clear to the Pharisees who said his healing work was devilish in origin. How could Satan cast out Satan, he asked. That would be Satan with a divided self. "Every kingdom divided against itself is brought to desolation," he pointed out, "every city or house divided against itself cannot stand." Former Yugoslavia demonstrates horrendously the truth of that warning as have, down the ages, Ireland, the Holy Land and, in former unhappy days, South Africa. Domestic politics have demonstrated the same truth. Both the Prime Minister and the Leader of the Opposition have taken decisive action at some time because of the risks which internal conflict creates for their parties.

The same danger applies to human beings. Inner conflict can threaten health and well-being. It is not comfortable to be, or to feel like, a divided self.

Such inner tension may manifest itself in various ways. Who has not said at some time: "Part of me would like to do this, but another part wouldn't"? A fear of loneliness may well compel some people to seek company and social involvement, but deep down the thought of losing their solitude is unbearable. The longing for a permanent, loving relationship may come into conflict with a deep-seated fear of commitment to marriage. Most of the time we can probably cope with conflicts of choice but, at other times, they may lead to worrying indecision or even a paralysing ambivalence.

Inner conflict can come also from the difference between what we *think* and what we *feel*, between our conscious rationality and our irrational unconscious. The pressures coming from the hidden, dark side of our being, feelings unacknowledged or unknown, can force us into behaviour at odds with our conscious intentions. (As St Paul had to confess it: "The good that I would, I do not, and the evil that I would not, that I do.") In the realm of sexual misbehaviour, life is littered with personal tragedies that have ended outstanding ministries, brought the public punishment that society demands for unacceptable actions and the removal of talented people from professional registers. Would all who condemn remember that there but for the grace of God, go any of us!

"Thou desirest truth in the inward parts," sang the Psalmist. We need reconciliation and healing there too. The divided self, in the sense in which I have used the phrase in this Meditation, threatens the fulfilment of that longing for wholeness which is deep in the human soul but, as Bishop Stephen Neill wrote out of his own experience: "To suppose that Christian life can ever be anything but a conflict is sheer illusion." Inner tension is to be faced, not feared, accepted, not denied.

The resolution of conflict can be a wholly creative process. For everyone it involves the ancient maxim: "Know thyself." For those with faith it involves the glad acceptance of the power promised by Jesus to his disciples, the divine energy, the Holy Spirit.

To become aware of the divided self within us is to move forward on the journey of grace, the end of which is reconciliation, integration, wholeness and therefore inner peace.

THINK, FEEL AND ACT

One of the most delightful of pictures is that presented by the prophet, Isaiah, in an early chapter of his prophecies. The prophet, on God's behalf, has denounced, in anything but polite terms, the "rebellious children" which the divine Providence has "nourished and brought up". But for a remnant the country would have become a variation of Sodom and Gomorrah. Harsh words indeed but the prophet is relentless in his attack. "You rulers of Sodom and Gomorrah," he says in withering criticism, condemning them for meaningless ritual worship amid wickedness, bribery and corruption among their princes and complete failure in social justice. It is blood and thunder prophecy indeed to a people with bloodied hands and scarlet sins. Then, and this is the delight, Isaiah (on behalf of God, of course) seems to lay aside his wrath and turn to soothing charm. "Come now," he says, "and let us reason together" or, as the *New English Bible* puts it, equally delightfully: " 'Come now, let us argue it out,' says the Lord." After verse upon verse of diatribe in monologue, God says "let's have a dialogue," that is, essentially conversation between equals. Hand of iron in divine velvet glove it is "Obey with a will," that God says, but the picture, anthropomorphic as it is, has rationality at its centre. "You do not *think*. It is time to think."

It is a point made too by the prophet Ezekiel* when criticising people who enthusiastically gather to listen to the word of the Lord but then treat the occasion like an entertainment, "listening to a singer of fine songs with a lovely voice, or a clever harpist". They listen, do not think about what they have heard, and do nothing.

It is a pertinent matter in relation to our times. Do we really think about what is going on in our society, the descent into drugs, pornography and crime? Or do we just see it all but carry on accepting it as part of life?

There are limitations to *thinking*. It is often therefore necessary to go on to *feeling*, for what we think about things or people and what we feel about them can be very different. But the need to "argue out with God" the state of our life, the life of the church, the life of the world and to take some action in the light of it is a primary requirement of the committed life. We cannot possibly think seriously about the issues of war and peace, justice and poverty, human rights for all, drugs and crime without wanting to do something to improve the situation. Action is the fruit of thought seriously undertaken. Strength may be limited, age may be confining, time may be precious, but James's straightforward words: "You must not only listen to the Word, you must act on it" are a challenge from which we cannot hold back *if* we think about it.

* See also Meditations for April 25 and, particularly, May 9.

A Meditation for Remembrance Day

GRATEFUL REMEMBRANCE

"Except the Lord build the house, they labour in vain that build it." The words are familiar, but they must not be treated with contempt for they proclaim a profound truth. Those who take no account of the spiritual dimension to life risk failure in all they, as individuals or as citizens, try to do. God must be actively acknowledged in his world.

The season of Remembrance is a time for gratitude and grief, thanks and tears, but it is, at the same time, an occasion for personal and corporate rededication. There are those who still feel the pain of the First World War, for it cost them the love of their life and therefore the life they would have loved. The Second World War, the Falklands War and the Gulf War inevitably mean for many pride and pain, wounded bodies, damaged minds, longing, loneliness. Grateful remembrance commits us all to the effort to create a fair, just and loving society.

What can happen when God's way is ignored is dramatically illustrated in a short story contained within five verses of Psalm 106, especially when each verse is summed up in a one-word "chapter heading":

> Verse 11 – *And the water covered their enemies; there was not one of them left.* The chapter heading is "Victory".
> Verse 12 – *Then believed they his words; they sang his praise.* The chapter heading is "Thanksgiving".
> Verse 13 – *They soon forgot his words; they waited not for his counsel.* The chapter heading is "Indifference".
> Verse 14 – *but lusted exceedingly in the wilderness, and tempted God in the desert.* The chapter heading is "Sin".
> Verse 15 – *And he gave them their request; but sent leanness into their soul.* The chapter heading is "Destruction".

What a storyline! Victory, Thanksgiving, Indifference, Sin, Destruction. What a tragedy! For the story that begins with Victory ends in Destruction.

Why did the story turn towards tragedy? The clue to the answer must lie in the chapter connections. Two are natural enough – Victory to Thanksgiving, Sin to Destruction. One is understandable – Indifference to Sin, for indifference untreated becomes something more negative. The crucial question is: How does Thanksgiving move to Indifference so quickly? But post-war experience twice over confirms how easy it is, in a world dominated by materialism rather than God, to slip from the idealistic visions of victory to individual and corporate indifference.

It is an essential part of grateful remembrance to ensure that, as our initial text says, God is involved in all our "building", individual, national and international.

A Meditation for Remembrance Day

THE QUIET MIND

Asked to draw or paint a picture of "Peace", the majority of the pupils in a senior class chose to portray landscapes – hills and valleys, meadows and rivers. These are, of course, places of peace. But one girl's picture was different. She painted a city street, crowded with people, jammed with traffic. Above it, on a branch of the tree in the adjacent park, a little bird sang cheerily. It seemed at peace with the world. True peace is of that kind. It is an oasis of calm in a turbulent world.

Such is the quiet mind. It is serenity in the midst of strain.

The importance of the quiet mind was often demonstrated by Jesus. He needed it when he was under pressure from the multitudes seeking his healing. He showed that attitude when he was facing persecution or under threat of death. Taken before his accusers, he had to face false claims and listen to blasphemies, yet his response was striking. "*Jesus answered them nothing.*" This is the silence of dignity I have mentioned earlier.* It is a product of the quiet mind. It is expressed in calmness in the face of trouble, in tranquillity in the face of hostility, and in serenity in the face of tribulation and suffering.

The quiet mind is a gift of grace. We do not ourselves have the resources to create it. It comes as a gift from God. Behind it lies a spiritual perspective, an active sense of the embracing, loving providence of God and a conviction that, as Paul declares: "*Nothing* can separate us" from the divine love.

Remembrance Day is the day on which we share two minutes of silence. The noisy, turbulent world pauses to remember with mingled gratitude and sadness the sacrifices, suffering and pain of two World Wars and other conflicts. At the same time, we know that wars and rumours of wars are with us still and, what is worse, in a nuclear age. If we are going to be able to live in and cope with this world of conflict and violence, with the weight of human suffering it contains, we *must* find that inner peace. We must cultivate the quiet mind.

"Wait on the Lord. Be of good courage and He shall strengthen thine heart," the Good Book says. God will do more. If you will receive it, he will give you the quiet mind.

* See the Meditation for May 8.

LARK RISE

Many and moving are the memories each year on Remembrance Sunday, especially for those who lost loved ones in two World Wars and subsequent military operations. In the First World War, the loss of men in large numbers left many women without the possibility of marriage. Such was the waste of life on the battlefields of Europe.

Just how devastating that loss was came home last night when I attended a production of *Lark Rise*, by that extraordinary acting couple, Sylvia Read and William Fry. For 40 years they have been continuously presenting their two-person productions, an amazing record: 3,800 performances, 30 different plays (*Lark Rise* is their thirtieth production), tours not only all over the United Kingdom but in Europe and across the United States.

Flora Thompson's book is a classic. It documents the life and times of a tiny hamlet which she calls Lark Rise, near Oxford. Life was hard work in the fields, family life, and music in and outside the pub in the evenings. This production, in a tiny pub theatre in West London, moved to a dramatic and emotional climax. It ends with the stark reality that out of that tiny hamlet of 80 souls, eleven of the men who had gone to war did not return. The proportionate loss was staggering, the emotional consequence shattering.

The greatest public debate I ever heard was in the General Assembly of the Church of Scotland, a long time ago. It was on a motion that "War is contrary to the will of God." George MacLeod put the case for the motion and passionately pleaded for the rejection of war as something unacceptable to God; James Pitt Watson, equally passionately, argued the case not for war but for a just war. The decision went Pitt Watson's way, but the memory of the passion remains. It is a dilemma which is always present in attempting to be obedient to "the will of God".

Now that war is claimed to be of a different kind in that it is expressed as a "war on terrorism" (and that is to be an ongoing feature of twenty-first century life), it is hard to resist the culture of violence which conditions so much of life today. We live in our fortified houses, alarmed and barred where necessary. More and more public money goes into "law and order". We are checked at airports, asked to be vigilant over possible bombs. Such is our conditioning that it is hard now to see the (as it were) "simple" issue which MacLeod and Pitt Watson debated. We are more and more precisely where Jesus asked his disciples not to be. We are, however unwillingly, *of* the world.

"Wars and fightings," said St James, have their sources within us. Fear, frustration, resentment, bitterness, envy . . . these are the sources of war, and to these factors attention needs to be paid. Oh that the United Nations Organisation had not become so impotent today.

REFORM AND RENEWAL

"The church which is married to the spirit of its age," writes the famous Dean of St Paul's Cathedral, Dean Inge, "will be a widow in the next." It is a comment that relates deeply to the current debate on the much publicised terminal illness of the church. Nor is it only the institutional church which appears to be "nearly vanquished". It is, according to Cardinal Cormac Murphy-O'Connor, Christianity itself that is in defeat in that it no longer has any impact on the majority of British lives and their moral decisions and no influence on modern culture and intellectual life. It is New Age beliefs in which people find "glimpses of the transcendent". "Christianity faces its day of judgement" is the headline across the page of one national newspaper. Are rumours of its death (recalling Mark Twain) "greatly exaggerated"?

It is obvious that a large number of old-fashioned and unattractive buildings have become a burden on the church. Much of the language, liturgies and music are only meaningful to older generations. "I have no objection to churches," wrote Brooks Anderson, "so long as they do not interfere in God's work". It may be that now many have become, unintentionally, obstacles to living religion. But the constant sniping by media writers and presenters does not give proper credit to the faithful and effective service across the land of parish priests and ministers, of devoted lay people, of lively congregations well aware of the need for change and active in bringing it about. Reports of the death of the church are, as was that of Mark Twain, "greatly exaggerated".

It is not a new experience for the church to be attacked, criticised, written off. Centuries of history have demonstrated its capacity for revival, renewal, reformation, resurrection. Taking seriously informed criticism of its weaknesses, its best response will be a return to its fundamental belief. Too much of the church's contribution today is social commentary on current problems. It sometimes seems unwilling to do what the first Christians took for granted, "preach Jesus Christ and him crucified". Those words must of course be in the language and concepts of today, but they remain the heart of the gospel and that which the church must proclaim.

People are still religious. Surveys constantly show some 70 per cent say they believe in God. People still seek contact with transcendence, hence the explorations of so many in New Age religion. People still seek the inspiration of the Spirit, hence the progress of Pentecostal and other churches that emphasise the work of the Spirit. People still look to cults and sects for those fundamental beliefs the mainstream churches fail to emphasise.

There is a time for out-of-date structures, irrelevant language and attachment to buildings to die, a time to set aside all that interferes with the work of God. If the church believes, as it should, that the Holy Spirit is the agency of reform, then change and renewal are always possible.

GOD CALLS

"How shall they hear without a preacher?" St Paul asks the Romans, quoting words from the Old Testament prophet, Isaiah. The question may have contemporary relevance because virtually every denomination is facing severe difficulties in finding candidates for ordination. It is part of the decline of the church as an organisation and a symptom of that decline.

There is in contemporary society evidence of spiritual need, spiritual hunger and the search for meaning at every level of society. That is not the problem. It is simply that the church in its present structure, with a conservative (with a small "c") bias and a style and language out of touch with twenty-first-century life and needs, cannot survive as it is. But the church is committed to continual reformation from within. Whether that can happen without much more involvement by active young people tuned to contemporary needs and language, concepts and ideas, remains a question. Meanwhile, despite the Lord of the church having commanded his followers to "preach the gospel", there seems to be a widespread unwillingness to make a lifetime commitment to ordination in an organisation as uncertain of its message and unhealthy in its structure as is the position today.

It has always been the position, from Old Testament prophets to the preachers of today, from priests to pastors, from religious to church office-bearers, that a sense of call was essential to religious commitment. Does this mean that God has ceased calling people to his service, that the fault is not ours but his?

It is hard to believe, given the history of vocation, that this can be the answer. The words of Jesus to his disciples emphasise a recurrent biblical theme. "You have not chosen me," he said, "but I have chosen you." He himself, in his profound baptismal experience in Jordan, testified to the Father's affirmation of his Messiahship. When he was ready to tell the world in which he lived that he was called to preach, teach and heal, it was because the Spirit of the Lord was "upon him" and he must take up his ministry. In that sense of vocation, he was in the prophetic tradition in which he had been schooled.

It is the conviction of many, as it is of myself, that, called to preach, there was no choice. Happily, hindsight confirms that call has been affirmed over the years.

God calls, but only in the right atmosphere will the call be heard. It is the church's role in these declining days to make them waiting days, days of expectancy. It is a time for "unceasing prayer", profound theological reflection, disciplined life in the Spirit to try to bring about the conditions in which once again, however radically different the modern roles may be in a "church without walls", many are prepared to say, as did one prophet long ago: "Speak, Lord, your servant is listening."

WHAT PERVERSITY!

"The modern generation has no faith. There is a fatal perversity about it." Those words bring unhappy images into my mind. I see those huge advertisements designed to encourage (as it seems to be believed) a gullible public to smoke more, advertisements which at the same time carry (but only because by law they must) the chilling reminder that smoking causes cancer, and cancer brings death. What perversity is this! I read of terrible atrocities in Africa, and learn from a *Sunday Times* report that a British company has exported machetes to one of the sides involved in the butchery. Of so much arms trade it seems appropriate to say, "What perversity is this!"   John Rae's words in *The Custard Boys* touch a painful nerve: "War is, after all, the universal perversion. We are all tainted; if we cannot experience our perversion at first hand, we spend our time reading war stories, the pornography of war; of seeing war films, the blue films of war . . . " We condemn violence, rightly seek to ban guns and knives, yet in any evening's television, violence with knives or guns will almost certainly be featured. "You live in an age which is twisted and perverted" I read, and in our despairing moments, we fear we do.

The words with which I began, however, are not a statement about today – although they could be. *They are the words of Jesus to the people of his generation.* Paul writes to the Philippians as people living in an age "in which life is twisted and perverted". It simply leads to one conclusion. Human nature does not change. It is perverse indeed.

What does "perversity" mean? Contradiction, stubbornness, being wrongly self-willed, directed away from what is right or good, my dictionary tells me. It is the kind of condition of which St Paul talks in the passage to which I refer so often: "There is a law in our members that when I would do good, evil is present with me." And why does this theme – perversity – affect me so much now? Because it is so demonstrated in Jesus' journey towards Calvary.

Take Palm Sunday, for example. What perversity is this that Holy Week begins with the triumphal entry into Jerusalem and ends with Jerusalem crying "Crucify him, crucify him!"

Take the choice of Barabbas as the one to be freed, Jesus the one to be condemned. They liberate a murderer. They murder a holy man. What perversity is this!

See Pontius Pilate proclaiming Jesus' innocence, washing his hands and – despite his wife's warning – delivering Jesus to be crucified. What perversity is this!

Such perversity is caused by the fault that runs through human nature. It is the product of human disobedience and wilfulness. And to the human dilemma there is but one answer. It is the transformation of perversity, through divine forgiveness and grace into positive faith and commitment.

GRAPES, GIANTS AND GRASSHOPPERS

The focus in this Meditation is on three words: grapes, giants and grasshoppers. The purpose is to encourage the disheartened and support the despairing.

The three words come from the book of Numbers in the Old Testament. The story tells how selected men were sent ahead of the children of Israel to spy out the land of Canaan, given to them by God "to possess it". Two reports were brought back. The first enthused over "the land flowing with milk and honey", and grapes were produced as evidence of its grandeur. The second advised holding back "because there we saw the giants, the sons of Anak, and were in our own sight as grasshoppers; and so we were in their sight".

Grapes, giants and grasshoppers together symbolise our human problem. The *grapes* represent, as they did for the Israelites, our aims and ideals, our desires. The *giants* are the threatening obstacles in our way. The *grasshopper* feelings are those of sheer impotence when we are faced by overwhelming odds.

How should we deal with such situations? The story itself (Numbers, chapters 13 and especially 14) illustrate possible reactions. The first response (chapter 14, verse 1) is *self-pity*: "and all the congregation lifted up their voice and cried; and the people wept that night." It is a common, human reaction in situations of distress, but it achieves nothing.

The second response (verses 2 to 3) is no better. Why has God let this happen to us? "Were it not better to return to Egypt?" It is the *defeatist* reaction. It, too, achieves nothing.

The third response (verse 10) comes after an appeal from the leaders to get up, go on and fight. "But all the congregation bade stone them with stones." *Resentment* is a common reaction to frustration and failure. We put the blame on others but defeat no giants.

The solution of the problem, for the children of Israel, had to come in some other way. It did. The language is religious but the message is clear: "And the glory of the Lord appeared in the tabernacle before all the children of Israel" (verse 10). It was a demonstration of God's presence in power that transformed the people and sent them courageously on.

The biblical message is a consistent one, and Jesus repeated it to his disciples: "You shall receive power." Fortified indeed they were for their battle with the giant forces of a hostile world. The promise holds good for all of us. Take courage!

CO-OPERATORS WITH GOD

"I sought for a man among them that would stand in the gap . . . but I found none." The failure and faithlessness of chosen people is a constant theme in the Old Testament. It persists, too, in the New Testament. As the death of Jesus drew nearer, Judas betrayed him, Peter denied him and "all the disciples forsook him and fled".

To over-emphasise this somewhat negative aspect of the relationship between God and his people would, however, be unhelpful. The essence of the divine–human encounter related to "covenant" and therefore to trust. What is significant is that, despite the persistent tendency of human beings to fail, God chooses to work through them! It is this aspect of co-operation between God and his people that leads Paul to say: "We are workers together with him." We are co-operators with God.

What, then, is asked of "fellow-workers" who, in the words of God through Ezekiel (quoted at the beginning of this Meditation), must stand in the gap for him? There are three key concepts.

The first is *conversion*. Some people are uneasy with this word because it is too often associated with a dramatic, emotional, public decision at a particular moment. It is not, however, the way in which people come to faith that is important. It is the fact itself.

Conversion, by derivation, means "turning-point".* For many that turning point is an affirmation of the faith which has always been theirs. Whatever process we think of as constituting the turning-point in life, the greater need is that we know where we stand as a result of it. That is the first qualification for those who must stand in the gap today.

The second word is *commitment*. Conversion is the beginning of the journey of faith, not the end of it. Lifetime commitment is needed by those who must stand in the gap.

The third word is *concern*. It is not enough to affirm the faith and be committed to it. Discipleship involves both a coming and a going. The coming is to worship and fellowship, but we always come in order to "go into all the world" in service to it.

Converted, committed, concerned are those whom God needs to stand in the gap for him today. Will he find them?

* See also the Meditation for December 15.

THE LOVING HEART

Love is the heartbeat of God. Those who seek to be true to their faith must show the world the loving heart.

The New Testament, as we have noted before,* proclaims the primacy of love. "Love is of God," it says, because "God is love." Jesus himself emphasises the centrality of love by pointing to the two great Old Testament commandments. You must love the Lord your God with your whole being, "heart, soul, mind and strength," *and* your neighbour "as yourself," he says, because "there is no commandment greater than these". Paul adds his word: "Three things last forever – faith, hope, love. But the greatest of these is love."

Is this simply pious God-talk? An escape from reality? The real world is in the news each day – war, violence, prejudice, persecution, pain, suffering, death. Unloving actions, insensitivity to people and needs, the rape of the earth – the news bulletins are full of these unhappy things. So away with spiritual fiction! Come down to earth!

This is exactly what the Bible does! It talks of one who "came down to earth" to be "God with us". "God so loved the world that he gave . . . " This is the loving heart of God in action. The disciple has no choice. He or she must be as the Master and offer the world the loving heart.

Our admiration for the saints who have shown us the loving heart in action is boundless – Mother Teresa ministering to the poor, the sick, the dying; Alida Bosshardt of the Salvation Army, exercising her extraordinary ministry in the Red Light district of Amsterdam.** But the loving heart is offered secretly and anonymously too – the devout and devoted nun who spends the whole of her life with the destitute, the devastated and the dying; the priest whose ministry is to "reach out" to the lonely, the despised, the rejected of society, in the pubs and clubs of the teeming city, especially offering a ministry to those who are HIV positive; the hospice carers whose loving hearts help people to cope creatively with death and find healing through dying.

The loving heart is, however, not demanded only from others. It is asked of us all. Like the quiet mind, it is a gift of grace. May the God of Love continually create a multitude of loving hearts.

* See Meditation for August 1, and the whole sequence for that month on The Harvest of the Spirit.
** See also Towards the Light, December 22.

November 19

THE ADVENTUROUS SPIRIT

The Christian faith is an adventure. It involves taking risks. With the quiet mind* and the loving heart** there goes the adventurous spirit. There was a time when his disbelieving disciples were asked by Jesus to "launch out into the deep," there to make their catch. They had just completed a wholly unsuccessful fishing trip, toiling all night and taking nothing. Against their professional judgements, but out of respect for their Lord, they obeyed, launching out in faith. The size of the catch they brought in staggered them.

Abraham had to be obedient to God. He was willing to go wherever God sent him.*** The risks for himself and his family were considerable, but "he went out, not knowing whither he went." It was a total act of faith. In human terms, the adventure made no sense at all, but Abraham would, in due time, see where it was to lead in God's purpose for the children of Israel. Beyond that, it would lead on to God's saving acts for all people in the Incarnation. Only a man of faith could take such risks. His was indeed the adventurous spirit.

Christopher Logue has described the fear of those who were invited to "come to the edge". "It's too high," they said; "We might fall," they cried. But when the invitation was repeated a third time, there was a surprising and thrilling consequence. In response, they *did* come to that edge and take off. *They flew!*

Christianity involves risk. True loving involves risk. But the God who himself dared to "send his Son into the world" to live among us, was taking the risks of love. He expects his followers to demonstrate the adventurous spirit, too.

Paul told the Corinthians that they must be "fools for Christ's sake". This does not mean being irresponsible – that is indefensible – but sometimes a sense of responsibility is just not enough. Between sheer irresponsibility and safe responsibility there is a "creative irresponsibility" I have already described.**** It is the taking on in faith of tasks that most would dismiss as impossible. It is just there that the adventurous spirit is at work. It is risk-taking for God. But what great things are achieved by those who, in obedience and faith, commit themselves to the adventurous spirit.

* See The Quiet Mind, November 11.
** See The Loving Heart, November 18.
*** Also referred to in Risk-taking, November 29.
**** Ibid.

WRONG DECISIONS

There cannot be many people who would attract less sympathy than Judas Iscariot. His betrayal of Christ was monstrous for many reasons. He was after all one of the twelve disciples deliberately chosen by Jesus. Betrayal was therefore not the act of an enemy but of a friend. His betrayal of Jesus moreover was not of a criminal or a terrorist, but of an innocent man. How can there be any sympathy at all for Judas Iscariot?

But that statement made, and the condemnation of history recorded, is it possible to sense the awful inner turmoil that followed the betrayal, and feel some sympathy for Judas? For the inner pain that leads to suicide must be one of the most awful feelings in the world. For those feelings to be acted out implies a sense of confusion, frustration, horror, remorse and desperation too awful to contemplate and too frightening to feel. Judas had made the wrong decision and its consequences were appalling, its effects unchangeable. As a result of that irrevocable wrong decision, Judas "went and hanged himself". It may be just possible to feel a tinge of sorrow for him.

Life consists of making thousands upon thousands of decisions. Most will be decisions of the moment which have no consequence of any importance. Many will be more important decisions that do have consequences – certainly for oneself, possibly for others. Quite often there will be decisions of considerable importance to be taken of which the effect may be significant for others as well as for oneself. These decision-makers could include employers, football managers, teachers, military commanders, etc. When the decision has been wrong, we may feel guilt, regret, sorrow, recrimination, but all we can do is to decide to try to be wiser next time.

There is, however, a level of decision-making that falls into a higher category. These are critical decisions on fundamental policies, or life-directional decisions which, if they go wrong, involve agonising regret. There is the political leader who decides to go to war, who by that personal decision may bring about death, injury, imprisonment, on a large scale. There is the individual who feels constrained to make some witness on a matter of principle or religious obedience that affects the lives of others.

If a military commander or a political leader makes a decision tactically or politically that ends in defeat, massacre, destruction in terms of lives and everything else, how does he live with that decision? What is even harder to bear is the pain of never knowing if a crucial life-related decision was right or wrong? There can be agony in not only wrong decisions but in indecision.

Honest decisions made must be left in the care of One who knows what is in man and what can go wrong. Lasting inner peace may never be possible, but the divine forgiveness is. It may need a living faith to save us from our wrong decisions.

The Judas solution is no solution.

SUMMONS TO WORSHIP

Can any devotional literature surpass the Old Testament Psalms for sheer exuberance in worship? What wonderful images – floods "clapping their hands" (and in Isaiah, trees join in the applause!), beasts and birds, the elements, dragons and ocean depths, lightning and hail, snow and storms, kings, princes, rulers, older people and younger, men, women and children – all are enthusiastically exhorted to "praise the Lord". Musical instruments of many kinds are involved as is dance. What a symphony – and all of it a contribution to worshipping the Lord in the beauty of holiness! The grace, goodness and love of God demand that the call to worship must be heard. The sense of the divine providence compels gratitude and praise. No wonder the last five Psalms are called *The Hallelujah Psalms*! They constitute a resounding call to worship.

The providence of God, the grace of God, the unconditional love of God – the great themes do not change, but response to them today seems muted and tepid, far short of the enthusiasm that characterised biblical devotion. The felt need for worship is diminished by a blasé society, more influenced by markets, dividends, and instant gain than by real religion.

If preaching the Word and pastoral care are the first and second priorities of the church – and they are – the third must be the call to worship. There is nothing more inspiring than to hear the congregation summoned to worship. What follows must be expressed in the words and concepts of the twenty-first century, but it should nevertheless be dignified and spontaneous. Worship is not an informal entertainment using a presenter rather than a prophet. It is a devotional exercise in which every part of a human being is involved, an experience that touches the heart, stimulates the mind, nourishes the soul and energises the body. The product of divine worship should be a sense of "new creation".

Everyone is different in their expectations and responses. That means varieties of religious experience require appropriate emphases. For some, formal worship and the dignity of the liturgy must remain available. For others, considerable change in worship patterns is constantly called for to ensure that it is real and relevant for them. There are those for whom clapping floods and trees can properly become clapping hands that express charismatic zeal. The *Book of Common Prayer*, the contemplative music of Taizé, the mystery of Celtic spirituality, ordered traditional worship with its familiar liturgy, Quaker silence, religious dance – all these emphases and more are needed to meet the diverse needs of extrovert and introvert, religious and lay, traditionalist and radical, people who are in good heart and those who are broken by life.

A bleak uniformity cannot adequately respond to the spiritual needs of people today. Variety and difference within a common faith are essential. However it is expressed, let there be an exuberant response to the great call: "Let us worship God."

THE VALIDITY OF PRAYER

There is a need for discipline in prayer but is prayer itself relevant to today's, and tomorrow's, world? Increasingly, the number diminishes of those who believe with James (in his New Testament letter), that "effectual fervent prayer . . . availeth much." It is another part of the crisis of faith and doubt that is affecting the church corporately and people individually.

There are several reasons for the diminishing belief in prayer. Some are intellectual, some psychological and some circumstantial. Intellectually, many find the traditional concepts of the transcendent God "out there" no longer tenable and turn, as the much-publicised case of an Anglican priest facing such a crisis did, to what he called "Christian humanism". Emotionally, rejection by a loved one may destroy that other relationship of love, relationship with God. Circumstantially, the pressure to set aside faith may come most of all from reaction to the suffering of the world. More and more, the critic's question – "Why does God allow such suffering?" – becomes the believer's question too. Why has the God who, through grace, is the author of change, not dealt positively with the dreadful pain of starving, violated, damaged people?

The validity of prayer, and the particular form of it known as intercession, cannot be established on a purely intellectual basis. That is not to say, for one moment, that intellectual reflection is valueless. It is imperative that great intellects continue to reflect on the basic material of the faith. But while reflection on the material of the faith is essential, the material itself is not intellectually conceived. It belongs to what Paul called, in a profound sentence in his letter to the Ephesians, the knowledge which is beyond knowledge. It is in that second dimension of knowledge that the great mysteries of faith – the miracles of Incarnation and resurrection – lie. Jesus testified to this in his response to Peter's confession of his Messiahship when he affirmed that Peter's spiritual perception was not revealed by "flesh and blood" but was given "by my Father which is in heaven". Prayer belongs to that dimension. Its validity is not established by mental gymnastics but by spiritual perceptiveness. If belief in the efficacy of prayer has fallen victim to the crisis of faith and doubt, the need is not for increased academic and intellectual effort, but for a renewal of inner vision.

The discipline of prayer is vigorously encouraged by Jesus who specifically says "Ask . . . Seek . . . Knock . . . ", who commends the "friend at midnight", who pleads his cause to the point of nuisance but receives the answer he needs. If Jesus is the authority in matters spiritual and the Lord who demands obedience, there is no possibility of setting aside prayer as irrelevant. It was the "firm foundation" of his life and he expects his followers to make it that too.

The validity and efficacy of prayer depends not on our weak faith, but on God's providence and grace. When damaged by doubt, faith falters and fails; when perhaps because of tragedy, spiritual sensitivity becomes numb; when the divine presence feels distant – as it has done for many a saint – it is essential to remember that it is not our frail grasp of God that is important, but his "mighty grasp" of us.* We are in the embrace of a love that simply will not let us go.

---

* These lines are quoted in The Healing Light, the Meditation for December 21.

FAITH AND THE ARTS

That fine Scottish actress and comedienne Molly Urquhart once told me how hurt she felt when, determined to go on stage, she was ostracised by her rigid, Calvinistic parents for choosing such a career. Going into the theatre was, for them, "going to the devil". It is sad that she should be a victim of the sort of relationship between the church and the arts that so often in the past created such bitter barriers. For that conflict, both sides must share the blame.

Many people in the churches have felt strongly that drama in the theatre, cinema or on television has deeply undermined public standards and family life. In particular they have felt uneasy over (formerly) implicit and (more recently) explicit sexual behaviour, normal and abnormal, over the aggressive use of unacceptable language, and, especially within late-night television, a seeming fascination with deviation and perversion. At the same time producers, directors, actors and actresses seem to claim for their profession a mystique that compels them to require total freedom in artistic matters and, in doing this, damage the sacredness of intimate relationships and besmirch holy things.

"Art deals with life, death, love, sex, everything that makes the world go round," Sandy Nairne of the Tate Gallery is quoted as saying. It is perhaps in relation to the exploration of frailty, despair and degradation that church and arts may disagree. The arts seek *carte blanche* in presenting life as it is, in all its horror and obscenity, individual and corporate, public and private. The church may consider there is too great an element of risk in such portrayal, but it must also try to understand the integrity, where it is genuinely present, of artists, writers and directors in their believed pursuit of that which is good. After all, the church of the Bible is familiar with the need for risk in exploration. "Launching out into the deep" at Jesus' command produced a miracle. The children of Israel reached the promised land because their ancestor, Abraham, in obedience to God "went out not knowing whither he went".

The conflict between the arts and the church is unnecessary and destructive. Both are primarily concerned with the creative, the good and the beautiful. "Beauty," said Dostoyevsky, "will save the world." It is too great a claim, as Alexander Solzhenitsyn agrees, but he adds: "There is a special quality in the essence of beauty . . . The old trinity of Truth, Good and Beauty is not just the outworn formula it used to seem to us . . . " There is so much common ground. "Art and faith are concerned with what it takes to be human and with transcending the boundaries of human life," writes Donald Smith, Director of the Church of Scotland's Netherbow Theatre and the John Knox House Museum in Edinburgh. "Art satiates the need for human values" (Sandy Nairne again) "in an age when everything is transitory."

The case for co-operation rather than competition between faith and the arts is strong. They should not be, as Molly Urquhart found them, bitter rivals, but rather colleagues in the creation of that which is "good and lovely, and of good report".

WORSHIP AS THEATRE

"A setting for dramatic and important events" is one of the dictionary definitions of the word "theatre". In that sense, an act of worship can be considered true theatre. This does not for one moment mean that worship is play-acting, but it does suggest that all who come to worship and, significantly, all who lead it, are involved in something dramatic and important, and, therefore, exciting. How arresting then is the first statement in public worship, the summons to take notice of all that will follow. "Let us worship God." This goes far beyond genial greeting or general notices. It is the call to share in an important drama.

Equally solemn, but in an awe-inspiring, not gloomy sense, is the demand for attention when the call is made: "Let us hear the Word of God." Dramatic and important words follow, the spiritual depths of the Psalms, the cry for social justice and sincere religion of the prophets, the wonders of the Gospels, the theology and pastoral care of the New Testament letter-writers or the apocalyptic visions of the book of Revelation. There is so much exciting material in the Bible.

The word "theatre", in addition to its direct relationship to the Greek *theatron* (the verb *theastai* means "to look at") and the Latin *theatrum*, is related to the Greek *thauma* which means "miracle" and miracle by derivation (from Latin) means "wonder". This happy combination therefore links worship and wonder. True theatre! How privileged are those, clerical and lay, who take part in it.

"Give attendance to reading," Paul wrote to his young associate, Timothy. He was referring to the public reading of the Word. For that reason, writes Nels Ferré,* the distinguished theologian, publicly or privately "it ought not to be read like a newspaper or magazine, not like a book of essays or an anthology. It ought to be prayed as it is read. Devotionally the Bible ought to be prayer. To read the Bible aright is to accept such communion with God as it is in his nature to give."*

The Bible is the source of so much of our devotional material as well as being our "supreme standard" for the understanding of the faith. It is the ground of theology and the objective standard by which the validity of our beliefs and opinions must be judged. It is not a textbook of science, a medical dictionary or an economic manual. It is the record, to be read under the Spirit's guidance, of the self-revelation of God through the understanding of the people of Israel in the Old Testament and of the Christian community in the New Testament. Seen "through a glass darkly" that revelation may have been but the church has given it authority by recognising the scriptures as the Word of God. Dramatic and important as its contents are, so is the context in which they are read. The wonder of worship is true theatre.

* Nels Ferré: *Making religion real* (Fontana 1958).

ACCENTUATE THE POSITIVE

Definitions of health have often been attempted, but seldom satisfactorily accomplished. For that very reason, it is helpful to turn to other concepts in order to try to illustrate what good health means. The word "wholeness" is one popular synonym. It is a useful one in that it sees health not simply as physical well-being but as health in every aspect of our being . Wholeness is the achievement of health not only in the body but also in the mind, the heart, the soul. In other words, to be healthy means demonstrating a wholeness which embraces the physical, mental, emotional and spiritual aspects of our being, and does so in their relationship with one another.

That concept, however, still needs other terms to convey its full impact and, in the quest for them, two words are particularly useful. One is *harmony** and the other is *balance*. If harmony means, as the dictionary defines it, "the pleasing interaction or appropriate combination of the elements in a whole", a positive creative image is given for our understanding of wholeness. If balance is defined as "a harmonious or satisfying arrangement of parts and elements", it too points to creative positive design or composition. The achievement of such harmony or balance will, or certainly should, be expressed in positive attitudes to the world around us and the people within it. A sign of health in that total sense is a commitment to "love and serve the world".

Winter is a time when many feel depressed, and their depression may well be reflected in a jaundiced view of life and people. But a sense of reality about human nature should not lead to a negative view of life and people. There is so much that is positive and creative in a world created good.

The spiritual writer, Thomas Merton, seems, in his autobiography *The Seven Storey Mountain*, to reflect a very negative attitude to the world, revealing a manifest distaste for its ways before he went into the monastery at Gethsemane in 1941. Having left the monastery in 1948, his attitude has become much more positive. "I met the world and found it no longer wicked after all," he writes. "Perhaps the things I resented about the world when I left it were defects of my own that I projected upon it . . . I went through the city, realising for the first time in my life how good are all the people in the world and how much value they have in the sight of God."

"God sent not his Son into the world to condemn the world, but that the world through him might be saved." There is no statement more positive and creative than that. It may well be a sign of improving health when we find we are more ready to "love and serve the world" with all our being.

* See also the Meditations for October 5 and 25.

WORSHIP AND WICKEDNESS

"The book of the prophet Isaiah," writes the late Agnes Sanford universally known for her ministry of healing, "is the most glorious book of the whole Old Testament." She goes on, in lyrical vein: "The sweep of his poetry, the loftiness of his thinking and the brilliance of his clear-cut logic are beyond compare."

These are fulsome words, but not without justification. Setting aside critical questions about how many Isaiahs there were (it is widely believed that chapters 40 to 66 are the work of a second Isaiah, referred to as Deutero-Isaiah), the purpose of this Meditation is to feel again the power of those prophecies and to see something of the relevance that they have today. As with all the prophetic books of the Old Testament, the historical context of such utterances is important. That unfortunately demands a level of knowledge of Old Testament history when Israel and Judah were separate. Important too are the rulers and kings of neighbouring countries. What is important is that in relation to the specific questions which the prophets addressed, there are general lessons applicable to all times.

Isaiah, like other Old Testament prophets, was particularly vehement where social justice and human rights were involved. He condemned the property speculation of his times, alcoholism and the sins to which it leads such as bribery and corruption. The "daughters of Zion" who "walk with . . . wanton glances, moving with mincing gate and jingling feet" deserve his judgement too. And there is plenty more to condemn in a degenerate society where "your very rulers are rebels, confederates with thieves; every man of them loves a bribe and itches for a gift." The result is that there is no justice for the underprivileged members of society. "They do not give the orphan his rights, and the widow's cause never comes before them." It is a resounding judgement on a dissolute society and a demand for a social justice. These things are not matters of choice. They deny the very nature of the calling of a chosen people.

Another theme on which Isaiah waxes eloquent and rightly so is that of worship with wickedness for he sees much religion as it is in the words of George Adam Smith,* a long time ago, "smoky sacrifice, assiduous worship and ritual". He goes on: The people pray, they sacrifice, they solemnise to perfection. But they do not consider, they do not *think*. "I cannot away," says the Lord "with wickedness and worship."

Isaiah's is a damning indictment of formal religion, routine church attendance, ritual worship especially if that is taking place in a society such as that described above, our church lacking justice, honesty and integrity; a materialistic, ruthless, greedy society. There are things that are wrong today that parallel some of these unacceptable conditions of Isaiah's time. Would that we had the gift of prophecy given to the prophets of old to try to present to society the need to marry worship and social justice. In the economy of God, they go together.

* George Adam Smith, *The Book of Isaiah* (1896).
See the Meditation for May 18, also on Isaiah.

EQUAL OPPORTUNITY

That "all men are equal" is a statement often made – for example, by John Chrysostom, Bishop of Constantinople in the fifth century, and Abraham Lincoln in a speech at Gettysburg in 1863. It does, however, need further definition, not only in relation to political correctness, but to fit the facts of life. In terms of inherited physical and mental ability, economic and social circumstances and various other ways, inequality rather than equality describes the human condition, but Pope John XXIII put the matter more positively: "All men," he said "are equal in terms of natural dignity." In other words everyone should have the opportunity to develop their creative potential.

The Bible makes the same point. "God does not show favouritism," Peter declares, a lesson learned from his encounter with Cornelius. This statement of the divine attitude to people is one on which Jesus focused strongly in his recognition, in word and deed, of the importance of every living soul. That principle must therefore be a crucial element in the church's prophetic word to all who are responsible for political, economic and social policies. Everyone, child and adult, must be given proper access to education and culture in order to develop their gifts and talents and enable them to contribute to society and its welfare.

While the right of access to literature and culture in theatres, concert halls, opera houses, etc, remains paramount, the cost of attending performances is still a major limitation to the fulfilment of the fundamental principle of equality of opportunity. All credit then to one notable theatre, Shakespeare's Globe in London, for what it has done, largely due to the efforts of its Education Development Officer, Alastair Tallon, who recently ended ten years at the Globe, to ensure that being involved in such a theatre is not an élitist experience but one which is offered to every child in the borough in which the theatre is. Over the last five years, hundreds of children in the strongly multi-ethnic borough of Southwark, where many deprived children live, have performed on that stage, their schools (including Special Needs schools) having been invited to contribute some aspect of a particular Shakespeare play. Acting on the stage of "Our Theatre" (as they are encouraged to call it) will have given them a love for Shakespeare as well as a lifelong memory of being on stage at Shakespeare's Globe. This is a striking recognition of the value of every child and their right to dignity.

This programme was not, of course, created for religious reasons, but all who want to see opportunity given to all to grow through the arts will welcome the application of a fundamental principle in such a practical way. Those who, because of their religious faith, set infinite value on each life, will want to applaud a secular initiative that so fulfils the law of Christ. For whoever offends one of "these little ones" by denying them the opportunity to which they have a right is guilty of serious social sin.

"WHOSOEVER SHALL OFFEND . . ."

We live, move and have our being in a world that, from September 2001, is a changed world. The horrendous events that started on the eleventh day of that month have divided "then", that is before that date, from "now", have made a profound and disturbing impression on both individual and corporate psyches, and have set off a chain of reactions, the results of which no one can foresee.

The element of confusion centres on the questions of where we are and whither we are going. Where we have come from is at least known. But now profound anxieties about the consequences of that decision abound. As Mohammed Khan, who lost five children when a bomb hit their home and his five children died, said: "I am not Taliban, Northern Alliance or anything else. I am just an ordinary man who had a family which has been killed." The questions begin to touch deep places in the soul. And in the depths of winter they do so even more as hungry, starving masses – but all individual people the gospel insists are of unique importance in the eyes of the One whose image they bear – multiply. Must this go on?

It is the children damaged by war, hunger, disease, destitution and death that wound the heart. Whether bereaved by terrorist attacks in New York, killed or compelled to flee in Afghanistan, made the instrument of politics on their way to school in Belfast, blown up by car bombs, revenge attacks and conflict in the land where Jesus lived, taught, preached and healed, and not least in the city where he died – all this creates a huge responsibility on those who "offend the little ones". No wonder a Jewish university lecturer writes with such intense feeling after her young daughter was killed by a Palestinian suicide bomber: "It is time to tell the world that the death of one child – any child, be that child a Serbian or an Albanian, an Iraqi or a Jewish child – is the death of the whole world, its past and its future; that there is no vengeance for the death of a child because after that death, there is no other death, for there is no more life."[*]

"Please, save the children!" is the Jewish mother's final plea. New generations must not "learn war any more", be trained to fight and kill as happens in certain countries, be wholly influenced by the culture of violence as portrayed in sections of the media, or be used as pawns or playthings in adult games, political or otherwise.

The last word comes from Dostoevsky in *The Brothers Karamazov*: "Love children especially, for like the angels they too are sinless and they live to soften and purify our hearts and, as it were, to guide us. Woe to those who offend a child!"

[*] Quoted in Crown Court Church Chronicle, London.
This Meditation was written in January 2002.

RISK-TAKING

I am a great believer in creative irresponsibility, by which I mean the readiness to fulfil some project likely to be deemed unachievable by 99 out of 100 people, but which the inner spirit says must be undertaken. If such a task is successful, something very creative will have been accomplished. I would not, of course, for one moment defend sheer irresponsibility. On the other hand, being responsible, while laudable, can often be boring and limiting. Creative irresponsibility springs from the sense of adventure which lies between prosaic responsibility and indefensible irresponsibility. I know from experience how creative the products of that attitude can be. The action of Abraham in obediently going out not knowing "whither he went" is a fine biblical example of such valuable irresponsibility. To responsible planners (and even Jesus had a word about the need for planning resources before you set out on a construction project – see Luke chapter 14, verse 28), Abraham's decision to take himself and his extended family on a journey into the unknown must seem utterly irresponsible. In the human perspective it was. In the divine perspective, however, everything is different. Abraham's action, carried out in faith and obedience, was divinely creative for the history of Israel and, indeed, for Christian history.

There is something of the feeling of assumed irresponsibility in Paul's recognition of himself and other followers as "fools for Christ's sake". Who, in their senses, would choose to be weak, "a public spectacle", insulted, persecuted, hungry and thirsty, "ill-clad and homeless vagrants," for the sake of religion?* But Paul, and many since him, have found that the irresponsibility of "giving without counting the cost" for the sake of such a cause leads to the wonder of spiritual growth.

Adventurousness involves risk-taking, and that is at the heart of creative irresponsibility. Living in a world that brings about constant tension, unremitting pressure, overwhelming suffering – mass and personal – nervous illness on a huge scale, personal disasters and human tragedies, it is all too easy to drift into negative attitudes to life – defeatism, resentment, envy, jealousy, self-pity.

Our faith, with divine help and human support, must work hard to recapture the sense of adventure inherent in discipleship. The spiritual journey, with its risks and its adventures, may be deemed irresponsible from a human point of view, but those who are "on the way" know they are moving towards "new creation".

* From William Barclay's translation of 1 Corinthians, chapter 4, verse 10.

A Meditation for St Andrew's Day

THE ENCOURAGER

Andrew was not the most publicly prominent of the twelve apostles. There are, in fact, few references to him in the Gospel records. That reticence may reflect his nature – I see him as a rather shy, introverted man, in contrast to his "front of stage" brother, Peter, who was extrovert and outspoken (often to his cost, but glorious in his confession of Christ). Andrew's presence may be muted, but he was important to the apostolic band and represents so much that is important for the church today.

Andrew fulfilled the primary command of Jesus to "preach the gospel"; he became in particular the evangelist to Scythia. In that he took his leader's instructions seriously, he was faithful to that primary means of communication, the proclamation of the word. Andrew's witness to that function has certainly been taken seriously by the church of the nation of which he became patron saint, Scotland. The importance laid on preaching has been recognised in some traditions by the layout of the church buildings: the pulpit has been given the dominant central place with extensive seating provided for the many who would come to hear the gospel. That physical arrangement has sometimes led to a diminished presence for "the table of the Lord", but it does remind us that, unfashionable as it may presently be – the exposition of the word remains a priority for the church.

Andrew was not (as Peter, James and John were) present at the great spiritual experiences of the Transfiguration of Jesus and his agony in Gethsemane, but that he was one of the inner circle of the disciples seems to be implied by the reference in Mark to his being the fourth of the disciples who spoke "privately" to Jesus about coming events. If that is so, he was clearly close to Jesus, something that must surely have contributed to his character and personality. That intimacy helped him to bring others to Jesus. It is of the essence of the church's work to follow that example and bring individual people into a close relationship with Christ.

Andrew was an encourager. His role in the apostolic band seems to have been a facilitating one, as two incidents show. First, we are told that Greeks came to Philip saying: "Sir, we would see Jesus." To whom does Philip turn to make that meeting possible? To Andrew, of course. The other reference is to the call of Andrew to be a disciple. He willingly responds, but first calls his brother, Simon (Peter). "And he brought him to Jesus."

To make it possible for human beings with needs to see, to meet and to understand Jesus is – as it was for St Andrew – the essential purpose of the church. Academic theology has, of course, its place but it is not doctrinaire discussion or the intricacies of inter-church relations that bring salvation. It is those things for which such as St Andrew so simply yet profoundly stands that lead to life. To bring "good news", to nurture a relationship with Christ, to offer a ministry of encouragement – these are the first responsibilities of the church, now and always.

A TIME TO SMILE

"There is a time to laugh," declares the Preacher (Ecclesiastes) in the Old Testament. To remember the truth of that statement is essential for our health and well-being, physically, psychologically, mentally and, indeed, spiritually.

There is, of course, also "a time to weep"; as we all know, there is much weeping in the world today. Filled as the media is with reports of death and destruction, starvation and disease, doom and gloom, it is essential that, in the interests of balance (a useful synonym for health), we honour, cultivate and demonstrate the capacity to laugh. "Laughter," said Thomas Hobbes in *Human Nature*, "is nothing else than sudden glory."

The evidences of "the fruit of the Spirit" are "love, joy, peace, long-suffering, gentleness, goodness, faith, meekness and temperance". Some other qualities seem to belong to that harvest. They include compassion, empathy, friendship, the ability to encourage, and a sense of humour. That last one is surely a God-given gift. Religious people, especially those given to over-earnestness, need to discover, sustain and develop their ability to smile – at themselves, at pomposity, at their less worthy reactions to people, at their mistakes.*

Elizabeth Templeton, an outstanding Scottish theologian, notes in her essay on *The Possibility of Laughter*, Ronald Knox's suggestion that because only man has dignity, only man can be funny. She adds her own comment: "The possibility of laughter belongs intimately to our humanness."

There are, however, those who turn every situation into a joke in a way that destroys serious discussion. That is often a defence against their vulnerability, but it can become a characteristic flippancy which prevents career progress. There is a time to laugh, but it is not all the time.

Just because our world is a vale of tears, there is a responsibility on all who believe in a theology of laughter to ensure that the blessings of humour, happiness and pleasure are available to all. The value of the ability to smile is underlined in Mother Teresa's classic words:

> Let there be kindness in your face, in your eyes and in the warmth of your greeting. For children, for the poor, for all who suffer and are alone, *always have a happy smile*. Give them not only your care, but your heart.

There is a time to smile and a time to laugh.

* See also references in the Meditations for February 20, July 7 and October 30.
For a fuller exposition of the fruits of the Spirit, see the Meditations for September.

By Invitation

It might well have been battered Job who said it, but it was in fact Jacob. Contemplating one loss after another, he uttered his heart-rending cry: "Joseph is not, and Simeon is not; and you will take Benjamin away; *all these things are against me.*"

Repeated suffering hurt then, as it hurts today. We all know people who are dogged by disaster, suffer seemingly endless bereavements, wrestle with increasingly complicated illnesses, face one tragedy after another. Out there in the great world, too, there is an ever-increasing mass of anonymous and distressed human beings, victims of war, violence, rape, murder, fire, flood and hunger. It hurts . . . wherever it happens, whenever it happens. Is it just bad luck, unhappy coincidence, human circumstance? Or might it be, as in desolation it can feel to be, that God has turned his back and what we are experiencing is judgement?

It is not too difficult to sense the prophet Elijah's desperation, the feeling that he has been left to fight the prophets of Baal alone. "I've had enough," he cries to a seemingly indifferent God. "Lord, take away my life." There are times when the broken heart just has to confess: "I cannot go on!"

Jesus' disciples, caught in a storm on the Sea of Galilee,* had not reached that depth of desolation, but they were out there in the darkness in a tempest and very afraid. It was the fourth watch, around or a little later than 3am,* that time when energy – physical, mental and emotional – is at its lowest, a time when perspective is distorted, when mental turmoil ranges restlessly over insoluble problems. It is not a time to make decisions.

In that darkest hour, Mark tells us, "the winds were contrary," and the disciples were "toiling in rowing". Spiritually too, they were confused. They thought Jesus was a ghost. Mark even comments that "their heart was hardened". They had just seen the miracle of the feeding of the 5000 but, "dully comprehending" (William Barclay's translation), they doubted still the wonder of their leader's powers. What they did learn was that it is in the dark, fraught, fearful moments that the presence of Jesus can become dramatically real.

The story of "doubting Thomas" declares the same spiritual truth. "Jesus came, the doors being shut," John tells us. There are many who will testify that it was when in a personal crisis, with every option closed, they sensed the divine presence in their darkness in a most extraordinary way. This is no mere platitude. It is, in fact, a declaration of the doctrine of the Incarnation which means that God is "with us", seeking the lost, healing the broken-hearted and, in the words of Howard Thurman, "making music in the heart".

The story of Jesus' walking on the water also throws into relief a principle witnessed to by his actions on other occasions. As Jesus strode across the water towards the boat, he *"would have passed by them"*. This immediately recalls the story of the walk to Emmaus** when "the Stranger", evening drawing nigh, nevertheless *made as if he would have gone further"*. The message is clear. Jesus comes to needy people only by invitation. The disciples "willingly received him into the ship". The followers on the Emmaus road "constrained" him and pressed him to stay with them – and experienced a miracle.

Grace is a gift always on offer' an invitation. It must be graciously received.

* See also the reference in Little Miracles, Meditation for February 11.

** See further development of the Emmaus theme in the Meditations for January 8 and 9.

HEALING WORDS

"Take with you words." The order came from God to the Old Testament prophet, Hosea, as he called him to prayer and penitence. This is a week in which the leaders of nations have turned to words in efforts to prevent wars. The weight of responsibility placed on words has been great indeed.

Stricken, saddened, sorrowing humanity needs healing words. Happily there are words that can relieve the agony of doubt, be the vehicle for profound thoughts, minister to inner distress, bring peace where there is no peace. In the Christian vocabulary there are words of assurance and reassurance, forgiveness and renewal, acceptance and achievement. On the journey through life we must take with us words of healing.

It is not surprising that, when God chose to come into our world in Jesus Christ, the apostle John welcomed him as "the *Word* made flesh" who "dwelt among us". In that he was moved by the needs of suffering people, Jesus was "the healing Word" in action. He then sent his disciples out to "preach the gospel" by proclaiming it in words and to "heal the sick" which was the "acting out" of those words.

Let us, then, reflect on some of the healing words of the New Testament, for, as John Milton wrote in Samson Agonistes:

> Apt words have power to suage
> The tumours of a troubled mind
> And are as balm to festered wounds.

The words of Jesus so often brought solace to distressed and despairing people. "Come unto me," he said, "all ye that labour and are heavy laden, and I will give you rest." "Peace I leave with you," he said, "not as the world giveth give I to you. Let not your heart be troubled, neither let it be afraid."

Let us, his followers, take with us healing words. Such words can be an instrument of peace, an orchestration of joy, a symphony of the sounds of salvation.

THE PAIN THAT HEALS

Some twenty years ago, two friends of mine received the dreaded news that they had terminal cancer. One was told she would be able to continue her professional work for a further year at most. For the other, a year was all she could survive. In the same mid-life age-group, both had futures of creative potential, for each had many talents. Suddenly "the future" was limited. They both had appropriate medical treatment, considerable supportive pastoral help within the ministry of healing, and much prayer offered on their behalf. The first lady, whom I accompanied to her bank manager so that she could "put her affairs in order", is alive today and still engaged in her professional work. The second lady, enduring an illness the awfulness of which deeply upset us all, died fifteen months after the prognosis had been given. The similarities in many aspects of their stories are remarkable – age-group, diagnosis, treatment – and yet, as the New Testament says in another context, "one was taken and another left." That for me sums up "the mystery of suffering".

The perennially perplexing problem of human suffering feels to have taken on new and frightening dimensions in the cruel world of today. The innocent suffer on a huge scale in theatres of war and places of violence; in the destitution of hunger; in the hopelessness of homelessness. Individual suffering is manifest in the spectrum of pain, be it in the physical, emotional, mental or spiritual aspects of being or in all together. With ever greater stridency, the usually plaintive question is voiced: "How can a God of love allow such agonies?" Equally acutely, the question (which all involved in healing ministry must face) illustrated in the stories with which I began, exerts its own pressure: "Why is one healed and another not?"

The tension between faith and doubt becomes ever more severe in the face of these familiar but profound ultimate questions. The result of that tension takes those who suffer in two directions. On one hand, there is a steep descent into despondency, depression, anger, resentment and bitterness. On the other, a positive, creative process may just begin to evolve. Whether it is the purpose of suffering (as some would claim) or a by-product of it (as others believe), the experience forces us to look at, test, re-examine our fundamental convictions. Can our simple faith, or (for some) profound intellectual theological structure, cope with the devastating questions thrown up by life? "Lord, I believe," we may cry and, with the father of the sick boy in Mark's Gospel, add "Help thou my unbelief."

One of the most moving statements on the theme of (in the words of the title of one of Dr Martin Israel's books) "the pain that heals" was made to me and a thousand others by a serenely religious woman facing her life crisis. Within the space of a year both she and her husband had been told of their terminal cancers. Facing that situation together, she was able to say with conviction: "We do not know if our cancers have been cured, but we do know that through the experience, we are more whole than we have ever been."

In the midst of the darkness, it is still possible to sense the creative element in suffering. There are those who can testify to "the pain that heals".

CREATIVE ILLNESS

Visiting the sick is a responsibility laid on every priest, pastor and minister. It can be a trying and testing experience. I still recall the first case of terminal illness that I met in my first parish. Jane was fourteen and had incurable tuberculosis. I still remember too the middle-aged woman in that same period, incredibly deformed by rheumatoid arthritis. Nor can I forget (I am writing of some 40 years ago when things were different, medically and socially) the human wrecks gathered together in what was then the "poor house", cast down, cast out, and cast away by anonymous relations deficient in a sense of responsibility and devoid of humanity. The images remain, as does the sense of failure, with ministry to them all limited because of inexperience of life and an abysmal lack of pastoral training in the divinity college. And yet there was, too, the added blessing that came from contact with people acutely ill and in constant pain. It made such ministry a privilege and an honour.

There is nothing attractive about illness: it is to be avoided where humanly possible. Can one then speak, as Anthony Storr does, of creative illness? He uses the term several times in his book *Feet of Clay* (HarperCollins) when he discusses some famous lives under that title, among them Rudolf Steiner, Carl Jung, Sigmund Freud and Ignatius Loyola. He mentions it particularly in relation to Jung's "breakdown", an illness from which he learned so much.

It is not easy to sense the benefits of pain when each day of life brings a heavy quota of it (as happens to people I know). One of the benefits of full recovery is the ability to find some blessing in what has been a miserable experience. God does not "send" suffering, but it is the divine way to so order affairs that good can come out of evil and a blessing out of the burden of illness. Perhaps it has led to a positive change in lifestyle; a transformation of attitude; a corpus of experience that will enable us to minister to others with enhanced empathy. There are those known to me who, through something as serious as a psychotic episode, have found new life.

Illness brings limitations. It reminds us that we are not omnipotent, but human; that we do not always have the power to control our lives, but can be victims of its strains and stresses. It may lead to a healthy dependence on others and perhaps a greater dependence on divine grace.

Any illness that overtakes us, if we examine it with understanding, may well tell us something about ourselves that can lead to a change in direction, lifestyle and attitudes. None of us wants painful experience, but if and when it comes it may help a little to feel there is the possibility of learning something through it; that there is validity in the phrase "creative illness".

HEALING THROUGH SUFFERING

Each of our lives has its quota of suffering. Does the Psalmist really mean what he says, namely that suffering is good for you? "It is good for me that I have been afflicted that I might learn thy statutes" (Psalm 119, verse 71).

The result of such a platitude, often pronounced by preachers not suffering greatly, can only be anger, resentment and rebellion. In any congregation there may well be the terminally ill, the HIV sufferer, the relations of someone suffering from Alzheimer's Disease. Such negative reactions are understandable. But we must consider the concept of "healing through suffering" and look in two directions for help in doing so.

First, we go to the Bible. What the Psalmist said was that *with hindsight* he sees that he has learnt much through his "affliction". Paul, too, talks of "present suffering and future glory", while Jesus says something similar: "In the world you shall have tribulation, but be of good cheer, I have overcome the world." The Bible does seem to say that out of present pain there can come future blessing.

The ultimate authority is, second, the testimony of those who actually suffer greatly – like Lin Berwick.* Cerebral-palsied from birth, in a wheelchair for life, blind since her teens, Lin trained as a counsellor, works in the bereavement field, counsels the disabled in sexual problems, was a counsellor on a television programme and to a disability newspaper. An accredited Methodist Local Preacher, she speaks from her wheelchair. She also lectures, has written her life story and has set up a trust to provide holiday accommodation for disabled people. She knows she has grown greatly through her pain. "The best things I have done for God, I have done since I became blind," she says. God does not "send" suffering, but when it comes he is present to lead the sufferer, if the response is not bitterness but positive acceptance, towards wholeness.

Whatever suffering or pain comes, be it personal or corporate, may we receive the grace to grow through it. This is part of the ministry of healing.

* Lin is referred to in several Meditations, for example, those for January 16, July 21 and October 26.

THE CALL TO CARE

There is a devastating divine denunciation of the shepherds of Israel in the Old Testament book, Ezekiel. They are, in fact, the rulers of Israel who have failed in their "pastoral" responsibility to the people. The words of the Lord God are trenchant indeed! "How I hate the shepherds of Israel who care only for themselves! Should not the shepherd care for the sheep? You consume the milk, wear the wool – but you do not feed the sheep. You have not encouraged the weary, tended the sick, bandaged the hurt, recovered the straggler or searched for the lost."* This is a serious failure in public stewardship. Might the criticism be relevant to questions relating to our national life today? It is, too, a passage to be taken seriously by the church? If the church and its shepherds, its "pastors", fail the people in terms of pastoral care, they cannot possibly avoid judgement.

It is a long time ago that I was launched, with no specialist pastoral training at all, into ministerial responsibility for a large congregation containing people experienced in every walk of life. I arrived in my first charge two days before the funeral of an only son, killed in an air accident. That was but the first death in a year of bereavement such as the congregation had never known before. Tragedy followed tragedy. There was, for example, one occasion when I found myself with a senior office-bearer dying in one bedroom, while his wife – unaware of his condition – lay dying in another room. Yet another only son went down with his submarine. A respected elder collapsed and died on his farm. Such events demanded a level of pastoral skill I could not possibly yet have attained, so I learned pastoral care not in the divinity college, but in the parish. My own faculty of divinity in Edinburgh University is now one of those which has led the way in equipping students today to meet the needs of wounded people and the profound problems of society. Whatever help pastoral training can draw from psychology and similar disciplines will enhance its care and should be accepted gratefully.

The church must not, however, turn itself into a psychotherapeutic clinic, any more than it should become a political party or a social service agency because of its concern for political matters such as education, health, homelessness, etc. The church was created to preach the gospel, demonstrate the meaning of fellowship, bear witness to the spiritual dimension so ignored by the world and help its people grow in Christian maturity. Solidly grounded theologically, its function is to be the healing community expressing its love through pastoral care. The "words of the Lord God," through Ezekiel (quoted before but well worth recording again), express the wonder of such pastoral care: "I will go in search of my sheep and rescue them no matter where they are scattered in dark and cloudy days . . . I myself will tend my flock, I myself pen them in their fold. I will search for the lost, recover the straggler, bandage the hurt and strengthen the sick."** The pastoral task has been delegated to the church. It cannot ignore the call to care.

* Ezekiel chapter 34, verses 2 to 4 (*New English Bible*).
** Ezekiel chapter 34, verses 12 to 16 (*New English Bible*).

DISABILITY PRIDE

The debate was due to last for three hours so the capable, caring lady presiding over it helpfully suggested a half-time break "to give you all the chance to stretch your legs". But the debate was on disability. On her left, in wheelchairs, were two of the speakers, and several of the audience were in wheelchairs too. Everybody, including those with disabilities, laughed because the innocent slip had made a point. How easy it is to use language and images out of habit which, in sensitive areas, can cause hurt.

The question to be debated had been announced as "Do Disabled People want Christian Healing?" Asked to lead for the affirmative, I refused to assume I could answer this factual question on behalf of people with disability. The right question seemed to me to be: "Is Christian healing relevant to the needs of people with disability?" Interpreting the healing ministry as I do, the answer had to be an unequivocal "Yes." If the purpose of healing ministry is to make people whole in every aspect of their being, the question of disability does not apply. We *all* need healing. On that everyone agreed.

What had given rise to the debate was that some people with disabilities had had it decided for them by individual "healers" or mass evangelists that they needed to be healed of their disabilities. Some had been exhorted to get out of their wheelchairs and walk. Others had had prayers for deliverance from their disability said over them – without ever being asked if they wanted such healing. What right has anyone to assume that people want to be changed from what they are, and may always have been, into something others describe as "normal"? There is, after all, such a thing as disability pride!

People with disability may strongly object to that of which they are proud being taken away. "I am so liberated in my wheelchair!" said an Anglican priest at the debate. "I am deaf, proudly and profoundly so," affirmed Dr Mary Weir, a Canadian theologian.* "Deaf people need each other and need a pride in being who they are as the good creation of a loving God." It may be a difficult concept but, offered by people with disability, it must be heard.

Our misunderstanding of people with disability may well be due to our attachment to a "medical model" of disability; that is one which sees people with disability as being in need of "treatment" so that they can cope better with the world as it is. Ought we not rather to follow a "social model" which suggests that it is the world and its arrangements that need changing? It is we, society, who disable people by our attitudes.

We alone can decide if we want to change or be changed. It is therefore not for us to try to take away disability, by miracle or otherwise, unless disabled people want us to do so. It is rather our responsibility to enable those who are different to contribute their unique gifts for the benefit of humanity.

* Quoted in an address entitled "Made deaf in God's image" given at an international conference at the University of Kent and quoted in *Disability, Rights and Wrongs* by Ted Harrison (Lion, 1995).

TIME TO GRIEVE

Tennyson's statement that "death closes all" will, when tragedy comes, find an echo in some people. Others will find comfort in St Paul's assurance that "death has no more dominion" over Christ and, through him, his people. Either way, death hurts. It brings a deep sense of loss whether it comes as relief from long suffering, as the climax of a fruitful life, as sudden accident or at another's hand in murder or war, or through that most traumatic of experiences, the death of a child. Bereavement brings the need for understanding, sensitivity, support, sometimes closeness, sometimes distance. It is often a time for silence rather than words, presence more than advice, touch rather than texts. There is "a time to die", but when it comes, death hurts somebody.

I read with sadness a statement made by the National Funerals College which said: "The average British funeral is a miserable and disappointing affair." It goes on: "For those who are not well-known figures or members of churches – most of us – the contemporary funeral lacks meaningful symbolism, dignity, adequate time and comfort for those who mourn." The College, led by its founder-president Lord Young of Dartington with a United Reformed Church minister, Dr Peter Jupp, as its director,* is a body drawn from many areas of society. Its aim is to "stimulate better funeral practice for the sake of the dead and the bereaved". It has produced a "Dead Citizen's Charter", a consultative document for the public and for professionals.

Over the years I have conducted, I suppose, more than 1000 funeral services. Taking any such service is a major responsibility, whether for church members or others, for those who died from natural causes or someone who was murdered, the aged adult or the little child. In time of bereavement, mourners may be overwhelmed by feelings – grief, anger, guilt sometimes, pain always – or find themselves numb and unable to feel anything. Death hurts.

To minister appropriately and effectively to such diverse needs, and in such variable circumstances, involves inner resources. In every funeral, priest, minister or lay person must empathise as deeply as possible with the wounded in spirit; provide comfort and consolation, sometimes forgiveness and reconciliation, always peace and love; convey to everyone the assurance expressed in John Greenleaf Whittier's words: we cannot "drift *beyond* God's love and care".

There must be time to grieve. Jesus wept because the death of Lazarus hurt. He can therefore "bear our griefs and carry our sorrows". A time limit of fifteen or twenty minutes laid down by crematoria is enough for a service of committal that concludes an act of worship already held in a church, but it can be frustratingly insufficient when that crematorium service provides the only opportunity for generous thanksgiving, pent-up emotion, dignified grieving and unhurried intercession. All who take responsibility for funerals must ensure that, at a time of grievous loss, those who mourn have time both to grieve and to be comforted. People matter when death, whenever and however it comes, hurts.

* This Meditation was written in 1997.

LIFE AFTER DEATH

"For what is to die but to stand naked in the wind and to melt into the sun? And what is it to cease breathing but to free the breath from its restless tides, that it may rise and expand and seek God unencumbered?" So wrote Kahlil Gibran in *The Prophet* (Heinemann). The words are moving and the concept glorious. The poet-philosopher from the East proclaims the transforming power of death: "Only when you drink from the river of silence shall you indeed sing." The same promise comes from the New Testament. Death has "no more dominion" over humankind. It is, declared Paul, "swallowed up in victory".

This is a faith which has sustained many on their journey through life, but is it an affirmation of the idea or a denial of the real? Death is of today. When it comes as quickly, cruelly and violently as it may, it brings the agony of bereavement and the deep pain of loss. Be it in the humble home where the beloved partner is suddenly taken; in a plane crash, rail disaster or avalanche; in a hospital ward or as the result of indefensible cruelty in a prison camp; in the obscenity of the holocaust; in the bombing by an aircraft or in the searing blast of an atomic bomb destroying thousands – this is the reality of death. It is not easy to see the great vision through trauma, tears and torment. Can death be healing?

Death, it is often said, is today's taboo topic. Is it that it is too difficult to face, and so is set aside, denied, repressed? It was not in the divinity hall but in the parish that I encountered the pastoral needs of the bereaved. I was taught Hebrew, Greek, divinity, dogmatics, ecclesiastical history – but nothing dealing with dying and death. It is better now. There are many training courses for all on loss and bereavement. And there are individual teachers too, such as Elisabeth Kubler-Ross who "brought death out of the closet" in her seminars on Life, Death and Transition. Sadly, following a series of strange events which included the destruction of her home, office, books, papers, equipment, etc, and then a stroke, such workshops are over. Other bereavement organisations remain and develop – for example, Cruse, The Compassionate Friends* (a self-help organisation for those bereaved of their son or daughter through any cause), the marvellous hospice movement. To bring together the reality of death with a theology of hope remains a priority task in our times.

Blessed indeed are those who minister to the dying and the bereaved, who sit where those in grief and pain sit, who offer not theory but practical compassion, empathy and love, who bring to those enveloped in the darkness of desolation, a glimmer of light. Death is not an end but a beginning. "When you have reached the mountain top," says Gibran, "then you shall begin to climb. And when the earth shall claim your limbs, then shall you truly dance."

* 53 North Street, Bristol BS3 1EN.

New Horizons

The images of the good shepherd, the vine, the door, the bread and the light of the world – the "I am . . ." statements in John's Gospel – provide valuable insights into Jesus' understanding of his mission. His saying "I am the way" is, however, particularly revealing. Jesus is the road by which we reach our spiritual goal. In other words following Jesus is a pilgrim journey. Disciples are travellers on the way. Spirituality is not therefore a static condition. It is a developing process. It is (as Paul said) "pressing towards a mark". It is movement.

In the disciplines of pastoral care and counselling, the therapeutic relationship exists to enable people to see where they are, why they are there, and then to help them to move forward towards something better. Psychotherapy and analysis probe the deep inner places in order to create growth towards maturity, to take those who seek it on the inner journey towards "individuation". There is a similar need for movement in the discipline of theology. Surprisingly it was the great Swiss theologian, Karl Barth, who emphasised that need.

To say "surprisingly" may seem unfair, but Barth's *magnum opus* is *Church Dogmatics* and dogmatics is a word which sounds, as Sydney Carter would say, "fixed and final"! Something Barth said in two letters in 1956, one of them to his son Marcus, gives us, however, an insight so splendid that Professor George Newlands describes it as "one of the best pieces of advice ever given in theology".* Barth wrote: "A good theologian does not live in a house of ideas, principles and methods. He walks right through all such buildings and always comes out in the fresh air again. He remains on the way." This is a thrilling statement that is relevant not only to academics and theologians, but to all travellers on the pilgrim way.

The new century has underlined the need for movement in many disciplines. It is not that all that is traditional – with its "ancient landmarks" – - needs to be set aside as irrelevant. That that is far from the case is pointed to in Newlands' comment that "some modern theological reconstruction" has resulted in a "disastrous weakening of the classical Christian claims about the nature and activity of God."* The "eternal verities", as the late George Appleton called them, are still essential. So long, however, as faith is firmly grounded, there is gain indeed in exploring new ideas, reflecting on insights from other religions, assessing contributions from modern literature and culture. Leaving aside what is irrelevant but pondering the challenge of fresh ideas, we still "remain on the way" to new horizons.

There has always been, in healthy religion, a flexibility that is not in conflict with deep conviction. Thus theological adventure and risk have their proper place. The bonding of the conviction, biblically based, with freedom for honest exploration gives us the opportunity to widen the horizons while rooted in the faith. "Remain on the way" – but travel on!

* *God in Christian Perspective* by George Newlands (T and T Clark 1996).

COMMITTED TO CARE

There are times when communication is not a matter of "talking at" or "doing to". It is a matter of "being with". The doctrine of the Incarnation is a theological statement about "being with". Jesus would be called Emmanuel because, says Matthew, it means "God with us". Throughout his mission, Jesus was indeed God present with people, however awful their situation. That presence was a healing presence.

Jesus' ministry to Zacchaeus is a model for pastoral caring. It represents a "move towards" in compassion ("Today, Zacchaeus, I am coming to your house") and then a "being with" in a sharing of his misery. The result was Zacchaeus' public statement of regret and commitment to restitution.

This is an example of redeeming relationship in action, a true communication of the grace of God to someone in deep need.

Within such a healing relationship there is a *commitment* to *sharing and caring*, three words which aptly describe the life of the early church (Acts, chapter 4, verses 31 to 37). Meeting together in worship and fellowship, the church showed itself to be a community committed to sharing and caring ("they had all things common . . . and parted them all, as everyone had need").

Such a group had a dramatic effect on the world to which they witnessed for 3,000 were converted in one day. The apostles' teaching and preaching had contributed to this success, but the depth of their fellowship and the level of their caring was a factor too. What they *did* was wonderful. What they *were* said that "they had been with Jesus".

St Francis once went on a preaching mission, taking with him a novice who would benefit by the experience. The latter, on his return to the monastery, was bemused. "I thought we were going on a preaching mission," he said. "We did," replied Francis. "But you never preached to the people at all. All you did was minister to people with help and comfort." "Exactly," said St Francis. "We preached in the comfort we offered and in the love we showed. *We preached as we went*. It was thus we preached."

So do we all. The healing presence of another, whether spoken words are used or not, is in its commitment to caring and sharing, a prime means of communication.

IMAGE OF GOD

Religious words and phrases often slip off the tongue without any effort to analyse or understand them. Perhaps "made in the image of God" is one such phrase. It cannot refer to any physical likeness to God, obviously. It does not imply equality with God, for Christ himself said even he did not claim that. So just what does it mean?

The phrase first occurs in the creation story in Genesis where the words "image" and "likeness" are used together. Some translators have chosen the synonym "resemblance", while various commentators offer suggestions as to its meaning – "dignity as God's representative", "having the capacity for communion with God", "being able to make moral choices", "being capable of a covenant relationship with God" or (Martin Luther's suggestion) "the complete orientation of life towards God".

Here is another definition of "the image of God". It comes from an American theologian, Mary Daly,* and it offers a very positive, stimulating, exciting insight into those words. She says: "It is the creative potential itself in human beings that is the image of God." Perhaps the essence of the concept can be located there. God is the Creator but we too have the capacity to create! It is in our creativeness that we are like the God who has graciously given us this gift. This is good news indeed for it is a ground of hope and a call to action. And that leads to a second interesting comment from Mary Daly:* "Why must God be a noun? Why not a verb – the most active and dynamic of all?" The urge to creativeness! Creativity and spirituality are very similar things. What gifts are these!

Sadly so often in life negative thoughts and feelings intervene to "block" the creative spiritual flow. In the Genesis story again, the false pride of Adam and Eve in "seeking to be as God" closed the door to their paradise. In biblical theology, that is precisely what sin does. It negates the growth of spirituality. Similarly there are psychological "blocks" to creativity – envy, jealousy, resentment, intolerance, judgementalism. These, and other negative attitudes, can dam the creative flow. There are , too, corporate barriers that militate against creativity – racism, militant fundamentalism, corporate greed, group selfishness – the kind of blocks that prevent reconciliation and healing. Moreover, in a theological sense mistaken and unworthy views of the nature of God – a God whom we make too small, too anthropomorphic, too judgemental – can seriously obstruct creative growth and damage spiritual maturity.

True religion, however, brings us hope. The image of God in human beings is distorted by sin, but it is never totally destroyed. It is the work of the Holy Spirit to stimulate creative, spiritual growth as the great acts of salvation restore the image of God in us all. That is indeed a reason for praise.

* Quoted by Julia Cameron in *The Artist's Way*, Pan Books, Macmillan Publishers (ISBN 0 330 34358 0).

THE POINT OF NO RETURN

It is such a relief to know that Jesus wept, I wrote in an earlier Meditation. "Very God of Very God" he may be, as the Nicene Creed affirms. Classical Christology may theologise about the two-natures doctrine: "One person in whom are united two natures, a divine and a human, without confusion or change, without division or separation." What the shortest verse in the Bible, "Jesus wept," tells us is that he who was called Son of God was really and truly human. Led there by Mary, like her Jewish companions weeping over their bereavement, Jesus looked into Lazarus' grave and he cried. He was bereaved just as they were and he felt it deeply. He was indeed human. How close, however, are joy and sorrow. "The selfsame well from which your laughter rises was oftentimes filled with your tears," says The Prophet, Kahlil Gibran.* "Joy and sorrow are inseparable. Together they come . . . " It was the tears of Mary that took her to the tomb – and to resurrection joy.

Joy and suffering are together at other times in the life of Jesus and his disciples. With whom did he choose to share his glorious Transfiguration experience when the disciples saw him embraced in the light of his future glory? It was Peter, James and John. Who were the disciples he invited to be with him in the place of agonising pain, the Garden of Gethsemane? The same Peter, James and John. Those who shared the wonder of his Transfiguration would share the pain of his Gethsemane. It was for personal support, surely, that he took them to the Garden, but it was comfort they could not give. Three times he came to awaken them, heavy with sleep. "Could you not watch with me one hour?" he asked. He had had to face the mental and spiritual agony of reaching what William Barclay calls "the point of no return" utterly alone.

That loneliness brings us back to the evidence for Jesus' true human-ness. He was "panic-stricken" writes Harry Williams,** basing that adjective on Mark's record of the event. "The increasing realisation of what lay ahead came to him with such a sense of overwhelming shock that he was distraught in mind" (Mark, chapter 14, verse 33, William Barclay's translation). "All things are possible with you," he prays. "Take away this cup from me." What human yearning is in that prayer! But obedience, trust and love flow back! "Nevertheless not what I will, but what Thou wilt."

No suffering of ours can equal his, but when we too reach our point of no return, his understanding, sympathy and empathy are guaranteed. He has been there. He knows.

In every human need, the divine compassion is present to share our sadness and our gladness. He wept when Lazarus died. He surely weeps for you in your sorrow. As he shed tears for Jerusalem so, though the reasons are different, he surely weeps for Afghanistan. Because of his Gethsemane, he shares our little Gethsemanes. In every sorrow, and every joy, he remains Emmanuel – God with us.

* Published by Heinemann.
** In *The True Wilderness* (Constable, 1965).
The theme of the divine compassion is further developed in a number of Meditations, but especially that for September 16.

THE TURNING-POINT

I can still see the picture in my mind's eye although it happened so long ago. There was the great American theologian Reinhold Niebuhr, moved to mirth at the sight of his old friend and my teacher, John Baillie, in the quaint breeches and related garb worn by Moderators of the General Assembly of the Church of Scotland in their year of office. It was the light moment in an after-dinner speech, restricted to seven minutes, in which Niebuhr offered a profoundly moving analysis of "the human dilemma". This, as I recall his words, could not be resolved by philosophy however profound, by education however intensive, by scientific progress however dramatic or by psychological understanding however acute. There was only one answer to the depth of human need and that was "the grace of our Lord Jesus Christ".

The gospel proclaims that fundamental inner change is needed if new life is to be found. "Except you be converted . . . " said Jesus, "you cannot enter the kingdom." When speaking with Nicodemus, he called it being "born again". Conversion is then a necessary experience but, unfortunately, the word itself is often interpreted in too limited a way. As a result, it tends to divide rather than unite, and that is sad indeed.

There is no need for such conflict. The word "conversion", by derivation, means "turning point". An experience of inner transformation is a step on the way to salvation. *It is, however, the experience itself which is mandatory, not the way in which it happens.* For, just as there is diversity in the gifts of the Spirit, so there are various ways by which God brings about inner change.

"Youth is the time to go flashing from one side of the world to the other, both in mind and body; to try the manners of different nations; to hear the chimes at midnight; to see sunrise in town and country, to be converted at a revival . . ." says Robert Louis Stevenson in *Crabbed Age and Youth*. But this seems to limit conversion to a "revivalist" experience and to "the age of adolescence". It can be both, but it need not be either!

Inner transformation does take place at crusades, in mission halls, within the church, in that dramatic, public way that can be timed and dated. There are many admirable people who have been "saved", "born again", charismatically renewed in such circumstances. But there are others who have experienced "the miracle of grace" in less emotional, less traumatic, less public but equally convincing ways. There is a group – and John Baillie was one of them – who, as he commented, had never known a time, because of their upbringing by devout parents, "when Jesus was not my Lord". For them, confirmation of their baptismal vows and public affirmation was and is their transforming experience.

An adolescent experience? Yes, such a turning-point often is. But mid-life crisis, as Jungian thought confirms, can also be the occasion for fundamental redirection. It is the time when spiritual, creative life often emerges and the movement towards integration develops. This too is a miracle of grace.

When a prodigal son returned transformed, there was spontaneous joy, and rightly so. This – and not controversy about how it happens – is the appropriate response when someone "was lost and is found".

THE ETERNAL VERITIES

Prophets, priests and preachers are among those who have responded to the call to communicate the unchanging Word to a constantly changing world, but the proclamation of "the eternal verities"* must relate to the location, culture and time-setting of those to whom it is addressed. Ways have to be found to convey the great truths of the faith . . . the offer of a right relationships with God, the assurance of forgiveness, the promise of new life . . . in a way that will be understood.

When I first came to live in London, I found myself using phrases from my Scottish background which completely puzzled those to whom I spoke. "I am going to get the messages," I would say, only to encounter blank looks. Had I said instead: "I am going to do the shopping," there would have been no problem. The basic fact was the same, but it had to be expressed in a way comprehensible to people in another cultural context.

The New Testament demonstrates superbly the way in which these "eternal verities" can reach very different people. The essential truth which the gospel proclaims is that, through Jesus Christ, the restoration of a right relationship with God becomes possible. The concepts and words in which this truth is conveyed vary greatly – "entering the Kingdom", "receiving eternal life", "salvation", "redemption", etc.

It would be naïve to say that each of these words or phrases means exactly the same, for much academic discussion would be involved in expounding their history and precise meaning. What I seek to show is simply that the great truths must be described in different ways depending on the background, interests and history of those to whom they are presented. To one group one of these words or phrases will be meaningless, but to another dynamite – and *vice versa*.

What are the concepts to which we need to turn to be relevant today? Surely to words such as meaning, purpose, reconciliation, relationship. The world is confused by cults and theories, devastated by suffering (and suffering always raises the most difficult questions), depressed by feelings of meaninglessness and purposelessness. The gospel message must be a giving of wholeness to, and a reason for, life. God offers the possibility of inner peace through the finding of a purpose. Restored relationship with God will transform all other relationships – to others, to the earth, to our inner selves. In a world too often trivial and tawdry, a world of inner despair and outward devastation, a world increasingly devoid of the sense of the numinous, the faith must continue to be proclaimed – but never with arrogance, always with humility.

* The late Bishop George Appleton said his instruction when appointed to write this column was to proclaim "the eternal verities". He contributed his Meditations for some twelve or thirteen years.

A Meditation for Advent

GOD WITH US

Christmas came commercially in October. Christmas comes on to our horizon devotionally this weekend with the celebration of the First Sunday in Advent. We are preparing ourselves for the great event which J B Phillips loved to call "the visit of God". The Incarnation is exactly that for, as John tells us in his Gospel, "The Word was made flesh and dwelt among us." The Good News is enshrined in a name Jesus would be given . . . Emmanuel. It means "God with us."

This *is* Good News indeed. It dismisses for ever the picture of God as some distant divine power, dispensing judgement on recalcitrant people. Advent is the announcement of the coming of one who will feel and share all that happens in this "vale of tears". His birth will be lowly, identifying him with the weak and the poor. He will "have no place to lay his head" so the homeless and the refugee will find comfort in that. He will be "despised and rejected of men, a man of sorrows and acquainted with grief" so he can empathise with the isolated, the sad and the bereaved in their pain. He will endure acute suffering of mind, soul and body, so those who are mentally distressed, emotionally wounded or desperately ill will be strengthened by his ability to feel for them. He will meet death when but a young man. The dying, older and younger, will be grateful and glad to know he is "with" them. He is indeed "the man for others", "God with us".

J B Phillips's faith was founded on the gracious relationship made possible by the "divine initiative", the act of love for which we give thanks in Advent. We love God because "he first loved us" by coming to be "with us" in whatever circumstances we find ourselves, whatever we do. We are in the grasp of a love that "will not let us go". Phillips wrote: "Christ *is* everything. He is God shown to us in human form. He is God dying a criminal's death to reconcile men and women to himself. He is God triumphing over death. He is God entering human hearts and transforming them from within – a thing unknown in a pagan world either then or now . . . God has entered the stream of human history in *person*." *

Advent is for many the promulgation of a great theological doctrine. To others it is a simple (but not simplistic) statement of faith. God is "with us" in loving relationship, to give us the quiet mind, the adventurous spirit, the loving heart. He wills our good. He desires our wholeness. It is Good News indeed.

* From the entry for December 7 in *Through the Year with J B Phillips* (Hodder & Stoughton, 1974, later re-issued by Arthur James).

A Meditation for Advent

THE MAN FOR OTHERS

It is to a world of broken relationships that Jesus comes with healing power. "God was in Christ, reconciling the world to himself," wrote Paul (to the Corinthians) as he interpreted to them the great saving acts recorded in the Gospels. Christmas is the celebration of, and thanksgiving for, the Incarnation, the coming of one whose purpose is to heal relationships.

Reconciliation must therefore be the dominant theme in Advent worship, reflection and meditation. The Incarnation is God's reconciling act, an action which commits his servants too to a ministry of reconciliation. God, ourselves and our neighbour are related within a triangle of love, the true "eternal triangle" based (Jesus says) on the greatest commandment of all. Love is at the heart of the gospel and must therefore be expressed in a commitment to "bind up the broken-hearted", "the bleeding soul to cure"; in other words, to heal relationships.

How timely and relevant is the Advent message! There are wounds to be healed in our national life where prejudice creates inter-group tensions. Negative trends in our society as well as in individuals are the outward expression of the "shadow" within us – materialism, secularism, ruthlessness, selfishness, lust for power, insensitivity. The pollution of the atmosphere and the abuse of creation damage our relationship to the earth. Racial and credal intolerance drives wedges between people and destroys relationships. It is the old, old story encapsulated with dramatic brilliance and to traumatic effect in the Genesis story of the Garden of Eden. There the disobedience of our representatives, Adam and Eve, distorted their relationship with God and consequently their relationship with each other (mutual blame and resentment), with the earth ("cursed is the ground for thy sake"), and within themselves (guilt).

It is in order to restore a right relationship with God, with ourselves, with the earth and with each other that the child born in Bethlehem became "the man for others" who lived, preached, healed, served, suffered, died and rose again for all humankind.

The gospel offers reconciliation to a divided world and integration to broken people. It brings Good News for the healing of relationships, through the way of love.

A Meditation for Advent

BEING, NOT DOING

It was late in the afternoon when we motored into Prague. Because of communication failures (this was Czechoslovakia of some years ago), our agent had failed to secure a hotel booking for us. I sought the assistance of the state tourist office, but they were unhelpful and totally indifferent to our difficulties. I tried the "unofficial" hotels, but Prague was busy. Everywhere was full. It was only at the last gasp, and with anxiety increasing, that I found one sympathetic receptionist who was willing to try to do something to help us. The room was spartan in the extreme, but it was at least "a roof over our heads".

Reflecting on that uncomfortable adventure at this Advent season, I felt sympathy with Joseph in what was essentially the same situation in Bethlehem. The town was busy and accommodation unavailable. Though Mary was far advanced in pregnancy, there seems to have been indifference to her need. "There was no room" – even in the inn. It was an innkeeper, at least sympathetic enough to allow them to use his stable, who gave them a roof over their heads.

It is worth reflecting on the two factors common to these stories – in different ways and for different reasons. They are busy-ness and indifference. Both can damage spiritual health.

Indifference represents an absence of focus and vision alongside a lack of conviction and commitment. "There is nothing so fatal to religion as indifference," comments Edmund Burke. In public and community affairs, indifference to political responsibility creates flabbiness and, more dangerously, cynicism. In personal attitudes it becomes lukewarmness, and an unacceptable weakness. But the worst feature of indifference is its inability to remain as indifference. It always, if not dealt with, develops into something worse. Sin is frequently the product of untreated indifference.

Busy-ness too requires attention. Over-activity, though usually undertaken for what seem good reasons, can stifle spiritual growth. Prayer, for example, is probably limited to late-night spare moments, when physical and mental exhaustion reduce it to a gesture rather than a discipline.

The danger of over-busy-ness is its inherent capacity to eliminate the solitude so necessary to the spiritual life. It has to be questioned too for other reasons. It can be a rationalisation of our unwillingness to go to "the desert place". It may be a defence against the pain of life in general or a bereavement in particular. For the ability to be active, let us be profoundly grateful; blessed indeed are those who, like Martha, for our comfort are "care-full" and "troubled about many things". But there is also Mary's "better part", so commended by Jesus. That needs time and demands priority.

It is never a gain to replace *being* by *doing*. That is why Jesus struggled, not always successfully, to ensure his solitude.

A Meditation for Advent

THE ENERGY OF LIFE

"Love," said Robert Browning, "is the energy of life." Henry Drummond, whose spiritual classic *The Greatest Thing in the World* is "an analysis of love," happily made that statement his own. Drummond goes on: "The power to set the world right, to renew the springs of affection, comes from Christ . . . The ingredients of love are all in relation to the known today and the near tomorrow, and not to the unknown eternity." The springs of love have their source in the Child of Bethlehem. Jesus was, in a way that only faith can comprehend, "Love incarnate, Love divine".

It was on a garden lawn in Kent that Drummond offered to a gathering of missionaries his spontaneous exposition of Paul's "hymn of love" in 1 Corinthians, chapter 13. The great evangelist, Moody, was due to speak to the assembled company but confessed to being "tired out with eight months of solid preaching" and introduced instead "a substitute recently returned from Africa, Henry Drummond". Intuitively, the audience realised that it was listening to an historic declaration on the nature of "the spectrum of love" and its ingredients. Later, that address would become a devotional classic as *The Greatest Thing in the World*.

The nine ingredients of love which Drummond presents are one-word summaries of Paul's statements about love. They are patience, kindness, generosity, humility, courtesy, unselfishness, good temper, guilelessness and sincerity. They are to be lived out in the real world on the pattern set by Jesus, Love incarnate.

But the real world we contemplate this Advent season is daunting indeed. Millions starve, Kurds die, Yugoslavia destroys itself, bombs wound and kill, Russians queue for food in freezing cold, cancer claims its huge quota of victims, AIDS' deaths increase, mental illness spreads, children are grievously abused, accident, natural disaster and violence bring bereavement to countless families (including police families). Do words about love have any relevance to all this?*

But there is no reason for Christmas without the Child of Bethlehem, the Word become flesh, Love incarnate. His followers have a binding commitment to proclaiming and trying to practise the healing, reconciling, redeeming, renewing power of love. When "Love came down at Christmas", it was in the form of a little child. Three decades or so later, his disciples set out to conquer the world in his name. His followers today have no choice. To proclaim the power of love remains their primary responsibility. The world must learn that love is the energy of life.

* This Meditation was written in 1994.

A Meditation for Advent

THE HEALING LIGHT

The Saviour comes! So Advent proclaims that "the people that walked in darkness have seen a great light!" It is the season which announces annually the coming of the Servant-king, in love. He comes to "heal the broken-hearted", to "preach deliverance to the captives", to be "God-with-us". The Advent candles symbolise the presence of the light shining in a world of darkness. The Saviour comes to bring (in the words of the title of a book by Agnes Sanford) "the healing light".*

The light shines the more brightly because the darkness is so great. In Yugoslavia tanks have trundled along roads trodden by tourists, while the whole land groans under the pain of internecine conflict. In Iraq Kurds huddle fearfully in flimsy tents, desolate and desperate, facing death through hunger and the winter's cold. In Ireland, the passing years bring killing after killing, the searing pain of bereavement numbing those of every faith – and none. The tormented faces and stricken bodies of the starving young and the dying old are there before us on our television screens, victims of hunger, disease, war and inhumanity. How great indeed is the world's darkness!

The Psalmist speaks of the darkness "which hideth not from Thee" and claims that "darkness and light are both alike to Thee." God is not only in the light; we encounter him in the darkness too, he seems to say. But looking at such world situations, dare we talk of meeting God in the darkness?

There is no place in genuine religion for pious platitudes and doctrinaire declaration about growth through suffering, especially if offered by those who suffer little to those who suffer appallingly. Yet somehow Paul can say that "*nothing* can separate us from the love of God revealed in Christ Jesus our Lord."

Paul had a right to speak in these terms. He suffered persecution, peril, imprisonment, beatings, hunger and cold. He knew too the inner darkness which made him cry: "Who shall deliver me from this death?" But it was through his darkness that he learnt the truth about relationship with God. We may lose all sense of God in our darkness, but he never loses touch with us.

> Let me no more my comfort draw
> From my frail hold of Thee;
> In this alone rejoice with awe
> Thy mighty grasp of me.**

God is in the light, but in the darkness too. It is there that He offers us "the healing light".

* *The Healing Light* by Agnes Sanford published by Arthur James.
** An earlier reference to these lines is in The Validity of Prayer, the Meditation for November 22.

A Meditation for Advent

TOWARDS THE LIGHT

I remember being taken, when very young, to a cave in the south-west of England. The memory is hazy, but I do recall the bleakness and darkness in the passages leading to the centre of the cavern. Electric light bulbs had recently been inserted into the walls to facilitate safe passage, and round each light a hint of green was beginning to appear. I realised then that where there is light and warmth, there is growth.

We meet God in the darkness, communal or personal. We have reflected on the need to accept our dark (or shadow) side. Here is further encouragement to do so.

Finding the ability to love our unacceptable self somehow brings the possibility of growth in that area of our being. The "surrender" of our negative side to God creates new possibilities of service. The encounter in the darkness can lead us towards the light; and where there is light, there is growth. Paul, who had a very aggressive side to his personality, illustrates the miracle of grace. He fiercely persecuted "the disciples of the Lord" and actually "approved" of the murder, by stoning, of Stephen. When he was so dramatically converted, his personality structure did not change, but the way in which he expressed it did. The destructive aggression for which he was so widely known was now, through the miracle of grace, a creative energy that drove him on through those demanding missionary journeys, with their perils and persecution, stripes and imprisonment, and all manner of painful experience.

Major Alida Bosshardt* of the Salvation Army spent 27 years ministering to prostitutes in the red light area of Amsterdam. I remember her saying to me: "Sometimes I feel like a kind of Christian prostitute." What I "heard" in that comment was that, had she not been called by God to this great ministry, she could easily have become a prostitute herself, because of her need to love and be loved. But then "amazing grace" made her the Incarnation of caring love to the hundreds of red-light girls she knew by name. She gave them love and received back so much from them. The road she took led her to the light; but, unredeemed, she could so easily have gone towards the darkness.

Advent brings the good news of the coming of God incarnate, love in action, leading whoever will towards the light.

* See my reference to Major Bosshardt in The Loving Heart, the Meditation for November 18.

A Meditation for Advent

INNER LIGHT

Advent announces the coming of light into our world of darkness. It also brings encouragement to us all as we wrestle with our own darkness. Of our inner conflict, the war between good and evil, we are constantly aware. It is that battle within which has driven good people into depression and some towards "the dark night of the soul". Yet the gospel truth is that the God whom we encounter in the darkness offers us the gift of inner light.

It needs courage to face the dark, negative side of our being. But the challenge faces everyone for "*all* have sinned and come short of the glory of God." In that we all have a shadow side to our personalities, there is comfort. The spiritual trauma is not unique to us. We are not alone in our darkness.

We need, next, to be aware of the sheer power of that shadow. Whether we speak, as we do in religious language, of "temptation" or, as we do in psychological terminology of the pressures within us that come from "the unconscious", the experience is the same. The need to "act out" our secret desires can lead us into behaviour unacceptable to church and society. How great then is the condemnation that comes from congregation and community of someone who, with grace and discipline, has "contained" some temptation down the years, but has failed once. Judgement and rejection, personal and official, too often ensue. Yet the only proper response to such failures can be, "There, but for the grace of God, go I."

The only way to deal with that dark side, the unacceptable self, is to face it and accept it, not reluctantly but positively. It is already known to God who accepts us as we are.

It is moreover that wholly unconditional acceptance of us by God that demands that we accept others' darkness too. But how can we so love others if we cannot learn to love ourselves? We love our neighbour as we love ourselves.

To acknowledge the reality and depth of our darkness is to open the way to the healing light. The Incarnation is the Good News of the coming of the Light of the World. He comes as love in action to redeem our darkness.

A Meditation for Christmas

THE CHOICE IS OURS

In the divine synchronicity that brought so many factors together so significantly, or as the Bible puts it "in the fullness of the time", Jesus was born in Bethlehem. It had somehow become the place of expectation and seemed to draw so many people, of different kinds, to it.

Mary and Joseph went there for ostensibly practical reasons. "All the world" must be taxed, said a decree of Caesar Augustus and each person had to fulfil the instruction in their own city. At a very late stage in her pregnancy, Mary was taken by Joseph from Nazareth to Bethlehem. But there were deeper reasons. Had not King Herod been told that it had been prophesied that out of Bethlehem would come "a Governor that shall rule my people, Israel"? If the fullness of the time had come, Bethlehem was where Mary and Joseph just had to be.

It was to Jerusalem first and then on to Bethlehem that the so-called "wise men from the East" travelled, having seen the star of "the King of the Jews" appear. Their motivation was clear. They wanted to honour and worship him and they expressed their feelings in the famous and time-honoured gifts of gold, frankincense and myrrh. They were wise indeed. Intuitively they avoided returning to Herod, as he had asked them to do, to protect Jesus, and they journeyed home another way.

Then came the shepherds to Bethlehem "to see this thing which had come to pass". They found themselves in a mystery (in, again, the biblical sense) which they could not comprehend. Carrying out their pastoral responsibilities, they had seen and heard first "the angel of the Lord" and then "a multitude of the heavenly host" announcing the birth of "a Saviour who is Christ the Lord". The days in which they lived and the background from which they came were much more open to psychic and spiritual dimensions than our predominantly materialistic atmosphere allows. Aware that something of unusual significance was happening, they immediately left their flocks to go to Bethlehem to see that which "the Lord has made known to us". They moved, we are told, with haste, to find Jesus.

Events in Bethlehem throw into relief two kinds of people, those who have no room for Jesus and those who do. So will it ever be. Discipleship is a free choice.

The choice then is yours, is ours. Though Jesus seeks people with the cords of love, he is open to rejection still. Those who have no room for him are free to say so – and they will. The fundamental question that is put to each and all is that which was put to Simon Peter so long ago: "Whom do you say that I am?" The response from Peter was: "You are the Christ, the Son of the living God." It was the response only possible by faith. So must that response still be.

Indeed, the choice is ours!

A Meditation for Christmas

THE MYSTERY OF BETHLEHEM

"Let us go even unto Bethlehem and see this thing which is come to pass." The immediate response of the shepherds on hearing the angelic Good News was to hurry to the manger to see the child, born to be "a Saviour, Christ the Lord". Christmas is the season when, in imagination, we are all invited to make that same pilgrimage, there to reflect on "the visit of God", the Incarnation, God-with-us.

The Incarnation is a "mystery", a word which in biblical terms involves two elements, the "secret" plan of God and the medium through whom the secret is revealed. As we encounter this true "mystery", let us reflect on two of the key figures in the story, Mary and Joseph.

Mary – gentle, gracious, intuitive and sensitive – knew that she was part of a mystery. In the *Magnificat*, her song of praise, she made her statement about obedience and privilege. To Jesus she gave not only a mother's natural gifts. She knew her son was "special" and so whatever he said or did became something over which she would "ponder in her heart". Mary is an inspiration to us all.

Joseph sometimes seems but a background figure, present but unobtrusive. His contribution to the mystery is moving, for his offering was *an attitude of mind*. Reflect on what he was asked to do. The girl he married was already pregnant. That would normally produce anger and rejection in a young husband. The explanation he was given was that his wife was "with child by the Holy Spirit". The only possible response to that would be utter disbelief. Yet Joseph, with extraordinary sensitivity, accepted without question what was happening and sought only to understand his role in what came to be called "the Incarnation". As a result this man of God was full of care for both mother and child, alive to their special needs and acutely perceptive over any threat to the baby Jesus. Joseph's commitment and faith are a challenge to some attitudes that we may have but need to change.

The mystery of the "divine synchronicity" must move us profoundly for it demonstrates that, "in the fullness of time", Jesus came. Time, geography, the preparation of a people and prophecy combined to make that the moment for "the Word to become flesh". Behind the proper pageantry and celebration of Christmas, there shines out the Good News of the coming of the Saviour in love, his only purpose being the redemption of humankind.

A NEW SONG*

There is a certain irony, unintended as it may be, in football crowds on Cup Final day singing a line from the second verse of "Abide with me". Henry Francis Lyte seems to equate "change" and "decay" when he writes: "Change and decay in all around I see." It is not, alas, distant from the truth. Whether it be behaviour, public and personal mores, media content, tabloid trivialisation, rampant materialism – there is much that is disappointing "all around".

That said, let us immediately banish the view that change means decay. Change is, in fact, a dynamic concept. Responsibly and appropriately approached, it represents a positive, creative, progressive opportunity. It focuses on new attitudes and revised lifestyles. Medicine strives to change ill-health into good health. Psychology aims at growth through therapeutic relationship and self-awareness. The aim of politicians is – or ought to be – the creation of a better society. The prime purpose of religion is to offer a way to new life through prayer, relationship, the means of grace, worship, the energy of the Spirit. It seeks to replace doubt with faith, meaninglessness with hope, fear with love. It is therefore not surprising that, in any biblical concordance, there will be a long list of entries under the word "new".

Newness of life is a central theme of the New Testament, summed up in the words from Revelation: "Behold, I make all things new." There is the *new* commandment Jesus gives the disciples. There is the *new* covenant or testament of which he speaks at the Last Supper. When anyone comes to be in Christ, St Paul writes, there is a *new* creation. The exuberant language of Revelation speaks of a *new* Jerusalem and of a *new* heaven and a *new* earth. But the theme is also an Old Testament one in both the Psalms and the prophets. Repeatedly there is the exhortation to sing a *new* song to the Lord. How often the Psalmist affirms with gladness that "he put a *new* song in my mouth." When it comes to God's relationship to his people Israel, prophet after prophet registers the promise of a *new* heart and a *new* spirit (Ezekiel), a *new* name (Isaiah), a *new* covenant (Jeremiah). "*New* things I do declare . . . Sing a *new* song to the Lord!"

How glorious is the potential of the willingness to change or be changed! How necessary it is in our world today to believe in the possibility of newness of life!

Whether we talk in the language of theology about justification, sanctification, salvation, redemption, grace; or in the language of psychotherapy about growth, maturity, individuation; in human language about joy's triumph over gloom, faith over doubt, hope over anxiety, love over fear, the ultimate theme is the same: "All things are made new." When such enhanced faith is experienced, it will be the easier to join in chorus with the Psalmist:

> You turned my wailing into dancing;
>> you removed my sackcloth and clothed me with joy,
> that my heart may sing to you
>> and not be silent.
> Lord my God, I will give
>> you thanks for ever.**

* There is a contemplative Meditation with this title on September 27.
** Psalm 30, verses 11 and 12 (*New International Version*).

A Meditation for the end of the Year

A Second Chance

Blessed are those who are given the opportunity of a second chance! Everyone knows human failure, and the weight of it can be very depressing . . . whatever the cause. It may be a broken marriage for which we feel responsible; grief over failures in relationships, personal or professional; the guilt that arises over secret sins and the persistent pressures from within us that tempt us to act out our unacceptable desires. Repeated failure then leads to inappropriate guilt and that can destroy initiative, hope and spiritual enthusiasm, but those with a lively faith should never equate human failure with hopelessness. The doctrine of forgiveness is the very heart of the gospel. Its product is inner peace.

New life stems from (in Emil Brunner's phrase) "the divine initiative". God is the author of each "new creation". To develop the spiritual life, involves an important spiritual law. It is that growth in grace depends on co-operation between God and human beings. The gift is from God but *we* have a crucial part to play.

This law is evidenced in various aspects of the religious life, for example in the practice of intercessory prayer. Our petitions contribute to the possibility of change in people and situations. For that reason, Jesus commands his followers to be "importunate" in prayer. "Pray without ceasing," says Paul similarly to the Thessalonian Christians.

Consider also the sacraments. The efficacy of the sacraments as means of grace depends on various components – God's repeated promises, the use of the appointed elements and the presence of faith in the recipient. If that last factor is absent, something essential to the sacrament is missing and it cannot fulfil its purpose.

Look too at the ministry of healing. As we contribute to the development of our illnesses, so must we play a part in our healing. God wants us to be whole, but if we are not prepared to change wrong attitudes, habits or lifestyle, our healing cannot be accomplished.

God wills our salvation, our wholeness, but to effect it he needs our obedience, commitment and self-discipline. That opportunity of a new beginning is always on offer and should be gratefully and gracefully grasped as a new year approaches. Growing in grace is an exercise carried out in collaboration with God. Out of it, spiritual growth will surely come.

A Meditation for the end of the Year

LANDMARKS OF FAITH

Many people have told me that they shared the Queen's assessment of her 1992 as their personal *annus horribilis*. The memories of that year will remain, for all experience becomes inextricably woven into the tapestry of our lives. That said, 1992 must now be laid to rest.* With God's help (for there is a fundamental spiritual law of co-operation between God and human beings), there is always an opportunity for a new beginning.

At the point in history at which we stand, that seems an impossible dream, but it is part of true religion to believe in "miracles". After all, "miracle" is, by derivation as we noted earlier, something that compels wonder. God's mighty acts in creation and redemption are the miraculous landmarks of the faith, demonstrating the divine power at work in the world. In a universe created by a loving Providence, redeemed by a loving Saviour and energised by a living Holy Spirit, there must always be the possibility of "divine surprises".

Given the enormity of human suffering, the obscenity of violence in much human behaviour and the reality of human selfishness and spiritual corruption, is this merely the language of fantasy and fiction? "Angels, martyrs, saints and prophets" (to use the categories of St Stephen of Mar Saba in the eighth century) and multitudes of believers today answer "No!" The Incarnation, the crucifixion, the resurrection and the coming of the Holy Spirit are the grand landmarks of the faith, beliefs founded on (in Paul's phrase) "the knowledge which is beyond knowledge". Add to them the most profound doctrine in the Creeds, "the forgiveness of sins", and there is a spiritual structure in place that offers faith to the lost, hope to the confused and love to the fearful.

"Remove not the ancient landmark," warns the Old Testament. When familiar landmarks disappear we lose our way. Similarly, when religion loses its markers, spiritual confusion inevitably follows.

Sadly, these are the characteristics of our times. In a world that is struggling politically, economically, socially and morally, with consequent disorientation in all these areas, it is the more essential that the church itself should not – through academic public discussion appropriate in theological circles, but only partly heard, partly understood and possibly misinterpreted – undermine its faith and discourage the faithful. The church must rather proclaim with "boldness" the "things which it most surely believes".

As the new year unfolds, there is a need to re-establish the landmarks of the faith, for it is in the eternal verities that we can find what the times demand – and I have already mentioned – a sense of direction, a sense of perspective, a sense of adventure and a sense of destiny. With them, and with God's help, we can set out to create an *annus mirabilis*, a year of "wonder, love and praise".

* This Meditation was written for the end of that year.

A Meditation for the end of the Year

PEACE RESTORED

As we move into an unknown, uncertain and unpredictable new year, the gift that we all most need is that of inner serenity. And a gift it is, however meditation, relaxation and other human techniques may help to develop it. "My peace I *give* unto you," said Jesus to all his disciples. "Not as the world giveth, give I to you." The divine gift is, in essence, quite different from anything the world can offer. "Be still and know that I am God," exhorts the Psalmist, again. In a world of insecurity, literal and spiritual, having a still centre in the depths of our being remains the strongest element in our effort to cope with the strains and stresses, personal and corporate, that will surely face us in the coming year.

To many, this opening statement will feel to be no more than religious verbiage, irrelevant to the facts of life today. How can we possibly feel any sense of inner harmony and calmness faced as we are by the appalling cruelty of violent crimes, the scenes of starvation it is almost impossible to watch, the suffering of the innocent in serial killings, sectarian violence and sexual abuse? How can we now believe that there is a Providence "working his purpose out as year succeeds to year"? What purpose is there in prayer when pressing petitions for peace, healing and unity seem to remain unanswered? It is not surprising that, in a world like ours, religion is being dismissed as irrelevant, and faith is treated with indifference.

Yet the miracle persists! The Bible, though despised and rejected, attacked and abused, subjected to radical and often hostile criticism, survives and continues to be the highest-selling book in the world. The church, especially where it has been persecuted and faced with obliteration, is alive and strengthened by its sufferings. Many people testify to miracles of healing, reconciliation and inner change.

For those who have lost faith, hope and, especially, serenity, the Old Testament provides an encouraging reminder: "He heard my cry – *and gave me back my peace*."* The miracle of grace is expressed in words of restoration – reconciliation, reformation, regeneration, redemption, renewal. They all speak of the possibility of a return to a right relationship with God, and consequent loving relationships with others, self and earth. Peace is restored.

In a world which Jesus assured us would be one of tribulation, serenity can be recovered. The gift of God's peace is always on offer.

* Psalm 55, verse 18 (*New English Bible*); also referred to in the Meditation for September 6.

A Meditation for the end of the Year

INSPIRATION

The preacher was not wholly happy with her sermon. "I was all over the place tonight," she said. That same sermon "moved me to tears" confessed the young woman who had been in the congregation.

The equation is familiar to all who preach the gospel. Sometimes a sense of elation is the immediate inner response to having sincerely tried to preach the gospel, a feeling of "that went well". At other times, it can be a feeling of disappointment, even despair. The preparation was done, the effort was made, but somehow the sermon had not "worked", that is the message had not been heard. Yet in each of these situations, over and over again, gratitude will be offered for that second sermon, the one over which we felt dissatisfied. This means surely that there is another element at work that somehow makes what seems weak, strong. Perhaps too the reverse is true. Preachers need to be cautious when they think they have done well.

When the disciples were first sent out by Jesus they had clear instructions to "preach the gospel". "Do not worry about how you are to speak or what you are to say. What you are to say will be given you at that time, for it is not you who are the speakers; the speaker is the Spirit of the Father speaking in you." In other words there is another factor at work in the situation, an energising element certainly but more importantly an inspirational one. To inspire means to breathe in. There is, as the disciples learnt at Pentecost, something powerful, unidentifiable but real, that comes in the honest pursuit of the work of the Lord. It is something which changes weakness into strength, which gives to those of limited education such as the disciples, insight and wisdom of a high order, which enables those who, though preachers, are as subject to temptation as every other human being is, an ability to communicate that they don't understand. It is an exciting experience. What greater satisfaction can there be than being called to preach?

In reaching the end of this book of 367 Meditations, products of a ministry allowed and encouraged by the editors of the *Daily Telegraph* over twelve years, it may be permissible to offer a comment on the reality of the promise of inspiration in the service of Jesus. In beginning each new sequence of thirteen Meditations twice every year, how often have I said (to Jillian who has typed and retyped every single one of them): "I don't know where another thirteen Meditations can come from." It is a sense of helplessness that can be severe. But over and over and now again particularly it has been done. The ultimate effect is therefore a truly humbling one, for it is to that inspirational Spirit, blowing as that Spirit wills, that, however poorly, however well, the gospel, spoken or in writing, is preached.

CREDO

Commitment to a belief depends on two factors. The first is the testimony of personal experience, the second the confirmation of that experience by some external authority. The subjective factor, experience, needs objective affirmation. For non-religious people that external confirmation will most likely come from the experience of others, the validity of their similar experience, especially if multiplied by many examples, confirming the authenticity of one's own experience. Religious people will find their external authority in another specific form depending on their church background. Some will find the authority they need in the tradition of their church with its record of God's grace to people down the ages. Others, especially those like myself in the "evangelical and reformed" tradition, will test their experience against "the word of God".

Such external authority is essential. Human nature is flawed and the flaw extends to all aspects of our being. The problem is what Paul describes as that "law in our members" expressing itself in his famous statement that when we "would do good, evil is present with us". The world of psychoanalysis similarly demonstrates how easily we fall victim to psychological mechanisms that threaten the reliability of our experience. We can rationalise a situation and make ourselves believe that we are taking action for one reason when unconsciously we are doing it for another. We can confuse the will of God with wishful thinking. The imagination can run riot and endanger the reliability of our deductions from experience. To have validity and authority for our beliefs and to feel confidence in them the subjective and objective factors must come together.

For me, the external authority is that supreme rule of faith and life (as we declare in our ordination vows), the Bible, thus giving biblical authority to our experience. When revelation to ourselves is confirmed by God's revelation to other people in many ages, and authenticated by its inclusion in the canon of scripture, we stand on solid ground. It is the Holy Spirit at work in history and in our own experience.

The four convictions which for me provide such stability and lead to commitment are the doctrines of providence, forgiveness, salvation and healing. I find my experience of providence compelling and convincing. Looking back on all the failures, successes, dangers, decisions, crises I can see that ultimately all things work together for good in extraordinary ways. I see apparently unconnected events brought into some kind of miraculous juxtaposition in such a way as to move faith forward.

I read the Gospel statements about forgiveness and from my experience know how true they are. I read the theory of what the religious vocabulary calls salvation, or redemption, or new life, or meaning and my deepest intuitions confirm that it is true. I believe in the healing power of the risen Christ. It is on record. But I know it from experience.

This reflection on authority and experience seems to have turned into a personal credo, but it just may encourage others to believe and make their commitment.